BEYOND HORIZONS

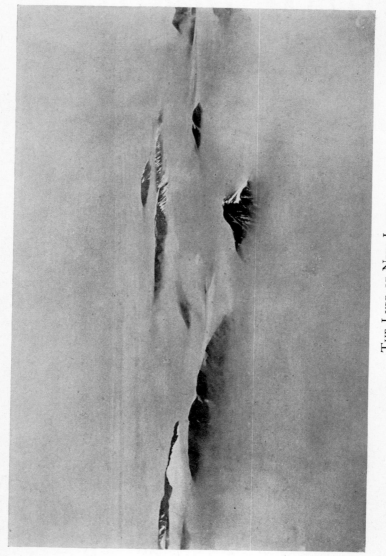

THE LURE OF NEW LAND
Nicholas II Land as Seen from the Graf Zeppelin

BEYOND HORIZONS

By

LINCOLN ELLSWORTH

LIEUTENANT COMMANDER, UNITED STATES NAVAL RESERVE

DOUBLEDAY, DORAN & COMPANY, INC.

Garden City MCMXXXVIII *New York*

PRINTED AT THE *Country Life Press*, GARDEN CITY, N. Y., U. S. A.

The quotation from "The Explorer" from
Rudyard Kipling's *Five Nations* is used by
special permission of Mrs Rudyard Kipling

Acknowledgment is made and thanks are hereby expressed to the *National Geographic Magazine* for the assistance rendered the author in preparing this material, and to the *American Geographic Society* for the material used in the Appendix

CONTENTS

PART I PREPARATION

CHAPTER		PAGE
I	Morning Mists	3
II	Victorian Father	11
III	Country Stars	29
IV	Western Sunsets	36
V	Extracurricular	40
VI	Canoes and Indians	49
VII	The Rim of the Unknown	55
VIII	The Race for the Pacific	61

PART II ARCTIC

I	Interval for Adventure	73
II	Galahad of the Ice	85
III	After Sheep for Science	91
IV	Desert Days	97
V	War Interlude	101
VI	The Turning Point	108
VII	Portrait of a Viking	113
VIII	Will against Will	122
IX	To Kings Bay	137

CHAPTER		PAGE
X	THE GREAT MOMENT	144
XI	THE JAWS OF THE ARCTIC	156
XII	STRUGGLE	163
XIII	ESCAPE	181
XIV	START OF THE NORGE	193
XV	BEYOND THE POLE	213

PART III   ANTARCTIC

I	FIRST LIFE	235
II	ARCTIC DE LUXE	245
III	PLANNING	250
IV	HYMENEAL	256
V	DOWN UNDER	258
VI	A SETBACK	263
VII	FRESH START	267
VIII	THE ICE AGE	278
IX	DEFEAT	287
X	NEW BLOOD	298
XI	PREPARATIONS	304
XII	FRUSTRATED	310
XIII	THE FLIGHT	316
XIV	GROPING	335
XV	IN LITTLE AMERICA	345
XVI	NOT "RESCUED"—"AIDED"	355

The Lure of New Land . . . . *Frontispiece*

Facing Page

Lincoln Ellsworth 4

Mr and Mrs Ellsworth with Her Sister (Mrs W. R. Linn) and Their Mother 5

Clare and Lincoln in 1888 5

Amundsen and Ellsworth beside Their Planes Just before the Start 180

Saturday Night Mess at Kings Bay and Eight Hours Later 181

Route of the Norge across the Polar Sea, May 11–13, 1926. Also Route of 1925 Flight 196

Ellsworth's Flight Bridging Antarctica for the First Time 197

Lincoln Ellsworth and Mary Louise Ulmer (Later Mrs Lincoln Ellsworth) 260

Some of the World's Finest Scenery—but Seldom a Human Eye to See It! 261

Ellsworth Plays Host to a Saucy Little "Neighbor" in Antarctica 276

All That Projects above the Surface when a Blizzard Engulfs the Polar Star Is the Snow-choked Engine . . . 277

Two of Antarctica's Rare "Growing Things"—Beards and Icicles 340

Facing Page

BELIEVING HER OWNER "LOST", THE WYATT EARP FLIES SYMBOLS
    OF GRIEF 341

THE OWNER COMES ABOARD! 356

THE FRINGES OF ETERNITY 357

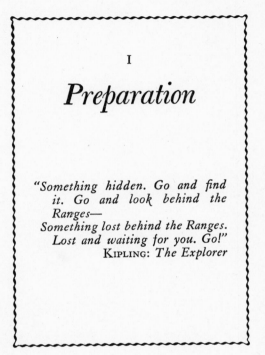

I

Preparation

*"Something hidden. Go and find
it. Go and look behind the
Ranges—
Something lost behind the Ranges.
Lost and waiting for you. Go!"*
KIPLING: *The Explorer*

I MORNING MISTS

LIFE IN AMERICA began for the Ellsworth family as early as 1646, when Sergeant Josiah Ellsworth, youngest son of John Ellsworth, of Derbyshire, England, was living in Windsor, Conn.

For me, in the eighth generation of his descendants, life really began with the Chicago World's Fair. I can't remember much of anything before that. On the twelfth day of the Fair I reached my thirteenth birthday. It doesn't seem to me now that I missed a single day's attendance. My father was one of the Exposition's directors, and I had a season pass. Though ours was a religious household, we even went to the Fair Sunday afternoons to hear the symphony concert and sometimes, though I suppose it bothered Father's conscience, Sousa's band.

My little sister Clare and I knew every painting, every statue, and every vase in the Fine Arts Building. Father was chairman of the Liberal Arts Committee and before the Fair opened went to Europe to invite the governments there to send art collections. I retain the appreciation of fine paintings he taught us in those days.

But I remember the Midway best. My favorite concession there was the ferris wheel, on which I rode many times. Among the ethnological exhibits the Javanese people interested me most. But I liked it all—the Austrian Village, the Streets of Cairo, and the rest of it. In the Exposition proper was the Eskimo Village, where native mushers of the Arctic, wearing parkas even in the hot weather, cracked their long dog whips.

At this time Theodore Roosevelt, of New York, was already known for his love of outdoor life. He built the Boone and Crockett log cabin on "Wooded Island" and presented it to the Fair. A long-haired hunter was in charge of this exhibit, which was

3

a place of fascination. When the Fair was dismantled, my father bought the log cabin and moved it to his farm at Hudson, Ohio, where I spent the more pleasant years of my boyhood.

My mind is clear about few events that happened before the World's Fair. I cannot remember the name or appearance of any playmate other than my sister and cousins, and so I assume that I had none. I must have been a rather solitary child. My health was delicate, and I suffered from constant colds. Yet when we went to the country, I grew strong immediately. Cities stifled me then, as they do now.

My mother I remember as a beautiful lady whom I loved dearly. As did my father, she liked horses. Her sister, my aunt Nellie Linn, lived to be eighty and rode almost to the day of her death. At least once Father and Mother visited England and took coaching trips through the shires.

Mother was fond of the theater, and it was in a theater that she took the cold which resulted in her death. Out of the still-dark confusion of that week jumps a vivid picture—my father, his face gray with anxiety, running into the house with an oxygen tank, with not a glance for me standing in the last wet leaves of fall. She died shortly after, and I thought the world ended.

Not long ago I was examining one of Father's diaries, when I came upon the entry: "On this day, 1888, my dearest Eva contracted pneumonia." I followed on. Every anniversary day of the illness was noted, then the death. Father had happily remarried years before the date of these entries. In his secret nature, which he found it so hard to break through, he must always have observed those sad November anniversaries.

My sister Clare and I were born in a house on Ellis Avenue on Chicago's South Side. Its grounds were spacious. I remember a colony of pet rabbits I had in a corner. When Clare grew old enough, father built a playhouse for her in the yard. There was a big stable—shining carriages arrayed in rank, blooded horses pawing and nickering in the box stalls, a harness room gleaming with polished straps and bits and smelling of leather, grease, and sweat. A little boy or girl could reach up and jingle the strings of sleigh

LINCOLN ELLSWORTH

Above: Early Daguerreotype of Mr and Mrs Ellsworth with Her Sister (Mrs W. R. Linn) and Their Mother.

Below: Clare and Lincoln Taken about 1888 at Their Ellis Avenue Home in Chicago.

bells hanging on pegs. In fact, one of the clear impressions remaining of Chicago in that day is of the beautiful horses on the avenues and boulevards. My father was very fond of driving in a handsome turnout.

Just across Ellis Avenue from us lived young George Ellery Hale, then head of the Yerkes Observatory and later in charge of the Mount Wilson Observatory. He built a private observatory on the roof of the Hales' Ellis Avenue house. I used to stare across at that dome in awe, wondering what mystery it concealed. We children were told that he looked at the stars there, through a telescope. It didn't seem to me that Chicago's stars were worth looking at. Even the gas lights on the street corners dimmed them.

But as I say, I have to probe my mind to get even a blurred impression of my first twelve or thirteen years. I can't say now whether my childhood was happy or unhappy. Certainly, the things I remember most clearly are the unpleasant things—my small mishaps, things that frightened me. I suppose a truer characterization would be to say that my childhood was dull. I wasn't much interested in anything.

An example of my early indifference arose just the other day. In going over my material for this book, I happened to remember that in 1889, the spring following my mother's death, Father took his mother, little Clare and myself to London with him. I hadn't thought about this for years. Having tapped the memory, though, other details came to me.

We crossed, going and coming, on the old North German Lloyd liner Lahn. In fair winds it hoisted a mainsail to help out the propeller. In spite of rough weather, during which Clare was miserably seasick, we made a fast crossing to England—twelve days. I had an upper berth, and I remember the cockroaches on the stateroom wall. This was in the day of ten-course and twelve-course dinners. Whether the sea air sharpened my appetite, it seemed to me the Lahn served the best food I ever tasted. After polishing off everything from hors d'oeuvres to fruit, I'd pocket a handful of walnuts and munch them in my berth after I'd gone to bed.

In London Father took us to Morley's Hotel, on Trafalgar Square.

I used to look from the window and admire the wonderful stone lions. Father had business on the Continent—this was the trip on which he acquired the most famous of his art treasures: Rembrandt's "Portrait of a Man"—and during his absence installed us with a private family in Shevening. The Crystal Palace was not far away, and we used to go there for the fireworks.

The point is that in 1889 few American children of my age had ever crossed the Atlantic Ocean. To millions of them that journey would have been the great adventure of their youth, yet I was so little impressed by it that it almost passed out of my memory.

Besides having this trait of indifference, I was very timid as a small boy. I always looked under the bed for intruders before I could go to sleep at night. Even coming into a deserted room in play, I would inspect the corners and under the furniture before risking myself in the place. Once our coachman lifted me off the ground by my head. It must have frightened me badly, for the memory of it remains while I have forgotten the coachman himself.

But I had a more dreadful experience. Walking home one day, I passed on the sidewalk a rough-looking man who acted insane, for he kept wagging his head and muttering to himself. Naturally, when I had gone by I turned and watched him. He felt my inspection and looked back. Then, scowling horribly, he turned toward me and pulled a revolver from his pocket.

Almost frozen with terror, I legged it home as fast as I could run, hurled myself through the front door, and hid under a lounge in a remote room. There I stayed the rest of the day, imagining that every sound in the quiet house was the footstep of the crazy man, coming to shoot me.

My sister, who never knew fear of anything, used to tease me for my timidity. To her I was a fraidy-cat—I, eleven years old; she, six, and a girl besides. I couldn't stand it—she simply had to be frightened, too. So in our play I would hide behind trees and jump out to startle her. If I really scared her and she cried, then I hastened to soothe her, for I was very fond of Clare. Our companionship continued, and until she died she was the staunchest friend I had in the world.

Clare was my constant playmate as long as we lived on Ellis Avenue. We played tag among the trees, and until I was a big boy, eleven or twelve years old, I played dolls with her. Now and then I would stop to see if I couldn't get into the pantry for bread and brown sugar. She had an old nurse called Nana, who used to take us sometimes into South Park to visit the zoo. Father was one of the South Park commissioners.

A crooked nose which I carry today reminds me of another childhood disaster. I owned a boy's-size "ordinary"—one of those original bicycles with a big wheel in front and a little one behind. Riding on the sidewalk one day, the front wheel struck a pebble, and over I went, head first. A broken nose was the result.

Often we went to the Linns' house to play with our cousins Howard and Mabel. There was a third cousin, Dwight Linn, but he was too young then to count. I was named after Uncle William Linn and was always called Linn Ellsworth at first—called that by Father, in fact, until the latter years of his life. About the time I could write fluently enough to take an interest in my signature, I began—though for what reason I have forgotten—signing myself Lincoln Ellsworth and eventually gained that name by common consent. My Uncle William, who was a Chicago cotton broker, was not exactly pleased by my rejection of his godfatherhood.

We always had good times at the Linns'. They had a big yard and a pet goat, which we children could drive. Mabel and Howard Linn had two cousins, living next door, making six of us, which was more society than I ever enjoyed on Ellis Avenue. With such a group, hide-and-seek became possible. The Linns were an outdoor family. Their house was full of stuffed birds and animals—trophies of the hunt. Whenever Uncle William came home after duck shooting, we had great family dinners.

Dreary Sunday mornings. They meant Sunday school and sermon in the Congregational Church. I am a religious man today, though not in a church way. Though I have never prayed, even in the most desperate situations, I have always retained a blind faith in God and His Providence. This faith was never stronger in me than when I stepped into the plane at Kings Bay, Spitzbergen, to fly with Roald

Amundsen to the North Pole. Many people, my own family among them, thought we were committing suicide, but I never had a moment of doubt or fear. If my pulse quickened, it was only with elation at having at last realized my ambition.

School was a horror. I couldn't do anything with school—always the dunce of my classes, always falling behind. It was to be this way throughout my school and college days. Not until, years later, I found my true interest in life did I discover that I could master a subject, no matter how difficult, if it helped me in what I wanted to do.

I knew casually that Father was building one of Chicago's first skyscrapers, the Ellsworth Building. In the early nineties, however, occurred an event which left an impression. On a site at 1827 Michigan Avenue, Father built a house for himself. We moved into it in 1892.

It was, I believe, the first private residence built in Chicago of the new weathered, or tapestry, brick. But it was more than a new house. It was a house of a new type. Chicago was abandoning the front porches and sweeping lawns of its village days. This was a house of the Eastern, metropolitan sort: square, tall, spacious, almost filling its site. It stood next door to the metropolitan granite home of Ferdinand Peck. A clipped hedge separated our tiny lawns.

I really believe Father put up this building primarily to house his art collections, which had quite outgrown the old place on Ellis Avenue. In consequence, the largest, most important room of the new house was the art gallery. But by the time we moved in, the gallery, too, was inadequate, and the whole house—halls, library, and drawing rooms—became a museum of paintings and Chinese porcelains. Years afterwards, when Father was preparing an endowment for Western Reserve Academy, he sold his entire art collections to Knoedler for the lump sum of one million dollars.

Recently I was in Chicago and drove past 1827 Michigan Avenue. The brick house, blackened by the smoke of forty years, is still there. It has become a funeral home. Sic transit gloria mundi.

The library was a room in which I spent many hours. There were numerous volumes which I was not allowed to touch—notable first editions, a collection to be adorned before the century ended by the Gutenberg Bible. Two permitted books held a morbid fascination for me. One of these was bound in snakeskin. The other, entitled *The Dance of Death,* was more horrid, for it was bound in human skin. One side of the skin was tanned to the color of ordinary leather, but the other had been left natural. Not for worlds would I have touched the corpselike human side of the binding.

A famous visitor who came often both to the Ellis Avenue house and to 1827 Michigan Avenue was Eugene Field. Field could never keep money and brought his financial and domestic worries to my father. He could not have come to a sounder adviser, one of Father's favorite sayings being that he would rather see a boy or girl put by ten cents than ten dollars, since it is the little things that make big ones. I have no doubt he poured many a depressing aphorism into the ears of the improvident poet. Eugene Field wrote a poem entitled "When I Was a Boy" and dedicated it to James W. Ellsworth. It is included in *Love Songs of Childhood.*

Another familiar figure in our home was George Inness, the painter. Father always kept a room at the Union League Club in New York, where Inness had his studio. On his visits to New York Father would watch Inness at work, sometimes buying his canvases off the easel. When the painter died in 1894, it was discovered that James W. Ellsworth owned some of his most important pictures.

Another artist friend of Father's was Frank D. Millet, the Chicago painter.

During the World's Fair period, famous men and women flocked to the rooms at 1827 Michigan Avenue. One of the most familiar was Daniel H. Burnham, the young architect, for whom the Exposition was such a personal triumph. But of all those who sat at Father's dinner table, the lion was Paderewski.

I feel sure today that that year of 1893 was the happiest of my father's life. To mingle on terms of friendship with these great figures in painting, architecture, and music was the greatest gratification he ever knew, as the fragments of writing he left about himself surely attest. The son of a plain farmer, the grandson of a revenue officer, he always thought himself a reincarnation, to have such an appreciation of art.

After dinner Paderewski usually played for the company, and on those occasions my sister and I were permitted to come down and listen. I must confess that the music bored me a little, but I never tired of looking at the thin, sensitive face of Paderewski and his great shock of sandy hair. He remains a clear memory with me.

What I have written above about comprises my recollections of my boyhood in Chicago. There is a little outside testimony, which I may as well note here to make the picture as complete as possible. One is a story—a mere legend to me—that when I was a baby my father carried me outdoors into the darkness to see a comet and that I cried to him: "Sky ship, Papa! Sky ship!" If I did, it was prophetic of later interests.

A close friend of Father's was Mr Dunlop, president of a railroad out West. He lived in Chicago and became a widower about the time my mother died. During Mr Dunlop's extended stays in the West, he was accustomed to leave his daughter Mabel with us in charge of our English governess, and she thus became almost a member of the family. When Mabel Dunlop grew up she married Slavko Grouitch, a diplomat, who is now Jugoslav minister to the Court of St James.

After my return from the Arctic in 1925, Mme Grouitch contributed some recollections of those Chicago days. She pictures me as a fragile boy with an almost transparently white skin and fine blond hair. She says I was highly imaginative, a statement which, considering my memories of fear, I can scarcely doubt. My upper room, with its plain iron bed, was almost austere, she says, but my shelves were full of adventure books. There were maps on the wall, a globe or two. If so, I have no remembrance of it.

In the library there were some other books about which I have deferred mention. They were on a low shelf, easily reached by a boy of twelve, and with their drawings and charts I could entertain myself for hours. Atlases. Too heavy to hold up like an ordinary volume, I opened them on the floor and lay on my stomach to pore over them.

In those colored maps were white patches marked *Unknown* or *Unexplored*—many more white areas then than there are today.

"Why don't people go there?" I wondered. "What can be in those white places?"

It hardly occurred to me then that I should be one to find out.

II   VICTORIAN FATHER

LIKE any well-brought-up child of that period, I called him Papa. Today's affectionately irreverent *Dad* or *Pop* would have shocked parents of the last century. Raising children was a serious business in the eighties and nineties, its foundation stones being discipline and parental respect.

There is no doubt that he was fond of my sister and me. I have a general recollection of being often held on his knee when I was small. But we saw so little of him! Just when we were growing up, his business enterprises were rapidly expanding in size and importance. He traveled constantly—to New York, to Montreal, to Europe—and when he was in Chicago business held him from morning until night.

Then, too, he had a reserve through which I was never able to break, either as a child or in later manhood. He couldn't open up, as we say nowadays. But if his shyness or sense of parental dignity shut him off from his son, how much more impenetrable must have been his armor to outsiders! In his last years he wrote a few autobiographical notes, but even in them his reserve did not yield to the frankness that ordinarily comes to old men whose work is done. His accounts of his transactions omit essential details, no doubt on the theory that they were his business and nobody else's.

He paid the penalty of being all his life a lonely man, secretly hungering for companionship. In his brief memoirs, surpassing in feeling the stern satisfaction expressed in the accounts of business triumphs, appears this emotional outburst, so rare in him, in reference to his association with the eminent painter George Inness:

"What wealth in life it brought me, a richness that made me perpetually rich and gave companionship forever after!"

These words bring tears to my eyes even now, for in them I seem to hear his secret loneliness crying out. If I did not have for him the warm affection a son feels toward a less austere and preoccupied father, I at least had an immense respect for him, and a great admiration. One of the things that made me persist in the Antarctic in the face of sickening discouragements was my determination to name a portion of the earth's surface after my father. I knew that if I could cross that ice-locked continent I was bound to discover new territory. On the most recent map of Antarctica a segment of 350,000 square miles of mountain and high plateau is lettered: "James W. Ellsworth Land (U.S.)" That much I could do for him.

He was the most methodical man I ever knew. When he was at home in Chicago, 5 P.M. was a sacred hour in our household. It was Papa's diary time. Each afternoon he reached the house—a tall, spare man wearing the heavy, though carefully trimmed, mustache of his era—at approximately the same moment. He went directly to his study, sat down at his desk, and entered the day's events in his diary. He was not to be disturbed during that work.

For thirty-five years, wherever he was, he kept his diary. In all that time I don't suppose he missed sixty days. When there are omitted entries, they usually come in groups—a blank week, even a blank fortnight. When the diary resumes, there is no explanation of the gap or no summary of what happened in the interim. Each day's entry begins by noting the weather, the temperature, the date, and the place. At sea, it notes the day's run. For the rest, it is chiefly a list of the persons he met each day. It took an extraordinary event in his life to draw mention in the diary. Even when I was lost in the Arctic, and he was frightfully worried, there are only one or two diary references to me. However, he was very ill then—dying—which could explain his silence. The only entry is: "No word from Lincoln."

In the beginning he kept each year's diary in a leather-bound, vest-pocket notebook. Always frugal in the use of little things, he adopted a microscopic hand for his diary, so that one tiny notebook would last out an entire year. This handwriting he continued to the end of his life. It is so fine and small that even people with sharp eyesight need a glass to read it easily. In later life he discovered a book in which he could make daily entries for five years—a book fitting comfortably into an overcoat pocket. He was writing in the fourth book when he died. The four limp-leather volumes occupy not over six inches of shelf space, but through them marches the procession of his days for the last twenty years of his life.

He was full of maxims of the Benjamin Franklin type. One favorite was: "Whatever is worth doing at all is worth doing well." Opening a package is worth doing, and so he always untied the string and saved it. I never saw him cut a string, and I don't believe he ever did cut one. After his death we found bales of string. He even collected strings. We found a deep drawer full of string specimens—a bushel or two of them—and so far as anybody could tell, there were no two alike.

Another eccentricity of his was that he would never let a servant lay a fire for him. He considered himself an expert and always built his own fires. He would never permit the wood ashes to be cleaned out, saying that fires were hotter and the combustion more efficient when wood burned in ashes. At Schloss Lenzburg, the historic Swiss chateau which he bequeathed to me, the ashes still lie two and three feet deep in the medieval fireplaces—ashes from fires of his building. The caretakers would no more think of removing them than they would of putting a bomb under the castle itself.

Father was an indefatigable collector. Besides his art treasures, he gathered collections of all sorts of curious odds and ends. One, which he kept in Hudson, was a collection of bottles. In Europe he collected the barber signs of many lands, ancient and modern. These also he shipped to Hudson. I have always understood he bought Castle Lenzburg to acquire a famous table which had belonged to the Emperor Frederick Barbarossa in the tenth century. After a recorded history dating back to 823 A.D., the *schloss* had become in the 1890s a boys' school. A later owner refused to dispose of the Barbarossa table alone but expressed willingness to sell the castle, which was and still is a white elephant, contents and all. Father wanted the table so much he made the purchase.

The feudal halls and galleries of Lenzburg are still redolent of his spirit. Nearly every movable object in the castle is a collector's piece. On the bottom of every chair, every table, every pewter mug and copper pot is pasted a label giving the price Father paid for it in Swiss or French francs, German marks, or Italian lire, with the dollar equivalent worked out at the exchange rates of the moment.

In young manhood he was an excessive smoker. Deciding that the habit was both extravagant and deleterious, when he was in his early thirties he broke it off abruptly and never touched tobacco again. After that he thought nobody should smoke. I was a grown man and getting along in life, too, before I ventured to tell him that I occasionally puffed a pipe. He never quite forgave me for it. My habit of smoking, never excessive, gave point to the most dramatic moment of my whole life's contact with Father, as I shall relate farther along in this book.

Once when he was going over his Ellsworth, Pa., mining property with the chief superintendent, he saw four car trimmers smoking pipes as they worked. Father told the superintendent to stop them and see that they never did it again. The official protested that the order was too drastic; car trimmers always smoked, everywhere; you couldn't stop it.

Father said: "You will stop it here, or I will close down the mine."

At that time the mine was producing 10,000 tons a day and was one of the greatest coal operations on earth. Yet I am convinced Father would have carried out his threat, if his order had not been obeyed.

Opposed as he was to tobacco, from the earliest time I can remember he always had wine on his table. But his use of wine was typical of his exact and methodical nature. He put a modest and rigidly fixed limit upon the amount he could drink at a meal and never exceeded that allowance. At the same time, he was fond of sitting long at dinner, especially when he grew older. To make his ration of claret last through, he would dilute his glass with water, about half and half.

In temperament he was very nervous and high strung. Except for a few stock stories such as all fathers, I suppose, relate to their children, he never told me very much about himself. Most of what I know about his life has been told me by his friends, or I have read it in the memoirs on which he worked during the final months of his life.

There was one episode of his youth which he loved to recount as showing his early business acumen, and I will condense it here. His father, a prosperous farmer and commission merchant at Hudson, Ohio, used to send him with his drovers when they took shipments of hogs to Buffalo. Though Father was only sixteen or seventeen years old then, he noticed that the hogs were sold right off the cars in Buffalo before being fed or watered. He persuaded Grandfather to let him take a shipment alone. Then, in the Buffalo stockyards, he refused to sell his fat Ohio hogs until they had been watered. The increased size of the check he brought home convinced Grandfather that the teachers at Western Reserve Academy, where Father was then enrolled as a student, were wrong when they said his son ought to study for the ministry.

Father's will and purpose, when he made up his mind to do a thing and believed he had right on his side, were almost irresistible. Nothing could stand against them, not even constituted government. He wrested the famous Rembrandt portrait away from the Princesse de Sagan, its owner, by sheer determination and ruthless insistence. That story, which he tells in his autobiography, I will relate now.

After Father left his aged mother and us two children in London, he went to Paris, where he met the younger Durand Ruel, the picture dealer, Father already being known in the European capitals as a buyer of works of art. The younger Durand Ruel—Charles—said he was just going to the *hôtel* of the Princesse de Sagan to care for some of her paintings, the princesse being at her summer home in Trouville, and he asked Father to accompany him. There Father saw the Rembrandt "Portrait of a Man", recognized it at once as a great masterpiece, and inquired if it could be bought. Durand Ruel said probably not, though some time previously the princesse, complaining that her son was spending too much money, said she might have to sell some of her pictures and asked Durand Ruel *père* to value them. On the Rembrandt the elder Durand Ruel had placed a valuation of 140,000 francs, which was then $28,000 in our money.

Desire for the Rembrandt obsessed Father. He was not as wealthy then as he became later, and the price was a sheer extravagance for him. Yet for three nights he tossed sleepless in his bed, remembering every brush mark of the painting, its signature—"R. van Ryn, 1632", and on the opposite side: "Aet. 40"—imagining it on the wall of his library on Ellis Avenue, thinking of its fame. There was only one other Rembrandt then in America—"The Gilder."

How well I was to know later that "strange frenzy" which seized my father then! We were both collectors—he of works of art, books, and antique furniture, I of remote solitudes and scenes on which human eyes had never before looked. Lust of either can possess a man like a temporary madness. At the end of three days Father's prudent nature yielded, and he cabled Chicago for a transfer of 140,000 francs. Then he sent Charles Durand Ruel to Trouville to negotiate the purchase.

From Trouville the younger Durand Ruel telegraphed that the Princesse de Sagan would not sell. Father's reply was this:

"The picture is already mine. I have bought it at your valuation, and I expect its delivery."

Charles again telegraphed a refusal. Father was no more yielding than a granite crag. He simply repeated his first telegram. It was too much for the Princesse de Sagan. That poor lady was afraid to let her countrymen know that she was selling to America one of France's great art treasures. She replied that if Father would make the payment in unidentifiable French bank notes, he could have the picture.

Charles Durand Ruel brought back an order signed only by the princesse's valet on the back of her visiting card. In a panic lest something might yet occur to upset the sale, Father rushed from the Durand Ruel gallery, picked up two sashed and capped porters in the street, and with their handcart went clattering over the cobbles of Paris to the Hôtel de Sagan. The card gave him a dubious admission. He pushed past the servants, lifted the Rembrandt from the wall, and carried it out to the cart. I should have liked to see that procession back to the gallery—the sweating *porteurs* in their peg-top corduroys and blue shirts and Father, tall, erect, determined, steadying the precious painting in the cart as he strode on his long legs beside them.

Father left the Rembrandt safely with Durand Ruel during his visit, and when we returned to New York he kept the masterpiece in his cabin.

Two other episodes in his career illustrate that determination of his which could penetrate all resistance. So far as I know, only once in his life did he meet failure in any major exercise of his will. Unhappily, I was the one to defeat him then, though there was nothing else I could do.

It is not my intention to give any complete account here of my father's life beyond the mention that in the twenty-five years between 1873 and 1898 he rose from a clerk, at $1,500 a year, with a Chicago wholesale coal company to the presidency of the Union National Bank of Chicago and directorships on the Postal Telegraph Cable Company, the B. & O. Railroad, and other large corporations. In 1874 he married my mother, who was Eva Frances Butler, of Chicago, daughter of a pioneer paper manufacturer. She died on her wedding anniversary, November 4, 1888, and the next day was Clare Ellsworth's third birthday.

My father's greatest business achievement was his development of the Ellsworth coal mines in Washington County, Pa., south of Pittsburgh. This enterprise was so typical of his genius that I must touch upon it a little.

The nature that could untie parcels and save the strings, and could price-tag the most trivial purchase for a collection, could also envision an industrial operation on a scale that might daunt any individual capitalist today. The Ellsworth mines were a single-handed enterprise for Father, yet the surface by-product plant alone contemplated an investment of $100,000,000. Few operators of the present would care to tackle such a development without partners. There were hundreds of problems to solve, and a mistake or misfortune anywhere along the line might result in disastrous ruin.

It was typical of Father that, in picking up this coal field, he took what other men rejected. The bituminous coal was rich and plentiful, but it lay deep—four hundred feet down—and the entire body was full of natural gas, very hard to control. Some of Father's closest business friends advised him to keep out of it. More than one company had gone broke in that field. In fact, the gas had virtually stopped mining in the district. Consequently, coal rights there were cheap.

Father untied and saved string, despising waste and having only contempt for the waster. The smoke cloud above Pittsburgh he saw not as the banner of prosperity but as a shameful flag of waste. Besides polluting the sweet air, that smoke represented to him enough electricity to turn every wheel in the Pittsburgh district, including the railroad wheels, enough ammonia to double the fertility of the farms in all that section of country, besides dyes, perfumes, cosmetics, medicines, flavors, and all the other products of coal tar. In other words, my father was the pioneer by-product coal operator in the United States. From every ton of coal his mines produced, he expected to get by-products to the value of $1.50, leaving still metallurgical coke worth almost as much as the coal itself.

His life philosophy was simple. He often spoke and wrote it in a single sentence: "It is the little things that go to make the large ones." A single executive mind, no matter how capable, might be confused by the complexity of the entire operation in Washington County, yet a good businessman could take care of the details one by one as he met them. The sum of the details would make the whole operation. I wonder how many industrialists today would dare risk their solvency on any formula or business recipe.

When endowing Western Reserve Academy, Father wrote this advice to the students:

"If a proposition is fair, it cannot fail. I have handled questions that looked monumental and which to accomplish might look like a question of luck. But there should be no such question in anyone's life. Whatever is worthy can be successful, but success will not come unless the most inconsequential and seemingly the most trifling undertaking is done well. It is this discipline, practiced over and over, and over again, that perfects. Never mind if, in perfecting some object, it does not seem worth while, because of taking too much time. All right; let it be a waste of time, if, whatever it may be, the doing is done in the best manner possible. Unravel and go over it again, spending all the time necessary to make it perfect—that is what counts in one's life and brings immense returns later."

In precisely this methodical way, Father went about the development of his coal mines. He optioned some sixteen thousand acres of land in Washington County but before buying a square foot of it he sank test holes in every acre to study the depth and quality of the vein and determine whether it was cut out anywhere by rock. Meanwhile, samples of the coal were going to the principal by-product laboratories of Europe—to the London Gas Works and the chemical centers of Germany. The Germans reported it one of the richest coals they had ever analyzed. Railroads in France and Italy tested it in their locomotives.

Such a huge output as Father contemplated had to find foreign markets. The French railroads were receptive. The government lines in Italy spoke of a fifty-year contract. American coal had to meet in Europe the competition of Welsh and Cornish coal carried in subsidized British bottoms. But the French had begun to subsidize their colliers, which meant that Father must have a fleet of vessels of French registry. His own ships entailed a knowledge of continental ports, and Father made a personal study of the harbors and dock facilities at Saint-Nazaire, La Rochelle, Bordeaux, Genoa, and Venice. At Genoa no space could be procured for coal storage.

Father's Italian engineers designed aerial yards built above the railroad tracks and holding 80,000 tons of coal.

Thus he conquered the details of the operation and allowed the main proposition to take care of itself. During this period of two years he was constantly in Europe, spending much of his time at the by-product mines of Germany, shuttling back and forth across the ocean like a commuter. Meanwhile, four great mine shafts were going down in Washington County. Father had made one miscalculation, but a serious one. It had been his theory that if enough entries were driven through the coal body, the mine would drain itself of gas, with the help of ordinary ventilating machinery. As it proved, the gas made faster than the fans could drive it out, and the mine remained dangerous. Open lights were forbidden, and all mining work had to be carried on by compressed air. The difference in cost between compressed air and electricity, which was proscribed in gaseous mines, might easily have been the difference between success and failure, to say nothing of the increased efficiency of labor in a well-lighted mine, breathing good air.

About this time occurred an accident that showed Father's consideration for animals. It was a rigid rule in the Ellsworth mines that no coal could be shot down until the fire boss had pronounced the air safe. One morning a cutting gang disregarded the rule. There was an explosion which set two mines on fire. Both had to be pumped full of water from a creek.

No human lives were lost, but the mule boss reported that when he was herding out his stock, one of the mules broke away and disappeared. Father, who was at the mine that day, was frantic at the poor mule's plight. The pumps had started; the animal would be trapped and drowned. Father offered a thousand dollars to anyone who would bring the mule up alive. Several miners tried it but were driven back by gas and smoke. When the mine had been pumped dry, Father was comforted to learn that the mule had been peacefully gassed to sleep before the water caught it.

Gas remained a menace not only to life but to the success of the whole enterprise; and in that firm way of his, which would not take no for an answer, Father demanded better ventilation. The engineers shook their heads helplessly. The mine's 25-foot fans were the most powerful made. At a conference with ventilation men in Pittsburgh, a young engineer from the mine said that he had just read in a technical journal about a new fan invented in London. It was called the sirocco, and it showed promise. Two days later Father was on the ocean bound for England. The sirocco was a small high-velocity steel fan. Father saw it cleaning a gaseous mine in Northumberland and knew that his problem was solved.

Sirocco fans put sweet air into the farthest corners of the Ellsworth mines. Still in Father's path stood the state regulation forbidding the use of electricity in that mining field. The official in charge could not be moved. Father's answer was a mandamus action in court. The best experts in America testified that the mine was safe, and the judge ordered a permit granted.

On the edge of the gaseous territory operated the Buffalo & Pittsburgh Mine. It also applied for a permit to use electricity. Following the Ellsworth precedent, the state granted it. A short circuit caused an explosion which killed 182 men and bankrupted the company. The Buffalo & Pittsburgh Mine had no sirocco fans.

At Ellsworth the power was being produced at a central plant burning coal to make steam. At Newcastle upon Tyne Father saw the waste heat from the beehive coke ovens generating all the electricity the Northumberland mines needed. Upon returning to Pennsylvania, he scrapped half a million dollars' worth of new boilers and substituted two central power plants operated by waste oven heat. Incidentally, this change saved the labor of fifteen firemen.

Another waste remained—a waste of human efficiency. Washington County was dry by local option, but the express company brought in hard liquor from Pittsburgh, its agents virtually doing a bootlegging business. Every Saturday night brought a carouse, and not until Wednesday could the mines get a complete force of men.

Father went to the county judges. "I have a stupendous enterprise at stake," he told them, "and I must control the use of strong drink." He asked for licenses to sell beer.

Impossible. The law was the law—the people had voted it. Father took the judges to the property, showed them his model town of Ellsworth, where he was encouraging his employees to buy their homes—showed them the model schools, the public library, the healthy children wearing good clothes sold at cost. Once a week this utopia was invaded by a general spree in which the miners lost time and squandered wages with bootleggers.

The judges yielded, as everybody and everything had to yield when Father determined upon a course. By a quibble that called the taverns clubs, licenses were granted for two taprooms, one in residential Ellsworth, the other in Cokeville, the industrial center at the shafts. Beer only went across their bars, the best beer obtainable and retailing at three cents a glass, with no drinking limit set between the hours of 5 and 9 P.M., when the taprooms were open. Bootlegging ended, the fights and shootings stopped, and a sober force of miners reported for work every weekday morning.

By 1907 Father had the cheapest-per-ton bituminous mine in Pennsylvania—in a territory where experts had pronounced costs prohibitive. Government had begun to regulate business, the attack led by that same Roosevelt who had built the World's Fair log cabin. A law was proposed, prohibiting mines from owning their own railroad cars. Father saw ruin in it; and when, in the spring of that year, a group of interests approached him, he jumped at the chance to sell—nor did he ever again engage in mining except to conduct a private operation exclusively to provide engine fuel for the Canadian Pacific.

Of all his achievements, Father himself was proudest of his work for the World's Fair. He could justly claim to have been one of a small handful of Chicago men who made the Exposition the artistic and cultural triumph it became. As originally projected, the Fair was little more than a political scheme to get some federal money for Chicago. The East was horrified when Chicago won from Congress the right to hold the exposition celebrating the four-hundredth anniversary of the discovery of America, expecting the prairies to produce some sort of glorified country fair, with prize cattle and pumpkins. Except for James W. Ellsworth, Lyman

J. Gage, and one or two other Chicago men of wealth and taste, it might have become just that.

Against his will and almost without his knowledge, Father was elected to the Exposition's board of directors. He had been opposed to the Fair at first but, having accepted his election, acted on his precept that whatever is worth doing at all is worth doing well. And, typically, though he was but one of forty-five directors, he acted individually and secretly, keeping his counsel even from his fellow directors.

It was assumed that the presidency of the board was to be a plum for some politician. Father threw a bombshell into the organization by insisting that the president must be Lyman Gage. When another director said that Gage would not accept the place, Father called on the financier in his office in the First National Bank and whispered a secret into his ear. It was that the secretary of state, James G. Blaine, was about to appoint James W. Ellsworth as special envoy to solicit from the governments of Europe the loan of their great art collections for the Exposition. Gage accepted the presidency. Evidently this was not going to be a country fair.

Next day Father was enroute for a final conference with Blaine at his summer home in Bar Harbor, Me. At Boston he stopped off to see Frederick Law Olmsted to ask him, on no authority at all but his own, to become the man to lay out the exposition grounds. Olmsted laughed. The greatest landscape artist of America devoting his talents to a country fair? Father told him about his errand in Bar Harbor, and Olmsted agreed to go out to Chicago and at least look over the site.

Parenthetically, to the end of his life Father always referred to it as the Exposition. Never the Fair. He was as touchy about it as San Franciscans are about their late fire.

When Father returned to Chicago from that trip, in his microscopical hand he wrote Olmsted a long letter, giving his own idea of what the Exposition ought to be. Even the directors at that time were assuming that the Fair would cost $5,000,000 to build, that being the amount of the stock subscription. In this letter Father set the estimate of $15,000,000. After Olmsted was engaged to lay out the lagoons, canals, courts, and walks, at the first meeting with the architects, when everything was still vague as to what to do, the Boston artist produced this letter; and Father's vision of the Exposition was adopted as the general plan.

During the entire construction of the Fair buildings, it was Father who fought the battle of the architects against the parsimony of the directors, most of whom could not get the original figure of $5,000,000 out of their heads. Even the leading business and financial figures of Chicago in those days were rough, tobacco-chewing men, profane and plain spoken. One of the directors, a Mr O'Dell, then president of the Union National Bank, publicly upbraided Father on the street, calling him a finicky troublemaker, and predicting that if he kept on, there wouldn't be any Exposition at all. This was in the summer of 1892. Four years later Father had the pleasure of throwing Mr O'Dell out of the Union National and taking the presidency himself.

But by Christmas of 1892 it seemed as if Mr O'Dell's prophecy and that of other directors, for whom the country-fair idea was good enough, was about to be realized. On a Saturday the Exposition treasurer telephoned Father that he lacked $50,000 of having enough in the treasury to meet the Monday pay roll. Father sent him his personal check for the amount and then had a showdown with the finance committee, which by this time had all but capitulated before the force of his determination. In every dispute that arose in the board meetings over Exposition costs, Father would win by answering that he personally would see that the costs were met.

Now that the treasury was empty, the badgered finance committee called upon him to make good. Father replied that if the committee would promise to stop entirely trying to raise any more money and turn that responsibility over to him, he could guarantee that the Exposition would be finished and opened on time. Only too glad to make such an arrangement, the committee agreed, and from that time on Father was in complete charge of the finances.

His attack was immediately upon the railroads. Everyone who had subscribed for stock in the Exposition Company had also obligated himself to take bonds in double the amount of his stock subscription. Since the railroads were by far the largest stockholders, they were the place to go for quick money. But the worst panic and financial depression in American history before 1929 had begun; and the railroads, their revenues diminishing fast, welched out of their Exposition bond obligations. Whenever they knew Ellsworth was in the waiting room, the railroad officials sent word that they were out.

Father met them at their next directors' meetings in the Morgan, Vanderbilt, and other financial offices of New York and Boston. The Eastern financiers saw what a disaster it would be for America if the Exposition went into receivership and in every instance ordered their railroads to take up their pledges. Even so, there was not quite enough ready cash provided. When the Fair opened on May 1—its scheduled date—the Exposition Company owed Father something over $800,000 which he had advanced out of his own pocket. But, as everybody knows, or did know then, the gate receipts paid everything off and even returned a profit to the stockholders.

So it is no wonder that my father held the memory of the World's Fair in such affection. He was responsible for the design of the Columbian half dollar. At the close of the Fair he induced Marshall Field to endow the celebrated Field Museum, starting with some two million dollars' worth of Exposition exhibits. At first the Museum occupied the Fine Arts Building. After the Fair closed, with Mr Burnham he worked out the plan for improving Chicago's lake front by connecting Grant and Jackson parks with parkways. In the *Life of Daniel H. Burnham,* that great architect is quoted by Charles Moore, the book's author, as naming but one man responsible for the Chicago Exposition as it proved to be—James W. Ellsworth.

"Mr Ellsworth," the quotation ends, "almost alone among the directors at the beginning, saw the vision."

In our home after 1893 we had an invariable custom. I have already mentioned how Father liked to linger at table. Whenever there were guests, which was nearly always, we sat for an hour—

exactly an hour—after the coffee was poured, while Father ex-
patiated upon the World's Columbian Exposition.

I feel sure that my father, after he passed middle age and had
time for contemplation, must have looked back upon the phenomenon of himself with something like astonishment. As I remarked above, he felt he must be a reincarnation of some previous
life. To explain himself, he examined his lineage, tracing back to a
coat of arms and a village in Cambridgeshire, England. The origin
of the name Ellsworth is thought to be Norse. When honoring me
with a medal after my North Polar flight with Amundsen, the
Norwegian government called me "one of ours." I hope I am, for
there is no breed of men I admire more than the Norwegians.

Father's maternal grandfather was William Dawes, whose great-
grandson, Charles G. Dawes, became Vice-president of the United
States. One of our collateral ancestors was Oliver Ellsworth, second
chief justice of the United States, appointed by George Washington.

After my exploratory flights in the Arctic, Yale University gave
me the honorary degree of master of science. To receive it, I traveled to New Haven from New York by train. Two of my faculty
friends met me at the station.

"Nice gesture for the New Haven Railroad to make," one of them
remarked.

Seeing that I did not understand, he pointed to the name on the
side of the Pullman car from which I had just stepped. It was
"Oliver Ellsworth."

I am not in the least superstitious; but, perhaps because I have
spent so much of my life in the solitudes, coincidences like that
always strike me forcibly. In spite of reason and logic, I can't help
but feel that they are significant. A series of most fortunate coincidences rescued Amundsen and me from the Arctic, as I shall
tell later, and I saw the hand of God in them.

There have been a number of curious coincidences in my experience. For instance, one of the heroes of my life has been Wyatt
Earp, who seems to me to typify better than any other man the
spirit of the pioneers who conquered and civilized the West. I had

worshiped the memory of Wyatt Earp for many years, had read everything about him I could find, and had collected his mementos and relics, before I learned that he began his career as a frontier marshal in the town of Ellsworth, Kan.

An even stranger coincidence arose just the other day. I must explain that when I am away from New York it has long been my custom to take a daily 18-mile walk. In New York I substitute for walking an hour of wrestling with a professional, but when away, wherever I may be, to keep fit I must do my eighteen miles on foot. And exactly eighteen miles. I have found that to be just right for me.

When I was waiting in Christchurch, New Zealand, for the start of my first Antarctic expedition, I quickly found an 18-mile walk for myself. A favorite walk of mine, which I have taken many times, is at the Grand Canyon—nine miles from the brink to the bottom, nine miles back again, the eighteen miles, of course, including a mile of descent and a mile of climb.

In October 1936 my wife and I motored to Windsor, Conn., where the Ellsworth family originated in America. The place is full of Ellsworth memories, chief among them being Oliver Ellsworth's country homestead. When in Windsor he always used to walk from his home to his Hartford office in the morning and back again in the afternoon. They told me the distance, but in my excitement I could not take anyone's word for it. Setting the car's trip-mileage meter at zero, I drove by the most direct route from the office to the country house. It measured exactly nine miles!

Both my grandfather and my great-grandfather, on Father's side, were cripples. Great-grandfather was Elisha Ellsworth, the doughty revenue officer. While pursuing smugglers, his cutter was caught in a winter storm and blizzard on Lake Erie. To keep from freezing, everybody had to stay below. Someone had to steer the vessel, so my great-grandfather rolled a hogshead of molasses to the wheel and stood in it to protect his legs. The expedient was too late. His legs were frozen and, after his rescue, had to be amputated.

Grandfather lost a leg, too, but in less gallant fashion. When he was a boy the Ohio country doctors administered mercury for every ailment. Once, while he was saturated with the drug, he caught cold and developed a case of mercury poisoning, resulting in the loss of one leg. During his active life he got around with a crutch and cane but wound up his days in a wheel chair. He died when I was three years old, and I don't remember him.

In 1904 Father bought the famous Villa Palmieri, in the hills north of Florence, Italy. Every visitor to Florence knows this place, for it was in the Villa Palmieri that Boccaccio wrote the *Decameron*. Marie Antoinette had lived in it, and Queen Victoria. Its latest owner, the Earl of Crawford, had restored the gardens according to Boccaccio's description of them.

Father loved the Villa Palmieri and spent, I believe, the happiest hours of his life there. Of the two residences in Europe, my own preference was for the more rugged Lenzburg in Switzerland. He could scarcely understand this. He could never understand how I could deliberately choose a life of hardship in the wilderness or on polar wastes, when I might have the comfort of a Park Avenue penthouse or a Florentine villa. We both loved nature, but in different ways. He wanted his nature tamed—a well-cultivated Ohio farm, or an Italian garden. Of what he couldn't understand he was apt to be intolerant. Though my years in the open made a competent engineer of me, in Father's memoirs he gives this fact only a grim, grudging approval.

It was in the Villa Palmieri that he died—while Amundsen and I were working desperately to get our plane off the North Pole ice. His methodical habits endured to the last moment, and also his indomitable will. Pneumonia had carried off my mother. It was to take my sister, Clare Prentice. And now it had gripped him—and he was seventy-five years old. Yet not even to himself would he admit that he had the disease. His diary continues to the very end, but not once does it speak of pneumonia. His throat was bothering him, that was all. He had throat trouble. He did not write that diary for public consumption. It was his personal record.

He died on June 2, 1925. Even on that day he wrote in the diary. Two doctors from Florence visited him at two o'clock in the morning. In his matter-of-fact way, he noted down their visit. His judgment must have told him that when specialists ride into the country after midnight for a consultation, the case of the patient is desperate. If so, he chose to put that deduction aside and ignore it. They came to see about his throat.

But now his will and determination were opposed by a stouter adversary than even his son had proved to be some months earlier. With the entry about the specialists, the microscopical writing ends. He must have written this in the morning—perhaps before the first flush of a June dawn filtered into the lovely garden under his windows. The rest of the day's space is filled out in a somewhat bolder hand: "Mr Ellsworth died at 5 P.M. today. We were with him at the end." And the entry is signed by the initials of the two nurses who had accompanied him from New York.

Five o'clock! His diary hour found him with his eyes closed forever.

III COUNTRY STARS

NOT LONG after Mother died Father sent us two children to live with Grandma Ellsworth on the farm near Hudson, Ohio. Except for the year of 1893, when Father brought us back to Chicago to see the World's Fair, I was never again to regard any city as home.

The farm was about three miles out on a road running east from the village. Even in 1888 the farmhouse was an old building. It was a square three-story structure of red brick, with a slate roof. Across the front ran a porch. Fine old elms shaded most of the grounds, but the front yard near the road was sunny and enclosed a big fenced-in strawberry patch. Back under the trees was an artesian well, with a well house above it.

In back were capacious barns, sheds, and other outbuildings such as pertained to any prosperous farm of the Western Reserve. The

front barn was used only for horses—both the carriage horses and
the draft animals—with a central part for carriages. Here, too, there
was a fine harness room. A great haymow was above, ventilated by
cupolas in the roof. Behind this barn was the cow barn, and both
barns were connected by an open-sided shed one hundred feet long.
Under this shed the farm hands exercised the horses in winter.

The driveway from the road to the carriage barn was cindered
and packed hard, and it was just one hundred yards long from
the front gate to the bottom of the carriage ramp. When I discovered this momentous fact, I turned the drive into a running
track. The country air was proving good for me, and already my
thoughts were turning toward athletics. Indeed, before I left for
boarding school a few years later, I sponsored a track meet on our
driveway, the runners and hurdlers being my cousins and some of
the boys of my age from the academy in Hudson.

The parlor of the old house, as I remember it at first, was a dark,
gloomy room always icy in winter. It had slippery haircloth furniture—chairs and sofa. On the center table was a bouquet of artificial flowers under an inverted glass bell. A bundle of dried
cattails stood on the hearth. The sitting room, with its hard-coal
base-burner and its worn carpet and rocking chairs, was much more
comfortable.

Soon after we went there to live, Father remodeled the house,
softening the square ugliness of the original building by adding
wings and putting in a central heating system. A brook ran through
the fields, widening into a horsepond near the barns. Father
dammed this stream, dredged the pond, and created a lake ten
feet or more deep. Then he named the farmstead Evamere Hall
after Mother. The pond became Evamere Lake.

I have forgotten to tell about my father's love of trees. He considered himself an expert in the management of shade trees and
particularly in the transplanting of big trees. He maintained that
no shade tree, such as an elm or a sugar maple, was ever too big
to transplant successfully, given the machinery for handling it. In
fact, he once wrote a sort of treatise on this subject. His practice
in northern Ohio was to dig up trees for transplanting in the dead

of winter, when their entire root systems could be moved in a frozen ball of earth. Even at the Villa Palmieri he heightened the romantic beauty of that place by planting many cypress trees.

In improving the farm at Hudson his talent for trees received its greatest exercise. The road to town was the usual country road of Ohio before the advent of the automobile—deeply rutted, rocky on the hills, full of mudholes in spring. With his children living there, Father planned to spend more time at the farm than he had since his boyhood, but he wanted a good road over which to drive his spirited horses to town. Therefore, at his own expense he graded, widened, and dragged the entire three miles between Evamere and Hudson, and gave the county one of its first smooth roads.

Still he was not satisfied. He wanted beauty through which his shining spokes could spin or his sleigh bells jingle; and so, with the consent of the township and the adjacent property owners, he lined both sides of those three miles of good road with sizable elm trees, scouring all that part of the state for good specimens and moving them in for miles. Today the road in summer is a shady tunnel under an arch of elm branches.

Not all of Father's improvements at Hudson were so directly selfish as this. To close this subject, let me note that before he finished his work there he built the Congregational parsonage, converted an old gristmill into a community club, employed experts to lay out a model-village plan, thus anticipating Henry Ford by a decade or two, besides purchasing and endowing Western Reserve Academy, where he had received his education.

Evamere Lake had a utilitarian as well as decorative purpose, for it provided ice for the household. Father built an icehouse at one end, and every winter the hired men harvested it full. There was still plenty of ice left for skating, however, and in summer we swam in the pond. Curiously enough, I have no memory of how or where I learned to swim, but I assume it must have been here. Father also stocked the lake with fish, but none seemed to survive but suckers.

After the World's Fair a new set of tenants took up residence in Evamere Lake. I have already mentioned the Roosevelt log cabin that came to the farm at this time; but Father bought many other things of the Exposition when it closed, including the Fair's ornamental poultry—peafowl and the swans, Muscovy ducks and other waterfowl that shared the lagoons and canals with the Venetian gondolas. Fresh from this foreign contact, they nevertheless made themselves at home on a bucolic Ohio pond, sheltering in winter in a house built on the bank. I disliked the peacocks, who were always screaming around the house by day; and during the spring nesting season they and the male swans would chase us children.

Remembering how enamored we were of the Linn children's goat in Chicago, Father bought us one in Hudson. We also had a pony to ride; but the goat and pony were, I believe, the only pets we had, except that I managed a coop of bantam chickens. Grandma Ellsworth had a spidery black-and-tan dog of the breed that used to be called rat terriers. I didn't care for this animal, which barked at me and sometimes nipped at my heels. In fact, I have never been a dog lover and never owned a dog that I can remember.

We used to play tricks on the farm chickens. I would tie two kernels of corn to the ends of a string, then call two trusting hens and feed one kernel to each. In the tug of war that followed, the game was to see which chicken could pull up the other's kernel. I also discovered that by tucking a chicken's head under its wing and rocking it back and forth, I could put it to sleep. As the poor fowl, after being set down, tottered in dreamland, Clare and I would scream with laughter.

The sheds and vacant lofts in the barns filled up with debris from the World's Fair. Father bought all the direction signs that had been on the grounds; for instance, lampposts, and many other souvenirs. The most startling was the golden arm, globe, and surmounting eagle of Daniel French's heroic "Statue of the Republic", which stood at one end of the Grand Basin. This was, I believe, the largest statue ever erected in this country, except the Statue of Liberty. The little finger was almost as tall as I was, and we had no barn large enough to contain the arm itself. At his death Father bequeathed Evamere Hall, its buildings and their contents, to Western Reserve Academy. As one result that institution has the best museum of Columbian Exposition relics that exists, I suppose.

I think it must have been after our return from London that we went to live on the farm. At least, I know it was summer; and we came back in the summer. My first clear memory of the farm and the country was of seeing the stars there—liquid as quicksilver and as bright in the unrelieved darkness of a country night, with not even the distant glow of a city to diminish them. I knew then why Professor Hale liked to study them through his telescope. But I saw them first through foliage—under trees—and I had to step out to find clear spaces through which to look at the sky. It was summer.

My Linn cousins in Chicago were cousins on Mother's side, but Hudson, Ohio, was Ellsworth territory. Aunt Emma Ellsworth lived on a farm about ten miles from Hudson, and her two children, Henry and Ruby, became our first playmates. After the house was remodeled, I had a big room on the third floor—a former attic space fixed up for a boy's bedroom. A bay window had been put in at one end; and, because of some architectural necessity, the floor of this window alcove was raised about a foot above the floor of the bedroom, forming a natural platform.

To youngsters the suggestion was obvious, and Clare and I soon used my new room to play school in. Besides the advantages of its window views and its spaciousness, this room contained a treasure —a large revolving globe map of the earth mounted on a standard. Whether it traced to my memory of Dr Hale's telescope in Chicago or whether the revelation of country stars had stimulated my interest, I became very astronomically minded about this time. A natural reader of maps, I saw the world as a whole on this globe, as if I were seated on the edge of the moon; and one day, when I was "teacher", I turned the globe and expounded to Clare what the earth looked like from the moon.

Clare was fascinated. Under such encouragement, I developed this theme until I had what I called a lecture entitled "A Trip to the Moon", delivering it to a spellbound audience of one. When our

cousins Henry and Ruby next came to Evamere, Clare begged me
to repeat the entertainment for them, which I did. They must have
liked it, for I remember being called upon to give it every time
they visited us.

My memory of the "lecture" itself is confused, possibly because
my talk itself was confused likewise. At any rate, as I think back
now, I seem to have regarded myself in some fashion as being on
both the moon and the earth at the same time. This daydream
developed until I conceived the idea of a balloon in which people
could rise to the moon and look down upon the world's spaces
where men had never been. Who could provide such a balloon if
not the government; and who was the government if not Mr Butterworth, our congressman from that district, who was a friend of
the family and sometimes visited us, when Father was in Hudson?

So I wrote to Congressman Butterworth, outlining my plan and
venturing the hope that I might be taken along as a passenger. The
statesman replied, in a letter which was preserved for me, that
while the suggestion was praiseworthy, the project, he feared, was
too vast for even Congress to undertake. Thirty-five years later I
was actually in a balloon, the dirigible Norge, crossing a wide
area of the unexplored Arctic. I can, therefore, only regard this
early mental adventure as prophetic.

But life at Hudson was not all imaginary journeys into space,
not all field meets on my cinder track. I was still the diffident,
obstinate, half-rebellious sprig of humanity, uninterested in the
usual boyish delights, living within my own imagination and dully
bored by it. While I remember Hudson with more pleasure than
Chicago, still my years there are none that I would want to re-
capture. I was not yet awake to life.

Grandmother died, and Clare and I went on in care of a housekeeper and our governess, Miss Johnson. One of the miseries of
existence was violin lessons. I suspect they were Miss Johnson's
idea. A violin teacher came down from Cleveland once a week
and gave lessons to me and another boy, who lived in the village.
I had to practice two hours every day. As soon as I escaped from
home surveillance, I hung up the fiddle and the bow forever.

School continued to be an abomination. They started me in the public school in Hudson. I was a big boy—going on ten years old —but when the teachers examined me for my scholastic attainments, they unhesitatingly put me in the First Reader. The most vivid recollection of public school is a fight I had—my first fist fight —with a schoolmate who taunted me about my backwardness. I came out a bad second in this encounter, for my enemy kicked me in the stomach with his knee, knocking the wind completely out of me. I never forgot it.

I crawled along through the *McGuffey's Readers* for three or four years, but hated the Hudson schools so much and cried so hard to get out of them that Father finally entered me as a day scholar in Western Reserve Academy. Here I acquired my first chum, John Findley, who later became the Congregational minister at Hudson. By this time I had learned to play tennis and had laid out a court at Evamere Hall, and John came and lobbed tennis balls at me.

The safety bicycle had come in, and of course I had my "wheel", too. Even at this time physical endurance was becoming an ideal with me. My favorite Saturday ride was to Cleveland and back, twenty-six miles each way—no mean pull, considering the dusty, rutted roads of that day. Later in my school life I became a distance runner; and, since I have been adult, the only athletic sport in which I have engaged, except for a year of crew while in college, has been wrestling. I am still a good wrestler. When I was thirty, I was not afraid to meet any wrestler of my weight in the world, amateur or professional.

Also about this time I had a girl, though for the life of me I can't remember now who she was or even what she looked like. I had inherited Father's liking for horses and had learned to handle the most spirited steeds in the stable. I used to take my girl buggy-riding. In fact, I think I must have wooed her for the express purpose of presenting a correct man-of-the-world appearance when driving a horse for pleasure.

It was the same story with me in the academy as it had been in the village primary school. I couldn't apply myself to study, and my marks were deplorable. Father saw us children only on rare occasions. At home I was under the authority only of women employees, and I was growing headstrong. I needed strict discipline, evidently, in a wholesome Christian atmosphere. In lieu of a father's training, schoolmasters were indicated—boarding school. Father sent me to the Hill School in Pottstown, Pa. The year was 1895, and I was fifteen.

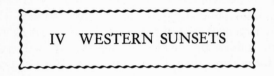

IV   WESTERN SUNSETS

AFTER I HAD GAINED recognition as a polar explorer, the headmaster of Hill School wrote a letter to a friend of my father telling what pleasant memories the school still kept of me and reciting various virtues I was supposed to have had as a student. I'm afraid the good professor was thinking of somebody else. Certainly from the scholastic standpoint I was no ornament to Hill, and honesty makes me admit that I look back upon my experience there with no such pleasure as that expressed by the headmaster in his letter.

Any school was jail to me. After each vacation I used to spend the first week shedding tears of homesickness. Dull as was the village of Hudson, I preferred it to school. Even a case of pneumonia which I contracted at Hill School remains in my memory as a happy episode. Lesson books couldn't follow me into the infirmary, and afterwards I was sent home for convalescence. Such had my recuperative powers become, and such was the tonic of freedom, that within two weeks I was out skating on our pond.

Hill School fully met Father's specifications as the institution for me. Its discipline was rigid, though kindly and fair. Its Christian atmosphere expressed itself in daily morning prayers, afternoon song services, and evening prayers, while Sundays added church and Sabbath school. There was also compulsory military drill, the one mass activity I rather liked. I rose to be color sergeant.

The school was far from being a factory for veneering the sons of rich men with the appearance of education. The one thing the masters insisted upon was good marks; and if you couldn't get those in class, you made up for it during vacations. As a result, I never enjoyed a real vacation while I was a student at Hill. I worked with a tutor through every one.

For me the one bright spot was Epps Candy Parlor at the bottom of the hill, where a boy could gorge on a new concoction then sweeping into popularity—ice-cream soda water. The school authorities frowned on Epps, but we used to sneak off and go there; and hidden up in the springs of my bed were usually stores of forbidden candy, cakes, and nuts. The universal punishment for demerits in studies and deportment was to be held "on bounds" Saturdays, while the good boys enjoyed a holiday. One accepted a pound of prison to gain an ounce of freedom. I was always on bounds, and my inner resentment took the form of pranks and practical jokes none too gentle—pitchers of water balanced over doors, and such things. In the dormitory cottages each floor had a monitor who watched the hallways. So we climbed out of our windows and gained entrance to other boys' rooms by way of the roof.

When I entered Hill School a sanguine faculty, grading me by age, size, and years of previous schooling, put me into the Third Form but dropped me back to the second as soon as they heard me try to recite lessons. Nevertheless, I take pride in recording that I did get through prep school and received a diploma of graduation—in five years. I even passed the entrance examination for Yale, though with conditions. In some fashion I was coached and rehearsed to ultimate success—for me, considering my ineptitude for study, more than a success—a veritable triumph. I was twenty years old at graduation—two years above the average.

My first roommates at Hill were Erskine Smith and Linn Adsit. Linn later became captain of the Princeton track team and held the intercollegiate record for the half mile. He died at an early age. Erskine Smith is now a well-known civil engineer. A close friend, though not a roommate, of mine then was Bob Carey, who is now governor of Wyoming. I also went around with the Elkins boys of West Virginia.

Later I roomed with Walter Stokes and Tom Guffey, of Pittsburgh. Tom was a queer boy, one of his hobbies being to collect knives. To frighten us, he sometimes sneaked into the room after lights were out, carrying a knife, its long blade gleaming in the faint luminosity from the hall. He scared us, too, for neither Walter nor I quite knew what Tom might do with a knife on those occasions.

Though I was terrible as a student, I did well in certain other school activities. In athletics, for example. Our track coach was Mike Sweeney, who then held the world's record for the high jump. I was on the cross-country team and also on the track team, running the mile and the two miles. My best time for the mile was 4:59. I competed one year on the Hill School team in the interscholastic meet at Princeton. My chief rival at Hill in distance running was Hermann Hagedorn.

Encouraged, perhaps, by my former success as a home lecturer, I also went in for public speaking at Hill School and won four gold medals. Here my principal competitor was Russell Bowie, now a well-known clergyman of New York. I joined the Dramatic Club and used to take female roles in the school plays.

Really I ought to have brought away from Hill School pleasanter memories than I did, for it was a beautiful place with fine old trees and lawns and the buildings enclosing a quadrangle, English fashion. Though at the time it seemed a sort of nightmare I supposed I had to live through, my five years at Hill were far from being time wasted. By making me apply myself to studies, the faculty inculcated in me habits that stood me in good stead later. I can truthfully say that Hill laid the foundation of my life, and I would not want anything I have written here about it interpreted as ingratitude.

On each floor of our dormitory cottage at the school lived a professor as mentor. The one on my hall was Charles J. Hatfield, who is now a doctor in Philadelphia. He was a young Princeton graduate and taught English, I think, at Hill, though I never had a class under him.

Professor Hatfield must have detected in me a love of the outdoors, for, just before I was graduated, he suggested that we spend part of the coming summer vacation together, making a trip to Yellowstone Park. Father was agreeable and would put up the money for the expedition, and as soon as the commencement was over we left for the West. That brief trip did more for me than all the schools and teachers I had known, for on it I found myself at last though I was not to know it for yet a little while.

Our railroad tickets took us from Philadelphia to Idaho Falls. In St Paul we had to wait between trains. I strolled from the station, and in the window of a pawnshop I saw a pair of brass knuckles—the first brass knuckles I had ever seen. I went back to the station and asked Mr Hatfield if I shouldn't buy us some of these for protection in the wild and woolly country into which we were heading. He laughed and said he thought not, and I accepted his advice, though somewhat dubiously.

In Idaho Falls we got in touch with Ellis Buck, a typical rancher of the old days, who knew the country and agreed to guide us in. I can remember his appearance as clearly as if it were yesterday —his corduroy trousers, the vest he wore over his shirt. He never wore a coat, and out of one vest pocket always dangled a Bull Durham tag.

Buck provided a cook, and we started out with nine horses— five pack animals and four with saddles. We carried a tent, blankets and tarpaulins, and provisions for a month. Our itinerary took us into the park at the Gardiner entrance, near Old Faithful geyser, and we were in there an entire month, camping all the time, and riding six hundred miles by the time we got back to Idaho Falls. I found out during that month that I didn't need the brass knuckles or any other weapon.

The gorgeousness of the mountain scenery, the marvels of nature that fill the park, and the free, rough, healthy life in the open delighted me as nothing ever had before. For once I was taking an eager interest in things. If it served any purpose, I could give an account of those thirty days almost day by day. Hunting, of course, was prohibited in Yellowstone Park, but we saw lots of game—antelope, elk, black bear. I think I really began to study bears at that time. And the coughing and calling of the elk by night —I can feel the thrill of it yet.

But sunset on the Continental Divide—the mountain peaks pink in it! I saw Western sunsets, and for me the East, with what that word connotes in comfortable, safe, routine existence, was to be no more.

V   EXTRACURRICULAR

I ENTERED Sheffield Scientific School at Yale with a condition in almost every subject. At the end of the college year I had more conditions than ever and was dropped.

Nevertheless, that year began my real education. It started me on a course which has never ended and never will end until I die and which has made me a well-educated man, though my education is highly specialized to my work.

Three of us freshmen—Harry Ferguson, George Morgan, and myself—had a set of rooms in the Hart Building. Ferguson and Morgan were as indolent and indifferent to studies as I was. We scarcely ever even opened a textbook. Speaking for myself, I only went through the motions of being a college student, attending classes but without the faintest notion what they were about. The social side interested us more. I became a Delta Psi and a member of St Anthony. Ferguson was also dropped for conditions at the end of the year. Later, he buckled down, worked off his conditions, and went through to graduation, rowing one year on the Yale four-oared crew. His family owned Fisher's Island, and he is now in charge of the real-estate end of that development.

Harry Ferguson was a man after my own heart, for he liked big-game hunting, and I had brought back from Yellowstone Park a head full of daydreams of adventure in the wild and untrodden parts of the continent. We burned plenty of midnight oil in our quarters but not over our proper studies. While more serious freshmen were probing mathematics and physics, Harry and I were discussing the merits of high-powered rifles.

Then, too, a marvelous book came out that year, or at least I found it that year. It was Theodore Roosevelt's *Ranch Life and Hunting Trail*. I devoured that book like a man starved for reading, sitting until the small hours night after night with it, rereading favorite chapters again and again. From textbooks and Sheffield professors I didn't gain a thing that stuck in my memory, but I think I could pass a fair examination on *Ranch Life and Hunting Trail* today.

How well I remember those chapters! The one in which T. R. tells how, as a frontier sheriff, he walked into a saloon filled with desperados, held them up and cowed them with his gun, and herded them all into jail. And the chapter about hunting big-horn sheep—Ferguson was fond of that one, too. A dream of going together to hunt sheep began to take form. But the whole book filled me with that "passion for the West." I knew then I'd have to go back.

Being dropped from Yale did not specially depress me, for I had expected it. It did, however, leave me at loose ends; and, as much to pass the time as anything else, I took my first job that summer —as a chainman and lamp carrier for the surveyor in Father's coal mines at Ellsworth, Pa. I hardly saw daylight all summer, going down into the mine with the first shift in the morning and not coming up until evening.

It was during this period that I had one of the closest brushes with death of my whole life. Never in the Arctic or the Antarctic have I been in such danger as I was early one morning when my helper and I were pumping a railroad handcar up to the mine from Ellsworth. We were on a stiff grade, the track bending sharply around the shoulder of a hill, a high bank on one side of us, a deep drop on the other. I was pumping the front handle, riding back-ward, when my helper suddenly straightened up, a look of wild alarm on his face, and dived off the handcar down the embank-ment.

I followed him while he was still in the air, for even as he yelled at me I heard the clank of a locomotive's driving rods behind me. As I rolled down the slope, I locked my arms over my head, expecting the handcar to come down on us; but as I picked myself up at the bottom, I saw pieces of it tumbling down the embank-ment below us, while, above, a switch engine, bringing a string of eight or ten loaded cars from the mine down to the main track, rocked and rattled by. On the grade, the engine had been coast-ing. It made little noise and was right on us before we knew our danger.

Business must have been good at the mine that summer. On the handcar I had an open bucket of white paint I used for making bench marks on the roofs of mine galleries and entries. When the engine hit us, it took that whole gallon of paint over its nose, and it was never in the roundhouse long enough after that for the gang to clean it. All summer I'd keep seeing it—a rusty black switch engine with a streak of white on its face like a pinto pony.

Although I learned something about surveying that summer, I wasn't fond of work underground; so when Harry Ferguson wrote me from New York urging that we make a reality of our ambition to hunt bighorn, I was his man in a minute. That September we went to British Columbia.

Our primary destination was Ashcroft, B.C., a town of perhaps two hundred souls on a branch of the Fraser River. We traveled via the Old St Paul & Soo Line, now the Canadian National Rail-way. Our deliberations at Yale had brought us to the conclusion that a Manlicher 6.5-mm. rifle was about as good a gun as you could get for bighorn; and Harry had bought two in New York, together with plenty of ammunition.

Hospitality was openhanded in Ashcroft. Though we were un-known, the local bank cashed our checks without question; and in the hotel it was the honored custom that drinks imbibed before breakfast were always on the house. In fact, the bartender always set out a rank of martini cocktails to greet the guests as they came from their bedrooms. There may have been a smack of guile in this generosity, since a man who starts drinking martinis before breakfast can usually be relied upon to liquor out the day.

Our next objective was the settlement of Lillooet, on the Fraser River, where we intended to find a guide and an outfit. It was a journey of some thirty-five miles, and the only commercial transportation was the four-horse mail stage. On the day we made the journey our fellow passengers were a very surly prospector, on his way up into the North Country, and three Chinese, going to wash gold along the Fraser. The white man resisted our friendly advances, no doubt considering us Eastern tenderfeet, which indeed we were; but the Chinese were sociable, and we liked them best. I remember they gave us some Chinese candy—delicious stuff which I have never been able to find since.

It was going to take us several days to assemble our outfit in Lillooet, so we went to the little hotel. When we opened our two duffel bags, we found that into each one our generous landlord back in Ashcroft had slipped a quart bottle of whisky. While waiting in this frontier town, we were fascinated by the Indians, who were spearing salmon in the Fraser River from platforms they built on the rocks.

Speaking of salmon, let me interpolate here that the most fun is to watch a grizzly bear catch those fish. He lies on the bank as if dead, one inert paw dangling in the water. Then, quick as lightning, the paw flips up, and back in the bush ten or fifteen feet flops a big salmon. Then Mr Grizzly ambles back to devour it.

We also watched the Chinese placer miners washing gold at Lillooet. It was all sluicing and hard work. Nobody but a Chinaman would bother with those placer beds, since the most a miner could take out in a day was two dollars' worth of dust. The Chinese thought this good wages, though, and our friends of the stagecoach joined several dozen other Celestials working along the river.

For our hunting guide we engaged a man named Martley, a

picturesque frontier character wearing buckskin shirt and pants, moccasins, and, of course, the usual Stetson. He was an old hunter who knew the mountains well. He engaged a man to serve as cook and wrangler, and we assembled a pack outfit for a month in the wilderness.

Had we been wiser then in the ways of the Canadian Northwest, we might have noticed that Martley's name, along with others, was posted in the barroom of the hotel. It was against the law in British Columbia for a publican to sell liquor to a man pronounced by the court to be an habitual drunkard, and Martley was on the index expurgatorius. If we had realized that, greenhorns as Ferguson and I were, I think we would have ended with him then and there, for a man with a constitution shattered by drink is a bad man to take into the wilds.

Early one September morning we started out from Lillooet, making our way up the stream valleys to the foot of the Coast Range. There we made camp, though we did most of our hunting above the timber line, climbing up on foot from this base and hunting as we went. Each type of mountain country, the wooded slopes of the mountains and the bare regions above, had its own life, as we discovered; but we were primarily after sheep and goat, who live above the timber, the goats on the rocks, the sheep on grassy slopes.

This was really game country, and we got lots of it. We shot six mountain goats, as I remember, and brought back several bighorn heads as trophies. We also shot plenty of black-tailed deer. Whether we got any bear on that trip I'm not sure, but we did begin to observe their habits. This is as good a place as any to tell about some of the differences between grizzlies and black bears. What I am about to say is known to every Western hunter, but they are things which I have also observed during many years on the trail.

If in some hunting area the black bears suddenly disappear, you can be sure that there are grizzlies about. Black bear are afraid of grizzlies and flee from a country when the grizzly moves in. The black bear is stupid; the grizzly, smart. If a black bear knows a hunter is coming, he fades quietly from the vicinity. The grizzly stands up and looks over the brush for the hunter. If you shoot and wound a black bear, he will howl and run. The grizzly bites at his wound and is likely to come after the hunter. The two varieties differ utterly in character.

One morning I went alone with Martley for a day with the bighorn, Harry Ferguson for some reason preferring to remain at the camp. I had grand sport that day, bagging several head, caching the game to be picked up another day. About the middle of the afternoon Martley began asking to go back, but the hunting was so good I kept on, aware that we could follow the trail down to camp as easily after dark as by daylight. Just at dusk my guide suddenly sat down and began to cry. He said he couldn't go another step. His alcoholic physique had simply caved in.

For me this was no laughing matter. I couldn't desert Martley. In his exhausted state he might freeze to death. On the other hand, I had on only a khaki hunting suit—breeches and high-laced boots—and faced the bitter cold of a September night in the Cascade Mountains high above the timber line without even a blanket to cover me.

However, I had to put up with it. We collected brush and made as good a fire as we could and then tried to sleep, but sleep was impossible for me. The cold which had set in at sunset drove into my bones. During the day I had shot and skinned a mountain goat, and I had this skin folded up in my pack. I tried to use it for a blanket, but the moment I got it out and unfolded it, the cold froze it hard as a board. Nevertheless, I got under it, but it kept sliding off every time I moved. Finally I gave up and spent the night sitting at the fire, alternately roasting my stomach and back. Martley, too, was too cold to sleep, even in his buckskins, and he did the same. I breathed so much wood smoke that night that the smell of it sickened me for a month afterwards.

With the morning sun came warmth at last and unconquerable drowsiness. We both slept in the sunshine until midafternoon and then, with Martley again able to travel, made our way down the mountain, reaching camp just at nightfall.

The high-laced leather boots—the Eastern sporting-goods store's idea of the correct thing for hunting—show what a tenderfoot I was then. Moccasins, which the Westerners wear, are much better. After you ford a stream in moccasins, you can wring them out and put them on again fairly dry. Their disadvantages are that they flatten and callous the feet and that they wear out quickly. Later, when I was on the U.S. Biological Survey in the West, I used to carry a sackful of moccasins with me, wearing out a pair every three days.

The best footgear in the wilderness is ordinary tough Oxford shoes. They protect the arches and soles of your feet, you can dump water out of them after wading, making them almost as dry as moccasins, and their great advantage over leather boots is that you can get them on easily on a frosty morning. A wet and frozen boot is almost impossible to put on.

On this trip Ferguson and I carried an ordinary four-wall tent. That also shows how green we were. In Indian country, by far the best tent is the tipi. You can carry the tarpaulin for a tipi in a small compass, and in a tipi, when you're held in by wet weather, you can have a fire, the smoke going out naturally through the top. Furthermore, when traveling you can always find tipi poles up ready for your tarpaulin, for when tipi Indians break camp, they leave the poles for others to use.

Upon our return to New York I entered Columbia University, taking courses in mineralogy and mining. There is not much to say about this year, except that I made the freshman crew, rowing Number 2 oar under the coaching of Ned Hanlon. I was the lightest man in the boat. We beat the Yale freshman crew that year on Lake Whitney but lost in the regatta at Poughkeepsie.

At this time the newspapers were full of the prospect that the United States might drive a ship canal across the Isthmus of Panama. The French company had sold its franchise to us, and with President Roosevelt urging the project in Washington, its early accomplishment seemed to be assured. Actually, the digging did not start for two years after that, but nobody in 1902 foresaw the obstacles the Republic of Colombia would put in the way.

Even in Canada Harry Ferguson had talked to me about Panama, and that next summer he suggested a trip down there, I think with the idea that we both might land engineering jobs with the canal builders. A word from Harry was enough for me, and August found us on a steamship wallowing down through a Caribbean whipped rough by the southeast trade wind.

The isthmus was reeking with yellow fever, malaria, and half the other plagues of the world, but that meant nothing to two young fellows burning for adventure. In Panama City we made the acquaintance of the chief of police, who one day showed us a small gold idol of Inca times, saying he had picked it up in a Colombian mountain village. Ferguson and I decided that we could find more Inca relics if we went there, too. A cattle boat was conveniently leaving for the South, and we were aboard as passengers.

We debarked at Buenaventura, a Colombian port on the Pacific, a town rising on stilts from a coastal swamp, and our subsequent expedition took us through to the Atlantic—across the Andes on foot, following the coffee trails.

I shall never forget our first and only night in Buenaventura. The one hotel was crowded, and the only place offering itself to us as a shelter was a corrugated iron coffee shed on the dock. This, we thought, was better than nothing, until we found that most of the available room on the coffee sacks was already taken by the Negro stevedores. Nevertheless, we were tired and found places for ourselves and presently slept as soundly as the laborers. In the morning Ferguson's eyes were swelled nearly shut, and my ankles had doubled in size, from flea bites.

We got out of Buenaventura as quickly as possible, crossed the low coast range of the mountains, and came down to the village of Cali, our first objective, in the narrow but very fertile valley of the Cauca River. Thence we quartered northeastward across this valley, climbed the high Central Cordillera of the Andes, dropped down into the valley of the Magdalena, and followed that great river north to Honda, the head of navigation.

This was a foot journey of about two hundred and fifty miles, much of it through rugged country. We knew no Spanish, except the phrase, *"Cafe con leche y huevos."* But the Colombian people we found very kind and hospitable. Most of the time we were far from towns and hotels and had to stop with farmers and plantation hands, but the meanest hut never turned us away when we asked for shelter. Instead of the *huevos,* they always gave us chicken. Hungry as we were, we had to wait until our host killed and plucked a fowl and roasted it in the outdoor oven. In the high mountains we nearly froze every night, for we had only tropical clothes, and the cabins were unheated.

In fact, from our point of view the Colombians had only one flaw, and that perhaps should have been excused them. Not many North American Yankees had ever been in their part of the country, and they were very curious about us. We had practically no privacy. At night when we undressed for bed, we were afraid to light our candle, for we knew everybody would be watching us through the unshuttered window. In the morning when we opened our eyes, we saw a ring of faces glued to the pane, regarding us.

However, it all became worth while when at last we stood on the ridgepole of the Andes and looked down into the great flood plain of the Magdalena Valley, one of the finest scenic spectacles in South America. I have neglected to mention that during our marches we sustained ourselves by munching a local sweetmeat called *pinoche,* which is simply raw cane sugar wrapped up in banana leaves. And, incidentally, we found no Inca treasures.

At Honda we boarded a wood-burning, paddle-wheel steamer, being the only foreigners on the passenger list. The passenger quarters were screened from mosquitoes by cheesecloth. Everybody, officers and all, ate yellow soup and pulpy fish at a long table in the dining room. Ferguson and I amused ourselves during the three days of the voyage by shooting alligators on the bars and mudbanks with the rifle we carried. Near the mouth of the Magdalena we turned westward into a canal and came out at Cartagena.

During the week we waited for the United Fruit steamer that was to take us home, we two American boys were much impressed by the pretty girls of Cartagena sitting behind their barred windows and being serenaded evenings by young fellows with guitars. One morning while we were dressing in our hotel Ferguson suddenly yelled and tore off his shirt. There on his bare shoulder perched a scorpion.

Back in New York, I began a second year at Columbia University. But my story here was just about what it had been at Yale. It is true that after my glimpse of the West mining and mineralogy were interesting me more than had the subjects at Sheffield, but my heart wasn't in college work. School was still prison to me.

Then, in the spring of 1903, I read, or somebody told me, about a magnificent railroad enterprise in Canada. The Grand Trunk was about to build from Moncton, N.B., to Prince Rupert, B.C.— a clean transcontinental span—and wanted men for their exploratory surveys.

This was engineering more like—driving across prairies and mountains, cutting through swamps, tunneling hills, bridging rivers! I didn't want to be a mining engineer and spend my life burrowing underground like a mole. When I explained my real desires to my father, he approved of them, realizing by this time that I would never make any great go of book education.

No more college for me! Unceremoniously, just before the spring examinations began, I quit Columbia and took a train for Canada.

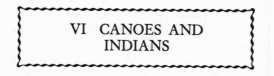

VI CANOES AND INDIANS

IN MONTREAL I found the offices of the Grand Trunk Pacific Railway humming with activity. Survey gangs were being recruited and sent off every few days. I had hoped that my work in the Ellsworth mines might recommend me as one of the engineering force, since I had learned something about the transit and could even run levels. The most this experience got me, however, was a job—a humble one, but still a job—as axman at $40 a month and found.

I was taken into a party headed by an engineer named Allen. To us was assigned what was known as the English River Division, and our job was to run an exploratory right of way from a point on the English River to Winnipeg, a distance of about two hundred miles. It was practically all through virgin wilderness full of lakes, streams, and rapids, and covered with forest and dense underbrush.

As soon as our gang was made up—one transit man, one leveler, and six axmen—we were loaded, two to the bunk, on a C.P.R. tourist sleeper and shipped to Rat Portage, Ont., on an arm of the Lake of the Woods. Camp equipment awaited us there, and we pitched tents on the shore of the lake until Mr Allen, the engineer in charge, who had remained behind in Montreal, could join us. Mosquitoes darkened the air, but we had so much work to do, freighting our supplies out from the C.P.R. station in Rat Portage, that we paid little attention to them.

Mr Allen brought the camp cook with him, and we still had to wait several days at the lake until the boss hired wagoners, horse wranglers, and other white labor, as well as a number of Indians to serve as guides, hunters, canoemen, and also as stake men and axmen on the survey gang. When we were at full strength we numbered twenty-five to thirty men, of whom one third were Indians.

This was hunting country of the Ojibways, a tribe for whom I gained great admiration. They were picturesque fellows, dressed in cotton shirts and those blue jeans known universally in the North Country as "Levis." They wore moccasins and around their waists wrapped woolen *voyageur* sashes in many bright colors. In camp they slept in tipis, and at dusk, after they had eaten, they would sit around their fire and sing wild, haunting tribal chants.

When we were ready, we struck camp and loaded ourselves, stock and baggage, aboard a stern-wheel Hudson's Bay Company steamer, which took us northward through little lakes and connecting streams, finally dumping us out on a flat rock in the heart of the wilderness. After that we had to fend for ourselves. The first big job was to portage our supplies through the woods to our starting stake on the English River.

There we pitched a camp and began to get acquainted with each other. I found that my fellow workmen were nice fellows and pleasant companions. I liked them all, even the cook, a Canadian who was too fond of his liquor. Being perpetually saturated with alcohol, he sweat like a horse all summer. We'd come in at night to see him mixing up a mess of bannocks, perspiration dripping steadily from his chin into the dough. One night I found a cigarette butt in my raisin pudding. But one got used to such things. I had a fellow axman who had been all over the world and was blasé. "There's nowhere left for me to go," he would say. "I've seen it all." Then he'd switch a big cud of chewing tobacco from one cheek to the other.

Mr Allen was an old-time exploratory engineer, rough but considerate of his men, and he seemed to be able to live just as methodical a life in the wilderness as he might in a house in town. Driving rights of way through desolate country was an old story with him. My typical memory of him pictures him sitting at the little smudge fire he would build every night in front of his tent. The mosquitoes swarmed all along the English River. On a forked stick near the fire hung his socks, as he sat barefooted, peacefully smoking his evening pipe. He always dried out his socks every night. That country was half under water, and we had much wading to do. The rest of us put on our socks damp every morning.

Perhaps the most interesting man with the survey gang was the head Indian, Moses, our surveying poleman. He was responsible for our rough line, and by Indian instinct and sense of direction he could run a line so straight that a transit man had trouble finding anything in it to correct with instruments. As I said, this was Ojibway hunting ground, and Moses knew all the watersheds and every other topographical feature. He made only one error, but that mortified him almost to death. One day when we were hacking his line through the bush, we brought squarely up against a long granite precipice. Moses could never explain how he made that error, nor could any of the rest of us. We had nothing to do for three days, while the Indian found a new route that avoided the wall.

When the exploratory right of way was cut through to Winnipeg, the Grand Trunk, in appreciation of Moses' work, presented him with a handsome pair of Zeiss binoculars.

At first there was no room for me in any of the dormitory tents, and I was ordered to make a bed for myself in the cook tent. Once when I was asleep there, a midnight thunderstorm blew the cook tent down on me, and I spent a miserable night on my hands and knees, holding up the canvas. It rained cats and dogs all the rest of the night, and there was no other dry shelter to which I could go. When I was discovered under the flattened tent in the morning, there was only laughter at my plight. Nobody had sympathy to waste on a mere axman.

In making our beds, we whites adopted the Ojibways' type of bed—four birch logs laid in a rectangle, the inner space being filled with boughs. At each corner we drove a post, the four posts supporting a mosquito bar.

As I mentioned, the Indians had their own tipi camp, but we often went over to talk with them in the evening. Sometimes they gave us bannocks to eat. The bannock of the North Country is a sort of soda biscuit, but I have never tasted any as light as the Ojibways could make. Our own cook's bannocks couldn't compare with them. We usually had one of the Indians out hunting, and when he brought in a black bear, the Ojibways always asked for the suet. When blueberries were ripe, they made a sort of pemmican of blueberries and bear fat, stuffing it sausage fashion into the cleaned intestinal membranes of moose. They were great tea drinkers, and even when working in the bush would stop every three hours and make tea. The boss knew Western Indians too well to interfere with this custom.

Tea was also the only hot beverage in our camp. Our staple foods were jam and bacon, salt pork, rice, bannocks and other hot breads, and such game as our hunters brought in. The salt pork we brought in with us had a peculiar taste, most of us thought. The Ojibways drew salt pork and other rations from our supplies, and when the weather grew hot some of them developed boils. They declared that the salt pork was causing their trouble. Mr Allen made an investigation and found that the salt pork was really horse meat sold to the company by an unscrupulous contractor. We dumped nine barrels of it into the river.

Our practice was to work out of a camp as long as the morning and evening journeys did not cut into the working day and then move the camp on ahead of the survey. That made it all canoe work for us back and forth between the camp and the job. The English River is merely a series of detached waterways connecting a string of lakes. In these passages were many rapids. I became a good canoeman before that year was over. The Ojibways used their own birch canoes, but the company furnished Peterboro canoes to its white men. When paddling, we always stripped to the waist, and thus became brown as nuts. We always carried a blanket in a canoe, and when we reached a lake with a ripple of breeze on it, we hoisted the blanket as a sail. This was a welcome help in the evening especially, for we worked on the right of way until dusk and only got back to camp after dark. That is how hard the Grand Trunk was pressing the work. The blanket was heavy as a sail, and, with wind on it, it took good boatmanship to keep a canoe upright. Once a canoe in which I was riding did upset and spill everything out. We all had to swim to shore and later had to dive to recover our tools and other equipment.

The work itself was arduous, especially for the axmen. Through timbered areas it was all chopping to clear the route. Often the woods receded from the water-level grade and gave way to thick brakes of birch and cottonwood saplings and scrub spruce and pine. Wild raspberries and other briers tore at our legs. Then it meant hard work with the brush hooks. A crash in the thicket, and there was a moose. A yell from one of the Indian stake men just ahead, and everybody would scurry for shelter. That yell meant he had stirred up a nest of hornets. Most of the country teemed with game. On some of the lakes the wild duck were so thick we killed them with our canoe paddles.

Once, when we were moving camp, another axman and I took a

pack horse and attempted to avoid a detour of the river by cutting across overland to the north. By some miscalculation, we strayed from our correct route and lost ourselves in the woods, a possibility which anybody who has ever camped north of Georgian Bay will understand. For three days we must have traveled in circles. We had no guns with us and began to starve. Finally we knocked the horse in the head with an ax and feasted. Horse meat and wild berries kept us going until we finally found the river—a great relief.

After we dumped the spurious salt pork into the English River, the camp was very low in food supplies. In fact, we had little in the commissary but rice and sugar. An Indian runner had been dispatched to Rat Portage for fresh stores, but the arrival of these depended upon the steamboat which had brought us in, and its trips were infrequent. So many men could not depend upon the variable luck of a single hunter, and we seemed to be in for a series of alternate feasts and famines.

Three of us then asked permission to go down the river to a point where there was a fairly short portage over to the Canadian Pacific Railway and to a water-tank settlement called, as I recollect, Englehart. At this place, we understood, there was a section house stocked with supplies for the Canadian Pacific road gangs. We thought we might buy and transport back enough food from that depot to keep our camp going until the Rat Portage shipment came.

Mr Allen consented and gave us an order on the Grand Trunk to pay for whatever we might procure. It was a 100-mile canoe trip to the portage, then a stiff hike through woods and swamps; but when we finally reached the section house, the keeper refused to sell a thing to us. We were from a rival line, and he had no authority to help us. He did, however, take pity on us three, for we had had little to eat during our two-day journey, and began frying eggs for us. I'm sure I'm not exaggerating when I say we ate a dozen apiece.

But I loved it, hard work, hardship, famine and all, and especially in the winter, when snow weighted the boughs of spruces and firs, and we had to brush away in the zero temperatures the powdery crystals in order to find bare, frozen ground in which to drive our stakes. When the cold weather came, the Indians installed tin stoves in their tipis. These had to be stoked with wood every three hours; but, although no watch was kept and the Ojibways all slept at once, somebody would always wake up at the exact time and replenish the stove.

Having an interest in something, too, showed me that I could learn as easily as any other man. Although I did not especially covet promotion, in the fall I was raised to chainman with the survey party. When at the end of winter our cleared and staked route reached the outskirts of Winnipeg, I had changed from a callow college youth into a bronzed and toughened man of the open. For a year I had been eating with the appetite of a wolf, yet I did not have an ounce of fat in my body. I was drawn to the wire edge of condition, hard as nails and fit for any trial of physical endurance.

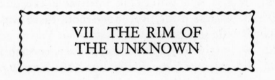

VII THE RIM OF THE UNKNOWN

AS I LOOK BACK on them now, I realize that those months along the English River were the happiest of my life. If they were ever matched afterwards, it was four years later, when I was townsite engineer for the Grand Trunk at Prince Rupert and lived in my log hut above the booming coast of the North Pacific.

When we reached Winnipeg that spring, Engineer Allen found a commission to go on and make the exploratory survey of the Beaver Hills section in Saskatchewan. He had to recruit a new gang for this, and I jumped at the chance to enlist, putting in the entire summer and fall of 1904 on the prairies of the young province.

This was different work than we had known along the English River and not nearly so pleasant. We were cutting a straight line through swamps, wading waist deep much of the time and grubbing willows out of gumbo muck. We seemed to be always wet, cold, and miserable. Yet it was good work, too—a man's work, opening up a new empire for settlement.

Boom towns were springing up all along our new right of way in Saskatchewan, so it was not necessary for us to move with a camp outfit. We could work out of these settlements, staying in their raw new hotels. Every other business shack was a real-estate office. Homesteaders and land buyers from Minnesota and the Dakotas, from eastern Canada, and from England were flocking into the wheat country. Grain elevators were mushrooming against the horizon.

One night when, dead with fatigue, I came to one of these hotels, I found that my only chance for a bed was to share one with an Indian half-breed. He had been assigned to a tiny room above the kitchen, and it received much of the heat of the wood-burning range below. While I did not appreciate the stuffy warmth of the room, there were other of God's creatures who did. As I was dressing in the morning, I found that the molding on the walls was three layers deep with bedbugs.

Nevertheless, on this job I learned to love the spaciousness of the prairies, and I carried on this feeling for clean, flat horizons into the deserts and polar snow fields I was to explore later. To this day I prefer these things to mountains, though I love mountains, too. But mountains hem one in. Only on their summits can they match the freedom conveyed to the soul when a man stands or moves always as the center of a perfect circle stretching, flat and unobstructed, to the round rim of the earth.

When the Beaver Hills work was finished, I could run a transit and call myself a surveyor. I had been away from home nearly two years, and so I returned to the East to see my sister and my father. On Father's earnest request, I consented to work that winter as a leveler in his coal mines. Once again there was a period of several months during which I scarcely saw any daylight.

That winter, though, I made a short trip to New York, and while there I met Madison Grant, an attorney who is now head of Bronx Park and a trustee of the American Museum of Natural History. The Alaska gold rush was still on, Chilkoot Pass and the Klondike were fresh in people's minds, and the beach workings at Nome were producing fabulous tales of sudden riches. Grant had become interested financially in a gold property in the Kougarock country, not far from Teller, Alaska, north of Nome. It was a hydraulic proposition on which the company was to start development in the spring, and Grant thought he might work me in on that job, if I cared to go.

I did care to go. Grant then introduced me to Andrew J. Stone, who had been engaged as general manager of the Kougarock Mine, and he hired me as assistant to Chief Engineer Jim Kelly. This was the same Andrew J. Stone after whom are named the black bighorn sheep of the Cassiar Mountains in British Columbia. I went back to the coal galleries in a happier frame of mind. The West had called me again.

In April I joined Mr Stone, Jim Kelly, and other members of the development party in Seattle, and we all went north together on the SS Victoria. Incidentally, it was to be this same old Victoria that, twenty-one years later, was to bring Amundsen, Nobile, and myself down from Alaska after we had completed our transpolar flight in the dirigible airship Norge.

We found Nome still the Nome of the great gold rush. All the famous figures of Alaskan story were still there—Davidson; Lane; Lindbergh, the pioneer gold miner of Alaska. Wyatt Earp, for whose stalwart courage I was later to build up such admiration, had been there the year before. I acquired a souvenir of a type dear to my collecting spirit. In the annals of Skagway the most famous duel was the gun battle fought between Reed, the claim surveyor, and Soapy Smith. Smith was shot dead, and Reed died next day. In Nome I bought Reed's old transit and used it all that summer at Kougarock.

Storage eggs, guaranteed fresh in February, were a dollar apiece in Nome on June 1, the date of our arrival, and other prices were in proportion. All of Nome's streets were planked, and the wooden sidewalks were raised up on posts out of the mud. In front of the Golden Gate Hotel, where we stopped, you had to watch your step, for there was a loose board that flipped up if you trod on the end of it. Gambling houses were wide open, and the stakes were terrific. Miners tossed their entire fortunes on the tables.

Raw gold—dust and nuggets—was the universal medium of exchange. Wherever anything was dispensed commercially, from hotel hospitality to love, stood scales. There were gold scales on every store counter, behind every bar, and, I may as well tell, in the parlor of every prostitute. The current value of gold was $18 an ounce.

As its bow toward the moral conventions of civilization, Nome confined its harlotry to a restricted district, but this district functioned with something of the businesslike precision of an Automat cafeteria. Each girl occupied her own private hut or cottage, and these houses of shame were enclosed within a high stockade having a single entrance. Visitors checked in and out through a turnstile.

The girls of the Division gave Nome its only feminine society and therefore mingled freely with the male population in all public places—the saloons and gambling houses, restaurants, and hotel dining rooms. One girl, often seen on the streets, was a memorable figure, because every time she smiled, she revealed a diamond set into a front tooth.

But she was nothing compared with Major French's horses. Major French was a New York man who pined for the lost diversions of a gentleman. When he struck it rich, he imported from the States a smart four-in-hand turnout in which he rumbled over Nome's planks. To display his prosperity, he had had a jeweler set diamond solitaires in each polished forehoof of his stylish nags.

In Nome we assembled an outfit of four-horse wagons and then started overland for the Kougarock country, 120 miles north. From the time we arrived in Nome, it took us a month to reach the mining claim, for, after the beaten trail pinched out, the going became very bad. Much of the country was a sort of Arctic morass, in which the only solid footing was on the niggerheads lifted three feet high above the muck by frost. You had to jump from one to the other. Try that some time with a 75-pound pack on your back, and you'll find it's no fun.

Along the travel routes of northern Alaska then were road-house hostelries spaced every few miles apart. These were log or board structures of a single big room—a bar across one end, the other walls lined with bunks in tiers, a hot tin stove in the middle. When the guests retired at night, they hung their socks to dry on ceiling hooks above the stove. If you reached one of these havens late at night you found the air steamy from drying apparel and noisy with the snores of men. In Nome and along this route I ate sour-dough bread and biscuits for the first time. Sour-dough bread is so good, I wonder that our city bakers don't include it in their offerings.

We reached the Kougarock property on July 5, just in time to witness the aftermath of a tragedy. North of us was Taylor Creek, and here there was one of the roadhouses such as I have just described. The day before our arrival being Independence Day, the transient boarders at the roadhouse celebrated in the only way possible for them to celebrate there—at the bar.

This celebration was especially wet, because a miner of the neighborhood had found a fifty-dollar nugget in his washing pan and came to the roadhouse that day to spend it. By afternoon the general spree reached the horseplay stage, the gang's drunken idea of good clean fun being to head up the nugget-finder in an empty pork barrel and roll him around. It occurred to them presently that it would be even more fun to roll him down the 20-foot cut bank of the creek. The stream was at freshet stage, and the man drowned because his companions were too drunk to help him.

Until we got our own camp buildings up, we stayed at this road-house. The engineering job was to run a ditch from Taylor Creek to the mine, a distance of fourteen miles. This work took all sum-mer because of the character of the country. Our nearest town was the Bering Strait settlement of Teller, fifty miles away, and we went there for our supplies. I may note at this point that when the company later began to work the Kougarock Mine, it fizzled out and never amounted to anything.

At one time during the summer, the other engineers went down to Teller, leaving me alone at Kougarock with nothing to do for three days. There was an Irish prospector trying to develop a placer claim not far away, and he had asked me to survey a ten-mile ditch line for him. Singlehanded, he expected to dig a ditch eventually and thus get a head of water that would enable him to wash gold in profitable quantities. I took this opportunity to do him the favor he asked.

When I had his line staked out, he wanted to pay me, but I refused, knowing that he was none too prosperous. Besides, I had been glad enough of his company and of the work to occupy my time. He insisted, however, upon giving me a ten-dollar gold piece for a souvenir, and I have always kept it as a memento of my only gold-mining experience. Before we left Kougarock, my Irish friend went down to Nome for the winter. He got into a quarrel there in a gambling house and was stabbed to death.

On our way out in the fall, we were treated to a rare and really pathetic spectacle of nature. The trail to Nome at one point passed through a lake country, the lakes being connected to the sea by a stream system coming out at Teller. These lakes were a breeding ground for salmon. Salmon after spawning commit suicide by starvation, during which period their flesh becomes soft and wormy and unfit for food.

Just before we reached these lakes there had been a sudden freeze-up, and tens of thousands of aged dying salmon had been caught in the ice, their bodies half in and half out. Sometimes their heads were out in the air, sometimes their tails, but the lakes were yellow with their frozen bodies, acres and acres of them. For them it was journey's end, as their fry, under the ice, were even then making their way to the sea to start another of their age-old mystic cycles of life.

Two or three times that summer I went down to Teller myself —the same Teller where Amundsen, Nobile, and I landed with the

Norge in 1926 after flying from Norway across the North Pole. I stood on the beach there looking out into the Bering Sea. Just around the corner of Cape Prince of Wales was the unknown Arctic Ocean. I was on the rim of one of those white spaces on the map which had fascinated me as a child, to look into which I had petitioned Congress for a balloon.

Perhaps those memories did not come to me then, but I did wonder how men could live year after year in Teller, staring out across gray tumbling water in summer and in winter over a limitless white field of pack ice, and never once have any curiosity about what lay in those distances. For the Arctic then was really the unknown. Even Peary had not yet stood on a polar headland and seen the mirage to the northwest that gave rise to the myth of Crocker Land—a myth I was to help dispel.

Thus, during those centuries of human sleep called the Middle Ages, dull men in Europe stared out into the Atlantic without any curiosity that transcended the horizon. Then came a Christopher Columbus, and the world at last began to move.

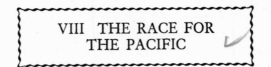

VIII   THE RACE FOR THE PACIFIC

ONLY A FRONTIER COUNTRY, where the land was anyone's for the taking, could have witnessed such industrial wars as our Western railroads waged about the middle of the last century in their struggle for rights of way. Engineering and construction gangs took almost the status of roving private armies; and in one instance, when the Santa Fe was racing the Denver & Rio Grande, breastworks were actually thrown up, and rival picket lines watched each other over the sights of rifles.

Now, fifty years later, and in less violent fashion, the same drama was to be repeated on the last frontier—the Canadian Northwest.

With incredible speed Mackenzie and Mann had slapped down ties and rails on top of the prairie and thrust their Canadian Northern Railway through to Edmonton. The Grand Trunk's exploratory surveys had also reached that city, and in Edmonton both rivals faced toward the Pacific, dreaming of a great port and terminal there through which the torrent of the new wheat of the prairies could flow by cheap ocean transportation to all parts of the earth.

Rumors of the impending race reached me in Pennsylvania, where I had become resident engineer in charge of the layout and construction of 180 by-product coke ovens at the Ellsworth mines. I had come down from Alaska with the Kougarock engineers, and Father had persuaded me to give up my wanderings and settle down into a steady job with him on his Pennsylvania coal property. For five months I allowed myself to be chained to this work. By the break of spring 1906 I had had all I could endure of the smoke, dull labor, and dirty snow of a bituminous mining town in winter, and, much to my father's disappointment, I threw up my job at the mine and went to Edmonton.

There I reported to the famous engineer Van Arsdol, who was in charge of the entire survey for the Grand Trunk from Edmonton to Prince Rupert. Van Arsdol was a veteran engineer of railroad construction, having been with the Canadian Pacific when it was pioneering into the West. A tall mighty-boned man, I remember him most clearly as always gripping a pipe with a stem at least eighteen inches long between his strong teeth.

On my previous record with the Grand Trunk, Van Arsdol hired me—as a full transitman now—and attached me to the gang headed by a Swedish engineer named English. The Canadian Northern engineering gangs were also in Edmonton, waiting for supplies. The objective of both sides, everybody well understood, was Yellowhead Pass, the nearest and easiest crossing of the Canadian Rockies, and it was to be a race. To Mr English's party fell the honor of staking and clearing the line from Lake St Ann, near Edmonton, to and through the pass.

Under Van Arsdol was a wonderful surveyor named Jones. He

combined instincts of direction equal to an Indian's with the science of a civil engineer and could almost smell the best grades through new country. Jones needed no assisting party whatsoever. He would go out alone with a single guide at the beginning of summer and not return until fall, but then he would bring back in his head and notebooks the equivalent of a topographical map of a new region, no matter how broken it might be. The previous summer Jones had spent in the hilly Pembina River country, and it was his tentative line that we followed to the Athabaska and to Yellowhead. He was now out alone charting grades through the mountains beyond the pass in British Columbia.

That our Grand Trunk crew beat the Canadian Northern engineers to Yellowhead was due partly to Jones's valuable preliminary work and partly to the strategy of Van Arsdol. We knew that the C.N.R people still lacked necessary supplies, and to steal a march on them and possibly stampede them, Van Arsdol started us out one night at midnight. Dismayed by this surprise, the C.N.R. started its men out badly prepared, with insufficient food and outfit. A shortsighted and niggardly policy of support never caught up with this bad beginning, and the poor Canadian Northern surveyors were hampered the whole way by their miserable equipment.

Here was where Van Arsdol's long experience on Western surveys proved its worth. He supported our party with a crew of expert packers, who kept freighting out food and other expendables from Edmonton and caching them in depots always ahead of us. By the time we had used up the supplies from one cache, we reached the next one, and so on.

On the other hand, we ourselves had started without riding horses, having only pack animals with our outfit, and as a result had to foot it all the way. I carried my heavy transit and tripod the entire distance. When, in August, we reached Yellowhead Pass, 270 miles out from Edmonton, my shoulders were as calloused as a blacksmith's palms.

We ran our line from Lake St Ann to Pembina, thence to Lac Brule, and from there to Yellowhead. It was fast and sometimes wild and exciting work, especially after we crossed the watershed and reached the Athabaska and water rushing for the Arctic Ocean. The expedition was hard on our stock. In the Pembina country two or three of the horses died from eating wild parsnip, the so-called "locoweed" of the West. If a pack animal bogged down in a swamp, we had to hunt a tree in which to deposit our instruments, and then it was everybody pull. Along the Athabaska the going was even worse. The river was deep and swift, and its banks were precipitate. Here we lost two fully loaded horses, packs and all, who fell off the cut banks. There was no chance to rescue them. There was no game in this country, and we were absolutely dependent for food upon the loads carried by our stock and upon the caches.

We crossed the Athabaska River at the point now called Jasper City. Years later I was in Jasper City again, engaging a guide. Standing against the Dominion Park office was an old dugout canoe with outrigger which looked familiar from a distance. I went up to it and read the sign: "Used on the first Grand Trunk survey crossing."

This crossing was a nasty bit of work. The only way to get the horses across was to swim them, but the water was so deep and icy we had to stone the animals to make them go in. Each one landed on the other side a mile down from the starting line, so strong was the current.

The management of a horse when fording a dangerous stream is something that takes knowledge and a cool head. I once blundered for an instant when making such a crossing, and it nearly cost me my life. Although this incident occurred years after my surveying experiences, it is convenient and not entirely irrelevant to tell about it now.

I was hunting in the country north of Banff with a guide named Graham. Panther Creek was swollen by the spring freshet, but we decided to ford it. Graham's horse got across all right, but my own animal, when in the middle of the flood, got scared and turned downstream. Now, the one thing a rider should never do, when his horse is fighting to hold his footing in deep swift water, is to touch the reins. I forgot this injunction for a moment and pulled my horse's head around to turn him in the right direction. At once he lost his footing, and we began to be swept down together.

His struggling legs were hitting mine, and I took my feet from the stirrups. Instantly the eddying current pulled me from the saddle and sucked me to the bottom, rolling me over and over against the rocks. Strong swimmer though I was, I could not get off the bottom. I tried to hold on to the rocks, but my fingers slipped off. I had been wearing a brand-new Stetson, and as I lost consciousness, my last thought was: "There goes my new hat!"

A short distance below the ford Panther Creek entered a canyon, and at the head of this canyon a small island split the current into two streams. When I came to, I found myself washed up on the beach of the island, and still more in the water than out. I was so drowned and cold, it was an hour before I could pull myself up on the dry bar. Meanwhile, I had discovered my horse lying on the gravel bottom beside me. The animal's head was split from nose to ears, and it died not long afterwards.

Graham had lost sight of us when we were sucked under and was now riding the other bank in frantic search. By the time he located my half-unconscious body, night was falling. The only possible way for him to rescue me was to return to the side from which we had started, the water between that side and my island being fairly shallow. But Graham himself felt that he had forded the creek safely more by good luck than anything else and did not dare risk another crossing in the dark. A mishap to him would now leave us both in a bad situation, far from help.

He therefore camped on the bank opposite to wait for morning. All through a terrible night, wet and shaking with cold, I watched the blink of his fire. Then the morning sun brought warmth and strength to me, and Graham got across.

Back in 1875 the Canadian Pacific Railway, then pushing west to the ocean, surveyed a route through Yellowhead Pass but later abandoned it for its present more southerly crossing. There was no city of Edmonton then on which to base, and that engineering party packed oxen instead of horses and later killed them for beef.

Wherever we could in the 1906 survey, we followed the old cutting. Often I set up my transit over the C.P.R. stakes, which were still there after the rains and snows of thirty-one years. It used to be the custom of Western engineers to use pieces of soft iron ore, called keel, as chalk for marking their stakes. The old C.P.R. stakes had weathered to the color of granite, but their marks were as bright and red as the day they were chalked on. They had good keel in the seventies.

As the survey neared Yellowhead Pass, one day we came up to an old prospector seated on a stump and regarding us as casually as if railroad surveys were a commonplace with him. I stopped to chat with the old Irishman, and he told me he had just come out of the Peace River country, in the northern part of Alberta, which was then opening up for settlement. This interested me, and I asked him many questions. Back along the Pembina we had seen the trek of settlers toward Grande Prairie—covered wagons drawn by oxen; men, women, and children, riding or walking, little trudgers clutching their parents' hands—our own pioneer West repeated on the last frontier.

The fame of this new wheat country to the north was then almost legendary in the Canadian West. Peace River! Its very name suggested a land flowing with milk and honey. The pioneers of Alberta and Saskatchewan heard tales of this paradise as eagerly as the Children of Israel once listened to the reports the spies brought back from the Promised Land.

As I talked to the old prospector, I knew I had to see the Peace River someday.

With the completion of the survey through Yellowhead, the English party's work was over. For want of something better to do, I went down to Seattle. There I heard of a survey about to be made by the Puget Sound Railway along the Palouse River in the Coeur d'Alene Mountains on the eastern boundary of Washington. I struck for a job and was hired as assistant to the chief engineer.

There is little to say about this work. The job lasted only three or four weeks, as we ran merely a reconnaissance line. I occupied a tent with the chief engineer. He had dyspepsia, and I had to step outdoors to smoke. I don't know if the railroad ever built on our line.

Then came wonderful news from the North. Before leaving Edmonton for Seattle, I had applied for more work on the Mountain Division of the Grand Trunk. Now came an unbelievable offer—nothing less than chief engineer on the job of laying out the townsite of Prince Rupert, the Grand Trunk's Pacific terminal.

Though the site of Prince Rupert was then only an uninhabited section of mossy hills and cedar forest, everybody in Western Canada expected the future town to rival Vancouver in size, and in no distant time, either. Of course, I accepted the commission at once and went to Prince Rupert by sea. Mine was the first tent raised in the coming metropolis. Though Prince Rupert never realized the extravagant hopes of the early 1900s, it has become a town of six or eight thousand people, making it an important place in that country.

How I gloried in this job! Twenty-six years of age, in five years I had changed from a discontented college boy, unable to pass a successful examination in any subject, into a civil engineer holding a post of responsibility with a great railroad.

The townsite as I found it was a wooded island in the mouth of the Skeena River, down which the Grand Trunk was coming. The timber was all red cedar. Though hilly, the island was actually a palpitating peat bog. Even the hills were composed of peat moss. There is an enormous rainfall at Prince Rupert—120 inches annually —as well as a 20-foot tide. Everything had to be up on posts. When I arrived the island was full of black wolves who howled every night when the moon was full. One day they drove a deer into the bay. We lassoed it and had a feast of venison.

My first job was to make a topographical survey to establish levels and heights and then lay out streets, business sites, and town lots. The mossy hills were covered with a spiny cactuslike shrub called the devil's-club. In climbing about, we were always grabbing devil's-clubs, getting our hands full of needles.

We planked our main streets and built wooden sidewalks. Other Grand Trunk gangs were moving in. A dock was built on piles; steamers began unloading merchandise and building materials into new warehouses. Carpenters hammered at the first business blocks and houses. A post of the Royal Northwest Mounted Police moved in. I admired the trim, determined young constables and for a time was tempted by them to join the force. The red cedars we cleared from the streets, we used as fuel. In memory I can still smell the aromatic smoke that issued from Prince Rupert's chimneys.

One day when we were in the hills about a mile back from the harbor, we heard a crashing sound, as if some careless sailors were throwing barrels off their ship onto the dock. One of my men exclaimed that there was a fight in the bay, and we rushed back to the edge of the hill and looked down on the harbor, a hundred feet below. There we saw a sublime spectacle in nature—two killer whales attacking a bull whale which they had cornered in our bay.

Never have I seen such ferocity and never two hunting animals display such teamwork. The strategy of the killer whales—huge beasts themselves, twenty-five to thirty feet long and weighing several tons apiece—was to drown their prey by keeping his head under water, at the same time driving him to strand in shallow water, if they could. This they did by leaping clear of the water, like a salmon, and coming down on the whale's head.

The thresher whales struck their victim alternately, and their timing was like that of a boxer. As one slid off the drowning whale's shoulders, the other was in the air. The thudding of their bodies carried plainly to us, a mile away. To avoid injury to themselves, the killers turned their black backs when in the air, exposing silver bellies to the sky, and came down on their quarry with their shoulders. The bull whale lashed with his tail, coughed, blew, and struggled to escape from its torment. We watched the mighty contest for an hour—until dusk set in and it was too dark to see any more. When we made our way down to the water front, the din of battle had ceased, and next morning the bay was quiet. We never knew the outcome of the struggle.

Though the Grand Trunk rails were yet a thousand miles from Prince Rupert, business, led by real-estate speculators and dealers, followed hard on the heels of the building gangs. Population was increasing so fast that we grew more sanguine of the future than ever; and when I had completed my work on the island, the company moved me over to the mainland, six miles south, to clear and lay out residence streets, thinking that the town would spread to that point.

I took with me a corps of Japanese axmen, and my first order to them was to build me a cabin of red cedar logs on the edge of the sea. In this I disposed my belongings, I had a Japanese cook and factotum to take care of me, and I was never happier in my life. I was the only white man at this place, but I liked my Japs— nice fellows, all of them. Once when they were celebrating a holiday, they invited me to their feast. It was a dinner entirely of Japanese dishes, with saki wine to whet the appetite.

April 1907 found my work at Prince Rupert finished. I came back East to see my people, doing nothing thereafter for several months. Then I grew restless again and went to Montreal to try to find a job, for I had fallen in love with railroad civil engineering. There I met one of my old division engineers of the Grand Trunk who had gone over to the Canadian Pacific to work on the survey for double-tracking that road. He had drawn the Smiths Falls (Ontario) section and hired me as transitman.

This survey took from September to January. Our party lived in a boxcar, which was shunted along to keep pace with the survey. Our route lay through French Canadian country, and the towns had funny names—St Polycarpe, St Clet. The French Canadians seemed very suspicious or shy people. They were always peeking at us out of their windows. Yet we liked them on closer acquaintance. This district is wonderful apple country, and we went through just at harvesttime.

That winter the Canadian Pacific Railway was sponsoring a course at McGill University, Montreal, in railway surveying and practical astronomy. My service with the company in Ontario entitled me to a scholarship, and I remained as a student until the end of the scholastic year. This time I had no trouble in mastering my subjects, for I knew they held great practical value for me.

I remember my room in Montreal. It was in an old stone house at 60 Drummond Street, six blocks from the C.P.R. Station. A fireplace in every room was the only heat. My landlord's name was Sait. For some reason I've forgotten now, I left a trunk there, to be called for later. I never did go back for it. There was an expensive transit in it, too.

During this stay in Montreal I made the acquaintance of an old friend of my father's, A. D. MacTier, then general manager of the Eastern Division of the Canadian Pacific and later a vice-president of the line. Father knew all the principal officials of the C.P.R., since for many years he had supplied engine coal to that system, first as a wholesale dealer in Chicago and afterwards as a coal producer in Pennsylvania. Some years he had their exclusive supply, furnishing three million tons or more.

Father was pleased that I made this contact as well as with all the work I had been doing for the Canadian railways. He realized now that it was better to leave a boy to his natural inclinations in choosing a career. In fact, he wrote as much once in his letter of advice to the students of Western Reserve Academy, citing my progress in civil engineering as an example. He still hoped, though, that eventually I would return to my heritage and manage his business after him.

But that was never to be. In fact, as it is easy to see now in retrospect, my course at McGill ended a distinct phase of my life. Never again was I to practice civil engineering, except as an aid to navigation. Henceforth, with time out for the war and its aftermath, I was to be an explorer, first for technical bureaus in Washington and other scientific societies, and afterwards as an independent leader of expeditions into the Arctic and Antarctic regions.

II

Arctic

And we shall see old planets change
And alien stars arise
And give the gale our sea-worn sail
In shadow of new skies.

I INTERVAL FOR
ADVENTURE

THE STATEMENT which closes the preceding chapter needs a slight qualification. Though after leaving McGill University I put away my transit instrument forever, I was not to come so quickly into a career as explorer. There was an interval of five years during which, always homesick for frontiers, I more or less deliberately sought hardship and adventure in wild and little-trodden regions.

It was during this period, I believe, that I accepted a commission from Baxter & Company, New York timber dealers, to investigate the hardwoods of the jungles of Yucatan as to their value for railroad ties. There is not much to be said about this trip, except that I studied various woods and brought back samples.

In Yucatan I stayed with the American consul on his ranch near the ruined Mayan town of Chichen Itza. Again in soft tropical nights I heard serenading guitars, and sometimes after supper the ranch hands baited bulls in the corral for our amusement.

Mayan relics interested me more. Of course, I visited Chichen Itza and Uxmal, and I also saw isolated Mayan ruins in the jungle. That whole peninsula is but a limestone cap upon an underground lake or sea of fresh water. In places the cap is broken through to the greenish water below. One of these holes or "wells", as they call them in Yucatan, was on the ranch of my consular host, who had fished Mayan images and pottery out of it. While I was there he had a professional diver at work systematically exploring the bottom. In this way he recovered a considerable collection of Mayan antiquities, which he presented to Harvard University.

In the late summer of 1909 I kept the promise made to myself on Yellowhead Pass that someday I would visit the Peace River. That summer I was hunting along the coast of British Columbia and fell in with an old prospector washing gold in the coast range. He spoke of an ambition to prospect the placer beds of the head-waters of the Peace River, his plan being to freight on down the river to the prairies before the freeze-up and then cross overland to Edmonton—a journey of about a thousand miles. I jumped at this chance to accompany him and thus make both our dreams reality.

We started from Port Essington, at the mouth of the Skeena River, where I had opportunity to see once more the booming town of Prince Rupert. We followed up the Skeena to its sources, crossed a narrow divide, and, dropping down, came to streams whose currents discharged eventually into the Peace; the Peace River, flowing toward the Arctic Ocean, and the Skeena, falling into the Pacific, heading within fifty miles of each other.

At navigable water we made a trade with a Sikani Indian for his dug-out cottonwood canoe and in this craft made the entire water journey. We stayed for some time in the mountains, prospecting streams flowing into the headwaters of the Peace. Sometimes I hunted, though without much luck. The Peace River basin was not good hunting country. In the upper part there were a few bear and moose, but out on the prairies game almost disappeared.

I have already spoken of two narrow escapes from death—once in Pennsylvania when I was nearly run down by a locomotive and again in British Columbia when fording a swollen creek. Here at the head of the Peace River I was to have a third providential escape. Vast dangers, such as the inhospitality of polar waste or equatorial desert, man can overcome by intelligent provision. It is the moment of incaution or carelessness that may plunge him into instant peril and even cost him his life, whether he be on a city street or mountain trail.

While my partner panned for gold one day, I took the dugout and a shotgun and paddled far up a stream, looking for game. That evening I was returning empty-handed as usual and very hungry, for we had had no meat for several days and were subsisting on beans and rice and what wild berries we could find.

At one point the stream rushed around a narrow bend and

then broadened out into a quiet pool, dammed back by a long gravel bar at the lower end. As I rounded this bend and looked over the pool, my eyes were gladdened by the sight of a fat porcupine out on the tip end of the gravel bar having a drink. For just a moment I deliberated. It was a long shot to make with the gun. If I missed or only wounded the animal, it would get into the thick underbrush on the bank, and dinner would be gone. On the other hand, if I tried to paddle closer, I might alarm him while still out of good range and risk the same disaster. In less time than it has taken me to tell this, I decided to race him for it, and, noiselessly digging my paddle blade into the pool, I bent my back and shot for the neck of the gravel bar.

Luck was with me. The porcupine was so interested in drinking he did not see his danger until too late. He turned and made for the underbrush with surprising speed, but the bow of my canoe was already grounding. I sprang out into the water, instinctively grabbing the shotgun by the barrel, though I expected to find some piece of driftwood on the bar with which I could dispatch the animal. But there was no stick or club there, not even a big stone. The porcupine was right at my feet. I seized the gun barrel with both hands, swung, and brought the stock down on the porcupine's back.

Both barrels of the gun were loaded, but what was worse, what I never dreamed, both were also cocked. Seldom in the years I have spent on the hunting trail have I been so careless. As I hit the porcupine both barrels went off, and I received a terrific shock. My left arm dropped paralyzed, and as I sank to the gravel, stunned, my only thought was that I had blown out the whole left side of my chest.

Beside me lay the porcupine, its back broken. My gun was a ruin, for, from the double stress of the blow and the explosion, the stock had broken off. But as my strength returned and my arm began to gain sensation, I sat up and as well as I could peeled off my shirt. My arm and left side were already livid, and they turned a wonderful black and blue by morning, but there was not a single shot perforation. Two heavy charges of buckshot had passed harm-

lessly between my arm and side. Had the porcupine been a frac-
tion of a second slower, had I swung the stock two inches farther
to hit him, I wouldn't be writing these reminiscences now.

So we had our feast of meat that night. It was during this summer that I learned the best way to roast a porcupine. All hunters
of the Northern wildernesses know what a delicious meat roast
porcupine is, resembling roast suckling pig so closely that few can
tell the difference. But most white hunters, even old-timers, skin
their porcupines before roasting, usually getting their hands full
of quills. The Indians taught me a better way—simply to gut and
clean the carcass and then roast it skin and all. The skin and quills
char to a crust that is easily scraped off, leaving the juicy meat
underneath perfectly cooked.

When frosty nights in the mountains heralded the coming of
winter, we dropped downstream to the first Hudson's Bay Company trading post on the Peace River, at Fort St John, B.C. The
post was an ancient log structure (built in 1803) scrupulously
whitewashed and on its little plateau set like a gem against the
high bluffs behind. Here for the first time I saw Beaver Indians,
whose headquarters this post was. Once a year they assembled
here to receive their treaty money, and here they sold the proceeds
of their hunts, receiving in payment trade valued in "skins", a
"skin" then representing thirty-five cents.

A hunting party had just come in, bringing dried moose meat,
and pelts of beaver, mink, and wolf, and I watched them. Cross-
legged on the counter, silently puffing clouds of tobacco smoke,
sat their old chief, Ignace, then over eighty years of age. The
younger men were unloading their pack ponies and spreading
their furs on the counters to be valued. The air of the low-ceilinged
room reeked with the smoke of tobacco and kinnikinnick, an
Indian tobacco substitute made of the underbark of the red willow. All afternoon the silent, smoking powwow continued. Then
payments were made, and that night tomtoms beat in the lodges
and the gambling chants carried across the desolate waste.

Though of a lower type than the Ojibways, whose acquaintance
I had made in Ontario, the Beavers are, or were, an interesting

tribe. I am not sure if there are any of them left today. There were only about two hundred, and those mostly women, in 1909, when privation and disease were steadily eating into them. They were nomadic hunters, never settling down in permanent villages, but following the movement of the game winter and summer and disdaining the comforts to be gained in winter by camping near a Hudson Bay post, as did the Crees and other tribes of the Northwest. Since game was scarce on their hunting ground, they starved half the time.

With them it was either feast or famine. I have seen a Beaver squaw take the putrefying skins of animals previously killed and gorged and boil them for soup. Yet despite their precarious existence, few human beings had their physical endurance. When hunting in poor country in summer, a Beaver brave would tie a bandana around his forehead to keep perspiration from blinding him and dog-trot all day long after moose, covering fifty miles.

The factor at Fort St John was hospitable and treated us to fresh vegetables out of his garden. I had heard so much about the hunting prowess of the Beavers that I wanted to watch them in action, if I could. The factor knew of a hunting party then encamped down the river about forty miles, so we bade good-by to him and resumed our journey. We found the camp about three miles above the mouth of a good-sized tributary of the Peace called Moose Creek; and one of the hunters, a young brave named Oule, consented to let me accompany him on a three-day hunt which would start next morning. Later I discovered that Oule was the most celebrated hunter of his tribe. His tribal name was "The Wolf", given to him because of his ability to run a moose down in deep snow and kill it with a knife.

These Beaver Indians lived and traveled in clans of a dozen or so families. Each family hunted alone in turn, and when game was killed the others moved in and feasted on the meat as communal property. Scarcity of men had made the tribe polygamous. Oule had four wives and lived with each three months of the year.

My partner and I made camp some distance away from this village to be apart from its dogs. Hordes of mongrel curs, all with a strain of wolf blood, followed these hunting clans. In winter the Indians fed and harnessed the strongest dogs to sleds but in summer left them all to shift for themselves. They became the wiliest thieves imaginable. The only safe way to keep food supplies was to cache them on platforms held up on tall poles.

Having grunted his consent to have my company, Oule left me to fend for myself, as I supposed; yet when I reached the Indian camp at dawn next day, I found a cayuse saddled for me. With Oule went two of his sons, aged fourteen and twelve, and two tough old Huskies, who were good bear dogs. We started off single file at a clip that made it hard for me to keep up, though I was a good horseman. We followed an Indian trail—a mere matter of a blazed tree here and there or a broken branch to indicate the way. We crashed through thickets with no slackening of pace. Twigs and thorns tore my face, and I had to lie flat on the pony's neck to avoid being swept off the saddle by low branches. Yet Oule and his sons never once looked back to see how I was faring. The two Huskies loped behind me.

After three miles of this, we dropped down to the mouth of Moose Creek. Here we found fresh bear tracks and a place where a bear had had colic from eating too many blueberries. But we were after moose, not bear, and turned and followed the boulder-strewn creek bottom up through a canyon which ended at a valley of as rough country as I had ever seen, full of ridges and knolls and covered with a tangle of fallen timber. It was an ideal haunt for moose.

Across the creek was a grassy flat on which stood the poles of old Indian lodges. We forded the stream and dismounted. Without a word being spoken, Oule picked up his small rifle and strode off into the brush, while his sons built a little fire and got moose meat and tea from the saddle bags. They put on water to boil, and then lay down on the ground and slept. Oule was gone a long time. At last I heard shots in the distance, and presently I saw him coming on the run down from the ridge that edged in the valley. When he reached us he threw down three teal and two mallard ducks he had shot.

We roasted moose meat, ate it and cold bear-fat-and-dried-blue-berry pemmican and drank tea, then mounted again and went on up Moose Creek. All afternoon we rode, jumping our ponies over fallen trees, cutting overland to avoid bends and dropping down cut banks again, crossing and recrossing the creek many times. I grew sore and stiff from the unaccustomed exercise and was hard pressed to keep up with the Indians.

Toward sundown we came to a clean grove of standing pine, where there was grazing for horses and shelter for men. This was Oule's destination. Leaving the two boys to make camp, he and I rode on together for half an hour. Then, tethering our horses to some willows beside the creek, we started on foot up the rough hillside.

Dismounted, I was at an even greater disadvantage. Oule traveled always at a half trot, jumping over logs and rocks as if they were nothing. Athlete though I was, I could not keep up. I slipped and fell over logs and several times had to call out to keep from losing my guide. Among the hills on top were many ponds black with wild duck. Deciding that there were no moose near, Oule shot several duck with his 22-caliber rifle. He also carried a 30-30 for bigger game. To capture one duck which was only wounded, he waded out in the cold water to his shoulders.

We kept on through the high country but found no sign of moose. Finally we came out to the edge of the valley again. The sun was just setting behind the opposite side and the whole wilderness below was filled with pink light. Oule was about to start the descent, when he stopped as if transfixed and pointed down at the distant river. I looked but could see nothing. Oule spoke two words: "Moose! . . . Come!"

He started down the long slope on the full run, leaping logs like an antelope. I made no attempt to keep pace with him now, realizing that I would be sure to find him at the creek. The two Husky dogs seemed to be staying with me. Then, far below, a shot echoed through the valley, then another and a third, and in the distance I heard the two dogs baying their hunting cry. How they had got there so quickly I could not tell, but I knew Oule had found big game. Three more shots were fired below, and then the dogs ceased their baying.

It was almost dark when I reached the creek and saw Oule on the opposite bank. In response to my question, he said he had killed a moose, which was lying in the stream. It was too late now to take care of it, so we found our horses and groped back to the pine grove.

There we found the family that was to hunt the country just above this. When they learned about Oule's moose, they camped there for the night. Next morning we all went upstream again and found the moose, a yearling cow, in the middle of the creek where it had fallen. It was too heavy for us to pull out on shore, so we constructed an island of rocks and brush and dragged the carcass out on that. There Oule skinned and quartered it. These Indians wasted nothing edible. Even the intestines were washed in the stream and kept for casings for bear-fat sausages.

This triumph demanded an immediate celebration. As Oule worked on the improvised island, his boys built a long hot fire on the bank, and over it arched willow saplings by sticking both ends in the ground, so that they looked like the ribs of a covered-wagon top. To these supports they hung slabs of moose meat to grill in the flames and heat. By the time Oule finished his work, the feast was ready.

Never have I seen human beings wolf food as those Indians did then. With their sheath knives, they cut off long strips and, holding them up by one end, swallowed them down, half a pound at a time, as I have seen Italians eat macaroni. In their alternate famines and seasons of plenty, the Beaver Indians developed the digestions and eating habits of wolves or wild dogs. The men put down pounds and pounds of roast meat apiece, and the squaws almost as much. The frosty air that morning had sharpened my appetite, but though I gorged myself to the chin, I could not consume nearly as much meat as the younger Indian boy.

When the feast was over, the visiting family went on to their hunting ground, and we packed our animals with the hide and meat and herded them down on foot to our camp at the grove.

The remainder of that day we rested, but the following day Oule and I hunted moose again. We saw none but brought back wild duck as usual.

Despite their ability as hunters, the Beavers were poor marksmen with the white man's guns. Oule, the best of them, had needed six 30-30 bullets to dispatch a yearling cow. On our way back to camp that last night he showed me a feat of another kind of marksmanship that left me gasping with astonishment and admiration. As our horses came around a shoulder of the canyon, ahead of us, at least a hundred feet distant, we both saw a partridge drumming on a log. Quick as a flash, without dismounting, Oule whipped out his sheath knife, caught it by the tip of the blade, and with a flick of his wrist and forearm threw it at the bird. The spinning knife followed the trajectory of a rifle bullet and neatly pinned the partridge to the log.

When we got back to the camp on the Peace River, the wild geese were flying south, and once in the night we heard the high distant note of a wild swan. Storms were brewing in the north, the aurora was painting the sky to the zenith, and the great white cold was beginning its annual push out of the Arctic. If we were to keep ahead of it, we must hurry; so we packed our cottonwood dugout, said farewell to our Indian friends, and early one morning started down the Peace, to hunt gold or game no more.

When the Peace came out of the hills into the prairie and began its placid, meandering flow to Great Slave River, then it became the river of my dreams. Only its steep banks were fringed with fir trees, and in this setting slept the green river, its quiet bends and reaches turning to molten silver at night under the full moon. Above, at the tips of the topmost firs, undulated the prairie to the horizon in every direction.

The land flowing with milk and honey—not for the hunter, to be sure; but when those leagues of black fertility should be broken and seed scattered, then would burst into richness the last empire of North American wheat!

Down this great quiet flood we paddled, stopping only at settlements and Hudson Bay posts for supplies. We turned into a southern tributary and stroked our Rocky Mountain dugout to a final town. There we procured horses and rode southeastward to Edmonton, following a trail over which were still creaking belated covered wagons of the season's migration. It was one of the last authentic scenes in the winning of the West.

Yet I myself two years later played a part in a sort of momentary recrudescence of the days when the buffalo blackened our prairies and ranged from the Alleghenies almost to the Pacific Coast and from Mexico to the Arctic Circle. In the fall of 1911 I engaged in a buffalo hunt and shot an old bull which, I have every reason to believe, was the last American bison to fall before the gun of a white hunter.

The last extensive herd of wild buffalo existed undisturbed until 1907 on the Flathead Indian Reservation south of Flathead Lake in the Bitter Root Mountains of western Montana. This herd was the property of Michael Pablo, a Mexican living at Ronan in the Flathead Reservation, and was of Canadian origin, Pablo having in 1873, when buffalo were still plentiful, purchased its nucleus—a dozen calves—from an Indian who had herded them down from Canada. The contours of the Bitter Root Mountains afford mild winters in the valleys of the Flathead country and provide abundant grazing on the hills. Consequently these buffalo never left that sanctuary and by 1907 numbered several hundred head.

When it became certain that year that the Flathead Reservation was to be opened for homesteading, the Canadian government, mindful of the ancestry of this herd, bought it from Pablo to repatriate the buffalo in the preserve in northwestern Alberta. Expert cowmen then conducted a great roundup which lasted four years and resulted in the shipment of seven hundred head by rail to Edmonton. By the end of 1911 the roundup was regarded as complete. Only a few unconquerables were left in the Flathead country, and these—wise old bulls, principally—had taken to the high wooded fastnesses of the Bitter Roots and could be captured alive only at the greatest difficulty and expense.

Almost unbelievable romances of the wild occurred during this roundup. Cattle cars were too flimsy to hold the mighty animals, if they stampeded. A bull buffalo could go through the heavy slats of a freight car as though they were paper. When obstreperous bulls were shipped in stout cages, they died of heartbreak. Near Edmonton two old bulls broke out of a cattle car and actually made their way down to Great Falls, Mont., a distance of twelve hundred miles. There they destroyed a farmer's wheat crop, and one was shot for his sins. The other, with perfect instinct, turned west to reach the country he called home. He managed to avoid towns, railroads, dogs, and hunters, and rejoined his outlawed brethren in the Bitter Root hills.

It was my luck to see part of the roundup, during which time I made the acquaintance of the Canadian commissioner of parks. To shoot buffalo in Montana was forbidden by law, but these renegades held the status of private property, being owned by Canada. From the Canadian commissioner I obtained written permission to hunt them; and, armed with this authority, I made my way down to Kalispell and to the house of Michael Pablo at Ronan, where I was received with true Mexican hospitality.

No need to tell here of the fruitless days and weeks I spent looking for buffalo. I went up the Camas Valley once with a half-breed guide and again with one of the men who had taken part in the roundup. Winter was setting in. Once, caught by a blizzard in the mountains, our horses played out and had to be lashed and dragged by their jaws through driving snow, wind, and darkness to get them back to camp, which we reached at midnight. When at rare intervals we saw buffalo, they were so far away that by the time we came to the spot they had vanished. Once, just at night-fall when we were in camp, we saw three fairly close at hand; but snow fell in the night and covered their tracks.

On my third hunt I started out of Ronan alone, took the stage up the Camas Valley twenty-two miles, and then, carrying only my rifle, crossed a range of hills on foot to Garceau Gulch, where lived a half-breed whom I had encountered on one of my hunts, and who told me he knew how to find buffalo. He provided ponies and took me into a range of hills to the west of those I had hunted.

The first day we saw neither buffalo nor their tracks. That night we made camp in a trapper's cabin and next morning rode the windy ridges again through deep snow. Then that afternoon we found what we sought—the fresh track of a buffalo, leading off the ridge down into thick brush below. The slope was too steep for our horses, so we left them on the ridge and followed on foot. As I clambered down, it was only by chance that ahead, through the brush, I caught the movement of a great shaggy form against a clump of spruce trees. It was our buffalo.

He was an old bull, a veteran of the mountains. Surprised, he had either caught sight of us or scented us, for he was looking in our direction, head raised, nostrils thrust forward. Then the badgered old monarch turned and went down through the brush again, and once we saw him stop for a moment and listen.

We climbed to the back of the ridge, mounted, and rode along to head him off. When we thought we had gone far enough, we plunged down into the brush until we came to the edge of a clearing. There we waited and listened. Suddenly a dead tree crashed down on the opposite side, and the old bull charged out into the opening, then came to an abrupt stop as he saw us silhouetted against the snow. Evidently he had been running, and his heavy bulk had grazed a rotting, tottering spruce tree. For a moment he stood undecided, uncertain what we were, wolves or men. He was not much more than a hundred yards below us, and my guide and I fired at the same time.

Both shots went home and shook him. Pumping our high-powered rifles, the half-breed and I fired a second and a third volley, then a final shot, and we had him. He dropped to his front knees, struggled to rise, then sank down and went rolling down the mountainside, bringing up against a big boulder. There he lay still.

I was a young man then and full of a hunter's lust for new and rare trophies; but, instead of the fierce elation I had expected to feel at killing a wild buffalo, when we reached our game I was filled with profound regret and melancholy that I had done this thing. No use to tell myself that the bull was very old and would not have lived long in any event. This rugged old fellow had been

one of the few last free representatives of a species that only a
generation earlier numbered countless millions.

Because he lived alone on this ridge, he may well have been the
one that escaped at Edmonton and made that gallant flight of
nearly fifteen hundred miles through settled country back to the
peaceful and hospitable valley where he was born. At last, hounded
by man and forsaken by his own kind, he had sought a refuge high
in the rocky fastnesses, sleeping in the thick brush, watering each
morning and evening at a little spring where we later found his
tracks, and every day climbing to the rocks above to gaze across
the valleys at distant hills upon which he perhaps saw others of
his kind whom he dared not join.

Night was at hand. The level light of a sinking sun lay like blood
on the snows of the Mission Range far to the northeast. With a
heavy heart I helped the half-breed cover the carcass against the
coyotes, and then we mounted and rode in silence down to our
camp in the valley.

II GALAHAD OF
THE ICE

IT WAS a meeting with George Borup in 1912 that crystalized
my ambition to become a polar explorer. In a general, indefinite
way that dream had been forming for some years, and particularly
after I discovered and read Fridtjof Nansen's book *Farthest North*.

But first I must note that for several years New York City had
been my home, as much as I could call any city home. After my
father had closed out his businesses in Chicago, he sold the
Michigan Avenue place and bought a residence at 2 West Sixteenth
Street in New York. During the rest of his life he owned and
occupied at different periods three other New York houses. From
West Sixteenth Street he moved to 18 East Fifty-third Street, then

to 12 East Sixty-ninth Street, and finally to 603 Park Avenue, the house he owned when he died.

For the sake of the record, let me insert that my sister Clare attended Miss Spence's school in New York City and in 1908 married Bernon S. Prentice, a banker well-known in the sporting world as a tennis champion, enthusiast and patron.

It was in one or another of these houses that occurred those contacts with my father which will figure in the remainder of this book, and to one or another of them that I would return from my trips and expeditions to make impatient visits, moping about the streets and clubs of New York, my nerves fretted by the disagreeable aspects of congested humanity, my secret spirits often a ferment of vague hopes and unhappy frustration.

In the period between 1908 and 1912 I was at particularly loose ends when in New York. It was then I formed the habit of visiting the American Museum of Natural History in Central Park West. There was little in the museum that did not hold interest for me, but what captured my imagination most were the exhibits of Arctic and Antarctic exploration—the vivid paintings of polar scenes: Eskimos hunting the walrus, dogs dragging sleds over the pack ice, and, above, the aurora borealis in resplendent colors. Here were the very sledges pulled by explorers into the polar wastes and upon the walls, relief maps showing the routes they had traveled. I could spend hours tracing those journeys stage by stage, imagining the hardships and the human fortitude displayed; for I, too, had stood on the edge of the unknown in Alaska and gazed northward across it.

In 1909 Peary returned from the North Pole only to learn that Dr Frederick Cook had entered a prior claim to its discovery. The ensuing controversy focused American attention upon polar exploration as nothing had ever done before. It led me to read Nansen's book, which fascinated me more than anything had since Roosevelt's *Ranch Life and Hunting Trail*. I realized now that the polar regions, north and south, offered the last great fields for heroic enterprise in the service of science and humanity.

In the spring of 1912 occurred two major events which once more whipped up public interest in polar exploration. Amundsen emerged from the Antarctic continent with the news that he had reached the South Pole in December 1911. The reverberations of this event had not died down when a rescue party came out of Antarctica with the bodies of Captain Robert Scott and his companions and a tale of heroism and self-sacrifice without parallel in the annals of exploration. Scott, too, had attained the South Pole, only to discover that Amundsen had beaten him there by a month; and on their way out the young British leader and his men were overwhelmed by a blizzard on Beardmore Glacier and frozen to death. Scott at once became the national hero of England, and even the stirring events of the war have failed to dim the luster of his memory.

During that same year occurred a third event in polar exploration of more immediate concern to myself. Peary had stood on Cape Columbia, west of Greenland, and off to the northwest, at a distance he estimated to be one hundred and fifty miles, had seen the mirage which he called Crocker Land. Upon his return, Peary said he was too old to attempt the exploration of this supposed island, and the challenge was picked up by that young Galahad of Arctic exploration, George Borup, who, while still a Yale undergraduate, had been a member of Peary's supporting party.

Borup, now a senior at Yale, interested another member of the Peary supporting party, Donald MacMillan, and secured the backing of the American Museum of Natural History. Then, in the spring of 1912, he announced a forthcoming Crocker Land Polar Expedition to continue and complete the lifework of the veteran Peary in the Arctic.

At this news I grew excited. Here suddenly had developed a chance such as I had been seeking, more or less unconsciously. There was reason to believe that my application to join Borup might at least be considered, since the American Museum was backing Borup and MacMillan, and I had become well acquainted with Dr Henry Fairfield Osborn, president of the Museum, who was also a close friend of my father. Dr Osborn approved of my ambition. Of course, he would not interfere with Borup's choice of personnel, but he introduced me to Colonel Borup, George's father, who was then living in New York. We saw Colonel Borup in the University Club, and he willingly gave me a letter of introduction to his son. With this in my pocket, I took the train to New Haven.

I met George Borup in his college room, which was full of mementos of the Arctic. Colonel Borup was one eighth Cherokee and proud of his Indian blood. The racial tang showed in George Borup's high cheekbones and intense face. I presented my letter, told him of my hope and ambition, and then gave him a statement of my qualifications.

"Do you smoke or drink?" was the first thing he said.

I told him that I did both, in moderation.

"One can't have habits in the North," he said.

Neither tobacco nor alcohol, I assured him, had fastened upon me to such a degree that I could not easily give them up for indefinite periods. His attitude on these points was, of course, a little absurd—the attitude of a very earnest and very young man. Not that an out-and-out alcoholic should or even could penetrate far into the polar regions, but the temperate use of stimulants would not harm anybody there. Explorers ordinarily do not take liquor on their expeditions for the reason that it is too heavy and bulky to carry. Tobacco, on the other hand, is light and compressible into small space. On every polar expedition I have known, the men have carried tobacco, and it has been their solace in hardship and peril.

Nevertheless, George Borup's attitude toward smoking and drink seems to me still to have been a fine thing, attesting to the purity of his young ideals. With him the goal was what counted, and all nonessentials had to be sacrificed to that.

I left him without knowing what impression I had made. Then one day Colonel Borup called me up in New York to inform me that his son had picked me for the third member of the Crocker Land Expedition. We were to divide the work among us. My job was to be the civil engineer and attend to maps and topographical work.

Never in the years that have followed have I felt more honored than I did then. When I subsequently went into the polar regions, it was always as a leader of expeditions I had initiated and helped finance. Borup picked me on my merits alone. My training, physical equipment, and relish for the work won the place for me.

Many still remember the tragic end of these high plans. On the very day after Colonel Borup told me of my selection, George Borup was drowned off New London, Conn., trying to save the life of a friend after their motorboat had upset. He died in an act of self-sacrifice.

Though this experience was brief and seemed abortive, it was to have profound consequences with me. For a while I planned to go on with Donald MacMillan alone. We decided to postpone our start for one year, and I decided to use that year in improving my professional equipment for exploratory work in the Arctic. That fall, through the influence of the American Museum, I entered the school of the U.S. Coast and Geodetic Survey at Cheltenham, Md., under O. H. Bauer, head of the Magnetic Observatory, studying observations with sextant and theodolite and measuring magnetic intensities and compass variations.

Meanwhile, I was cooling rapidly toward the whole Crocker Land project. MacMillan seemed to be turning it into a mere trading voyage; and, after I knew him better, I began to question his qualities as a leader. By this statement I intend no reflection on MacMillan's character as a man or a companion. Leadership is a special thing, and the success or failure of a perilous or desperate mission may depend entirely on the leadership it gets. There should be nothing personal in a man's estimate of the leadership under which he expects to serve in the polar regions. If he doubts, he should not join the expedition. No man understood the value of leadership in the North or South better than Roald Amundsen, nor was any man ever a better leader. To the end of his life Amundsen kept up his friendship with Dr Cook, never forgetting that it was Cook's ability and steady optimism that brought them out safely from the Antarctic.

Besides these doubts of mine, my father was stubbornly opposed to all this folderol of Arctic exploration. As a result, I withdrew from the Crocker Land Expedition but kept on with my training for polar work. In Cheltenham and Washington I was meeting many government scientists. When I finished the brief course with the Geodetic Survey, I went next with the U.S. Geological Survey to learn plane-table work with a topographical unit being sent to Teachipec, Cal., at the Santa Fe railroad pass. It was very rugged country there, offering a good test to topographical map makers.

This was another brief period of training, lasting only three weeks, but quite long enough to give me a distressing experience. A sharp chip of gravel flew into my eye and defied all efforts to remove it. Suffering that excruciating misery which only a sore eye can cause, I had to ride down to civilization to find a doctor. For three days and nights I went without sleep.

Returning to New York, I found my father on the point of departure for Algiers. He invited me to go with him, and, for reasons of my own, I accepted. I had found out that the Royal Geographical Society of London was to give a course that winter in geographical surveying under the eminent scientist Reeves, inventor of the worm screw on sextants and many other improvements in navigating and surveying instruments.

Already, at the inception of my definite purpose to become an explorer of the polar wastes, the signs were beginning to point to the inevitable clash between my devouring ambition and my father's inflexible will. Now at the start his attitude was a sort of stubborn impatience that refused to listen to argument. As diplomatically as I could, without connecting the course in London to my most cherished hopes, I left Father to bask in the winter sunshine of North Africa while I went up to the January fogs of England.

The next few months I spent with parties of geographical students in the suburbs of London, making route maps. Of the laboratory equipment I had to buy then, I have left only my pocket compass. For good luck I carried this across Antarctica on my flight of 1935. When in the fall of 1936 I went to London to receive the medal of the Royal Geographical Society, in my address to the members I mentioned this fact.

During that winter in London I attended the great memorial service for Captain Scott in St Paul's Cathedral. Scott's epitaph, three words carved on his tomb, seems to me about all any man could desire to have said about him when dead—"A gallant gentleman."

Also while taking the course in London I would go to the zoological gardens in Regent's Park to see the emperor penguin that Shackleton brought back from the Antarctic in 1909. I used to watch the strange dignified bird for hours—and this, too, was a memory I took with me when my turn came to penetrate into that inhospitable land.

III   AFTER SHEEP FOR
SCIENCE

FROM THIS TIME ON I was never to abandon, even temporarily, my determination to become an Arctic explorer. Until at last my ambition was fulfilled, there was scarcely a day in which I did not think of the North.

My dream then was for an Ellsworth Arctic Expedition, but that required financial backing. I had a modest private fortune, but it was tied up in trust, and my income was far too small to finance the feeblest of attempts to advance into the frozen unknown. All through this period Dr Osborn, of the American Museum, remained an influential friend who believed in me. He appealed to many, including my father, for funds to back me, even approaching the National Geographic Society in my behalf. But I had no reputation as an explorer to win the confidence of others, and Father was adamant.

Until 1914 the airplane was a flimsy, experimental contraption so uncertain in performance that a flight across the English Channel or from New York to Philadelphia was front-page news. Then the war began and so stimulated aero invention that every month of it advanced mechanical flight as much as a peacetime year could have done. As airplanes increased in power, range and dependability, I saw them only as vehicles of exploration.

On a visit to Washington in 1914 I even sought and secured an interview with Admiral Peary to discuss the feasibility of using airplanes in the Arctic, taking lunch with him and his daughter, Miss Marie Peary, who later became Mrs Edward Stafford, at the Peary residence. After I left, Peary turned to his daughter and predicted a successful future for me in exploration. Only recently Mrs Stafford wrote and told me about this episode.*

But this slightly anticipates my story. When I came back from London in 1913, I was 33 years old. Having now a definite purpose in life, I could no longer be content with the aimless, Micawberlike existence I had been leading, always waiting for something to turn up. I had to have some definite work—congenial work and yet work which should be preparing me for my destiny. I sought it among the scientific bureaus of Washington and in December of that year secured an appointment as field assistant in the U.S. Biological Survey.

The office or branch of the work to which I was assigned was "Distribution of the Animal Life of North America." This meant hunting for science, exploring for new varieties and species, and studying the habits of all creatures of the wild. I entered upon this work with enthusiasm, for it was exactly to my taste. In the three years I remained with the survey, my job took me from Lower California to Alaska.

My first assignment was to investigate wild mountain sheep in the vicinity of Death Valley in southern California. I did my hunting in the Panamint Mountains, going in with a four-mule team from Bigpine in Owens Valley on the eastern edge of the Sierra Nevadas. My driver, I remember, was a man with one wooden leg. They are all Nelson sheep in that part of the Western moun-

*Peary's words, as quoted by Mrs Stafford, were: "Keep your eye on that young man. He has not only youth and courage but ability and imagination. He will go far."

tains, named after E. W. Nelson, chief of the Biological Survey.

But these sheep, while all of one variety, present a most striking instance of adaptation to environment. On the wooded eastern slope of the Sierra behind Bigpine lives the typical Nelson sheep. Travel only five miles eastward, and you are across Owens Valley, in the desert, and among the foothills of the Panamints, and here is a Nelson sheep quite different in appearance. Its hair is shorter and of a lighter color than the Sierra sheep, and its ears are noticeably longer. Here it has become a desert animal.

The struggle for survival in the desert is of a ferocity unmatched anywhere else on dry land. All desert animals have enlarged ears. Cover for hiding is scarce, and the quarry must hear its hunter before it is seen. Dissection of the inner ear of a desert animal also shows a more sensitive organ of hearing. The rats of Death Valley have such long ears that they are known as kangaroo rats. Nobody knows where they get water to drink. Nelson sheep in the Panamints butt over the barrel cactus and drink the water it contains.

It was during this winter in the Panamints and Death Valley that I began to love the desert. The grandeur of desert mountains and the glory of color that wraps the burning sands at their feet are beyond words to describe. To the seeing eye the desert is always revealing new beauties and wonders. Desolate and sterile though it appears to be superficially, study discovers it to be full of life, both flora and fauna. To its lover it becomes an eternal fascination.

Then, too, you are astonished to find out that in the desert mountains people manage to eke out a fairly happy existence. Almost every fertile patch in the Panamints is occupied by a tiny ranch, growing grapes as its principal product. The ranchers make their own wine, and there is always a hospitable glass for the stranger passing by. A delicacy of the Panamints is wild honey, made by desert bees that find their nectar somewhere.

An old sheepherder came to me one day in the Panamints and said he knew where there was a funny stone in the ground. It was black, he said, and its peculiarity was that when you hit it with a hammer it rang like an anvil. I suspected at once that this must be a meteorite and went with him to see it. We found it on a hillside—a foot of pure meteoric iron sticking twelve inches out of the ground. We dug and excavated a celestial fragment nearly four feet long and weighing 425 pounds. I paid the herder to haul it to the railway and then shipped it to Washington, where it joined the meteorite collection in the Smithsonian Institution. An analysis showed that the iron contained both platinum and iridium.

On another occasion that winter I was caught out in a blizzard in the Panamint Mountains. No one who has not experienced it can realize how cold a desert wind can be in the southern California mountains. For a shelter I found a deserted stone house. It had no roof, but its walls broke the icy wind. When the storm was over the weather turned bitterly cold. I had a long walk in snow ahead of me, and to keep my feet from freezing I bound them in gunny sacks which I found in the hut.

During the winter I shot six mountain sheep for specimens. Now and then I went out to the railroad towns for rest and a brief change of scene. In that country the most popular gem is the turquoise, which is found in the desert. The largest turquoise I ever saw worn by a human being was on the little finger of a bartender in a saloon in one of those towns. It reached from his knuckle to his fingernail, and whenever he poured from a bottle, he kept his little finger straight out.

My second trip for the Biological Survey took me to the Cassiar Mountains in northern British Columbia. I went with Edmund Heller, who had been not long before, the field naturalist with ex-President Theodore Roosevelt's African hunting expedition. Later Heller lost his life while studying the buffalo of Yellowstone National Park for the Biological Survey. He was a fine comrade and one of the greatest American naturalists.

We went in through Fort Wrangell on the coast, freighted up the Stikine River, scene of the first gold strikes in the North, to Telegraph Creek, where we boarded a Hudson's Bay Company scow that took us to Dease Lake, the source of the Stikine. From the lake we struck northward two hundred miles through wooded mountainous country, virtually unexplored. It was the end of May 1914 when we went in, and the snow was deep and winter lay on the country when the scow brought us out on its last trip in November. War had broken out in Europe, but we did not know it until we came to the Hudson's Bay post on Dease Lake.

It was marvelous hunting country that we were in—the finest I ever knew. We shot moose, sheep, caribou, and deer, besides all manner of small game. Heller's memories of African hunting were still fresh, but he said there was better sport in the Cassiars than in Africa—better, he explained, because African animals come to the hunter, whereas in the Canadian mountains the hunter had to go after the game.

As a matter of fact, there are two ways of hunting in the Northwest: one, to lie in wait for the game; and two, to travel and jump the game. The latter is the Indian way and is far preferable as sport. I have no use for the ambush system in hunting big game. We had with us for a guide an Indian who was the best man for that purpose I ever knew. He was fast and tireless, loved to travel, and could scour a whole section of rough country in one day. He used to wear out two pairs of moccasins every week.

I learned much of professional use to me on this trip with Heller. We divided the work in camp, he taking the birds and I the mammals. With our field notebooks beside us, we had to dissect the game, at least enough to study food habits, skin it, and preserve specimens by taxidermy. Heller was an expert taxidermist, and I learned something of that art from him. I also gained a certain knowledge of anatomy. When we had a considerable number of specimens prepared, we sent them back to the lake by some of our Indian boys, and from there the Hudson's Bay Company freighted them out to the coast.

The work was so hard and our travel so incessant that we developed enormous appetites. One day we shot a fine fat yearling sheep. That night we roasted it entire over our fire, and the three of us—Heller and I and the Indian guide—ate the whole animal. It was a little too much for me, though. I have never been able to stomach mountain sheep since.

Toward the end of our stay in the mountains, when the nights had grown frosty and ice had begun to skim the lakes, I had an experience that has ever remained vividly in my memory. The Indian guide and I had been out for sheep since daybreak but had drawn only blanks. It was just at dusk, and we were making for camp as fast as we could, having had nothing to eat since morning. As we passed a little grassy draw in the mountains, I happened to look in, and there I saw three caribou feeding. One had an immense spread of antlers. The other two were younger. I drew the Indian's attention to them, and he at once urged me to go after the big one. There was nothing then I wanted quite so much as a hot meal and a fire.

"No," I said. "I'll get him tomorrow."

"Tomorrow?" said the Indian gravely. "Tomorrow—one hundred miles." He swept his arm toward the distant ranges. "Caribou travel like hell."

But the prospective comforts of the camp were too much for me. We went on, and I gave up the big head for lost. That night it snowed heavily, and the storm lasted two days longer. On the first good day the guide and I started out again after sheep. It was not long before we spotted a flock of six ewes and two rams. The Indian and I crawled up toward the rim of a precipice to watch them. They seemed to be feeding toward us, coming slowly. I crawled up to the edge and looked down. It was the same grassy draw we had seen before, and there were still the three caribou, feeding on patches of grass the wind had blown bare. For some reason they had violated the caribou practice of keeping always on the go.

It was a question now of caribou or sheep. That vast spread of antlers tempted me, and I took a shot at him. It was at long range, and I missed. The two young bulls with him ran off a little way, circled, and then returned to him. I fired again, and this time I hit him. Again the two younger animals only retreated a short distance and returned. My third shot brought him to his knees, and we climbed down to him.

Not until we drew near did the two young animals finally streak off. We came up to the dying game. It was an old bull, so old that its horns were brittle enough to be broken almost between the fingers, and its meat was worthless. But those horns had a spread of fifty inches. The astonishing thing was that this aged veteran of the North was totally blind.

As a scientist I would be the last one to attribute human emotions or impulses to dumb brutes. The fact remains that the two young bulls, against habit and instinct, had stayed with the blind senator of the herd throughout the storm and, unconsciously or not, were leading him to feed.

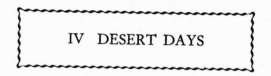

IV   DESERT DAYS

MY FINAL TWO YEARS with the Biological Survey I spent largely in Lower California, making three expeditions into that desert Mexican land, photographing and studying bird and animal life of all kinds, but still specializing in wild sheep. My most notable contribution to science there was the discovery of a new variety of coyotes. It was during these years that the desert fastened its spell upon me.

Soon after I got back from the Cassiars, I went to Lower California and spent the winter of 1914–15 there. I traveled in alone from Calexico, Cal., to a water hole in the desert called Tres Posos, where I engaged a guide, an old fellow named Captain E. W. Funke.

Funke was a rich Western character. In his day—which was the day of poaching and slaughter in the Aleutian Islands—he had been an Alaskan sealer. When the government began to protect and manage the seal herd, Captain Funke had followed the sea otter down to the kelp beds along the coast of Lower California. Now the sea otter were practically exterminated, and the captain was reduced to hunting and taking hunting parties out into the desert as guide.

He was a one-eyed man. Once when hunting and camping in the San Pedro Martir Mountains of Lower California, a blizzard caught him, and he came out of the experience with a frozen eyeball. During his years on the peninsula he had married a Mexican woman and had taken the status of a Mexican citizen. This was fortunate for me, since the fact enabled us to get in guns without trouble. A gun permit might well have been denied even to an American government explorer, or at least could not have been obtained without endless red tape. Mexico was then in the throes of the Villa rebellion, though the echoes of that struggle scarcely carried to the silent mountains and desert of Lower California.

In addition to the infirmity I have mentioned, Captain Funke also stammered. He prided himself on his old-fashioned courtly manners. When he talked to one, he always seemed to be bowing and backing away.

I have spoken of Tres Posos as a water hole. Actually the water was some distance below the surface of the ground. To reach it, the inhabitants scooped out of the sand great craters called *sinotes*. Ironwood and wild palm trees sent their taproots down to the water table and shaded this dry oasis. The wild palms were especially interesting. The palm is not native to the West Coast of North America. Nobody knows the origin of the Lower California palms.

Camping was simple. Since it never rained, there was no need for tents. One had to pack only a light cot, to keep the sleeper up above the rattlesnakes and scorpions, and a blanket to roll up in, sleeping under the stars or an ironwood tree. I know of few outdoor experiences more pleasurable than to wake up in the gorgeous dawn of the desert, opening one's eyes upon the lacy branches of an ironwood overhead full of silent birds. The poet wrote:

> *Full many a flower is born to blush unseen,*
> *And waste its sweetness on the desert air.*

He could not have been speaking of our Western deserts. Desert life advertizes itself to but few of the physical senses. No desert flowers are fragrant, no desert birds sing. The birds, though, are often brilliantly plumaged.

Not even an ax was necessary to a camp outfit. The desert was studded with the ancient stumps of vanished ironwood trees. With chips, dead cactus trunks—and the cactus growth of Lower California is the most varied in the world—and a few dry palm leaves, you built a fire around an ironwood stump, and it burned all night.

It was during this first winter in Lower California that I found the new species of coyote. They were huge animals, big as a wolf and double the size of our ordinary Western coyote. They were far too shy and cunning ever to let us get within rifle shot of them. The alternative was to poison them. This again presented a difficulty, since after taking a poisoned bait they would run a long distance and hide away before dying. We solved it by putting strychnine on tough meat and wiring that bait to an ironwood log. In taking the bait, the coyote would try to drag the log away. This effort wore out his strength, and he died within a hundred yards or so of the bait.

I collected nineteen coyotes that winter. After studying the specimens I sent to Washington, the Biological Survey pronounced the species new. So far as I know, it has never yet been named.

The following year I went into Lower California again with Captain Funke as guide. This time for companionship I took with me Harry Blagden, who had been with Dr Walcott's party on Mount Robson in Jasper National Park. We hunted at first up near the California border, where the Mexican government was then conducting a great experiment in irrigation. The desert shone with canals and storage lagoons. As a result, millions of aquatic birds had gathered there—tropical birds and migrants from the North. I never saw so many birds in one place before—heron, egrets, and all sorts of waders, as well as duck and geese. Later the irrigation project was abandoned, and now all that region is a waste once more.

Following that experience, we hunted for sheep down through the mountains, bagging six of them besides eight antelope and several red foxes of the desert.

We came out late in the winter, but I went in again almost immediately, this time alone with a guide named Denton. He was an old hunter who knew Lower California well, and I have never known a better shot with a shotgun. We feasted that trip on desert quail which Denton brought down.

Our route this time was an ambitious one. We traveled down the Pacific side of the mountains, looking for desert sheep, as far as Rosario, then quartered back northeastward, cutting across the mountains diagonally and coming out at the head of the Gulf of California. At one time on this arid trip we ran out of water. Our horses would paw holes in the sand three feet deep in their attempt to get a drop or two of moisture. Finally they played out on us altogether. On another occasion I ate some cold boiled potatoes we had been carrying in a tin pail. They gave me ptomaine poisoning, and I was very sick until I could get to a doctor in one of the towns. I had to go to bed for several days.

Except for an occasional shortage of drinking water, we fared well on this trip. The desert quail I have mentioned we supplemented with a wild dove of that country, a slender gray bird, smaller than a pigeon and very good to eat. For meat we had desert antelope. To get them, we sneaked up draws that were full of ironwood, smokebush, and paloverde trees, and jumped them before they knew of our presence. Desert antelope venison is the sweetest meat I ever tasted. We could have had beef, had we chosen, for we ran into herds of wild cattle in the mountains. They were ugly in temper, both bulls and cows, and even dangerous, if you were on foot, for then they chased you.

For dessert we had plenty of wild honey. The mountains of Lower California are full of bee caves; and the knowledge of how to handle wild bees to make them work for you is handed down by the local Indians from one generation to the next. To keep the coyotes out of the bee caves, the Indians block up the entrances to within an inch of the top. After the honey flow, the Indians knock down the barrier and smoke out the bees. They find the roof of the cave crowded with big two-foot combs. They squeeze the comb through ordinary men's socks and thus strain their honey.

This is a black honey, taken from the flowers of the desert agave, or century plant. It is good in flavor, though a little too rich. I brought home lots of it. My sister in New York liked it, until I told her about the socks. After that she wouldn't touch black Mexican honey, though I explained to her that the honey socks were bought new for strainers and were never worn by human feet.

Denton, who was a deep and steady drinker, found cheer more to his taste—tequilla, the universal beverage of Lower California. It is a potent brandy distilled from the fermented juice of the fleshy agave leaves. He stopped for tequilla at every mountain hut. When we went through, the tequilla mills were just doing their season's grinding.

But I seemed to have queer luck with guides in Lower California. Captain Funke was a character and so was Denton, though of quite another type. He was a silent man, who spoke only when necessary, but some mystery hung over him. He seemed to be constantly afraid of something, perhaps of pursuit or revenge. He couldn't sleep unless his shotgun was right at his hand, though there were no dangers in the desert that I knew of. Years afterwards I heard that Denton had died of alcoholism.

By the autumn of 1916 the guns of Europe were beginning to thunder on our side of the ocean. It seemed evident that the United States must sooner or later be dragged into the war. To get in ahead, I resigned from the Biological Survey and once more became a seeker for opportunity.

V WAR INTERLUDE

AVIATION was my goal. Quitting Washington, I went to New York, putting up at the old Waldorf. At breakfast and dinner in the grill I used to spend hours reading the newspapers, which were then full of the exploits of the Lafayette Escadrille. Service in that glamorous flying unit fascinated me. Colonel Bentley Mott was the American representative of the Lafayette Escadrille, and he was stopping at the Waldorf. I sought and obtained an interview with him.

Two obstacles stood in my way, one being my age—thirty-seven now. It was believed then that only boys made good war pilots, because of their daring and their light weight. Thanks to my good physical trim, however, Colonel Mott thought the authorities might waive the age rule for me. He promised to pave the way for me, if I could get to France. That was the other difficulty. America was still officially neutral, and it was impossible to secure a passport or passage for Europe in order to join a belligerent army.

While waiting for my chance, I went to Norfolk, Va., and entered the Curtiss Flying School but remained only a few days. The school was crowded with embryo pilots. Preference was given to youth, and I saw it would be months before the instructors reached me.

Back in New York there came a lucky break for me. Mme Slavko Grouitch, who in her girlhood as Mabel Dunlop had been almost a member of our family, had joined a Red Cross hospital unit, which had assembled and was ready to sail on the first ship. Through her influence, my enlistment in the unit was accepted, and I got into a uniform.

In the latter part of March we sailed on the French liner Rochambeau and had a slow and uneventful voyage until we came in sight of the French coast. I was sitting on the forward boat deck, half asleep in the thin spring sunshine, when the forward gun crew fired. Jumping to my feet, I saw off our starboard bow, half a mile away or less, the black back of a submarine and in the middle distance, plain as day, a lithe, steady torpedo coming toward us.

Everything happened then under perfect discipline and with no confusion. The forward gun kept firing, and the after gun joined in. Whistles shrilled, boat crews began getting down the lifeboats, the ship started zigzagging, passengers were wriggling into life jackets and taking their boat stations. Mme Grouitch was as cool as a cucumber, I remember. But there was no panic on board at all. Clever work on the bridge turned the vessel in time, and the torpedo slipped past the rudder. The U-boat had disappeared. Our zigzag took us nearer, and where the submarine had sunk there was only a great oil slick on the surface. We always thought our gunners hit it.

This occurred on April 7. Two days before the radio had told us that the United States had declared war.

America's entry in the war instantly upset the previous procedure in France. There was now no longer just a Lafayette Escadrille which an American volunteer might join, but the French began taking American students into the military aviation schools everywhere. A Franco-American flying unit began training at Tours on the Loire southwest of Paris. The examining physician, Dr Gros, who later became head of the American Hospital in Paris, refused to certify me as a student pilot, because I was fourteen years above the age limit. He did pass me for an observer, however; and I secured my release from the hospital unit and enlisted in French aviation as a private.

Then, in the beautiful confusion of theory and practice existing between Paris and the field, at Tours the French instructors at once set about training me to pilot an airplane.

But this is anticipatory. In Paris we first had to be photographed and fingerprinted. A detachment of eleven of us was sent down to Tours by train. At the station there we were loaded into a motor lorry and taken to the barracks at the flying field. Our introduction to the life of a war bird was grisly. Just as we turned into the grounds, two student planes collided overhead, and one came down in the garden of the *caserne,* killing the pilot. That same afternoon we recruits were put on a detail to clean up the mess and extricate the mangled body. Our dormitory windows looked over this garden, and whenever I saw the poppies there, I thought of that crash.

I found myself in a sort of Foreign Legion camp, with students of many nationalities in training, though the big majority were French. There were twenty of us Americans, including young Brewer, whose first name I forgot but who was the son of a Boston surgeon, and Gil Winant, who later became governor of New Hampshire, I believe. Most of the youngsters I trained with were killed later on.

Our instructors were French pilots, few of whom knew even a word of English. We trained in the old Caudron biplanes, the student sitting forward in the observer's seat, where he had a second set of controls. A poke in his back from the instructor behind him meant one thing, a rap on the head another. Time was more important to the French than human life. No one was supposed to fly solo until he had been up twenty-five times with an instructor, but after my fifteenth lesson my teacher reported me ready to fly and got on with somebody else.

It was with trepidation that I climbed for the first time into the cockpit alone. I didn't think I was yet ready to pilot a ship, and I was right. Orders were orders—I had to go. I tested my controls, made the ignition contact, and the engine began to roar. I gave her the gun, and then, to my astonishment and dismay, instead of heading down into the wind, as I had expected, the plane swung off to the right on a curve.

The biplane wouldn't straighten out for me. I tried to think of a thousand instructions at once and remembered everything except the right one, which was to shut off the power. By the time my ship had cut half of a huge semicircle, threatening to upset every moment, I remembered that little point. The biplane came to a standstill. Shaken by the experience, I somehow managed to turn and taxi back to the start. On my second trial, the plane again stayed on the ground, swinging to the left this time.

But now I was gaining more assurance. If I had to go up and kill myself, I might as well be about it and not shilly-shally around in circles. I gave her the gun the third time. We gathered speed, straight into the wind, and before I knew it I was in the air.

The moment that occurred, all my fears left me. I had not anticipated any trouble in taking off. The greater danger, I knew, was in landing. Yet once I was flying and my safety was dependent solely upon myself, I had every confidence. Flying over a ground mark set for the purpose, I shut off the motor and nosed down.

I had not yet acquired the "feel" of an airplane. The ship's responses to the controls, too, were different from what I had expected. Evidently my instructor had kept more control in those final lessons than I knew. I had trouble in keeping the coasting ship on an even keel. Nevertheless, I flattened out at the right moment and made an easy landing but with a rocking plane. One wing tip brushed the ground. Men rushed across the field to me, but the only damage was a broken strut. I hoped this wouldn't be counted against me as a crash. The French allowed a cadet only two training crashes. A third, and they kicked you out.

So I persevered, and within a week received my *élève* pilots' insignia—a silver oak wreath enclosing a single wing attached to a star. A little later I was promoted to the grade of sergeant. Then the American army took over the Tours camp, under Seth Low as commandant, and all the easy informality of French army discipline gave way to a rigid adherence to book and rule that left no play for individual imagination or initiative.

It bothered the American command at Tours to discover in me a soldier marked down on the records as an airplane observer yet who was actually sitting at the controls of a training ship. There wasn't anything in the Articles of War about that. I should have been in an observers' training camp, but there was no such camp in France. I imagine my case built up quite a file of perplexed letters. Pending a decision, they permitted me to keep on flying, which I did for three months. I may remark now that this was the only piloting I ever did.

So many things in the American army service seemed stupid to me. For instance, our authorities at Tours at once imported a hard-boiled sergeant and put us student pilots through daily rifle and bayonet drill. Why, I don't know, since military fliers don't carry rifles. And then the awful American uniform—the terrible puttees and the high collar of the tunic that was so uncomfortable in hot weather—there wasn't much sense about it.

While I was at Tours, Eddie Rickenbacker joined us for training and was in the air solo in no time. It disgruntled the rest of us a little that Rickenbacker, due to his influence at headquarters, received double-time credit for his flying hours, enabling him to get to the front sooner than anybody else. This favoritism justified itself, though, when Rickenbacker became the leading American ace.

While awaiting our turns to fly that fall, we cadets would sit on the grass talking and sometimes engaging in wrestling matches. They were bringing some husky youngsters into the Air Service, but I won every match. Nobody there could put my shoulders on the ground.

The military master minds finally solved my problem by sending me to aviation headquarters in Paris. It would never have done, of course, to tell an enlisted man anything happening to his interest, but I did gain the impression that I was to be commissioned in Paris and permitted to fly over the trenches. Instead of that they shoved me into an office, with a desk job, and there I stayed until the summer of 1918.

In common with the other noncoms and enlisted men in that office, I was treated like a servant by the commissioned officers. I might be writing some report, absorbed in it, when my major came in. First he pulled off his gloves and tossed them on my paper. If they smeared the ink, I only had to do the report over again. Next he tossed his swagger stick on the desk, scattering pencils and pens. I was supposed to rise, salute, give him my seat, take his cap and hang it up, and then stand at attention until he got ready to notice me.

There may be people who don't mind that sort of treatment, but I'm not one of them. The most I can say for the experience is that it taught me, as we say, to take it. Some years later, when Amundsen and I came out of the Arctic, this same major, who is a Philadelphia banker, tried to claim a friendship with me on the basis of our Paris association. He had only indifferent success.

One March afternoon I had had lunch and was sitting on a bench in the Tuileries Gardens, enjoying a cigarette, when there came a terrific explosion not three hundred yards from where I sat. A crater appeared in the park, and fragments of steel flew in every direction. I picked up a piece, which I still have, as a souvenir.

Everybody thought at first that it was an unannounced air raid, but it was the first shot from Big Bertha, the German long-range gun. Not bad shooting, either, to come that close to the Place de la Concorde, the bull's-eye of Paris, from a distance of seventy miles.

The air raids usually came at night; and, being off duty, I made it a practice during raids to sit in the rotunda of the Hotel Meurice, on the Rue de Rivoli, to be out of danger. I seemed to have but little company there; and once when I went in during daylight I discovered that I had really been sitting under a glass dome which a dropped buckshot could have penetrated.

Whenever I could—Sundays and other days off—I took out my camera in Paris. I always had my films developed at a little shop near the Place de la Concorde, and the famous French flying ace Guynemer used to bring his films to this same place. Several times we were in the shop together, and I had a good opportunity to observe him. He was extremely nervous, shifting position constantly, never still for a moment, but what I noticed most were his black eyes—the most deadly eyes I have ever seen. I grew to know, at least by sight, most of the famous French war aces. Nungesser and Lufbery were phlegmatic types, just the opposite of Guynemer.

The influenza epidemic swept into Paris that summer, and I was one of the first victims, contracting a bad case that developed into pneumonia. When I emerged from the hospital, my faint sergeant complaints about not being sent to the front as an aerial observer at length became audible in the ears of my superior officers. They sent me back to the States to enter an observation school. But scarcely had my travel orders been made out in New York than the armistice was declared, and thus ended my none too glorious career as a soldier.

But the war had done something for me. A great thing had happened to me in Paris—an epochal event. I had met Roald Amundsen.

He was at the Hotel Meurice as the guest of the French government while waiting for the Maud, the vessel in which he was to attempt, and make, the northeast passage to Alaska, to be equipped for a possible seven-year drift. I summoned up all my courage one evening, went to the hotel, and sent him my card, requesting an interview.

Always kindly and accommodating about such things, the famous discoverer of the South Pole came down to me at once. I saw a tall, long-limbed, rugged figure with a hawklike visage and eyes that bored through me and then seemed to look a million miles behind me into space. His skin was weatherbeaten; forehead baldness was creeping back into his iron-gray hair. In my ill-fitting uniform I must have presented a seedy spectacle to him. I stated my errand, and he sat down to hear me, in a very patient attitude.

So I began, telling him of my training and experiences and listing what I considered to be my qualifications for polar exploration. As I spoke I became filled with hatred of the menial service into which I had been trapped. I felt that I couldn't go back to it again—to be an office drudge, chained to a desk. I began almost to babble as I begged to go with him in the Maud. I could arrange for my discharge from the army. I had influential friends—United States senators at home, my cousin General Dawes was one of the high command of the A.E.F. Wasn't there any chance that he could take me?

I subsided, and for a long space he was silent, as if in thought. When he spoke it was in a tone of gentle reproof.

"Isn't it," he inquired, "a little bit late?"

I am satisfied that he forgot about this meeting, but that viking figure and those piercing eyes were to haunt me for years.

VI   THE TURNING POINT

THAT ARCHENEMY of my family, pneumonia, knocked me down physically to such an extent that for the next four or five years I was incapacitated for any such arduous work as exploration either in the Western wilds or, as my dream still beckoned, at the Poles. Two subsequent attacks of pleurisy put me on the shelf. To give myself every chance to recover health, I returned to the deserts of the Southwest.

It was during this period that I "discovered" the Grand Canyon of the Colorado, and by that I mean discovered it for myself. Since then I have never failed to make my annual pilgrimage to the Canyon. I call it pilgrimage, because there is something almost religious about it, with me. There I confront the Source of Great Truths that Dr van Dyke talks about. In the stratification and geologic horizons exposed in the canyon walls, I read the story of eternity.

At this time of wandering, too, I first visited Mount Wilson Observatory, at Pasadena, Cal., where Dr George Ellery Hale, whose housetop telescope I had gazed at with such awe when a child in Chicago, was in charge. My two favorite trails today are the trail up Mount Wilson and one that descends the wall of the Grand Canyon.

All during these years, however, the lamp of the aurora borealis kept burning steadily for me. I regarded my enforced leisure as a period for recuperating the strength I would need for supreme tests ahead. How I would get to the Arctic or when, I did not know; but I did know that I was going. In a letter to my father at this time, I wrote: "Just why the North has always appealed to me, it is impossible to say, but that there is a great field for scientific work no one can deny."

Indeed, I made one abortive attempt to get to the Arctic—with Stefansson, the Canadian explorer. Stefansson wanted to buy the ice steamer Carluk with which to continue his valuable exploratory work, and I tried to induce my father to put up the money for it. Dr Osborn, of the American Museum, also approached Father on this project but without success. He was as impervious as ever to plea or argument. I had to confess failure, and Stefansson secured the necessary aid in Canada.

About this time Father's attitude toward me underwent a change. I still remained his chief problem, the one sorrow and anxiety of his declining years. Paternal disapproval, well-meant advice, appeals, and commands having failed, he now tried to tempt me away from my ambition with riches. I could have a villa in Italy, a fine home in New York, if I would only settle down to a common-sense life such as ordinary people of means enjoyed.

But if bribery, this was the bribery of love, or perhaps of his pride. He could not tolerate the idea that all the money he had amassed should not of course protect his own flesh and blood from privation or worse. It shamed him in his own eyes and, as he may have thought, in those of his friends. They knew him as a man who had never been defeated in any main purpose of his life, yet I stood before him and them as a living symbol of his defeat.

He was in Italy, at the Villa Palmieri, when he tried this offer upon me, hinting that it was time for him to be making other provision for me as well. The letter I wrote in answer contained the following paragraph:

"You have spoken to me vaguely of the future—of a home, for instance; but if, instead of such a provision, its equivalent in value might be placed as a working fund in some national institution that is particularly interested in exploration, so that I might be able to continue the work, it would indeed mean infinitely more to me and to the world than that small value in material property could mean."

But my determination to go into the North was something more than a man's natural desire to accomplish something noteworthy for himself and valuable to science. It rested, too, upon deep psychological considerations. It must be remembered that I was born a physical weakling, timid and anemic. At the age of 40 I was both physically and professionally a self-made man. I delighted to match my powers against hardships under which men of lesser strength wilted. The whole chemistry of my nature demanded these convincing tests. What then must have been the appeal to me of the Arctic and Antarctic, where the resourcefulness and stamina of men meet the supreme ordeal?

In another letter to my father, I expressed this same thought.

"I do not want worldly goods," I wrote him, "castles or villas

or money with which to purchase luxury. I do want the opportunity
to make good and satisfy my inward self in the line of endeavor
I have chosen."

Father thought I was a fool to make such a choice and so did
many of his friends—hardheaded businessmen, all of them. Judged
by ordinary standards, perhaps I was; but I could only express the
nature God and circumstance had given me. Once in an hour of
discouragement I came upon some verses that seemed to gather
into so few words all that I thought about myself and my career
that I never forgot them.

> *We are those fools who could not rest*
> *In the dull earth we left behind,*
> *But burned with passion for the West*
> *And drank strange frenzy from its wind.*
> *The world where wise men live at ease*
> *Fades from our unregretful eyes,*
> *As blind across uncharted seas*
> *We stagger on our enterprise.*

That was the ideal I sought for myself—to go blind across uncharted seas and lands, struggling, conquering, the advance pioneer
of humanity.

Doors to the North would not open for me; and, with returning
health, I was not one to sulk. I returned from the deserts a little
thin but brown and strong and at once looked around for something to do. I met Dr Joseph T. Singewald, professor of Economic
Geology at Johns Hopkins, and he suggested an expedition to Peru
to make a geologic cross section of the Andes. There was then in
existence no adequate geological study of the rock structure of
those mountains.

The work promised results of value, I had nothing else to do,
and I had enough money to meet the slight costs of such an undertaking. In February 1924 the Ellsworth Expedition of Johns Hopkins University went to Peru. It consisted of three men: Dr
Singewald, his brother Quentin D. Singewald, also a Johns Hopkins
geologist, and myself.

Of the results of the expedition I need say little here. The important work was done by the two geologists, and Dr Singewald's report, a paper chiefly of technical interest to geologists, has been published.* We went in at Chimbote, crossed the three great ranges of the Andes, measuring their rock masses, and then came down the Huallaga River to Yurimaguas, on the upper Amazon, from where a small steamer runs to Iquitos, five hundred miles east. Thence by a regular Amazon River boat 2,500 miles to Para at the mouth of the river.

The Andes I found different from any mountains I had ever known. Their immensity and barrenness were depressing to the soul. The valleys are so narrow and deep, the peaks so high, the trails so steep, it was always up or down, climbing all the time. The altitudes bothered me, and I couldn't sleep much at night. At the Canal on the way down I managed to pick up a touch of Chagres fever, which the Andean fleas aggravated. Off and on I shook with malaria for the next two years. Even in perfect health, though, I wouldn't have enjoyed the Andes. There was no game—nothing to hunt. The only animal life that interested me much was the condor. There were plenty of condors.

The Peruvian Indians we found to be a worthless lot, spineless and unreliable. They would desert on the slightest pretext. There were not many llamas in that part of Peru, and we used mules for pack animals. One thing impressed me. All the Indians down there carried gourds of slacked lime and dried coca leaves. They made cuds of this mixture and, when chewing it, were capable of extraordinary feats of endurance. Years later I remembered this and carried a supply of Andean coca leaves on my flight across Antarctica. I never had to use them; but it is conceivable that their narcotic principle might lend a man that last ounce of energy needed to take him safely out of some desperate predicament.

Leaving my two companions to undertake alone the final stage of the Andean crossing—a thirteen-day raft trip down the Huallaga River from Uchiza to Yurimaguas—I returned to New York via Callao and Panama to get medical care for my malaria. The expe-

*In the *Bulletin* of the Pan-American Union, March 1925.

dition brought back to the States a representative collection of
fossils and rock specimens to be analyzed in detail in the Johns
Hopkins laboratories. The scientists were so enthusiastic over
what we had done that I agreed to return with them for further
.Andean studies as soon as they had deposited their collection with
the university and written a preliminary report.

A month later I was in New York, waiting to sail for South
America once more. I had, in fact, bought my ticket to Callao.
Skimming through the New York *Herald Tribune* one morning,
my eyes fell upon a small item buried inside the paper which
brought me to the alert, every nerve tingling. Among the arrivals
in New York from Europe the day before was Roald Amundsen,
the discoverer of the South Pole.

I went to the telephone and found out that he was stopping at
the old Waldorf-Astoria Hotel, at Fifth Avenue and Thirty-fourth
Street. I called him up, and when that long-remembered voice
answered, no novice seeing his first moose across the sights of a
rifle was ever more shaken and excited than I. I asked him for an
hour's interview, and in that kindly way he had he granted it
without any hesitation.

Late that afternoon I went to keep the appointment. The hour
I had asked for became two hours. Then we had dinner together.
Our talk continued afterwards in his room. When I left the hotel
that night, my head was in the stars. My second Peruvian expedition was in the discard, and life for me had turned a new corner.

VII   PORTRAIT OF A VIKING

FOR THE NEXT TWO YEARS I was intimately associated with
Roald Engelbregt Gravning Amundsen. By telling some of the
characteristic things he said and did during that time, and adding

observations of my own, I hope to convey to the reader something of the savor of that extraordinary man.

People who ever knew Amundsen always tell you first about his remarkable eyes. His long head and hooked nose gave him the look of an eagle, an effect which his imperial white mustache only accented. Yet his eyes were his most arresting feature. Years spent on the decks of vessels and amid limitless sweeps of ice and snow had given them a chronic squint. Through narrowed lids peered those gray eyes, boring through one as their gaze passed on into infinite distances.

Amundsen had come to America in the fall of 1924, disillusioned and embittered. He hoped to earn enough by lecturing to finance further explorations in the Arctic, but that, he knew, was an outside chance. He expected only to go to a cabin he owned at Wainwright, far in the north of Alaska, near Point Barrow, and there spend the rest of his days. He had packed up at home and had brought most of his most treasured belongings with him.

He loved Alaska. It was in Alaska he landed after both his northwest and northeast passages of the Arctic Ocean, and from Alaska that he planned to start for the North Pole in the Fram before he knew that Peary had already reached it. When we were coming down from Alaska after the Norge flight, as the steamer headed south into Norton Sound I saw Amundsen standing at the rail, his chin on his hand, looking at the receding coast of the land of his choice. I stepped beside him and observed that his eyes were moist.

"I suppose I will never see it again," he said.

He never did.

He was a virtuoso of exploration, following to his goal with a singleness of purpose shared by a painter at work on a masterpiece or by a poet aware that he is writing something imperishable. Nothing but his work and his goal counted with Amundsen. As a result, he neglected other sides of himself. He had no business sense, for instance, and was always in hot water over finances. He went into bankruptcy, and creditors hounded him for money. In his room at the Waldorf, I frequently heard a mysterious rustling of paper on the floor—another court summons for Amundsen being slid under the door.

Creditors never let him rest. Even when we reached Seattle after that voyage from Alaska and were in the midst of a civic welcome, the inevitable process server appeared. Poor Amundsen had to leave the dinner for a little while and take this fellow to his room in the hotel, to go through the same story once more.

Such persecution made an old man out of him before his time. While he did not consider that the world owed him a living, he did think he should be treated more leniently than ordinary men. People who met him casually complained of his chilly reserve. There was nothing of that about the real Amundsen. He was like a child whose confidence has been betrayed so often that it finally trusts nobody. So he encased himself in a shell of ice. Win his confidence and melt that ice, and a different being emerged. Nobody was warmer hearted, no boy could frolic more joyously than Amundsen in his fifties, as he was when I knew him.

He assured me profusely that he remembered everything about our meeting at the Hotel Meurice, but I never believed a word of it. Amundsen was not above a white fib now and then, if it made someone happier or if it extricated him from some trivial embarrassment. In all important matters relating to his own achievements or to his intercourse with his friends, he was scrupulously truthful; yet a little later I shall have to tell how he and I signed a certain contract, though we had privately agreed in advance not to follow its provisions.

No man more than the explorer is tempted to adopt the doctrine of ends justifying means. An explorer soon discovers that the world is full of busybodies righteously ready to save him, as they probably think, from himself. The only way to deal with such people is to agree to their terms and then go ahead as one pleases. There are enough legitimate discouragements in the work without submitting to artificial ones.

Having learned English late in life, Amundsen spoke our language with a strong accent. In the anecdotes that follow, I shall not attempt to suggest his broken speech by distorted spellings, since printed dialect has a comic effect. There was nothing comic about Amundsen. To Americans his accent only sounded distinguished.

He had an immense gusto for life. From those half-wild ancestors who voyaged to America centuries before Columbus was born he inherited a heroic appetite that included everything that could be called edible. His throat seemed to be lined with asbestos, and his digestion was that of an ostrich. When we were down on the ice in the Arctic, we lived on pemmican, oat biscuits, and hot chocolate. The rest of us alway had to set our mugs of boiling chocolate in the open air to cool, but Amundsen gulped his down in a minute.

"That is good," he would say as he set down the empty mug. "There are two times when a man is happy up here—when his belly is full of hot liquid and when he is in his sleeping bag."

When we started in the Norge a friend in Spitzbergen presented us with two big thermos bottles filled with a concoction of hot grease and meat balls. It tasted like garbage to me. Yet as we passed over the North Pole Amundsen helped himself to two mugs of this terrible slum and smacked his lips over them.

We had been down to Rome together to meet Nobile and inspect the Norge. On our way back to Oslo Amundsen turned to me suddenly in our compartment and said: "I know where to get the best coffee and rolls in the world." I asked where, and he said, "In Copenhagen." I told him that city wasn't on our route.

"Never mind," he said. "It will take only a day, and we have plenty of time."

We detoured to Copenhagen, and he took me to a pastry shop. It was the worst coffee I ever tasted, but it fulfilled Amundsen's expectations.

We were coming East from Seattle after the Norge flight. Being due to arrive in Chicago one morning at seven-thirty, Amundsen and I were up early to shave and dress. The porter brought us a telegram, informing us that a committee from the Chicago Geographical Society was meeting us at the station to take us to an official breakfast. This didn't suit Amundsen at all.

"I am very hungry," he informed me. "Let the rest of the party go to that breakfast. You come with me."

So we told the committee we had previously made a very important engagement. Amundsen and I then went to the Blackstone Hotel, where, though we had been three days on a train, he ordered and ate among other things four hard-boiled eggs.

"I remember liking these as a boy," he said.

He was a very modest and very democratic man. Of Nansen he said to me once: "Nansen is too kingly. He will not hobnob with the common herd." But Amundsen liked people. On his expeditions he was not only leader but comrade with everyone. Once he made a friend, nothing thereafter could shake his loyalty. He stood there on some rock of his own.

He never deserted Dr Frederick A. Cook and made it a point to visit him regularly in Leavenworth Prison. He told me it was pathetic to see Cook reduced to doing needlework.

"Only this I know," he said. "Cook pulled us all out of the Antarctic with his good spirits and his medical care. That is all the Dr Cook there is for me."

Amundsen's boyish nature took an amusing turn in that he appropriated several of my habits, though I was the younger man by ten years. I like to smoke a pipe in bed. Amundsen scolded me for it at first but later fell into the habit himself. I smoked a brand of French-Canadian pipe tobacco. Amundsen tried it a few times; then I discovered he had ordered fifty pounds for his own use.

For many years I have had the habit of eating but twice a day, omitting lunch and substituting a walk or other physical exercise. In Norway especially I followed this practice, since I couldn't stand so many heavy Norwegian meals. In Spitzbergen when I started out at noon to walk, Amundsen laughed at me. He said if he skipped a meal, it gave him a headache.

After our first polar flight Amundsen came over to America to deliver lectures. I met him on the pier and helped him through the customs. We got to his hotel about noon. I then suggested that while he was having his lunch I would go to the gymnasium for my regular wrestling bout with the professional. Rather bashfully Amundsen told me that he had taken up the no-lunch system, too.

About his past achievements he was very reticent. "There is nothing to tell," he would say. Yet during the many days of intimacy I passed with him he dropped several remarks about himself which I treasure in my memory.

One day he said: "I suppose my discovery of the South Pole will always be regarded by the public as the high point of my life—but not with me. My greatest achievement was the northwest passage in the Gjoa."

Then he related to me a miraculous incident of that passage, an episode that might have been taken from the sagas of the Norsemen. Skirting the Arctic Coast of America, the little Gjoa was caught in a gale and blizzard. Mountainous waves tossed the ship like a cork, visibility dropped to nothing, and the mariners could only drive ahead of the storm. Suddenly breakers were right under the bows as the Gjoa drifted upon a reef so close to the surface that the receding waves showed the rocks. Disaster seemed at hand, but just then an immense comber picked up the ship, lifted it across the reef, and set it down safely on the other side.

As he finished this story, Amundsen said: "When it is darkest there is always light ahead." This was a favorite maxim of his, and he said it more than once during those desperate days when we were on the ice near the North Pole. Incidentally, the Gjoa is now in Golden Gate Park, the explorer's gift to the city of San Francisco.

Amundsen was always the explorer, never the mere adventurer. Hardship and peril were incidental to his aim of adding to the store of scientific knowledge. I remember an occurrence on the Farm, the yacht which the Norwegian government lent us to take us to Spitzbergen for our airplane flight to the North Pole. We ran into very rough weather, and the little Farm was under water half the time.

Amundsen and I were bunking on couches in the dining saloon. Once after a series of dizzy pitches I saw him turn white, the perspiration beading his forehead. I was pretty seasick myself, and I said to him, "You know, Captain, I don't like the sea."

"I don't either," said that Norseman, who had spent thirty-two years of his life on salt water. "It is something we have to put up with."

He had no interest in visiting any spot to which another explorer had preceded him. The mere feat of getting to a difficult place had no appeal for Amundsen. This trait was never better shown than in the story of his discovery of the South Pole.

Amundsen secured Nansen's old ship, the Fram, with the intention of drifting to the North Pole, or at least drifting so close to it that the rest of the journey could be made with skis and dog sleds. Nansen had failed to do the same thing; but Amundsen thought that, by starting farther east than Nansen had, he might accomplish it. When he sailed in the Fram, his destination was the Bering Strait. He intended to enter the Arctic Ocean between Siberia and Alaska and catch a northerly current there.

He had proceeded thousands of leagues from Norway when he learned the startling news that Peary had attained the North Pole. At once that objective, the goal of all polar explorers for fifty years, lost its attraction for Amundsen. Without hesitation he turned the Fram around and headed for the Antarctic. He knew that Scott was already there; but, since the season would be exactly right, he hoped to beat the Englishman to the South Pole.

Amundsen landed on the Bay of Whales of the Ross Sea where Byrd later established his camp, Little America. Putting his lightly packed dog sledges on the shelf ice and taking with him Oscar Wisting and three other Norwegians, these five experts, all men who had practically been raised on skis, drove a swift straight line to the South Pole and back, a feat of skill and efficiency without parallel in polar exploration. Amundsen was back in civilization with his announcement before the news came of the Scott tragedy.

What an adventurer he was! This same flexibility of mind was illustrated in the famous story of how he sailed in the Gjoa to negotiate the northwest passage of the Arctic. As usual, his finances were in bad shape. He had his supplies and his men aboard the ship at a dock in Oslo when, just as a terrific thunderstorm broke, his first mate came to him with the news that his principal creditor was on the pier with officers to attach the whole expedition and was only waiting for the rain to stop to serve the papers. Amundsen seized an ax, dashed out into the cloudburst, and cut the mooring hawsers. By the time the squall ended the Gjoa was out of the jurisdiction of bankruptcy courts.

It was Amundsen's pride that three years later, the first northwest passage now a fact, he was able to pay off his creditors in full.

After our flight across the Arctic in the Norge, Amundsen, Byrd, and I formed what Amundsen in his book, *My Life as an Explorer,* called "probably the most exclusive club in the world." We named it the Polar Legion, and the only eligibles for membership were to be leaders of expeditions which had reached either Pole. Only we three could qualify, and Amundsen was then the only man who had reached both Poles. We adopted a beautiful pin —a polar bear in platinum clutching the North Star, represented by a diamond. Though they were dead, we voted in Peary and Scott as charter members and sent pins to their widows.

To inaugurate the Polar Legion we had a little formal dinner at the Metropolitan Club in Washington. In the course of the dinner Commander Byrd announced to us his intention to fly to the South Pole, a thing he accomplished three years later.

"And, Captain," said Byrd to Amundsen, "what a thrill it will be if I find your tent still there!"

Amundsen agreed but, it seemed to me, without much enthusiasm. After the dinner he and I walked together to our hotel through the frosty December streets of the capital.

"Of course," said the viking, shrugging his big shoulders, "Byrd can fly to the South Pole, if he wants to, but what is the use? I don't understand such a thing. I was there, Scott was there— there is nothing more to find. Why should anybody want to go to a place where somebody else had already been? Or go there for the sake of doing it a different way?"

That was his whole attitude toward exploration.

As we go along with the story, I shall have many other things to tell about Roald Amundsen that indicate his character. Two or three of his idiosyncrasies occur to me now. One was his hatred of being trailed. He couldn't bear to have anyone following on his heels. When our party marched over the ice in the North, Amundsen would always get far ahead of us.

That time we went to Copenhagen for the famous coffee and rolls, he and I took a walk through the residential part of the city in the afternoon. Suddenly, without looking around or even glancing at me, he said tensely: "Ellsworth, we are being followed!"

I whirled about, and, sure enough, some little boys were trailing us. It must be remembered that Amundsen was almost as much a national figure in Scandinavian Denmark as in Norway, and these youngsters were indulging a natural curiosity, quite unaware that they were also rasping their hero's pet phobia. Amundsen shooed them off, and, being well-mannered urchins, they vanished.

He was the only man I ever knew who said he could sleep better in the long polar day than at night in the lower latitudes. I have never quite believed him, thinking his boast to have been another of his harmless prevarications. Most men are troubled by insomnia at the Poles in summer. Your proper sleeping times get out of adjustment, the eternal light frets your nerves. My own slumber there is always broken and uneasy.

Though he could indulge in a mild, merry spree on occasions, Amundsen was not a heavy-drinking man; yet he had a trait of one. When liquor was available he always took a drink at five o'clock in the afternoon precisely. At about ten minutes to five he would begin to look at his watch. At one minute to five no persuasion could induce him to take a drink. At five he lifted his glass. Then, that ritual over, he might not take another drink that day.

He died as he had lived—heroically. The event is so recent that I need set down only the bare facts as reminders. In the spring of 1928 Umberto Nobile crashed in the Arctic with his airship Italia. Searchers at once answered the SOS. The Norwegian ace Lundborg rescued Nobile; the Russian icebreaker Krassin brought out the survivors of Nobile's party. Amundsen and another comrade of our Arctic flights, Dietrichson, volunteered for the search, flying as observers with the French pilot Guilbaud. Their plane was never heard from again.

Thus passed one of the heroes of my adult life. I am frankly a hero-worshiper and always have been. Three great men have stood out before my eyes—three who have inspired me most and whom I have tried most to emulate—Theodore Roosevelt, Roald Amundsen, and the Western frontiersman Wyatt Earp. Rated by their influence upon me, the greatest of these was Wyatt Earp, but the one I knew was Amundsen.

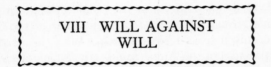

VIII   WILL AGAINST WILL

THAT FIRST LONG TALK I had with Amundsen in his room at the Waldorf developed many things, the most important being that henceforth we were to be partners in polar exploration. And partners we remained until a day in New York two years later. We had just crossed the continent from Seattle, our transarctic flight in the Norge a thing of history, and the newspaper reporters asked Amundsen what he intended to do next.

"I am now going to leave it to younger men," he said, and he waved his hand toward me. He knew he was through with the Arctic, and he was, except for his final death flight on a mission of mercy.

I opened the interview by telling Amundsen of my long experience in scientific exploration and of my almost equally long ambition to go into the Arctic. I told him of my belief in the airplane as a vehicle for polar exploration, certain that this would strike a responsive chord in him, since I knew about his frustrated attempt to fly north from Alaska two years before.

He replied that for several years he had thought of little else than flying into the Arctic. His attempt from Wainwright, where he had his cabin, had been doomed to failure from the start. He had been able to afford only an old obsolete plane, which indeed had cracked up when he attempted to land it on the tundra after its trial flight. Moreover, it was doubtful if this ship could have carried enough fuel for the Arctic crossing. Amundsen, in fact, intended to take skis and a folding canoe with him, fly to the end of the gas, and finish the journey on foot.

After the failure of this project, Amundsen had returned to Norway, where for more than a year he had been trying to get financial support for a first-class airplane expedition into the Arctic. He had pleaded and besought in vain. Newspapers and even aviators were skeptical of the ability of the airplane, as then developed, to fly successfully in the polar regions; and not even Amundsen's great reputation as the discoverer of the South Pole and as the only man in history to make both the northwest and northeast passages of the Arctic could induce men of means to put up money behind his scheme. At last, discouraged and broken-hearted, he had given up and had come to America to retire to his Wainwright hermitage.

Thus I came to Amundsen as a godsend, bringing not only new blood and enthusiasm to bolster his spirits but a chance as well to secure financing for some magnificent enterprise. It was only an outside chance, to be sure. I had to confess to the explorer that all attempts to persuade my father to back an Arctic expedition for me had met with failure. Still, I had a few thousands of my own. With that money we might do something.

As we talked Amundsen seemed to shed years of his age. By the time we had finished dinner we knew that we were congenial to each other and could form an efficient team. We spent the evening discussing plans. Amundsen became eager as a boy. The money I had might finance an expedition to Nicholas II Land, the big mountainous island north of Siberia. Though discovered, it had never been explored. Failing to do that, we might both go to his cabin at Wainwright and make a study of Arctic birds.

But our first ambition must be to fly clear across the Arctic. It interested neither of us merely to attain the North Pole. The myth of Crocker Land, to call it that, still persisted. To be sure, Mac-Millan had long since proved that the land Peary thought he saw off a Greenland cape was an illusion. Yet Dr Harris, of the U.S. Coast and Geodetic Survey, after studying tidal currents along the Arctic Coast of Alaska, had formed the theory of a large body of land lying between the North Pole and North America. A million square miles of the Arctic there were still unexplored; it was possible for that supposed land to be almost continental in size. Every explorer in 1924 believed in its existence, and its discovery was the great objective of all polar adventuring.

With now a definite plan to propose and an association formed with a man as thoroughly tried as Amundsen in polar travel, I thought it possible that my father might change his attitude and supply the money to finance us. Father was still in Italy when I had my meeting with Amundsen, but I wrote to him immediately, pleading for myself as I never had before.

"It seems to me that what I ask is not unjust," I said in my letter. "It is something due every human being born on earth—a chance to make good, where his own individual conscience is satisfied with the result." This opportunity, I went on, had come to me as "a great favor from God, as I see it."

I did not ask him for a gift of money but only a loan—an advance of a year and one half of my private income.

"I will pay every cent of it back, gladly undertaking any menial service afterwards in order to do so."

Father's reply was as uncompromising as ever.

Amundsen went out on a lecture tour, while I continued my efforts to secure American support. I went to Washington and saw General Mitchell, head of the army Air Service. He was sympathetic but said he could not give us army planes and equipment without an act of Congress. It would take many months to secure that, with the issue always in doubt. He advised me not to attempt it.

The Aero Club of Norway had been almost the only supporter of Amundsen in his previous campaign to form an Arctic air expedition. Amundsen got in touch with them again, and there were indications that we could rely on them for something, provided we could secure the major part of our fund in the United States. I had my nest egg in a Cleveland bank; Amundsen was lecturing. There was still hope that somehow we might finance our ambition.

Then Father returned to America, and I renewed my pleading. He was nervous and irritable, and the pressure I was putting upon him bothered him terribly. Wouldn't he at least see Captain Amundsen? I begged. Was that asking much—to give himself the opportunity of meeting familiarly one of the world's historic men?

"Bring him, then," my father finally cried. "Bring him."

It was the first break in his defenses, the first time his iron opposition had even sagged. Filled with elation and hope, I awaited Amundsen's return to New York.

I must present a picture of Father in 1924, when he was 75 years old. Though his hair and mustache were iron gray, he was as tall, thin, and erect as ever. His skin was as smooth as that of a man twenty-five years younger. Yet he was on a swift decline. His second wife, my stepmother, had recently died, and that had been a great shock to him. His old firmness of thought was giving way to an uncertain frame of mind that was most strange in him. He was beginning to vacillate in his judgments. Five years earlier, I believe, he would have refused to see Amundsen at all.

Three topics were then occupying his thoughts—the tribulation I was causing him, his memoirs on which he was at work, and the selection of a new barber. I can assure the reader that this last was almost as important with him as the other two. In his diary at this time there are as many references to the barber problem as there are to me.

Thus his nature rested as strongly upon him as ever. He was closing the final chapters of his life with the same precision that had opened them back in the seventies and eighties. His barber was an illustration in point. Upon his return from Florence he learned that the barber who always cut his hair was for some reason no longer available. With thousands of good barbers in New York, that might not seem a serious loss, but to Father it was a domestic calamity.

For years he had been accustomed to have his hair cut at home twice a month by one barber, who always came on the same dates in the month and at the same hour. Father virtually went into a contract for this work. The price was stipulated—fifty cents. Haircutting prices in the better shops were higher than that, but Father came from a generation that grew up with twenty-five-cent haircuts. This was also in the flush times when dollar tips were common in hotel barbershops; but Father would no more have tipped a barber than he would a dentist or physician.

Furthermore, the man had to be specially qualified—expert, of course. Once shown the style of the cut, he was to ask no more questions about it. He must always be prompt and reliable, and after each haircutting he would find his fifty-cent piece on the dresser.

To find a new barber, Father submitted to no experiments. He consulted with friends and interviewed their candidates. His diary has numerous references to these interviews. Eventually he secured a man who, I assume, proved to be satisfactory.

How vividly I remember that interview between my father and Roald Amundsen—the grim, old, white-faced financier facing the gray, bald but vigorous, weather-beaten old viking! It occurred on Sunday, November 9, in the house at 603 Park Avenue. Just at the stroke of noon Amundsen and I arrived, and Father received us in the library on the second floor. I introduced them, and then we sat down, the two older men eying each other.

Finally Father said, "I suppose you have something to tell me, Captain Amundsen?"

"What do you want to know?" asked Amundsen.

"About your experiences," said Father. "What this business is like."

Then Amundsen told of his past expeditions, speaking longer

upon the subject than I ever knew him to do again. As he talked, I saw he was making a favorable impression. Amundsen bred confidence. You knew by looking at him that here was a man who could take care of himself under any conditions.

"What about the dangers?" Father finally interrupted him.

Amundsen replied in substance as he had replied years before to a newspaper reporter, upon returning from the South Pole. The chief dangers of polar exploration could be discounted by making provision for them in advance. Unexpected dangers were no greater than those to which sailors, fishermen, and men in other ordinary walks of life were subjected.

Father looked at Amundsen sharply and said, "Suppose I don't help you? What will you do?"

That was the first intimation he gave that he was even considering our proposition. I held my breath for Amundsen's reply. The old explorer had had too many discouragements in his life to be downcast by this implied one. Slowly and patiently he said in his broken English:

"Well, Mr Ellsworth, I will do what I have always done. I will get along some way."

This statement completely predisposed my father toward Amundsen, and I may add that he never afterwards lost confidence in him. Before I could realize what was happening, Father offered to back us. It was a question of how much money. This we were not prepared to say so abruptly. Amundsen, however, had given much thought to costs and could give a general estimate. As a nucleus we would have to have two planes, specially built ones capable of landing on ice or water, powered with good engines, having adequate flying range. Such ships should cost about forty thousand dollars apiece.

Before Amundsen could go on further, Father broke in with the statement that he would put up $85,000. We ceased to argue. With $85,000 we were a long distance on our way to the unknown Arctic.

It all had to be put into writing, for that was Father's way— a contract, legally drawn. But when we met the following afternoon to complete this formality, Father had already begun to waver. It was with no enthusiasm that he read the document the attorney had prepared. He picked up a pen to sign but for a moment could not bring himself to it.

For ten years he had been trying to avert this thing. Now he had lost. On the table before him lay his articles of surrender. Out of defeat this man of triumphant business coups had to snatch some morsel of gain. What he chose to demand was so unexpected, so childish, so out of proportion to the main issue involved, that in any other circumstances it would have been ludicrous.

"Lincoln," he said to me, "if I give this money, will you promise me never to touch tobacco again?"

Before I found time to grow indignant at the absurd condition, I gave my promise, and he signed. Later I began to fume. What right had he to exact such a thing, to take from me a harmless habit that meant so much to a man whose life was devoted to solitude and physical hardship? And only because of an out-of-date Victorian prejudice.

Upon mature thought, I deliberately decided not to keep that promise. It had been wrung from me by coercion, which invalidated it. Would not the man who in his passion for possession wrested a Rembrandt masterpiece from a woman have done the same in my place? We were both collectors, he of rare works of art, I of still rarer things—experiences of standing where no man had stood before.

When Amundsen and I had signed and the lawyer had witnessed the paper, the explorer then did a graceful and unexpected thing. Taking from his brief case an old pair of Zeiss binoculars, he presented them to my father as a keepsake. No souvenir of Amundsen could have been more intimate, for they were the glasses he had carried on all his voyages. On the worn brass were scratched tremendous dates—that of the South Pole, those of the starts and completions of his two passages of the Arctic. After Father's death I received the binoculars from the estate.

At the same time Amundsen gave me the gold watch he had carried to the South Pole—dated and inscribed there by himself and the men of his party. Nothing could have indicated Amundsen's gratitude more pointedly than these gifts—historic trophies which, I think, no other man would have parted with under any considerations. They are among my most precious possessions.

Father's signature to the contract was scarcely dry before he was trying to back out of it, so far as I was concerned. He paid over the money but began a desperate campaign, one that verged on the unprincipled, to keep me from accompanying the expedition. In December Amundsen went back to Norway to take charge of that end of it. I remained in New York until March 1925, and a terrible winter it was for me. For four months I was placed in an attitude of opposition and hostility to my own father, a sick old man.

All his friends—men whom I respected, men prominent in business and the professions—criticized me unsparingly. With most of them I have never had any relations since. As the tension grew, I knew I was risking my future inheritance—the fortune that I had expected someday to devote to science. But I would have risked my soul to go on that flight with Amundsen. And all the time, too, I lived in the fear that Father somehow might succeed in blocking me away from my life's dearest ambition.

His first move was to send influential men to me, ostensibly on their own initiative and out of concern for him, to urge me to give up going into the Arctic and rest content with being Amundsen's backer and having my name attached to the expedition. When that failed, Father tried something else. Even in his old age he was still too reserved to grow sentimental with his son. The appeal to emotion he entrusted to his attorney, Harold T. Clark, of Cleveland.

Mr Clark came to me with a moving plea, speaking of Father's advanced age and how much he needed his only son by his side during the sunset of his life. My answer was that other

men's sons were not asked to sacrifice their careers because their
fathers grew old. My opportunity had come, and I was determined to take it. Privately, I may add, Mr Clark was on my
side. He fully approved of my ambition. As secretary of the
Cleveland Museum of Natural History, he had in the past
asked me to explore for that institution.

These two attempts had no consequence more serious than to
give Father a wounded, put-upon attitude that made me uncomfortable in his presence. Before I tell about his next step, I
must insert something about the history of the expedition before Amundsen left New York.

After Amundsen and I had agreed upon the several responsi-
bilities we would assume preliminary to the flight itself, the
famous explorer sent word to the newspaper offices and received
a large delegation of reporters in his room at the Waldorf. He
then broke the announcement of our expedition, saying that we
planned to fly from Spitzbergen in two planes, land at the
North Pole, refuel one ship from the gas left in the other, then
abandon the fuelless plane and fly on to Alaska in the other, our
objective being the unexplored area between Point Barrow and
the Pole.

Later, let me interpolate, we amended this plan—for public
consumption. The expedition's costs proved to be so great that
we had to accept important aid from the Aero Club of Norway.
But that organization categorically refused to go behind anything more ambitious than a reconnoitering flight to the North
Pole and back as a preliminary to a transarctic flight. Amundsen
and I signed such an agreement with the Aero Club, but our
secret understanding was that, if everything went well, we
would fly on to Alaska just the same.

In justice to the Aero Club we must remember that aviation
equipment in 1924 was not what it is today. No Lindbergh had
yet flown the Atlantic, and there were yet no nonstop transcontinental flights in this country. Airplanes in strength, power,
range, and dependability have vastly improved between that
year and the time I write these words.

After Amundsen had read our statement, the reporters asked us numerous questions. I have already said that Amundsen's English was very broken. Some people had difficulty in understanding what he said. At the end of the interview two of the reporters who had come late—typical hard-boiled New York specimens—turned to me and asked: "Say, what's the big idea, anyhow? What's it all about?"

The scornful air with which they asked this question, as if we were a couple of mild lunatics, annoyed me. I was a pure idealist then. When the reporters had gone, I said to Amundsen, "Let's not bother with the newspapers. Let's do this for the thing itself."

The wise old Norseman shook his finger at me.

"You can't do it that way," he said. "You have to have the publicity."

How well I learned the truth of that later!

Those reporters gave me my first contact with people who could not understand the value of polar discovery. Long ago I quit trying to explain it to anybody. The Arctic or Antarctic traveler soon finds out people are not interested in faraway things. Few have the imagination to project themselves outside their own narrow spheres.

The publication of our announcement brought in its train one unpleasant consequence for me. From a man in Philadelphia, who claimed to have lived in Alaska, my father received a letter, an excerpt from which read as follows:

"If you will investigate the circumstances connected with the attempted airplane flight of Amundsen from Alaska to Spitzbergen, you will never let your son go with him."

Father's reaction to this was to send at once for our family attorney. The lawyer reached New York next day. Father handed him this letter.

"Clark," he said, "I want you to go clear to the bottom of this thing. I have got to find some way to discourage my son from entering upon this wild scheme. This looks like what I need."

Mr Clark came to me at the Metropolitan Club, where I was

living, and repeated this conversation to me. Much as he sympathized with my aims, he said, he had his duty also as a lawyer.

"Good!" was my answer. "I hope you look up everything. It will help calm Father's fears and make no difference with me, anyhow, because I know Amundsen, and I am going with him."

With the assistance of Mr Hans Fay, consul general of Norway in New York, who knew Amundsen well, Mr Clark went over the explorer's record with a fine-tooth comb, finding out only what I have told above—that Amundsen had been inadequately equipped for his flight from Alaska, as he told me himself. True, he went into bankruptcy afterwards, but no discredit was attached to him. It was simply that, unable to do otherwise, he had gone into a desperate venture on a shoestring, and the venture had failed.

As to the man in Philadelphia, he owned a gold claim in Alaska. By ingratiating himself to Father, he hoped to find a purchaser for it.

Thus another threat was shunted off. Down in the New York Custom House Matt Henson, the Negro who was Peary's only companion at the North Pole, was doing a lot of talking about our suicidal plane expedition. Word of this was brought to Father, and he sent for Henson. When the colored man arrived, Father put the question to him: "Can an airplane reach the North Pole?"

"Absolutely not," Henson replied. "There is nothing at the North Pole but howling blizzards and ice piled up high like mountains."

In grim triumph Father repeated this assertion to me—quoting the only living man who had been at the North Pole. It made no impression on me. Besides what Amundsen had told me, I had read every book, I think, ever written about the Arctic, including Peary's books. Every Arctic traveler spoke of the calm, foggy, equable conditions of the summer.

Why Henson could make such a statement, I don't know. He had been in the Arctic twenty-three years with Peary, so he knew it was not true. My complete answer to Father, though, was Peary's own prediction of the conquest of the Arctic by airplane.

Thus everything Father could pick up—every rumor or loose statement—he used against me. His next move was the most disagreeable of all. He adopted a maddening attitude, assuming that I expected Amundsen to make a sort of demonstration flight to the North Pole first, alone, to prove that it could be reached by air. After that I was to fly there with him. In so many words Father insisted that I had agreed to that plan when he gave us the money.

I could not very well tell my father to his face that he was uttering an untruth. Perhaps in his frantic anxiety he had seized upon some word I had dropped or some half-understood statement of Amundsen at the contract signing and convinced himself later that I had made such a promise. I could only deny it. The thing was too absurd. Explorers do not make experimental discoveries before proceeding to make the real ones. Besides, our whole plan contemplated abandoning one ship at the Pole and going on in the other, though I did not tell Father that.

The winter wore on. Mr Clark was frequently in New York, for Father, in tying up the few loose strings of his life, was increasing his endowment of Western Reserve Acadamy. He had recently sold his lesser collections—rugs, coins, books, furniture, and other classes of collectors' objects—to Knoedler; and the proceeds, several hundred thousand dollars, had to be added with legal exactness to the school's foundation.

But Mr Clark found it hard to pin Father down to business. I had now become an obsession with him. He would break off in the midst of a sentence to talk about the dangers of the Arctic trip. Father was writing his memoirs, and to divert his thoughts from me Mr Clark would ask him about his early experiences. For a little while this ruse would succeed, but then Father would come back to the refrain:

"Clark, you are a lawyer. You must find a way to keep him from going."

On one such occasion Mr Clark replied: "Mr Ellsworth, you

have been telling me of all these important things you did. How old were you when you did most of them?"

"In my forties," said Father.

"Well," said the lawyer, "Lincoln is forty-four."

"Not the same thing," declared Father. "There's no comparison."

"Oh yes, there is," retorted Clark. "The spirit that moved you to strike out for great things is what impels Lincoln today."

"Mr Clark," said Father, a shadow of a smile on his face, "you leave me worse off than before you came—but I'm glad you came."

This frame of mind did not last long. Clark was scarcely out of sight when Father began making efforts to have my passport canceled, calling up Vice-President Dawes, United States senators, even the White House, and raising heaven and earth to have his will accomplished. I heard of this in a roundabout way, for of course his pleas got nowhere. The State Department had no legal reason to abrogate my passport.

Meanwhile, I had an increasing worry on another score. Through Amundsen's intercession, the Norwegian government and the Aero Club were providing ships, a base party, food supplies, and other necessities for the expedition. My part over here was to raise money for the purchase of parachutes, instruments, and various other expensive equipment for the planes. In Cleveland I had money enough of my own to buy these things, but I did not want to touch it, if I could possibly help it. The way things stood between Father and myself, this might be the only money I would have in the world when I emerged from the Arctic.

I tried the army and navy air services in Washington but with no success, though I merely asked for the loan of such equipment. The National Geographic Society could not help me out. I even approached Father for the money, to be refused, of course; but I told him that if everything else failed, I should have to use my own funds.

At last I could put it off no longer. I drew a draft on my Cleveland bank for $10,000 and waited for the money to arrive.

Instead, I received a telephone call from the bank, saying that my father had instructed them not to honor any of my drafts. What right had he to send any such instructions? I asked. The money was my own and I insisted upon immediate payment, for my time was short. The bank official pleaded with me. He acknowledged that they were legally obliged to honor the draft, but on the other hand they did not want to offend so important a depositor as James W. Ellsworth. Wouldn't I see him and straighten it out? I told them it was no use for me to try that, and that I expected the money.

Instead, they sent Mr Clark again. He saw me first to explain into what a delicate position this clash had placed the bank. It was better to take a little more time and settle such a thing amicably. I was willing for him to try.

He went to see Father, finding him, as he told me, in a terrible state of anxiety. At sight of him Father blurted out: "I won't have any responsibility for this expedition. I can't help but feel that I am sending my own son to death."

"Mr Ellsworth," said Clark, "do you know why Lincoln wants the ten thousand dollars?"

Father replied that he didn't.

"Among other things, he wants to buy parachutes. Do you want your son to go without parachutes? He is going, parachutes or no parachutes—that I know. Don't you think it's taking a little responsibility, if you force him to go without that safeguard?"

"Give him the money!" Father shouted. "Let him have the money! Let him have it right away!"

I had gone to Mr Clark's room at the Yale Club to await the outcome of this interview. When he came in, nodding encouragement to me, he called Cleveland on the phone and said: "This is Clark. Release the draft. It's all right."

"Just the same," I remarked, as he hung up, "we haven't heard the last of this yet."

As I spoke the phone rang, and I could recognize Father's rasp in the receiver.

"Clark," he said, "I've changed my mind."

Mr Clark answered: "I'm sorry, Mr Ellsworth, but it's too late. The draft has gone through."

There was silence for a few moments; then Father said slowly, "Well—I guess—I'm glad of it."

Nevertheless, I think he would have stopped me somehow, had it not been for my sister, Clare. Clare loved me, yet secretly she was one of those skeptics who thought I was going to my death. But she knew that I would rather die than not go. She knew that if I did not go I would be crushed in spirit for the rest of my days. So she interceded with Father in my behalf.

Father was furious with her, threatening her with all sorts of dire things in the future because she had dared interfere. Yet she fought on for me, risking her own future as I was. In his frame of mind then, Father might well have cut off his children with a pittance and left all his money to the Western Reserve Academy. I think it was Clare's influence that made him give up in the end.

When the time came for me to go, I went to Father to bid him good-by, a most dismal experience. I had hoped that he might come to the boat, but he didn't. He had, of course, the excuse of ill health, and the ordeal might have been too much for him. I am told, though, that after I was gone, a great calm came to him and a great confidence. Shortly afterwards he went to Italy. There he contracted pneumonia and died. One of the last friends to see him at the Villa Palmieri was Judge Sanders, of Squire, Sanders & Dempsey, the legal firm of which Mr Clark was also a member. We were then lost in the Arctic, but Father expressed his firm belief that I would return because I was with the great explorer Amundsen.

Clare came to the boat. She wept all the time, and that made the parting hard. When the ship backed out of the slip, I kept waving to her on the pier as she tried to smile and be brave but dabbed her eyes with her little handkerchief.

For a long time I stood at the rail with a heavy heart. The ship turned slowly in the stream, then moved toward the Battery, the procession of Manhattan skyscrapers marching majestically by. I watched until we were far down the bay and the New York spires had huddled together and shrunk. Then my depression dropped from me like a cloak.

It was a mild March day—the first hint of spring. Spring would soon touch the Arctic, too, and there lay my destiny. With a buoyant step I walked forward to watch the passage of the Narrows, lighting a cigarette as I went. The vessel was the Scandinavian liner Oscar II—the Peace Ship.

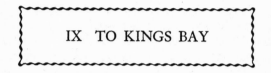

IX TO KINGS BAY

WINTER LINGERED in Oslo. The hills were still white with snow, the air was frosty. Amundsen met me at the pier. He was wearing a green Alpine suit and a hat with a feather in it. He informed me that during my stay I was to be his guest in his villa at Boenefjord, a suburb of Oslo twenty miles out in the country. There the explorer lived, next door to his brother.

But I was not to expect too much. Norway was not the United States.

"We live on just coarse, simple food," Amundsen warned me.

After that, breakfast was a bit of a surprise, for it was bounteous with jams and eggs, flaky rolls, coffee and rich cream. But that was nothing compared with lunch, or, I suppose I should say, dinner. The family sat down at noon, and it seemed to me we spent the rest of the day at the table. We had plenty of the delicious hors d'oeuvres for which the Scandinavian countries are so famous— fish in oil, cheeses of many sorts, salads and sausages—then soup, fish fresh out of icy waters, beef and mutton courses, and always roast native grouse, called *rupa,* which were then in season. Cakes and other sweets for dessert, and all through the meal plenty of fiery aquavit, the national drink.

No sooner was that feast cleared away than we began another— tea, I suppose, though for the adults it consisted principally of cakes and aquavit. Then, if one were hungry before going to bed —and on a cold night there are few satisfactions greater than sleeping under a huge Norwegian eider-down feather bed—one could have cheese, cold grouse, buttered rolls, and beer or aquavit. Thus for most of the day these gay, hearty people surrounded the festive board, eating and drinking, laughing and telling stories.

To prepare ourselves for these encounters, Amundsen and I used to start out after breakfast and take long country walks in the mornings; incidentally, flushing plenty of *rupa*. Those birds were so plentiful, in fact, that Amundsen or his brother could take out a gun and in an hour knock down enough to serve both families for dinner.

At the end of the second day of such feeding, I threw up my hands in surrender.

"After what you told me in Oslo," I reproached Amundsen, "I expected only black bread and soup; but, my heavens, you live better than we do in America." And I added: "Norwegians are certainly big eaters."

A twinkle came into the squinting gray eyes.

"You ought to see Swedes eat," said Amundsen.

That same evening I was to be guest of honor at a grand dinner given by the Luftseiladsforeningen—the Aero Club—in Oslo. We decided to drive in wearing our country clothes and dress in the hotel. But we had drunk so much aquavit that afternoon that when packing my bag I quite forgot to put in any collar. We were dressing in one of the rooms of the Grand Hotel when I discovered this horrible omission—and horrible it was, since, as Amundsen had said, this was Norway and not New York. All of Oslo's stores were closed for the night, and there was no valet service or lobby shop in the hotel to take care of just such an oversight.

Things looked black for me, when the room waiter entered, freshly starched for the evening. Amundsen pranced over to him, took his collar off the man, and presented it to me. The waiter said he could get another.

I passed a miserable evening. The collar was much too large for me. It was an old-fashioned wing type with rough edges and points that wore the skin off my throat. When the time came for me to speak my few words, I felt that I must resemble a cartoon.

Afterwards, when I gave the waiter's collar back to him, he said something in Norwegian. I looked inquiringly at Amundsen.

"He says he is going to keep it always as a treasure," Amundsen translated.

Can one imagine a New York bellhop or hotel waiter preserving the collar worn by even a successful explorer, to say nothing of merely a prospective one? But the Norsemen have been sea rovers and discoverers for a thousand years. Exploration represents their national genius, as business organization does that of the United States or invention that of Italy. Venturers for discovery's sake take the rank in Norway that other countries accord only to their idols of sport or entertainment.

Amundsen's villa in Boenefjord was a veritable museum of souvenirs of his voyages. Even the panes of the outside doors and ornamental windows were transparencies, both colored and black and white, of polar scenes. The top of his dining table was the long marble slab which he had used in the North when taking the observations that enabled him to fix the position of the magnetic pole in the Boothia Peninsula in northern Canada. On the return voyage in the Gjoa, one of his men had carved on this slab a map of the Arctic regions and the names of the crew of the Gjoa.

Later Amundsen gave me this tabletop, and I have it today. He also promised me his famous South Pole pipe, but after his death it could not be found. Perhaps he had it with him when he flew to hunt Nobile. After the Norge flight, he told me I could have the diary he kept during our 1925 attempt to cross the Arctic by airplane, but that, too, was missing from his effects.

In Oslo I met the men who were to go into the Arctic with us. Chief among them was Lieutenant Hjalmar Riiser-Larsen, Norway's leading aviator, who later was to establish a record as an independent air explorer along the edges of Antarctica. He was a tall heavy man, given to little speech. During our entire ordeal in the Arctic I never heard him express a word of either fear or hope. He took everything as a matter of course. But all the Norwegians I have ever known in the polar regions have been silent and reticent. One never knew what they thought.

Second only to Riiser-Larsen as an aviator was Lief Dietrichson, our other pilot. Then there were the two mechanicians, Feucht and Omdal, who were to serve the engines during the flight. Feucht, a German, had been assigned by the Dornier-Wal airplane factory in Italy, which also sent its manager, Herr Schulte-Frohlinde, to superintend the assembly of the two planes. In our supporting party were also a doctor, a pharmacist, a meteorologist, two newspapermen, a photographer, an expert mechanic from the Rolls-Royce factory in England, two guides who knew Spitzbergen, besides various laborers and the officers and crews of the Farm and Hobby, the two vessels that were to take us North.

Most of these people were Norwegians. Of the sextet who were to fly in the airplanes, only one—Amundsen—had ever been deep into the Arctic before.

Besides gathering together this personnel and securing our special Dornier-Wal airplanes, Amundsen had accomplished other important results during the winter. With the backing of the Aero Club, he secured from the government by act of the Storting the use of the Norwegian naval transport vessel Farm to serve as the mother ship of the expedition. The same act authorized the issue of special polar stamps, from the sale of which the incidental expenses were to be met.

Thus it will be seen that, though my father's gift to us procured the flying equipment and made the expedition possible, yet it was a Norwegian government enterprise. The Act of Assistance, in fact, specified that only the Norwegian flag should be carried and that the undertaking should be wholly under Norwegian command—Amundsen's. This was correct, since our own government in Washington had refused participation.

Furthermore, it was the way I wanted it myself. Amundsen was the veteran of polar exploration; I, the complete novice. I regarded the airplane expedition as my apprenticeship. When soliciting the money from my father, I pleaded my desire to go into the Arctic with Amundsen "even though it be a small part" I should play. I wrote that I would be proud "to serve under such a capable master as Captain Roald Amundsen." Yet, though the final authority was his, Amundsen always made me feel as his co-equal in authority, an equal sharer of the responsibility for the expedition, an equal participant in the credit for its achievement. That was his way as a leader.

For an auxiliary ship the expedition chartered the Norwegian motor ship Hobby, which transported to Spitzbergen the airplanes in parts, the other supplies, and most of the technical crew. Spitzbergen is a large island lying exactly halfway between the northern coast of Norway and the North Pole. A wisp of the Gulf Stream flows up to it, tempering the climate and keeping its harbors ice free during most of the year. Important coal deposits exist in Spitzbergen, the coast of which is dotted with mining settlements. These settlements, within 500 miles of the Pole, are the most northerly human habitations in the world. Spitzbergen, therefore, and especially the sheltered harbor of Kings Bay, at the northern end of the coal field, offered us an ideal base and, in fact, has always been used as a take-off point for Arctic expeditions by water or air.

We sailed from the port of Tromsö, far up beyond the Arctic Circle, where the Norwegian fjords have begun to face toward the Pole. The Norwegians regarded the voyage from Tromsö to Kings Bay with more anxiety than they did the polar flight itself, for the five hundred miles of Arctic Ocean between Spitzbergen and the Norwegian coast is a nasty stretch of water at almost any time of the year but especially so at the break of spring. Our boats were none too seaworthy for this voyage. The Farm, though dignified by the title of a naval transport, was really the king's yacht—a summer boat with thin sides vulnerable to ice. The Hobby was stauncher but had to be badly overloaded. There was no place aboard her for the huge cases in which the dismantled flying boats were packed except on her decks, which were piled high with crates. When loaded, she was top-heavy and resembled a small floating dock wandering over the ocean.

On April 9 the annual Arctic day had already broken at the Pole. Even at Spitzbergen, half a thousand miles away, nights had become mere midnight periods of twilight, so rapidly does one gain on the sun when moving up over the northern shoulders of the earth in spring. But at Tromsö at five o'clock in the morning, the hour we sailed, it was still dark as pitch, a cold rain beating against our faces, fog draping the harbor.

The Arctic Ocean did not disappoint us. Just outside of Skaarö Sound we ran into a thick gale and blizzard. The radio informed us that the storm center was still west of the coast. We therefore turned back, signaling the Hobby to follow, and about noon reached a quiet anchorage in the sound. Meanwhile, we had lost the Hobby in the thick weather. She had no radio and, as we found out later, had misread our signals; in spite of the tempest and her top-heavy condition, keeping on for Spitzbergen.

This was a great anxiety to us, for if anything should happen to the Hobby, the expedition would be wrecked. Prior to sailing, our two little boats had agreed to stay together to render mutual assistance, if it became necessary. At four o'clock in the afternoon the storm had moderated a little, and we decided to set out after the Hobby. We crept along the shores of the sound, peering into every fjord and inlet, but found no trace of the missing motor ship. Snow squalls frequently smothered us in. Outside, the storm seemed as violent as ever; but this time we did not turn back but in a whooping gale set a course direct for the island of Björneöen, off the south end of Spitzbergen.

I have voyaged in small boats on rough seas in my time, but never have I seen a vessel dance, pitch, and roll as crazily as did the Farm during the next forty-eight hours. Everyone was seasick, I think—even the officers on the bridge. As I have related, Amundsen and I slept in the dining saloon, and it was during this storm that the Norse explorer uttered his disparagement of the sea which I quoted in a preceding chapter. Our overcoats, hanging on hooks, at one moment were flattened against the wall as though pressed down by invisible weights; the next they stood out stiffly parallel with the floor. Everything loose slid together in confusion. A box of Havana cigars broke, and there were cigars everywhere in the dining saloon, even in bed with us. In the galley a loose galvanized pail banged about for hours, the cook evidently too seasick to care. The unspoken wonder of every man was: how is the Hobby, with her towering deckload, weathering such a sea?

On the second afternoon the storm abated somewhat, and a bunch of pallid explorers crept out on the decks. There was no sight of the Hobby across the tossing waters. Björneöen wirelessed that there was no ice in that vicinity, and we ran in close to see if the Hobby had sheltered in any of the island's coves. It was four o'clock on the morning of the eleventh when we passed the southern cape but daylight already. Failing to see the Hobby, we radioed to Björneöen to keep a watch for her and then went on.

Kings Bay had been free of ice all winter. As we were passing Björneöen the operator at Kings Bay informed us that two days earlier ice had moved in and that the harbor was now locked. This seemed a misfortune to us at the time, but it turned out to be a break of luck. That April kickback of winter gave our planes a runway of ice for the take-off and enabled us to load (divided between the two ships) a ton more of weight than the engines could have dragged out of water. Without that added capacity we could not have carried, in addition to absolutely vital supplies, enough fuel for the Arctic crossing as we had planned it.

The weather changed on the eleventh and by afternoon we had a brisk following breeze. About suppertime we began running through light ice. Next day it was all still weather, fog and ice. The ice was not heavy enough to bother an icebreaker, such as the Hobby, but it was dangerous for the fragile Farm. Men whose ancestors, however, had navigated the North Atlantic in open boats were not to be daunted at finding themselves challenging the teeth of the Arctic in a regatta pleasure craft. Less skillful navigation than Captain Hagerup's might well have sent us to the bottom during the storm. A less expert touch than Ice Pilot Ness's could have as easily brought us to grief among the floes as he smelt a passage through the fog. The fog cleared at sunset. At ten o'clock on the evening of April 12 there was still a faint sunset, and in it we saw the cape off Kings Bay. Four hours later we moored to the edge of the hard ice—three miles out from the coal company's dock.

Next morning Amundsen and I walked ashore over the ice to meet the coal company's resident directors, Knutsen and Brandal. Nothing would do those hospitable men but that all the members of the expedition itself should be entertained on shore with them during our stay. It seemed an imposition to me, since there were only the two directors' cottages and the industrial buildings, including a hospital. The miners lived in huts back in the hills.

Knutsen silenced our protestations by quoting a Norwegian proverb: "'Where there is room in the heart there is room in the house.'"

But the missing Hobby lay heavy on our thoughts. After accepting the offer of this hospitality, we walked back to the Farm again to keep watch. About seven o'clock that evening the lookout reported that some high structure was looming above the ice and drawing closer. We rushed on deck and with our glasses descried a heavy-looking crate approaching us to the sound of crushing ice.

"Comes Hobby! Comes Hobby!" shouted the Norwegians, and to the hurrahs of the crew the motor ship drew up to the edge of the fjord ice next to us, everyone and everything on board safe.

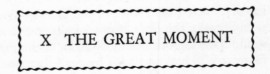

X THE GREAT MOMENT

TO GO BACK A LITTLE in the story, as soon as Amundsen and I, in New York, were assured of Father's gift to the expedition, Amundsen at once got in touch by cable with Hjalmar Riiser-

Larsen, an aviator who, though he had never flown into the polar regions, was accustomed to ice conditions along the Norwegian coasts. Amundsen had been discussing polar flying with Riiser-Larsen for some years and believed that he would go with us. Nor was he mistaken. Riiser-Larsen cabled back his consent, whereupon we instructed him to select the model and order two suitable airplanes, superintending their construction and test flights. Riiser-Larsen picked a brother flying officer of the Norwegian navy, Lieutenant Leif Dietrichson, as our other pilot. With these two air vikings at the controls, our lives could not have been in the hands of abler men.

Riiser-Larsen, of course, was familiar with the various makes of European airplanes suitable for service in the North. Nevertheless, taking Dietrichson with him, he visited several plants to look into their latest inventions and improvements and finally chose the German-designed, Italian-made Dornier-Wal seaplane powered with twin 450-H.P. Rolls-Royce engines mounted in tandem. The Dornier company designed and made the enormous DO-X that visited the United States some years ago—the first multimotored superplane Americans had seen.

Without becoming too technical, let me give some of Riiser-Larsen's reasons for selecting the Dornier-Wal. In the first place, he sought a ship with a duralumin hull. Wooden hulls he deemed unsuitable for landing on rough ice or in water filled with broken ice, because of the danger of stripping the bottom. Duralumin, even lighter than wood, will bend or dent under ordinary collisions but will not break much more readily than steel.

Several types of duralumin flying boats were then made in Europe. What determined the choice of the Dornier-Wal was the design of the hull itself. The lines of other hulls were such that in snow they would have to push the snow aside, in the manner of a plow. The Dornier-Wal hull had a lift forward that would enable it to climb over snow, like a toboggan, and was the only hull of that design in Europe. Another great advantage was that the ship had no wing floats to be torn off in the event of a forced landing, stability in the water being given by two flares or swellings of the hull, called *flyndres,* beneath the engine nacelle. We actually found that in light ice this flying boat could serve as an ice crusher.

The tandem mounting of the two engines, the propellers turning in opposite directions as one pushed and the other pulled, created such power that the heavy ship could carry a load equal to its own weight. There was, of course, no more dependable engine than the Rolls-Royce Eagle IX. Either engine alone could support the ship in air with a full load, and with a light load the plane could take off from water with one engine. For spare parts we took to Spitzbergen one complete reserve engine.

These machines the Dornier company built in its plant at Pisa, Italy. They were stock models especially modified for work in the North. The power plants, for instance, were protected against the freezing of oil or water in low temperatures. We carried a French heating device called Therm-X which kept the engines warm when the planes were grounded. The engine radiators were equipped with shutters. Even more important, the bottom of the hull was fitted with longitudinal strakes that gave it a grooved appearance and made it steer straight on ice or snow.

Instrument makers besieged us to carry their latest inventions, with the result that our pilots' dashboards were probably as well equipped as those of any planes that had ever flown up to that time. We had gyroscopes for blind flying and several special compasses adapted for use near the Magnetic Pole, where the pull is weak and compass oscillations swing over an arc of 180 degrees. The most interesting gadget was a new sun compass invented by Goerz, of Germany. This worked through a small periscope on the deck in front of the pilot's windshield. At approximately the moment of the take-off, the ship would be headed in its true course and the periscope turned straight toward the sun. A clockwork mechanism was then started which rotated the periscope at a rate exactly to compensate for the turn of the earth. Thus the periscope would always keep pointing at the sun. A series of reflectors threw an image of the sun's disc upon a ground-glass dial on the dashboard. As long, therefore, as the disc image appeared at the center of the dial, the pilot was on his course. This compass, however, did not allow for drift. Consequently, the ship might be merely paralleling its true course when the compass was registering correctness of route. This actually happened on the flight north.

But enough of these technicalities. The next day after the arrival of the Hobby at Kings Bay, we all went ashore to live until we started for the unknown, distributing ourselves through the company cottages and station buildings. Out at the edge of the ice, the company's steamer, Knut Skaaluren, which had just brought up the directors for the summer's mining operation, lay beside the Farm and Hobby. On April 15 the master of this sturdy, sheathed little vessel grew impatient and tackled the ice, breaking a three-mile track through to the quay much more easily than anyone expected. The Farm and Hobby followed, and on the sixteenth the work of unloading the Hobby began.

With what eager interest I watched everything! It was all new to me. A spirit almost of hilarity pervaded the camp, testifying to the inner tension of all. The station's sailboat repair shop was cleared out to give us a dining room and meeting place. Amundsen promptly christened this shed the "salon", and salon it became for all of us. Berge, the newsreel man, ground away at everything of the slightest interest to outsiders. Ramm, the reporter from Oslo, filed reams of copy, competing with our meteorologists for the use of the radio. We had the feeling of being the cynosure of the world's eyes, and it was to me, at least, tremendously exhilarating. Every day at noon Amundsen and I went to the wireless station to check our watches by the Eiffel Tower time signal.

Winter lingered in the lap of spring, "night" temperatures falling to 10 or 15 degrees Fahrenheit. But there was no night. After April 19, the sun does not set at all at Kings Bay. We had all taken a hand in dragging the heavy airplane crates over the ice and up the bank to the machine shop. There in the open air, amid icy winds and snow storms, the assemblage began under the direction of Superintendent Schulte-Frohlinde, of the Pisa plant. Day by day the great winged machines grew. Schulte-Frohlinde promised them ready by May 2, but it was actually the fifth of May before they had received their last touches. The two ships went by their identification numbers of N 24 and N 25, and we never changed those names.

The phonograph in the salon played tunes for those off duty. Cook Einer Olsen concocted marvelous rum omelets. My curiosity probed into everything. One fascinating workman was Rönne, a real, olden-time, before-the-mast sailmaker, who had been with Amundsen on both the Fram and the Maud voyages. He plied his talents from early morning till night upon articles we would need in the North. Canvas shoes, canvas suits, tents, sleeping bags came from his needle.

The canvas shoes—huge ludicrous objects—explained our senna grass. Among the supplies unloaded from the Hobby was a bale of that commodity, which struck me as a curious thing to take on an Arctic expedition. Here, though, we were drawing on Amundsen's long experience in the North. On previous expeditions he had discovered that a man, even with ordinary shoes, could keep his feet warm in temperatures of 60 and 70 degrees below zero, Fahrenheit, if he put them, shoes and all, into sacks filled with any fine hay like senna grass. Facing the possibility of a very cold ride in the open cockpits of airplanes, with strong downdrafts behind the windshields, we adopted this footgear, though because of the mild temperatures through which we flew, we never really needed them.

The air crackled with cold, the low sun painted mother-of-pearl tints upon the glaciers at the head of Kings Bay. Fridays were blissful, for then company officialdom and visiting guests had hot steam baths—ladies in the morning, men in the afternoon. Saturday was bath day for the coal miners. There were a number of women at Kings Bay—wives of officials and workmen, cooks, and so on. Among them I must mention Director Knutsen's housekeeper, Berta, a kind, efficient soul who, just as we started for the Pole, presented each plane with a delicious lunch to be eaten en route.

Another woman figured in all of Amundsen's later expeditions: Mrs—or in Norwegian, Fru—Clausen, of Oslo. Fru Clausen was the widow of a former mine boss at Kings Bay who was killed there in an accident. She became acquainted with Amundsen at Kings Bay and remained a great admirer of his. Whenever he started on an exploration, she always baked for him a store of oat biscuits such as only she knew how to make. We had a box of them in one of the planes when we flew and carried another the following year in the Norge. They were wonderfully good, in shape and size about like our ice-cream wafers, but full of butter and roughage. I enjoyed them more than anything else we ate in the North.

Here at Kings Bay I saw the important part the modern science of dietetics now plays in polar exploration. Gone are the old ship-and-dog days when diets were hit-and-miss and scurvy was a formidable enemy. All well-managed expeditions now carry dietetic experts with them, and diets are balanced not only for their calories but also for their vitamin contents. Our dietician at Kings Bay was Zapffe, the chemist. The daily ration per man which he prescribed for us to carry to the Pole was as follows:

Pemmican	400 grams
Milk Chocolate	250 "
Oat Biscuits	125 "
Powdered Milk	100 "
Malted-Milk Tablets	125 "
Total	1000 grams

This is a kilogram—a little more than two pounds—and is probably as concentrated and as efficient a diet as could be devised for an airplane expedition. Inasmuch as we carried thirty days rations for six men, our entire food supply weighed less than four hundred pounds. The only bulky item in the list was the oat biscuits, but we had less than fifty pounds of them all told, and their stowage offered no great problem. Incidentally, Fru Clausen's oat biscuits were only a sort of dessert for us. Our main supply came from a commercial bakery in Oslo.

A man back in civilization might complain that this diet—the menu for every meal—would become monotonous. Yet all polar explorers—and my experience coincides—agree that it is a mistake to attempt variety in expeditionary rations. When you have variety the temptation of tired men is to eat first the things they like best and leave the less favored articles to the end. As a matter of fact, you never grow tired of the polar diet, even though you eat four times a day. You think it is the best food in the world at the time, though when back in civilization you could scarcely be tempted by any of it. My friend Sir Hubert Wilkins, however, eats pemmican even in New York and always has a supply with him.

Amundsen taught me not to carry tea or coffee on expeditions. They were purely stimulants, he argued, and therefore nonessentials. It was better to have food value in a hot beverage, so we carried chocolate. During the days we spent on the ice, we five novices of the Arctic learned to love our hot chocolate so much that we all swore we would never again have anything else for breakfast. Yet so different is the polar appetite from that of normal existence that almost the first thing we asked for when we got out was hot coffee.

Though I had eaten bear-fat pemmican with the Indians in Canada, this was my first introduction to the factory variety. Pemmican is not a stock commodity in trade but is made to order for each expedition. As a result, there are as many kinds of pemmican as there are explorers. Ours that we carried in the Dornier-Wal planes was made by a Danish concern from Amundsen's own recipe. The base of all commercial pemmican is hard clean beef suet. This is melted down, and with it is mixed, usually, extract of beef and, often, various flavoring condiments. Amundsen's recipe called for powdered beef mixed with the suet. Lean beef was dried brittle in a cool temperature and then pulverized. Amundsen also added beans and peas, cooked, dried and powdered. Peary used to put raisins in his pemmican. Dr Dana C. Coman, of Johns Hopkins, who was with Byrd in Little America and also accompanied me as dietician on one of my Antarctic expeditions, added peppers to the pemmican, but I found that I grew tired of this savory brand.

Amundsen's pemmican was immensely fortifying, as may be

seen from the fact that it takes five pounds of raw beef to make one pound of beef powder. The warm mixed pemmican is poured into molds and cooled in cakes about the size of a cake of laundry soap and weighing a little less than a pound. Half a cake makes a meal. You shave it into your Arctic mug with a knife, add a little snow, then bring it to a boil on the primus stove, stirring until the lumps are gone. The result is a thick broth or gruel, nearly all fat, but impregnated with concentrated protein. You can also cut pemmican cold and eat the crisp shavings, if you like.

The so-called Arctic mug is simply a big handleless enamelware cup such as can be bought in any hardware store. The primus stove, which all polar expeditions carry, is a compact little gadget that works on the principle of a plumber's blowtorch—i.e., with an air mixer and forced draft. It burns either kerosene or gasoline. In the old sailing days explorers always carried kerosene for their primus stoves, but with the airplane in the polar regions has come a greater use of gasoline for fuel. Inasmuch as high-test engine gas is full of ethyl and therefore dangerous to burn in a tent or hut, the expedition must carry ordinary store gasoline for cooking. This is known as "white gas", to distinguish it from the engine fuel, which is always colored.

We also took with us as an experiment a new cooking apparatus called the Meta, which could burn alcohol as well as gasoline. For this, as a test fuel, we packed a small quantity of pure-grain spirits, which could be used as a human stimulant, if necessary.

I will not tire the reader with many more details of this sort, but I must mention our long debates over the relative merits of skis and snowshoes. Skis were better for fast travel over long distances, and the Norwegians were adept in their use; but their weight militated against them. Snowshoes are much lighter. We compromised on one pair of skis with ski staves for each man of the expedition and a reserve pair of snowshoes. Furthermore, each plane carried a sledge, which was simply a frame set on a pair of skis for runners. In an extreme emergency the sledges could be abandoned and the runners turned into two reserve pairs of skis.

Let me merely list a few other articles in our equipment: two motion-picture cameras, with 2,000 feet of film; two still cameras, a lightweight sounding apparatus (the operation of which I shall describe later), sextants, Arctic maps, and other navigational materials; a shotgun, a rifle, a Colt automatic, with ammunition, aboard each plane; a canvas folding boat and a tent on each plane; rucksacks, ski harnesses, axes and other emergency tools, logbooks, individual diaries, goat's-hair socks, Laplander soft-soled boots, telescopes, clasp knives. The sight of such things assembled ready for packing in the hulls of our planes made me tingle with the sense of imminent adventure. The total cost of the expedition was in the neighborhood of one hundred and thirty thousand dollars, of which my father and I together contributed about ninety-five thousand dollars.

On May 4 came a break in the weather. There was an unwonted mildness in the air, a whisper of a breeze from the south, a feeling of restlessness pervading all nature. Our meteorologists, in touch now with all northern weather stations of the earth, began to receive more favorable reports. Spring was touching the frozen North with a timid finger. The two mighty planes stood on their cradles, almost ready. Our hour seemed close at hand.

The company steamer Skaaluren had been keeping a channel broken to the open water. Amundsen sent out the Farm and Hobby to reconnoiter north of the island of Spitzbergen, to report on the position of the pack ice, and to hunt for a better field for the take-off than the ice of the narrow fjord. Scarcely had they gone than a northeast wind sprang up, and that night the mercury sank low. Next day the Farm radioed that the weather was still uncertain, with wind and sub-zero temperatures. Furthermore, the shore ice was so ridged and piled up that it offered no suitable starting place at all.

On the ninth of May the N 25 slid from its cradle. Riiser-Larsen took it out and taxied a few times up and down the fjord. On its strakes, or runners, the big hull moved almost as lightly over the ice as upon wheels. The pilot was mightily satisfied. A day or so later the N 24 came out for a similar test, Dietrichson at the controls. The Farm and Hobby returned. Every day the temperatures were mounting, though wind, fog, and sleet continued. Spring was trying to break.

A week more of waiting. The two planes were hauled up on shore at the heads of launching slides down which they could coast onto the fjord ice. The supplies went aboard, all carefully weighed and checked. It was evident that we were going to exceed the rated load capacity of the ships. In fact, when everything was aboard, including the crews, we were carrying on each airplane about a thousand pounds more than it was supposed to lift.

Even Director Schulte-Frohlinde wanted us to make a trial flight with these loads, but the taciturn Riiser-Larsen and Dietrichson shook their heads. "No—unnecessary." There was no doubt about the ships and engines being able to support this weight, if they got into the air. Rated capacity meant capacity of lift out of water, but we were to rise from hard ice. The experienced Norwegians feared no trouble in the take-off, nor was there any. The two planes rose like gulls.

May 18 was abruptly a good day, and we might have started then. The nineteenth and twentieth brought a return of unsatisfactory weather, but our chief meteorologist, Dr Bjerknes, notified us to be ready to start on short notice, as all outside reports were favorable. The base crew started gassing the ships. At evening on May 20 we were absolutely ready.

As we looked from our windows on the morning of the twenty-first, we needed no weather expert to tell us that the day had come. The pale Arctic sky was fleckless. A mild, light breeze blew down the fjord, which was exactly what our pilots wanted. Everybody was up early, swallowing breakfast and hurrying away to pack personal belongings in rucksacks and getting ready to break camp. It was understood that if the good weather held, we would leave in the late afternoon, when the sun, swinging on its rising orbit, would be in the west off our port beam on the flight north, and therefore in a favorable position for the sun compass. If all went well, the sun would creep around to our bows and we should be at the Pole at midnight. Midnight? No, the moment we reached there, midnight would change to noon. At the poles it is perpetual

noon, the sun always in the noon position. My throat swelled
with emotion as I thought of experiencing that transition.

The good weather held. In the early afternoon the ground crews
lowered the heavy ships to the ice. At four o'clock the ships were
orientated to the north and the sun compasses set going. Mechanics
started to turn over the engines to warm them. We six members
of the flying expedition had a special late luncheon in the salon.
On the plank table before each plate stood a thermos bottle full
of hot chocolate. At four o'clock we all went down to the machines.
The mine declared a holiday, so that everybody could see the start.

The clock hands moved to four-thirty. Director Schulte-
Frohlinde was inspecting every square inch of the two ships. Green,
the Rolls-Royce mechanic, listened to every engine, one after the
other, as they idled. Riiser-Larsen spoke to him in English—"Are
they all right?" Green smiled and nodded.

A few last handshakes, and we got into our clumsy flying clothes
—thick woolen garments faced with leather—then added Arctic
parkas, fur caps, sun goggles, heavy gloves. We buckled on our
parachutes. Five o'clock! Volunteers hoisted us aboard the two
ships. Amundsen and I took respectively the observers' places in the
N 25 and N 24—the forward seats in the very noses of the hulls.
Behind us sat Riiser-Larsen, in the N 25, and Dietrichson, in my
ship; behind them, at the engines, Feucht and Omdal. The crowd
drew back—a silent, wondering circle of men, some black from
the mining pits; a few hooded and cloaked women in the background.

Amundsen had a last word for the supporting party—written
orders. They could expect us back in fourteen days. The Farm and
Hobby were to maintain a patrol of the edge of the ice pack north
of Spitzbergen for six weeks, if necessary. Privately, we expected
the order to recall the ships would be the news that we had arrived
in Alaska. The command of the base party was distributed between
Captain Hagerup, of the Farm, and our reserve pilot, Lieutenant
Horgen, on the Hobby.

As Amundsen was speaking, I was nestling my feet in my senna-
grass overshoes. Ten minutes past five! Director Knutsen reached

up and shook hands with Amundsen and me. I don't know how any of the other five felt at that moment, but in me there was not the slightest trace of fear. I know that there were men in that silent throng who never expected to see us again. In New York and Oslo were plenty of people who regarded our flight as stark suicide. Even my own sister scarcely thought I would emerge alive. Yet if my pulse quickened then, it was only with elation that at last I had accomplished the ambition of my life.

The engines spoke, and we went bumping easily down the fjord to the starting place, almost at the mouth. Busy adjusting my parachute as a seat cushion, placing my diary and pencil handy for notes during the voyage, and settling myself comfortably, I scarcely noticed this taxi ride. The motors shut down, and both ships turned and faced the far-off quay and coal station. Then, like air pilots of any race, anywhere, ours for a moment or two twisted their heads and made a leisurely inspection of their ships and passengers. All set! Everybody and everything in place! N 25 roared and shot away from us in a flurry of snow and flaked ice. Dietrichson allowed her a quarter of a mile and then gave N 24 the gun.

For a moment we moved sluggishly—a heavy flat boat dragging over ice—then with the swiftly gathered speed of an arrow lunged forth after N 25 toward that distant glacier. Our engines yelled as they grabbed at the air. Eighteen hundred revolutions per minute! Almost before I could realize it, the grinding vibrations in the hull ceased, and we were in the air—high in air—as the dark ring of spectators and the coal station, its shops and sheds, black against the snow and dwindling to the size of huts, slipped under us.

In my seat forward, with all the flying machine behind me and only space ahead, above, and below, I seemed borne on mighty pinions. The twin engines shouted a song of strength and triumph, as Omdal tuned them to each other. I felt like a god. A bank, swing, and steep lift, and I found myself looking over the wall of the fjord into the North—looking over a fleecy sea of fog.

XI THE JAWS OF THE ARCTIC

FOR TWO HOURS we flew above the fog—two gnats in a void of sky and nether mist. Below each ship, off toward the east, traveled a double halo—two perfect wraithlike circles of rainbow with reversed colors—and in the very center of them the sharp shadow of the plane leaped along the eddies and billows of the fog roof. It was unreal, mystic, fraught with prophecy. Something ahead was hidden, and we were going to find it. Time and distance seemed to count for nothing. The steady clamor of the engines became second nature in one's ears and dropped from acute consciousness.

Now and then I saw down through holes in the fog to the sullen water of the Arctic Ocean, foaming under a northeast breeze. We huddled down behind our shields, for the wind cut like a knife. The sun swung northward on its arc, the eyes of our compass periscopes faithfully following. From time to time I made such sextant observations as I imperfectly could in the unsteady plane. The eighty-second parallel of latitude lay behind us; we were approaching the eighty-third.

Our two ships stayed close together, usually abreast. We had no radio communication with each other, since my plane, the N 24, carried no set. The apparatus had failed to arrive in time at Kings Bay, and we had agreed not to wait for belated equipment. But now and then a hand lifted in one ship to wave encouragement to the other. The engines on both planes ran sweetly, without a falter. One warmed with confidence in these powerful flying machines and in the skillful men at their controls.

Then all at once I was aware of a change going on below. The ocean's garment of fog was wearing thin and tattered. Through rifts I saw white patches on the water. Breaking waves? I wondered. But no, they were stationary, and I saw what they were—ice floes. The fringe of the polar pack! All my life, it seemed, I had been reading about Arctic pack ice, and for years I had dreamed of reaching it. Now at last I was beholding it with my own eyes.

But even that hint did not prepare me for what was to come. Abruptly the edge of the fog bank slipped under our wings, and ahead of us spread one of the most sublime spectacles the world could afford—the great frozen North itself. As Amundsen wrote of it later: "the most spectacular sheet of snow and ice ever seen by man from an aerial perspective." Ahead and to east and west as far as the eye could reach it spread, netted over with narrow cracks —the famous "leads" about which I had read—and off toward the northwest the sun drew a broad gleaming trail over it. I thought I had never seen anything so beautiful.

And we could see much of it, too. At 3,000 feet of altitude, a simple calculation told us that with glasses we could see between sixty and seventy miles in every direction. Thus, into one of those white patches of the map which had so struck my wonder as a child I was now helping to draw an explored band 125 miles wide. Heavy transport planes were not so fast then as now. Our cruising speed of 75 miles an hour seemed tremendous in 1925. Every hour we were putting behind us a journey that would take a sledge party a week to accomplish. Every hour we added to known geography more than nine thousand square miles of the earth's surface.

But it grew monotonous, that endless white expanse. I crouched behind my windshield and thought of many things. I thought of Andrée and Wellman, both of whom had had, so many years ago, this same dream of observing the Pole from the air. I thought of Peary. From his base camp at Cape Columbia to the Pole was only 413 miles—a shorter distance than we were traveling—yet it took Peary 23 years to negotiate that journey. With an airplane of sufficient range, a man now could go from Spitzbergen to the North Pole and return between supper and breakfast.

What a marvelous vehicle for the explorer the airplane had become! All honor to the men who fought over this trackless waste with dog sleds; but compared with the ease which modern science had lent to exploration and compared with the vastly magnified results, those former expeditions seem a pitiful waste of brains, energy, and money. We were compressing into a few hours all of the exploration that could have been packed into a former lifetime. Within the year other aviation engines would come roaring up the polar air lanes, but ours were the first to fly over either end of the earth.

Our two ships flew steadily together, side by side, with little dropping or rocking, their engines breaking the silence of the ages, their noses always due north. I had only to lift my hand above the windshield to feel wind pressure hard as a board. From time to time I glanced over at Amundsen. He was crouched in his seat, evidently writing his impressions in his diary. Now and then he took a sight through his sextant. The sun had swung around until it was dead ahead. Midnight. We had been flying for seven hours and must be close now. My shaky observations told me that we had reached a very high latitude.

We must land soon, but where? That level sheet below was deceptive from our altitude. Our binoculars showed it full of lumps and ridges. For our voyage, at least, the polar ice pack did not offer the open leads and smooth snowfields that we had been led to expect. The sun moved toward our starboard quarter, and it was one o'clock in the morning. If our course was correct and our speed calculations true, we must be right over the North Pole. As it happened, just then we came up to the first open leads we had seen that looked broad enough to land a seaplane in.

N 25 suddenly dipped and banked for a spiral descent over these leads, Amundsen waving to us to follow. Dietrichson let them drop 500 feet, then pushed his stick forward. As we corkscrewed lower we saw that even our glasses had failed to reveal the roughness of the polar pack. I have never looked down upon a more terrifying place in which to land an airplane. It was like trying to set down a ship on the bottom of the Grand Canyon. Great blocks of ice were upended or piled one upon another. Pressure ridges stood up like fortress walls. The leads that had looked so innocent from aloft proved to be gulches and miniature canyons. In them, amid a chaos of floes and slush ice, floated veritable bergs of old blue Arctic ice, twenty, thirty, and even forty feet thick.

Nevertheless, the N 25, with Amundsen, Riiser-Larsen, and Feucht, continued its descent, and we had no choice but to follow, since our strictest law of the expedition was that the two planes must at all cost stay together. The N 25 finally dropped into a narrow chasm surrounded by hummocks and ridges of such height that she disappeared from our sight instantly. One of the first things Dietrichson said after we had made our own precarious landing was that Riiser-Larsen must have gone mad to pick out such a hole. What we did not know then was that one of the N 25's engines had cut out, *and Riiser-Larsen was making a forced landing.*

For ten minutes longer we kept flying, looking for some field of level ice or open water bigger than a pocket handkerchief. We found a wider lead than the one Amundsen had chosen, but it was full of dangerous floating ice. At length, by flying up and down the lead, which ran east and west, Dietrichson spotted a tiny lagoon that was ice free. He pancaked down into this and made a skillful landing; but, even so, the ship's momentum carried it across, and it ran its tilted nose up on a heavy ice cake floating on the other side.

In the strange stillness that followed I was aware of Dietrichson yanking on the bell cord and yelling back to the mechanic: "Omdal, Omdal, the plane is leaking like hell!" His shout sounded far away to me, for I was temporarily deaf from the roar of the engines and propellers. The ship *was* leaking. In taking off from the ice at Kings Bay we must have sheared rivets and loosened plates on the hull's bottom, for we scraped no ice in landing.

But I paid little attention to this note of alarm. Thus far I supposed we had come down merely to take true observations of our position. Amundsen and Riiser-Larsen would be at work with their sextant. We must hurry in order to rise into the air with them. How we were going to take off did not then occur to my dulled brain.

Dazed by the abruptness of this new development, forgetting my heavy clothes and the vertigo that results from hours of flying, I jumped from the bow of the plane off onto the ice cake, for some reason taking my rifle with me. I expected only a hard surface but landed in two or three feet of soft snow, floundering and falling down clumsily and thoroughly choking up the barrel of the rifle.

I picked myself up and looked around at the white and blue chaos. In the utter silence this seemed to me to be the kingdom of death itself. Yet just at that moment a seal poked its head out of the water of our lagoon. We three men watched it swim closer in tame fashion until we could have touched it with a boat hook. It did not occur to us to shoot it. Why kill this harmless creature, when that very day we would all be back on Spitzbergen? Yet how often in the days that followed did we regret not having bagged that seal! It was almost the only animal life we saw in the North.

Dietrichson clambered out with the sextant and artificial horizon and together we made the observations. Great was the pilot's disgust when our final check revealed the position Lat. 87°44′ N., Long. 10°20′ W. We had started out from Spitzbergen to fly to the Pole along the twelfth meridian east of Greenwich; we had come down ten degrees west of Greenwich—more than twenty-two degrees off our course. The layman must remember that the meridians converge to a point at the poles and are very close together at 87° N. At the equator 22 degrees of longitude mean a distance of 1,500 miles. In the Arctic they represented only the 8-hour drift of an airplane in a quartering headwind.

Veteran pilots though they were, neither Riiser-Larsen nor Dietrichson had been aware of this westerly drift. In the frozen North there is virtually nothing that enables the aerial observer to determine drift and correct calculations of ground speed. Over the fog, of course, we had flown blind, so far as the earth's surface was concerned, and the ice fields, seen from a flying altitude, offered no landmarks on which to sight for drift. A suggestion had been made to us that we might blaze an Arctic air trail, so to speak, and fix drift sights by dropping paper sacks of aniline dye powder.

Somehow during the winter Riiser-Larsen had found time to test this scheme on the snows of Norway. He found that no practicable quantity of dye powder made a mark that one could see from the air.

As it was, we had flown the distance from Spitzbergen to the North Pole, but we were still 136 nautical miles from it. Our visible horizon at the altitude at which we had been flying just before the landing was 46 miles away. Thus we had looked at a point within ninety miles of the Pole. No other men had ever been so close, except Peary and Matt Henson. And we had established the fact that over an area of some seventy thousand square miles of the Arctic Ocean there was no land of any sort—no islands or even isolated rocks.

The thing to do next was to make contact with Amundsen. We scarcely knew in which direction to look, so engrossed had we been, after the N 25 disappeared, in hunting a landing area for ourselves. While Omdal pumped water from the leaking hull, Dietrichson and I climbed up all the high hummocks near by and searched the tumbled ice with our field glasses but could see nothing. Dietrichson wondered if Amundsen had taken off and gone to the Pole without us.

"It would be just like him," he said.

On second thought, however, we thought this unlikely. We would have heard the N 25's motors, even if we had not seen the ship itself. Dietrichson felt that the other plane must be near, and we kept up our search, but to no avail. We made our way back to the N 24 to learn from Omdal more bad news. The jar of the landing had disabled the plane's forward engine, and it would not turn of its own power.

Meanwhile, the water was gaining in the hull, nearly up to the fuel tanks. It was imperative that no sea water get into our gasoline, so we fell to with the handpump. After we had made some headway, we fastened the plane securely to the ice block with our ice anchors. Then we pitched our tent on the snow and took all our equipment out of the plane, lest it should sink suddenly and carry down our supplies.

When we had finished, our watches told us that it was mid-morning. We had not slept for more than twenty-four hours and were exhausted men. We set up our Meta cooking apparatus, the primus stove being on the N 25, and brewed mugs of hot pemmican soup. Then Dietrichson surprised us by producing from his ruck-sack a small tin of powdered soluble coffee. We melted snow and boiled water, and then into each cup of hot coffee Dietrichson poured a little of the alcohol fuel of the stove. We owed ourselves that drink.

Then, warmed and strengthened to take up our hard tasks again, we lighted our pipes to smoke and rest a little longer, feeling almost happy. Suddenly Dietrichson threw his hand to his face.

"Good God!" he exclaimed. "Something is wrong with my eyes!"

He was blind. To me, fresh from Prohibition in America, the instant thought came—"Wood alcohol!" And perhaps some such fear came to Dietrichson and Omdal as well. We bandaged Die-trichson's eyes and put him in his sleeping bag in the tent. Then Omdal and I squatted and smoked in silence, waiting, it might be, for blindness to come to us in turn. There could have been no more horrible fate than to go blind then.

But we didn't. Dietrichson's affliction proved to be a temporary one—that acute exhaustion of the retina called snow blindness. We had underestimated the power of the sun upon the ice and, be-cause our exertions fogged them, had grown careless about wearing our snow goggles. In fact, one of the minor miseries of our whole stay on the ice was the constant necessity of wearing steamy glasses. We were all more or less touched with snow blindness before we got through.

Dietrichson lay with bandaged eyes in his sleeping bag, awake or asleep, we could not tell. Men do not say much in such circum-stances. Omdal and I puffed and communed with ourselves.

The expedition was separated, one half lost from the other. Our own plane was badly wrecked. Even intact, there was no place from which it could take off. With only one engine to help, three men could not have dragged its great weight up to safety on the ice cake—and one of our party was blind. All around was this

chaotic confusion of ice, grinding and shifting with wind and current, leads opening only to close again with the irresistible force
of innumerable sluggishly moving tons—the deadly jaws of the
North.

A sorry introduction of the prentice to his chosen profession!

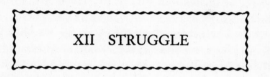

XII STRUGGLE

TWO THINGS were imperative:

1. To secure the N 24 against sinking with the engine fuel on
which our lives depended;

2. To establish communication with Amundsen and his party.

The latter we regarded as the more important. Divided, we
worked without any unified plan. Three men were powerless to
drag the N 24 to safety, but our united numbers might do so. We
were unaware of the condition of the N 25. For all we knew, she
was ready to fly at once, with sufficient open water for a take-off,
while Amundsen and the two others were spending their time
searching for us. One man at the pump could keep the water
down in the N 24's hull. The other two must continue the hunt.

A brief rest under the bandage had restored to Dietrichson's eyes
enough vision to permit him to get around. He had not slept; and
Omdal and I, weary as we were, had not even thought of sleep. In
fact, none of us slept at all during our first five days on the ice,
and we took very little rest. Men do not sleep when their lives
hang in the balance and salvation depends upon their own efforts.

From the near-by hummocks from which we had first looked
we had seen a higher hill of ice not far away. Dietrichson and I
decided to gain its summit, if we could, and use it as our observation point. We put on skis and started out, wary lest the 3-foot
covering of snow bridged hidden crevasses in the ice. The journey

proved to be not difficult, and when we reached the top of this hill, we spotted the N 25 instantly.

Gone were our hopes, or, rather, gone was our confident assumption, that Riiser-Larsen had landed the N 25 safely. She seemed in a worse plight than the N 24. Though a long distance away—three miles, we estimated—through our binoculars she presented a terrible picture. She was upended at an angle of forty-five degrees, her nose against a wall of ice that looked forty feet high. She seemed to us to have crashed against this wall and to have tried to climb it.

Now and then with our glasses we saw the tiny black figures of Amundsen and his companions; but, though we shouted and waved our signal flag, they did not see us. I returned to the plane and brought back some of the hydrogen sounding balloons which we carried for meteorological observations in the upper air strata. We tied pieces of flannel to these and set them loose, hoping they would drift over the N 25 and indicate our direction to Amundsen. But the N 25 lay northward and the wind was from that direction, so our balloons only floated south or were blown by gusts into the polar debris and entangled there.

After a while we gave it up and returned to the N 24, which sorely needed our attention. Omdal had been dividing his time between working the hand pump and trying to repair the disabled engine. Now Dietrichson and I took turns at the pump, so that Omdal could give his entire attention to the engine. Now and then during the next twenty-four hours one of us went to the ice hill to wave our semaphore flag; but it was not until afternoon of the second day on the ice—May 23—that Amundsen saw us.

Meanwhile, an encouraging thing was happening. All the ice was in slow but constant motion, and by the greatest good fortune in the world, instead of separating us farther, as it might well have done, the movement was drawing the two planes closer together. When Amundsen saw our flag, the N 25 was half a mile nearer than it had been the day before.

Now this is the log of our expedition to date: we started from Kings Bay at 5:15 P.M. on May 21. We landed at Eighty-seven Forty-four, as we always called our memorable position in after months and years, at 1 A.M., May 22. We discovered the position of the N 25 at noon of that day. Amundsen saw us first in the afternoon of May 23.

If I am able to give a complete and positive account of the days that followed, it is because I, as well as the others, kept a detailed log of events as they occurred. Otherwise, my memory of that long dreadful experience would have been a crowded confusion of struggle, heartbreak, and imminent death. Time exists at the North Pole only as a textbook fact. Day and night are merely calculations. It is day when the sun is in the southern sector; when it is in the northern, it is night. There are no dawns and sunsets, no moon or zenith sun, which serve the memory as aids in the lower latitudes. Events were fixed in time by the hands of our watches.

As soon as we established contact with Amundsen, we began to semaphore messages to each other. This was tedious work, since none of us was expert at it. It required two men on each side: one with the flag, the other with the book to call the signals. When receiving, one man used the glasses, the other decoded the signals as called. It took us two or three hours to exchange the simplest of communications.

While we would have been much more effective as a single party, the journey across the ice looked too formidable to attempt except in the direst of emergencies. Amundsen advised us to try to save our plane, as he and his assistants were trying to save the N 25. We reconnoitered and found that the ice cake to which we had moored our flying boat was six hundred feet in diameter. If we could drag the plane up upon this cake, it would be safe from sinking or being crushed, in the event that the lead closed.

Dietrichson and I, therefore, set out to construct a ramp by digging away the snow and ice. I chopped with the ice anchor, and Dietrichson shoveled with a wooden shovel Sailmaker Rönne had fashioned for us. Omdal, however, could not make the forward engine run. We opened the remaining engine out wide, and the three of us pulled, but the most we could do was drag the nose of the plane up on our ramp. Anyhow, she was now safe from sinking, if not from being crushed, and her fuel tanks were above water. It was the best we could do, and we secured her in that position.

This danger of being crushed became apparent. The breeze that had blown our balloons away from Amundsen had been favorable for us, since a north wind tended to open the leads. On the second day, though, it shifted to the south, and we could see the ice closing in. The whole field was alive with inert motion. Ice cakes in the lead would disappear, as if sucked under; others would emerge to the surface. The edges of the lead drew imperceptibly closer to each other. The implacable jaws were shutting on us, and we all felt that our plane would soon be caught in them.

With the shift of the wind to the south came, for some reason, a cold snap. When we landed, temperatures had been hovering around the freezing mark. Now we began to have continuously fifteen to twenty degrees of frost. The planes continued to converge in the ice movement. On May 24 they were not over two miles apart. There was nothing more that we could do for the N 24. The repair of the engine was a shop job. We signaled Amundsen that we were going to attempt to cross to him and started out.

We traveled on skis, dragging our sledge on which we packed supplies, including the canvas canoe. The going through the deep snow and over mountainous hummocks was terrible. At the end of a few hundred yards we gave up. To drag that weight farther was beyond our strength, weakened as we were by lack of sleep and insufficient food. From the supplies on the sledge we made up packs of fifty pounds each. As we rested, I recorded this episode in my diary, ending the entry: "We may or may not return to our plane again."

We pushed on. According to my diary, it took us two hours and fifteen minutes to travel the first two miles; and then, so roundabout had been the route we were forced to take to avoid crevices and ridges, we were little more than halfway to the N 25. At this point we came to a wide lead of open water and floating ice cakes. Without the canoe, which we had left back there on the sledge, we had no way to cross. Amundsen by signal advised us to go back. We followed the trail we had broken and reached camp at the end of a seven-hour trip, having covered five and one-half miles in about the time it took us to fly from Spitzbergen to Eighty-seven Forty-four.

The cold spell, continuing, began to seal the leads with new ice. The sea water, always poised at this season on the edge of congealing, froze in even a slight drop in temperature. Moreover, for some reason, though the sun shone all twenty-four hours, there was invariably a fall in temperature during the time designated as night. On the morning of May 26 our own diminished lead was frozen over with ice that would bear a man's weight. Furthermore, *we could now see* that the lead which had stopped us the day before was sealed.

Something akin to a miracle had been taking place. The ice movement, imperceptible as the movement of an hour hand yet just as obvious, had grown stronger during the night of May 25–26, and by morning the two planes had drifted within half a mile and in full sight of each other. Furthermore, the pressure ridges and heavy block ice that had floated between had all moved out, leaving a snow field still rough but low.

Here I may insert that in all the drifting that followed, the two ships never drew far apart. To that fact we owed our lives, since it enabled us to salvage the gas, food, and other supplies from the disabled N 24.

Through our field glasses we could now plainly identify the figures of Amundsen, Riiser-Larsen, and Feucht. We heard the hum of the N 25's motors, saw the blur of her propellers, saw Amundsen rock the wing up and down as if trying to break the hull loose from ice—but it did not budge. It still seemed to have its nose up against that berg of old ice. Amundsen signaled us to make a new attempt to join him, since there was good hope of extricating the N 25. Making up heavy packs of eighty pounds per man, we signaled Amundsen that we were coming and started out.

Well aware that the crossing of the new ice on the big lead would be precarious, we only shoved our feet loosely into our skis so that we could shake free if we fell into the water. We reached the edge of the lead and gingerly tested it. It seemed solid enough. Solid or no, we had to take the chance. If we were ever to get back to civilization again, we must unite our entire resources and work as a six-man team, and that at once.

We started out over the thin ice, separating to spread out our weight. Omdal went first, carefully shuffling one ski out ahead and carefully bringing up the other, as he felt his way. I followed, using the same tactics. Dietrichson came last. At this point we were out of sight of the N 25, an embankment of snow hummocks separating the lead from the plane's position.

All at once Dietrichson yelled behind me. Before I could turn my head, Omdal also cried out and disappeared, as though swallowed up by the earth. At the same instant I felt the ice sag under my skis. I slid sideways. The fact that there was a frozen-in block of thick ice right there enables me to tell this story now. Crawling on my stomach, partly on this safe raft, partly on the new ice, I reached my skis out to Dietrichson. He grabbed the ends and I pulled him in, breaking ice with his chest, until I could get hold of his pack. Then I managed to drag him partly out upon my cake, where he lay, panting and exhausted.

Next I turned my attention to Omdal. His head showed above water and he was calling hoarsely—in English, as it startled me later to realize—"I'm gone! I'm gone!" Gone he almost was. I spread out as widely as I could and wriggled toward him, pushing my skis out ahead. He caught them with the frantic haste of a drowning man. I pulled him through breaking ice until his pack was in reach. Then, partly supported by the firm ice, I could do no more and merely held on. Omdal was nearly unconscious. Blood trickled from his mouth, for he had broken off five front teeth on the ski points and ice edges. The strong current beneath swept his legs under the ice.

Dietrichson recovered enough strength to crawl over and hold Omdal while I cut off the man's heavy pack. Then the two of us managed to drag him out on our cake. Those at the N 25 had heard our cries. They strapped on skis and started to fight toward us, but before they could get far all three of us appeared among the hummocks.

They saw two of us floundering through snow almost waist-deep. Dietrichson and Omdal had lost their skis in the accident, which, in view of the possibility of a long journey over the Arctic ice, was a sheer calamity. Omdal was so badly done up that I had let him have my skis. We left his pack to be recovered later. Crawling from cake to cake, Dietrichson and I had managed to cross the rest of the lead safely, Omdal following us.*

Five days had wrought a shocking change in Amundsen. Sleepless toil and anxiety had graven in his face lines that seemed to age him ten years. In all his many adventures in the polar regions, I doubt if he had ever been in such peril as this or under such a strain. Yet in his manner he was his same old self, cool, clearheaded, resourceful. The first thing to do was get Dietrichson and Omdal into dry clothes, warm them with hot chocolate, and let them rest a while. We also bandaged Omdal's swollen and lacerated hands.

All the while we were hearing of our comrades' experiences, and we learned for the first time about the engine cutting out, due to a break in an air intake. Feucht had since repaired it, and the engine was functioning. Our own eyes showed us that the N 25 had not crashed into the ice wall, as we had thought. At the base of this cliff projected an old floe of firm but much thinner ice. The N 25 had nosed up on this and stopped without shearing a rivet. She was as ready for flight as ever.

But her position was dangerous. The lead in which she had found room to land had closed until there was now not enough water to launch a rowboat in. The squeezing, too, had locked the plane tightly in the grip of the ice. But Amundsen would not let us do anything to free her that day. At the N 24 we had been snatching food and rest as we could and paying little attention to day and night, but Amundsen was already enforcing an orderly routine in his camp—fixed hours for meals, for work and sleep, and for smok-

*In a public lecture on the 1925 expedition, delivered in the National Theater of Oslo, August 14, 1925, before the King and Queen of Norway, Roald Amundsen said: ". . . When Lincoln Ellsworth saved Dietrichson and Omdal from drowning, he saved the whole expedition; and I, therefore, deeply appreciate the king's act in conferring on Ellsworth, without whose generosity the expedition would never have taken place, the gold medal for the saving of life."

ing and talking. He knew there was no quicker way to break men down under strain than to allow them to live haphazardly. An ordered existence, moreover, engendered confidence. This calm and unhurried way of doing things seemed to symbolize the ability of intelligence to overcome the inimical forces of nature.

By the time we had stowed the supplies we had brought and Dietrichson and Omdal had recovered, it was late afternoon. We elected Omdal our cook, inasmuch as he now had no engines to attend to, and celebrated our reunion by having hot pemmican broth that evening. Usually we made pemmican soup only at noon and drank hot chocolate mornings and evenings. When we confessed to Amundsen that we had not been sleeping, he ordered us all to bed as soon as we had eaten. That night we disposed ourselves as best we could in the tent and aboard the tilted airplane and awoke in the morning much refreshed.

The next day we devoted entirely to moving the N 25 to a place of safety. The ice that half supported her was a tongue jutting out from a field or old cake several acres in extent lying beyond the miniature berg, which had frozen into it. To be able to slide the ship up onto this cake, we did as we had done at the N 24—hacked out a ramp. Our tools were pitiful—the ice anchor, one two-pound pocket safety ax, and three wooden shovels. We even took our sheath knives and lashed them to the ends of ski poles to make ice picks. Yet with these implements Amundsen estimated later that we removed three hundred tons of solid ice during the twenty-five days of our imprisonment together.

It took us all day to make the ramp, clear a level runway on the ice cake, and chop and shake the N 25 loose from the ice that gripped her. Then, as Feucht opened both engines out wide, the rest of us pushed and pulled, and the airplane slid up on top, out of immediate danger from the screwing pack ice.

This was May 27. That night we began to occupy the plane itself as a camp, thus escaping the continuous daylight, which was growing hateful to all of us. Amundsen and I occupied the cockpit, covering the top with canvas. The main compartment of the hull served as kitchen, dining room, and dormitory for Dietrichson,

Feucht, and Omdal. They laid skis across the floor to hold themselves off the frosty metal floor. Riiser-Larsen crawled back into the tail, where it was dark. •

We spent the next day, May 28, in relative idleness, scouting for leads or level ice for a take-off and making various observations. The reader must remember that we were still expecting some lead to open that would give our ship ample water. We had reason to expect it. Every polar explorer had told of the constantly opening leads in arctic ice during summer. At any hour, therefore, the wind might shift to the north, the ice would part, and we would soon be on our way back to Spitzbergen.

We took our first soundings of the ocean. Our sounding apparatus was a lightweight device working on the echo principle and made specially for us in Germany. A sea microphone connected with headphones, a battery set with a detonating cartridge of trinol, and a stopwatch were all there was to it. The observer timed the interval between the explosion and the return of the echo from the bottom. We took two soundings as a check on each other, but both times the echo came up in exactly five seconds. Sound travels much faster in sea water than in the air—nearly a mile a second. Five seconds indicated an approximate depth of 12,500 feet.

Curiously, the mountains near the South Pole are just about that high. It seems almost as if a great fist had struck the earth at the North Pole during a malleable stage, denting it in two miles or more and causing a corresponding bulge at the opposite end of the axis.

A sextant observation that day showed us to be twelve miles south of our landing point. Thus, besides the eddying motion of the ice, the whole pack was drifting along. We hoped it might carry us down where we would find game. How we regretted now not having shot that seal!

On May 29 Dietrichson, Omdal, and I took the sledge and canoe and skied to the N 24 to salvage the gasoline and remaining provisions aboard her. Though the two planes were remaining close together, it was a hard journey, as we had to take a circuitous route to avoid ridges, with always the chance of dropping through a snow bridge into a crevasse. At the N 24 we cut out one of the empty gas tanks and pumped it full from the others. We also stripped the hull of everything portable. It made a heavy load to drag. The roughness of the return journey splintered one of the stout ski runners of the sledge, thus further shortening our chances of getting out on foot. Then, on the return trip, we found that a new lead had opened across our path, too wide to cross with the sledge or even to jump. We had to leave the supplies there and cross with the canoe. Fortunately the lead closed again that night, and next day Dietrichson and Omdal brought in the sledge alone.

But the wind persisted from the south, squeezing in the polar pack. The bitter cold continued—always around 15 degrees Fahrenheit. The duralumin walls and ceiling of the hull compartment glittered with hoar frost from our breaths. The heat from the primus stove melted it, and it dripped down on our heads. The new ice froze thick in the leads that resisted pressure. On May 31, when we had been prisoners for ten days, our chances for launching the plane were no better than they had been the day we landed. At last we had to face realities.

We took an inventory that day. The brightest item was our fuel —enough and to spare for a flight back to Spitzbergen. We had conserved food and had ample, assuming that we could get into the air before the end of a month. But what reason had we to guide ourselves by that assumption? The optimism we had all been trying to show was false optimism. The chances were far likelier that in the end we would be left with the desperate expedient of trying to reach the coast of Greenland on foot and in the canoes.

"It is a hard journey," said Amundsen, "but it *can* be done."

Privately, I doubted it. Years in the wilderness and on mountain trails had inured me to hard travel, yet I considered that if I could make one hundred miles over that ice before I collapsed, it would be the supreme physical feat of my life. And if we ever reached Greenland, what then? Nobody cared to raise that point. A desolate coast, uninhabited, unvisited, perhaps gameless, and we would arrive without food, perhaps even without shelter, perhaps in terrible physical condition as well.

But men fight for their lives to the last inch, and we had to begin at once to prepare either for that journey or for a much longer stay on the ice than any of us had contemplated. To that end, Amundsen, as commander, put us on a ration of one-half pound of food per man per day, which was something less than half the ration Peary fed his dogs on his dash to the Pole over this same ice.

Furthermore, the commander ordered, until June 15 we would make supreme efforts to put N 25 into the air. There were three possibilities. The long-hoped-for lead might open, and that would solve everything. We might find smooth ice or frozen snow of sufficient extent to allow the ship to take off. Or we might clear a runway for the take-off. The last seemed by far the likeliest eventuality, but with our poor implements it also seemed a superhuman task.

On June 15 that order would come to an end, and every man of the expedition would become his own master, electing which he would do—stay with the ship or start for Greenland. As for Amundsen himself, he preferred to remain on the ice. He had faith in the Arctic's seasonal behavior. Sooner or later the wind would come to the north and the leads would open. He asked the rest of us to vote. What was my choice?

As Amundsen spoke, the poet Swinburne's line came to me:

Where Faith abides, though Hope be put to flight.

Reason and common sense had all but driven hope away, but faith remained. As I looked at my comrades, strong, coolheaded men, I could not believe that we would be defeated. I knew that we would win through, and I think we all shared this blind faith —or all but one of us.

A change had been coming over Feucht, our German engine mechanic. He had fallen into a mood of black despondency and presented the very picture of defeatism. In justice to Feucht, I must state that he came on the expedition on a moment's notice, with no knowledge of the conditions he must confront. Riiser-Larsen had engaged another mechanic, but at the eleventh hour the

Dornier-Wal company sent Feucht, because of his great skill with engines—a skill which he proved in the Far North.

Nor am I reproaching him with cowardice. During the days that followed I never heard him utter any word of fear, and I doubt if he felt fear. He was seized with an attack of melancholia—a disease no more avoidable than any other disease. His black mood persisted even after we escaped, for he insisted that Spitzbergen was only the bleak coast of some island where we would go on to meet the fate we had eluded on the ice.

In answer to Amundsen, I said I would prefer to wait until June 14 before making a decision. It seemed insane to start on a desperate foot journey, leaving idle nine hundred horsepower that could fly us back to civilization in eight hours. On the other hand, staying might mean seeing the food dwindle until death came by starvation. Not that—I should prefer to end it on my feet, making a fight.

Riiser-Larsen's turn was next. That sturdy Norwegian said with calm finality: "I will not stay here and die."

Dietrichson? My pilot thought he would stay with the N 25. Omdal? Omdal would go with the majority. Feucht? That man of shops and machinery muttered that he would not walk a step, even if everyone else went.

Riiser-Larsen was indefatigable. He seemed to take upon his shoulders the full responsibility of putting the ship into the air. He had picked out the model and felt certain that the broad hull of the Dornier-Wal would so distribute the weight that the ship would rise out of snow itself. Yet when he tried it alone, with the ship empty, he could not reach a greater speed than thirty miles per hour, and sixty miles per hour was the N 25's flying speed.

Just on the other side of the floe on which rested the N 25 was a very long lead which had never closed since we had been there and which was now solidly frozen over. On the morning of June 1 Riiser-Larsen, always out investigating, chopped a hole through this ice and discovered it was eight inches thick. He returned to us with something as near enthusiasm as his phlegmatic nature would permit him. This ice, he felt certain, would bear up the weight of the plane. It would be no great work to chop out lumps and clear a sufficient runway. There seemed to be good prospects that salvation was near.

With a definite goal to work for now, we all set about it with a will. It was necessary to construct a ramp from the floe to the lead ice, a drop of six feet. This we did by dragging in heavy blocks of ice for a foundation, filling in around these with smaller lumps, then leveling it with fine ice, which we broke up with our tools, and finally shoveling on a good surface of snow, which we packed down and allowed to freeze. It took us two days to build the ramp and level off fifteen hundred feet of lead ice ahead.

Meanwhile, that first night we established a new practice. It occurred to us that temporary leads, large enough for a take-off, might be opening at night, when we were asleep, closing again before morning. We could not bear the thought of even the possibility of such a tragedy, so we established a night patrol. Each man took his turn, skiing round and round our floe, watching for open water.

At 5 P.M. on June 2 we were ready for the start. We had our ship gassed, and all our supplies were aboard. I will not say we were excited or that our hearts beat high with anticipation, for that would not be true. A sort of blessed apathy had seized us, as, I have since discovered, it always seizes men under strain in the polar regions, and we accepted everything with indifference, the good with the bad.

Methodically we took our places in the N 25. Amundsen had the observer's seat. Riiser-Larsen and Dietrichson were in the pilot's cockpit. I stayed with Feucht and Omdal in the engine gondola. It was Riiser-Larsen's plan to hit the head of the ramp fast and drop down to the lead at high speed, since then there would be less danger of the new ice breaking under us; but with its load aboard and having to mash down three-foot snow, the plane could only crawl under full power. We slid down the ramp, but the ship's narrow nose, with nearly four tons of weight behind it, simply sagged through the eight-inch ice. Riiser-Larsen opened the engines wide, hoping she'd climb out, but we only broke a channel.

When we had moved about three thousand feet in this fashion, Riiser-Larsen gave up and shut off the power, and we prepared to spend the night in the lead. It was Amundsen's turn at the outside patrol. Hours later we were awakened by pounding on the hull and Amundsen's voice yelling that the plane was being crushed. I could plainly hear the grinding of ice against the metal sides. We jumped out into the midnight sunshine; and, while the two mechanics threw out supplies, the rest of us rocked the hull up and down to let the ice pressure in under it. Presently she was up on solid stuff, but it was a narrow escape. We all thought for a while that the ship would be crushed. The end of our fury of effort brought from Riiser-Larsen one of his rare remarks.

"Another chapter for our book," he said.

That same night, before the sun had swung round to its morning position, summer abruptly set in. The temperature rose to the freezing point and from that time on hovered there. A heavy fog rose, and after that we were never entirely free from fog. A mild breeze blew only strong enough to unfold our Norwegian flag. Indeed, if anything impressed us in those polar waters, it was the equable summer climate—one day exactly like another. It thawed slightly when the sun was in its day sector, it froze slightly when the sun was north.

I will not tire the reader with detailed accounts of our numerous attempts to get into the air and our equally numerous disappointments—the runways we hacked and hewed in the ice of this same long lead, only to feel the hull break through each time it slid on them. There were frantic periods when the ice closed in on us and we had to work like mad to pull the ship out in time. The squeeze the hull had taken that first time and its subsequent encounters with the ice loosened plates, and it began to leak. After that we pitched our tents on the floes and removed our most vital supplies when the plane was floating in the lead.

Fog stayed with us, but it was usually so thin that we could see the disc of the sun through it. Its actinic power was still there. Dripping with sweat, we removed our dark glasses, only to pay the penalty of snow blindness. I was totally blind in one eye for a whole day. Dietrichson was particularly susceptible. He had to lie with bandaged eyes for two days, suffering acutely from conjunctivitis.

One of our failures was especially heartbreaking—or would have been heartbreaking, if our minds and senses had not been dulled by the very monotony of failure. In plowing through the network of frozen leads, we had worked near to the N 24—so near that one night Amundsen and I pitched our tent on the floe that buoyed up our abandoned ship. That beautiful new mechanism was a sad sight. She had listed over, and one wing was solidly frozen into the floe. Indeed, she was so firmly held that we took away her ice anchor to serve us as a pick.

On the opposite side of this floe was the head of a lead which, after an examination, Riiser-Larsen thought offered us the best chance for a take-off he had discovered. The ice of the lead was thick and fairly smooth, but the chief advantage of this lead was its narrowness. Our pilot thought that a narrow lead might hold better. We cleared a runway, loaded ourselves aboard the N 25 once more, and slid down to the new ice. To our great satisfaction, the ice held!

Riiser-Larsen gave her the gun, and we gathered speed almost as swiftly as we had at Kings Bay. It was tricky work, though, because of the narrowness of the passage. About two thirds of the way down our runway, the lead widened and curved slightly. We hoped to be in the air before we reached this point, and we almost made it. Then, realizing that he would have to round the bend on the surface, Riiser-Larsen was forced to throttle down rather than risk a skid that would send us crashing to complete disaster against the side ice. As we slackened speed, the nose of the ship broke through, the tail lifted, and we stuck in that position.

We all jumped out to chop ice and bring the hull down on an even keel. Then we saw that the lead was closing fast, and it took sharp work to get the ship out of the trap.

Routine camp existence went dully on amid these disappointments. We became a terrible-looking crew. We lived in our clothes day and night, and, though often wet with sweat, we never bathed and seldom even washed. There was no time to waste on melting snow and heating water, and no fuel to waste, if we had had the time. Our hair became matted, our beards grew unkempt and stubby, until we resembled so many tramps in a hobo jungle. The sun glare through the mist burned our skin black. We were haggard and drawn from a starvation diet and killing work.

The morning and evening mugs of hot chocolate were twin tastes of paradise. Little things became irritating. It seemed a sort of personal grievance to the rest of us that Amundsen never drank any water. The pemmican made us all thirsty, but Amundsen drank only the chocolate. It was exasperating, too, to see him swallow the liquid boiling, as if it were nothing. We were all developing "polar nerves." If we had been talkative men, retailing experiences and life stories over and over again, I'm sure we would have been at each others' throats. But I have noticed that all men, whatever their nationality, grow silent under a long strain in the polar regions and commune with their own thoughts, if indeed they can be said to have thoughts. Norwegians are particularly taciturn. I never heard one in our party express a word of discouragement or, with the exception of Amundsen, a word of hope.

As leader, Amundsen expressed a steady confidence, though in no obnoxiously cheerful way. After our evening meal he and I usually took a turn together on skis around the ice, looking for fresh leads. On those occasions I sometimes asked him what he thought of our situation. He admitted that the outlook was not good but then added what he had said when he first told me of the miraculous escape of his little Gjoa from the Arctic reef: "When it is darkest, there is always light ahead." That was as far as his spoken optimism went.

Trivialities became obsessions. Mine was the management of my malted-milk tablets. When I had seen these packed on the ships at Spitzbergen, I had rather despised them as mere confections, but now they became precious to me. Every night after chocolate, each man received a dole of ten milk tablets. I always took mine to bed in my sleeping bag. As I hacked at ice and snow during the day, I would think for hours about those pastilles. If I could just save out one or two each night and hide them away, the night would come when I could have a feast. I never managed to carry out this plan. I was troubled with insomnia, and it always took my tenth malted-milk tablet to give me enough stomach comfort to induce sleep.

Amundsen and I took our secret resentment out on poor Feucht. That man, always glooming in a sort of waking nightmare or hopeless reverie, seemed a living reproach to us. When the rest of us were down on our knees chopping at ice, we would see Feucht leaning on his ski staff and simply staring down at the snow. It took a sharp word to bring him to his senses. To add to his misery, he developed an abscessed tooth and a swollen jaw. We came upon him one day leaning against the plane's hull as he tried to extract the tooth with a monkey wrench. The rest of us helped him complete a most rough-and-ready piece of dental surgery.

No minor tribulation was the fact that we ran out of tobacco. The planes could have carried a greater weight from Spitzbergen. How we regretted not having brought more tobacco! The only tobacco left was some strong navy twist that Riiser-Larsen had in his rucksack. He generously shared this with the rest of us. We rationed it to ourselves as stingily as we did food, limiting each man to one pipeful a day. The great moment came after the evening meal. Riiser-Larsen got out his twist tobacco, moistened it with snow water to make it burn more slowly, and then whittled a few scraps into each man's hand. These had to be rolled out loose between one's palms and then packed into the pipe. It was fearfully strong. We all hiccuped after smoking.

Feucht, lost in his black dream, stuck out his hand for tobacco, too. He rolled it as if he were not aware of what he was doing, dropping flakes of it in the snow. The sight drove Amundsen furious.

"The man does not want that tobacco at all," he would rage to me afterwards. "He just takes it to bother us—so it will not last so long."

Poor Feucht! I don't suppose he had the slightest idea he was annoying Amundsen.

I had a secret subtle revenge that I practiced on Feucht. When we ate in the plane's compartment, he always squatted opposite me. Besides the mug of chocolate and the malted-milk tablets, our ration gave us three oat biscuits. I slyly hid two of my biscuits in my parka, then pretended to eat, though I was only nibbling on the third one. I was waiting for Feucht to get through with his. Feucht and his biscuits got terribly on my nerves. His crime, in my eyes, was that *he was careless about the crumbs!* The rest of us caught our crumbs in one hand and dabbed them all up with our tongues. Feucht let his fall unheeded.

When Feucht had finished eating, I surreptitiously fished my biscuits out of my parka and munched them, being ostentatious about it. That seemed to make me feel superior to Feucht. By finishing my biscuits last, I convinced myself that I got more to eat than he did, and that gave me great satisfaction. Yet again, I don't suppose the man even noticed it.

Such are the conceits and aberrations apt to fret men's nerves when their lives hang long in the balance and they are cold and starved. But besides taking offense, I could, it seemed, also give it. One morning Amundsen said to me, a little maliciously, I thought:

"Ellsworth, what makes you sigh so much in your sleep? You are always heaving those big sighs. They keep me awake."

I was struck with astonishment and shame. I didn't know I was doing such a thing, though I did have vague recollections, when I awoke from troubled sleep, of having had difficulty with my breathing. What caused it, I don't know, for I never lost heart— not at any minute.

Could it have been some monster, long ago shackled into the deepest dungeon of my being, stirring and struggling for expression while its captor was sunk in the unconsciousness of sleep?

No. 7 Amundsen-Ellsworth 1925 Exped.

Amundsen and Ellsworth beside Their Planes Just before the Start.

No. 5 Amundsen-Ellsworth 1925 Exped.

Saturday Night Mess at King's Bay and Eight Hours Later.

XIII ESCAPE

JUNE 6. We had been on the ice fifteen days, and our position was hopeless as ever. No lead had yet exposed water broad enough for a seaplane's run. The ice of the frozen leads would not bear the weight of the ship. The plane could not reach flying speed on the snow.

Nine days to June 15, when we must take the supreme decision. Riiser-Larsen had already announced his intention to start for Greenland on June 15—on foot. If one man went with him, the remaining four might not be able to launch the N 25, if the providential lead appeared. If that man happened to be Dietrichson, there would be no pilot left with the ship. It was becoming evident that we must all set out on that frightful journey. I didn't like to think about June 15.

Wings brought us into the trap; wings must carry us out, if we were ever to see civilization again. That was the only conclusion common sense could draw. We still had left our third alternative, the superhuman one of clearing a runway on the old thick ice of the floes. But in fifteen days of moving around we had not seen a floe big enough to serve as a flying field.

A dense fog shrouded the ice on the morning of June 6. As soon as they had swallowed their breakfast chocolate, Riiser-Larsen and Dietrichson strapped on their skis, growled a word or two of farewell, and disappeared into the smother. They were off on a do-or-die hunt for what might well prove to be the unfindable—an ice cake that could serve our forlorn purpose.

The rest of us stayed with the N 25, which floated in the lead channel we had last broken—the last we were going to break. Now and then one of us pumped out water entering through the leaky joints of the mistreated hull. Amundsen and I wrote in our diaries, took a sounding through the lead, snapped a few pictures when the fog thinned at noon. Feucht brooded within his own spiritual fog. Omdal wiped and greased the engines. With some apprehension we noticed that the lead was slowly closing. Omdal started the Therm-X heaters to warm the engines ready for a quick pull.

Late in the afternoon Riiser-Larsen and Dietrichson returned, and we knew by their faces that they bore good news. Skiing in thick fog, they had had but little luck, but during a short break after noon they saw a big cake shining in the distant sunlight. They made their way to it, explored it, and estimated its north-and-south diameter at three hundred yards. This was none too long for a runway; but, on hard ice and lightened of all excess cargo, the ship might fly in that distance.

The good news was not entirely unmitigated. In the first place, this ice cake was more than half a mile away. Between it and our lead lay two floes separated by wide crevasses. These would have to be bridged. One pressure ridge lay as a barrier wall across the route. In addition, we had to lift the ship out of the lead and upon the first floe. And when we reached the big cake, the problem of a runway had still to be solved.

In other words, we were confronted with a job of Arctic road building. Instead of rock, gravel, and cement, our road metal was ice and snow. For tools we had such things as frail wooden shovels and sheath knives tied to the ends of ski poles. And it was no one-car lane we were called upon to construct, but a way wide enough to accommodate the 60-foot spread of an airplane's wings.

Because of the menacing movement of the ice, the main body of the pack now being only thirty feet away, we decided to move the plane up on top of the first floe that night. It was well we did, for during the night solid ice moved in where the N 25 had been. We started the engines and worked slowly up the lead to the point where we must build our ramp. By midnight we had the plane up safely on Floe Number 1. For our six hours of heavy toil we rewarded ourselves with a mug of hot chocolate apiece. That night we set no outside watch. Every man crawled into his sleeping bag and fell instantly into a veritable coma of exhaustion.

Next morning we were up early and at it again. We tackled first the most stupendous work we had yet undertaken—the cutting of the passage through the pressure ridge. It was a wall of ice fifteen feet thick. It took us an entire day to accomplish this—bitter work, on our knees, chopping with the pocket ax and the ice anchors, our legs wet to the skin from the melting ice, our hands, always soaking in icy brine, red, raw, and swollen from handling the tools. The leveling of sixty feet of this wall accounted for a great percentage of the three hundred tons of ice Amundsen estimated we moved during our stay.

The bridges across the crevasses required less grueling work but offered much more hazard and excitement. These chasms in the ice were really narrow leads, with open or thinly skimmed water at the bottom. It was a question of filling them up with ice until we gained a solid surface level with the floes.

We floated in big blocks as a foundation, hoping they might freeze in position. On top of these we threw down blocks we could drag or carry in our arms. As the upper weight increased, the foundation ice sank, so that we had to heave in a far greater quantity of ice than the mere cubic volume of the crevasse itself. It was also necessary to build the bridges extra wide, since the sides tended to slide off.

When we had a bridge level and bound it with packed snow, though it supported the six of us, there was every reason to believe that it would sag down under the weight of the plane. Therefore, it was necessary to send the ship across with all the speed its engines could muster through the snow. Moreover, it had to stop almost instantly on the other side. There was always danger of the crevasse opening wider and destroying our bridge, so we could spare no time to remove ice blocks and level a coasting runway ahead.

Riiser-Larsen took the N 25 across the bridges alone, the rest of us holding lines attached to the tail, ready to dig in our heels and brake when the ship was over. Thus we negotiated both safely, and before supper time on June 8 our plane stood at last on the lip of the big cake.

I have neglected to mention that this floe was south of the original position of the N 25 in the frozen lead. Therefore, the plane rested at the northern end of our proposed runway. This was favorable for the take-off, since the wind still continued to blow from the south. Riiser-Larsen had never lost belief in the essential ability of the seaplane to rise from snow. The wind blowing rather briskly that afternoon, he wanted to give it the chance then and there. I think none of us had much confidence, but we agreed. God knows, nobody wanted to stay there a moment longer than we had to.

We went over the course with our chopping implements, knocking off the heads of such ice lumps that projected through the snow. Then we went back to the plane and once more took our places. It was no use. The wind had died down, and the engines could hardly drag the hull through the sodden drifts. We merely bumped across the cake to the southern edge, stopping abruptly beside another lead when Riiser-Larsen shut off the power.

We now had to face the task we had been trying to avoid all along—that of shoveling off two and one-half feet of snow, heavy from thawing, and then leveling a runway in the blue ice below. Riiser-Larsen looked the ground over and, instead of taking the north-south diameter of the ice cake, chose a slightly quartering course, which, he estimated, would add a distance of over three hundred feet to our fairway. Speaking in metric-system terms, we would have a runway 400 meters long instead of one of 300 meters. We all knew more or less about flying, and each must have felt in his heart that 400 meters was none too long a run for a take-off.

On the morning of June 9 we began this work. Our chopping tools were of no use to us now. We had only our three wooden shovels. We set out to clear the blue ice along a path 39 feet (12 meters) wide. But this was no job of cutting in with a shovel and tossing the snow to one side. The shoveler had to walk to one edge and then throw the snow far, for it was necessary to leave on each side of the cleared track a 20-foot shelf to accommodate the wing spread.

Three men worked with the shovels while three rested or tossed out big snowballs. The wet summer snow was heavy as lead. So weakened were we by starvation and continued physical strain that after a few shovelfuls a man had to stand and lean on his shovel, panting for breath and gazing drearily out over the labor ahead. At the end of our first day of such effort, we stared disconsolately at only a hundred feet or so of runway cleared. At that rate it would take us from ten days to two weeks to make the runway.

To prevent the ship freezing into the wet snow, in the event of a cold snap, we decided to move it that evening over on the cleared ice. We found it impossible to turn the hull in the snow, ruining another pair of skis in the attempt. Then somebody thought of trampling down and packing the snow next to the hull, and presently we were all beating down with our feet a track to the runway. Over this, we discovered, the hull slid easily.

That gave us the idea that saved us. We decided to pack down the entire runway. Next morning we started it. We adopted a system. We marked out the work in squares, and each man was responsible for stamping down hard every inch of his area. Everyone could keep busy now, and that evening we had the satisfaction of seeing nearly three hundred and fifty feet of runway completed in addition to the stretch cleared the first day. We figured that we would complete the course in five days.

Next morning we had the further satisfaction of observing that the packed snow had frozen to the consistency of brick during the night. It thawed out during the day's rise in temperature but froze again the second night, and this succession kept up regularly. On that first day of trampling we heard a bird's cry overhead and through the mist saw a little auk flying northwest. Next day two wild geese dropped out of the fog and lighted near the plane. Somebody spotted them from afar, and Dietrichson, who was a crack shot, crept back to the ship for the shotgun. The geese seemed tame and stayed close, but this rich prize was too much for the famished hunter's nerves. He fired and missed, and the birds flew off to the northwest. We wondered if there were land in that direction.

At the end of the day, June 14, the last square inch of snow on the runway had been packed down. Five of us wearily plodded back to the N 25 at the southern end; but Riiser-Larsen stepped on ahead of us, carefully pacing the distance. At camp he greeted us with the closest approach to enthusiasm he had shown. He had made an error in his original calculation of the cake's diameter. We had a course not 400 meters long but 500 meters. The rest of us had been too dull witted, too sunk in fatalistic resignation to events, to notice the discrepancy between his estimate and the amount of work we had done.

Amundsen expressed the feelings of all of us.

"If somebody offered me a million kroner for those extra hundred meters," he said, "I would not accept."

After our evening mugs of chocolate, we took our places in the plane to taxi to the northern end, to be ready to take off into the wind early next morning, when the runway would be frozen. When about to start the engines, Riiser-Larsen suggested that instead of taxiing we try to fly. There was no telling how slippery this surface might prove to be. If we could get off now, why wait until morning? Amundsen and I nodded, and the pilot gave her the gun.

But the runway was soft from the day's thaw, and the strakes bit into it. The plane made no effort to rise. To lift, the wings needed mile-a-minute speed. We did, however, slide at thirty-six miles an hour, which was much faster than any speed we had attained before. When we stopped at the north end, Riiser-Larsen turned around to me and said: "I hope you are not disappointed, Ellsworth. We will do better next time."

I believed him. That night I had the outside watch. With my feet thrust loosely into the ski straps and a rifle slung over my shoulder on the chance that I might get a shot at a seal or wild goose, I shuffled round and round the big ice cake. Our night patrols were doubly anxious now, since the floe was beginning to show signs of the protracted thaw. Crevasses were opening in it here and there. Should a wide crack run across our fairway, it would be the supreme tragedy.

That night I had occasion to observe the solicitude and fidelity of Riiser-Larsen, his conscientious devotion to duty. While the others slept like the dead, several times our pilot drew himself up through the manhole in the plane's deck to observe the wind and feel the temperature. Weary as he must have been, responsibility for the morrow lay so heavily upon him that he could not sleep soundly.

Twice or more I visited the thermometer hanging on the side of the hull. We had our usual night drop in temperature—three Fahrenheit degrees of frost. As the sun moved down into the east, the breeze freshened from the south. Thus dawned, to speak of it that way, June 15, our Day of Decision, the day of our final trial.

Long before it was time for me to waken my comrades, Riiser-Larsen dropped down over the side of the hull. Together we inspected the runway. Yesterday's ruts left by our hull in the soft snow were now petrified grooves. The surface was crisp as a tile pavement. A truck would not have left a track in it.

So impatient was Riiser-Larsen to start that we woke everybody up ahead of time and started the primus stove to boil our chocolate. Riiser-Larsen kept urging us to hurry. The daily thaw was normally still two or three hours distant, but we shared an unreasoning dread that it might start earlier this morning. We gulped down breakfast and prepared for the great test.

The N 25 *had* to get off this time, that we all knew; and yet I think we all confidently expected her to. For now, for the first time, we stripped the ship of everything with which we could possibly dispense. Beside the runway we piled the expensive movie cameras, all the unexposed film, both rifles and one of the shotguns, all the ammunition except one hundred shells, both sledges and one of the folding canoes, half of our provisions, all the remaining skis —leaving only the light snowshoes aboard—even our field glasses. As an afterthought, we threw out our sealskin parkas and our stout ski boots, wearing only moccasins. In the mild weather the hull had long since dripped dry of the sea water taken in through its leaks. We could not have safely got rid of another ounce of weight.

It was not only for the sake of a take-off that we lightened the N 25. Riiser-Larsen was apprehensive about our fuel supply. We had burned plenty of gas during our various movements and take-off runs. It was questionable if we had enough to reach Spitzbergen. We could not afford one excess pound of weight, since it costs fuel to fly a pound six hundred miles.

We turned the ship south into the slightly quartering wind, and the hull slid easily on the packed frozen snow. Then we took our places for a long flight. Dietrichson, who was to do the navigation, got into the observer's place in the bow. So confident was he of success that he unfolded his charts, ready in the cockpit beside him. Amundsen took the co-pilot's seat beside Riiser-Larsen. This time I did not stay with the mechanics in the gondola. Whether I could not bear to see another disappointment or had a superstitious notion that it was bad luck to watch, I crawled back to Riiser-Larsen's sleeping quarters in the tail of the plane, where it was dark and I could see nothing.

The engines leaped into action. The hull moved, scratching and grating at first, then bumping—mighty bumps, spaced farther and farther apart. I did not need Omdal's shout, unintelligible in the tumult, to tell me that we were in the air. The bumping had stopped. Afterwards I found out that we took flight in those final million-kroner 100 meters. But then I did not care much. I experienced no particular elation but only a dull happiness when I felt the plane lift. We were all beyond sharp emotions.

I looked out through the manhole and saw that we were flying through thick fog, dark and clammy. From time to time during the next two hours I looked out again. Always the same fog. Sometimes we flew so low that we skimmed the ice for Dietrichson to make drift observations. It was a great job of blind flying the two airmen did in that fog, since for guidance they had only the magnetic compass, theretofore deemed useless in the Arctic because of its variations.

After a while I saw the manhole opening above me sharply bright. I looked out into clear sunshine. Below us was the fleecy ceiling of the fog bank, with the same double aureole following behind us and the jumping shadow of the plane in their common center. Up forward Amundsen was pointing the periscope toward the sun. I crawled back to my place. After a final day of punishing toil I had been on my feet all night, and I asked only to lie there torpid on the cold aluminum floor, too exhausted for true slumber.

The engines sang their steady song. Hour after hour, how many I neither knew nor cared, I lay there, my hairy, grimed, and salt-caked cheek pillowed on my arm. A confusion of shouting roused me, and I saw Omdal waving me forward. I crawled toward him.

"Land!" he yelled.

It shocked me to my senses.

"Spitzbergen?" I yelled back.

Omdal only shrugged his shoulders. But Feucht, still an image of gloom, yelled as if angry: "No Spitzbergen! No Spitzbergen!"

Again I stuck my head up through the manhole. Fog and ice were gone now, and below us tumbled a gray wind-flecked ocean. Off the nose of the plane, indistinct beneath the southern sun, was a faint shore line.

Something hit my moccasined foot. I drew down in and saw Omdal tossing cakes of chocolate at me. With safety in sight, our ration restrictions were off, and Amundsen broke open a carton of chocolate and distributed the cakes. I ate seven as fast as I could munch them down. As I squatted there, the engines cut off and began choking and backfiring in descent. Omdal gestured to me that we were landing, which meant that I must screw shut the roof deadlight to keep out spray. I treated myself first to a look. We were not at the shore, as I had supposed, but still some miles out, and as we dropped lower I could see that the ocean was rough. A little later I learned the reason for this maneuver. Even as the N 25 had had a forced landing near the Pole, so it was making another on the return. The stabilization rudders had jammed, and Riiser-Larsen preferred to taxi the rest of the distance rather than risk a dive.

I closed the deadlight, and the plane sat down roughly on the racing waves. The engines spoke again, but I was only regretting those seven cakes of chocolate. The light hull pitched like a cork on the combers, and in the airless dark tail I instantly became as seasick as I ever was in my life. For thirty-five minutes I had to endure this final misery, and then the plane taxied into still water.

We reached shore on our final spoonfuls of gas. Then we realized how much we owed to the skill at the plane's controls. Had Riiser-Larsen and Dietrichson not held a true course through those two hours of fog, we should probably have never come back.

We moored the seaplane in a little cave and then threw ourselves down on a flat rock, faces up to the sun. How good it was to feel the solid land again! Here there was not even danger of snow blindness. It was a different land than the one we left—not buried under snow now. Little auks and gulls screamed above our heads, in the fjords eider duck and geese were mating, the sunshine lay warm on greening moss and tundra.

Where were we? We took an observation by sextant which indicated that we were on the latitude of Spitzbergen, at any rate. To find our true position we should have to wait three hours, for an intersection line. While we lay on our rock, eating chocolate and oat biscuits, somebody yelled: "A boat!"

From behind a near-by point had appeared a little sealing vessel, heading out to sea. We shouted and waved our flag, but they did not see us, being engrossed, as we learned later, in the pursuit of a wounded walrus. We still had a modicum of gas, so we all piled into the plane and taxied after them. They soon discovered us, abandoned their walrus, and received us with every manifestation of joy.

Everybody was looking for us, they informed us—Norwegian government planes out of Kings Bay, Soviet ice ships farther east. They themselves had kept a lookout. We were now, they informed us, near North Cape, on that major island of the Spitzbergen group called North East Land—one hundred miles east of Kings Bay. Their sealing trip was over, and they were on their way back to Kings Bay, so we need only stay aboard.

We tried first to tow the N 25, but there was too much head-wind, and we beached her safely in a bay at North Cape. The tiny sealer was slow and took three days to reach Kings Bay, but we did not care. First we shaved and had the luxury of baths, even though they were baths out of pails. Then into clean, dry dungarees lent us by the sailors, and then into bunks to sleep, sleep, sleep. During the whole three days we woke up only to devour delicious seal steaks, smothered in onions, and omelets made from the eggs of the eider duck. And coffee—how good it tasted again!

We arrived at Kings Bay on June 18, exactly four weeks after our departure for the North. The aviators had sad news to break to me—my father had died in Florence on June 2. June 2! On that day we made the first of our unsuccessful attempts to fly from the frozen leads. At 5 P.M., the hour when Father passed away in his flower-girt villa, we were in our places in the N 25 looking at a different sort of scene—the dreary fog-hung expanse of Arctic snow and ice ridges. A moment later our plane was to lurch down the ramp and plunge its nose through the 8-inch ice of the lead.

There is little more I need tell about our polar flight. At Kings Bay, where we found the remnants of our support party, the wireless buzzed, the government at Oslo sent official congratulations, as New York papers headlined: AMUNDSEN AND ELLSWORTH BACK SAFE IN SPITZBERGEN. We remained at Kings Bay for a week—until the N 25 could be brought down from North Cape and loaded aboard the coal company's freighter Skollern.

We sailed on this vessel on June 25 and nine days later—the fourth of July—landed at Horten, the Norwegian naval base, not far from Oslo. This we did in order to fly the N 25 into Oslo next day to receive an official welcome. I wish I could describe that welcome and what it meant to me. I was entirely unprepared for its fervor. Escorted by Norwegian navy and army planes, we took off in the N 25—could this be the same ship that had so recently battled the Arctic ice?—and flew up the fjord. At the entrance to the harbor we dropped to the water and taxied, and then it began.

Past a long file of warships we taxied—naval vessels of Norway and other nations, including thirteen British battleships, their blue-jackets lined at attention on their decks. The quays and wharves were black with humanity. Whistles of all sorts of river craft howled and shrieked; airplanes circled overhead. The guns of the fort began booming a salute, and a great throng was waiting at the landing.

This spectacle and the thought that my father had not lived to hear about it swept me off my feet with emotion. The tears rolled down my face. Even the stolid Norwegians were affected; and as for Amundsen, he wrote later that it was the best memory of his life.

It continued on shore—the wildly waving and cheering throng, the frock-coated and uniformed committee of welcome, the triumphal procession through the city's streets, the state reception, and all crowned by the dinner at the castle given us by their majesties themselves. It was an intoxicating draught for one who had never known celebrity or the feeling of being treated as an important personage. It created an appetite that could never be once and for all appeased.

One or two things to add occur to me. In scientific results the expedition, though it failed of its original objective, had been well worth while. We made important observations of climatic and meteorological conditions near the North Pole, measured the depth of the ocean there, studied the drift of ice. We found out that summer flying conditions are favorable at the Pole, so long as an airplane does not land. More important still, our two routes had cut from the white zone a segment of 120,000 square miles. After our flight, geographers could say positively that on the European side of the North Polar Sea there is no land.

Amundsen's luck in the polar regions was proverbial. It was luck that saved him from the uncharted reef during his northwest passage, luck that gave him good weather at the South Pole in December, whereas in January, ordinarily a better month, the blizzards overwhelmed Scott and his party. And this same luck held during our polar flight. Consider these circumstances:

The engine of the N 25 cut out and forced a landing when we were over the first open water we had seen in the polar pack.

The two planes, landing three miles apart, drifted together, enabling us to salvage the gasoline of the N 24.

Our fuel lasted just to the shore of Spitzbergen; we could not have flown or taxied another mile.

Finally, the presence of a sealing vessel, right where we came to shore, saved us a hard and possibly disastrous trip, since between North Cape and Kings Bay there are nothing but impassable glaciers.

Is it any wonder that men who go into dangerous and desolate regions are prone to develop a blind faith in providence and to find mystic meaning in coincidences and similarities that others might pass unnoticed?

As we came down the Norwegian coast in the Skollern, Amundsen and I sat lazily on the collier's afterdeck one morning, content to bask in the July sunshine and gaze indolently into the fjords as the steamer passed their mouths. My sea chest was on the deck near us, and Amundsen idly studied its marks.

"L. E.," he said in a musing way.

"Yes," I replied, mildly wondering, "my initials."

"Yours," said the master explorer, a ghost of a smile playing on his lips, "and Leif Ericson's."

That I took for my diploma. Apprenticeship was over.

XIV START OF THE NORGE

BUT THE MYSTERY of the North remained a mystery. Our flight of 1925 had carried us higher on the European side than any other men had ever penetrated, but we could regard it only as a pathfinding effort—the pioneer demonstration of the practicability of the heavier-than-air flying machine as a vehicle of exploration in the polar regions. Soon the planes of others—Wilkins, Byrd, and Mawson among them—would be humming over Arctic and Antarctic snows; but Amundsen and I were first to venture with airplanes into the unknown at either end of the earth.

Beyond that horizon which we had almost seen, on the American side of the North Pole, lay a million square miles of the earth's surface, unexplored. What was in there? Land, everyone thought —Crocker Land, Harris Land, Keenan's Land, call it what you would. It was all hypothetical, all a theory.

Before we left Kings Bay on our way south, Amundsen and I had agreed to attack the Arctic unknown during the following year, 1926, on a truly grand scale. After our experience in the leads, we turned favorably toward the lighter-than-air ship, the dirigible balloon. Its advantages for the Arctic were immense flying range and ability to hover at low altitudes to allow explorers to make their observations without actually landing on the ice.

Because of initial cost and expense of operation, a German Zeppelin was out of the question for us. Riiser-Larsen, who took part in our discussions and who knew as much about existing European aircraft as any man alive, suggested the type of dirigible which Colonel Umberto Nobile was then building and flying for the Italian government. It was small enough to be within the means of a private expedition yet had almost the cruising range of a Zeppelin, and it was strong, airworthy, and easy to handle. The Italian airship N 1, which Nobile was then navigating, had attracted the attention of the aviation world.

I could promise to make my fair contribution to this ambitious project, and we struck hands on it. Thus was born the Amundsen-Ellsworth-Nobile Expedition, an enterprise which eventually drew in the governments of both Norway and Italy.

I had to hurry back home to settle my affairs, and Amundsen was coming soon to lecture in the United States. Before we broke up in Oslo, however, we sent Riiser-Larsen to Italy to see Nobile and negotiate for the purchase of the N 1. We had more than a little doubt that Premier Mussolini would sell the ship to us at all.

Accordingly, we were both surprised and delighted to learn that not only would Mussolini sell the airship to us for a transpolar flight but would do so on most advantageous terms—an equivalent price in lire of $75,000 with an agreement to repurchase the ship from us for $46,000, if we could return it in good condition. It amounted to little more than a charter and made the net cost of the dirigible to us considerably less than the price of one Dornier-Wal seaplane. The only concession Signor Mussolini asked in return was that for the honor of Italy five members of the old crew of the N 1 be signed on for the polar flight.

In Oslo we had also discussed the question of a pilot, in the event that we could secure the N 1. To Amundsen and me the ideal man seemed to be Nobile himself. Since he had both built and navigated her, he therefore must know more about her capabilities than any other man. The officials in Rome seemed a little surprised when we suggested Nobile as pilot, we learned afterwards. We asked Nobile his price. He named a figure, and we accepted it. Up to this time, it should be noted, we had no other thought than that the expedition would be known as the Amundsen-Ellsworth Expedition.

These preliminaries arranged, Amundsen approached the Aero Club of Norway for its participation in the enterprise and secured it on the understanding that $90,000 toward the cost of the expedition be raised in America. The Aero Club bore all the other costs, except that Italy supplied our navigational equipment. I was never afterwards able to get the exact expense account from the Aero Club, nor did Amundsen ever know to the penny what the expedition cost. But the Aero Club shouldered its full share. Not the least of its expenses was the construction of a hangar and mooring mast at Kings Bay, Spitzbergen, and the shipment of the necessary refill of hydrogen gas to that point.

No sooner had the Aero Club come into the picture and made our expedition an official enterprise than Nobile raised his price as pilot to $11,000 for the voyage. The Aero Club agreed to the increase, since it was now managing all the business details.

While the N 1 was being conditioned in Rome for the Arctic,

Amundsen came to America. I went down to Washington to hear him deliver the lecture that inaugurated his tour. The chairman was a young man destined to become much more famous in polar exploration than he was then. He was Commander Richard E. Byrd, a navy pilot, who had recently returned from the Arctic after serving as head of the aviation unit of Donald B. MacMillan's expedition in Greenland.

After the lecture Byrd confided to us his plan to continue the search for the evanescent Crocker Land the following spring as an independent explorer, using airplanes. The news of our airship expedition had been announced, so Byrd knew we would be at Spitzbergen. He asked us if we had any objection to his using Kings Bay at the same time as a preliminary base from which to fly to the north coast of Greenland, where he planned to set up the permanent base for his search.

Said Amundsen heartily: "We will welcome you with open arms."

Byrd asked numerous questions about Spitzbergen. We told him he could expect good ice in the fjord for a take-off until the end of May.

While Amundsen was on his tour, in the name of the expedition I signed a contract with the New York *Times* for the exclusive story of the flight across the Pole, the price being $50,000. We dealt with the *Times* alone because of its long identification with feats of mechanical flight and exploration of all sorts.

Later Amundsen dropped into New York and put his name to the contract, too. Scarcely bothering to read this document—or, if I did read it, it made no impression.on me—I folded my copy and put it in my pocket. I carried it, still unread, across the Pole to Alaska. Then I read it! Little had I realized what it obligated me to do.

In the winter I went over to Europe to complete the legal details of the transfer to myself of the title to Barbarossa's castle in Switzerland, Schloss Lenzburg, which my father had bequeathed to me, and at the break of spring met Amundsen in Oslo upon his return from America. There was no time, though, for another

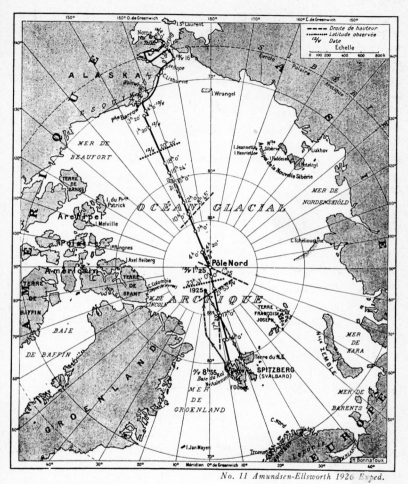

No. 11 Amundsen-Ellsworth 1926 Exped.

Route of the Norge across the Polar Sea, May 11–13, 1926.
Also Route of 1925 Flight.

ELLSWORTH'S FLIGHT BRIDGING ANTARCTICA FOR THE FIRST TIME

Drawn by Albert H. B[...]

jamboree at Boenefjord. A telegram was there, requesting us both to come to Rome at once to take part in the formal acceptance of the N 1.

Mussolini likes to do things with a flourish, and he was dedicating the polar airship with ceremony—a national event, in fact, with a protocol and speeches. We arrived on the eve of the celebration. As we stepped from our railway carriage in Rome a messenger handed Amundsen a telegram. He tore it open, and we read startling news. It was signed officially by the Aero Club of Norway; and it stated that unless we—Amundsen and I—could at once raise $25,000 to pay the insurance on the airship, there would be no dedication ceremony next day. The Aero Club itself could not so quickly produce such a sum, yet it refused to accept custody of the airship unless it were insured.

This was a pretty state of affairs. Entirely unaware of the hitch over the insurance, the Italian government was preparing for the ceremony next day, yet it looked as if we might have to call it off. However, I got busy with the cable to America and saved the day.

Next morning the machinery of preparation for the flight grated again. President Thommassen, of the Aero Club, came to Amundsen and me in our hotel with the request that we consent to add Nobile's name to the expedition. "For political reasons," he said mysteriously. He hastened to explain that such a change would in no way affect the leadership in the North.

Amundsen turned in his chair, faced me, and said: "You must decide, Ellsworth. For myself, I don't care."

Not without reluctance I agreed to the change in title. As soon as Thommassen had left, we sent for Nobile and told him what we had done. We explained that, of course, as our pilot his opinion must always be considered, but if any difference of judgment arose during the flight, the decision must be left to a vote of the three of us. This gave control to Amundsen and me. Nobile seemed to think this might constrict his powers as pilot and was emphatic in his insistence, but we would have it no other way. We went into the North under that arrangement; and when a difference of

opinion did actually arise there, as I shall tell later on, Amundsen
and I voted against Nobile.

After this interview, Amundsen said to me, chuckling: "If the
weather ahead looks good to us, it ought to look good to Nobile,
too." Amundsen always feared that Nobile might want to head
back to Spitzbergen after starting on the flight.

Thus, with everything settled in advance, we went ahead with
the dedication ceremony that afternoon—March 29, 1926. Mussolini
made an impressive speech. President Thommassen replied in acceptance. Mrs Riiser-Larsen broke a bottle of champagne over the
N 1's bow and rechristened her Norge, the Scandinavian name of
Norway. To the rolling of drums the Italian flag came down and
the Norwegian flag went up. The joint Norwegian-Italian crew
had already given the reconditioned airship a trial run along the
Mediterranean coast.

Great changes had been made in the Norge during the winter,
the main effort having been to get rid of all unnecessary weight
and thus increase her fuel capacity. She had been a veritable air
yacht with a big luxurious cabin. This cabin had been replaced
with another, much smaller, which was little more than a light
cage with canvas and transparent celluloid walls. The nose of the
ship had been strengthened and ringed for operation from a mooring mast.

The Norge, a semirigid type, was simply a skeleton of three-
quarter-inch steel tubing encased in an envelope of strong rubber-
ized fabric. She was 348 feet long. Her inner hydrogen cells had a
capacity of 672,000 cubic feet of lifting gas—about one third that of
the British R 34, which had recently crossed the Atlantic. To accommodate the cabin, the lower keel was broken, well forward,
and the cabin was roofless and integrated with the envelope. Thus,
one in the cabin could look up into the rigging beneath the gas
cells, or could stand and see up and down the whole length of the
keel. A light duck walk rested on the bottom tube of the keel,
and forward there was a duralumin ladder leading up to the air
valves in the space between the envelope and the gas cells.

Power was supplied by three Maybach engines of 230 H.P. each, two of them mounted amidships, side by side, the other aft below the keel. Each engine was enclosed in a nacelle in which a mechanic could ride protected from wind. The keel normally supported thirty fuel tanks connected with the engine nacelles by copper tubes. All oil tanks were insulated to prevent freezing. The radio equipment, specially designed by the Marconi company, was elaborate, both for receiving and sending. Power was supplied by an air propeller outside the cabin connected by a bevel drive to an inside dynamo feeding a storage battery. The Norge had a normal cruising range of 3,500 miles at 50 m.p.h. She had a useful load capacity of about eight tons.

After receiving her, Amundsen and I went back to Oslo, with the coffee-and-rolls detour to Copenhagen I have mentioned. On April 10 I ceremoniously accepted from U.S. Minister Swenson, acting on behalf of our President, an American flag to be dropped at the North Pole. On the seventeenth, at midnight, Amundsen and I sailed from Tromsö on a boat we knew well, the coal company's supply steamer Knut Skaaluren. This time the North Atlantic behaved, and we had a smooth passage. In fact, we did not even see any ice until we reached Kings Bay, where there was quite a bit of heavy stuff jammed in against the wharf. It took the Skaaluren six or eight hours to break this out, and at 3 A.M., April 22, we tied up at the dock.

It was a different Kings Bay than we had seen at the start of our 1925 flight. Then the fjord was covered with a sheet of ice that would have supported a steam roller. Now there was only dimpling water. On the other hand, the snow was much deeper on shore. Drifts banked to the eaves of the coal miners' cottages. Mountains, glaciers, and everything were buried in snow.

There were other changes. That of most flattering interest to us was a monolith erected by the people of Spitzbergen to commemorate our 1925 flight, the names of the six participants carved in the stone. I was also informed that a Spitzbergen mountain had been named for me. But the most conspicuous new feature of the scene was a huge green hangar to house the Norge when she should arrive. It dwarfed the coal company's plant. It was simply a strongly braced framework covered with canvas, which was painted to make it impervious to the wind. Inasmuch as the hangar's only purpose was to protect the airship from wind gusts, it had been left roofless.

Near it had been erected a mooring mast for the dirigible. Around the hangar were sheds filled with food, gasoline drums, and other supplies; and from this installation a donkey railroad, running through high embankments of snow, led down to the wharf. A day or so after our arrival, the expedition's base ship, the Heimdal, steamed into the fjord. The Heimdal had been busy all fall and winter carrying materials and workmen between Norway and Spitzbergen and also freighting the steel and cables for a special mooring mast erected at Vadsö, in northeastern Norway, and another put up at Oslo. As a result of the hard service she had seen, she arrived at Kings Bay with a damaged boiler.

A supply ship, three mooring masts, a hangar and railroad, to say nothing of the dirigible itself and the salaries and wages paid over nearly a year, indicate that our expedition was costly. The gross cost, in fact, ran to nearly five hundred thousand dollars; but there was a return of more than half of this amount in the sale of press rights and motion pictures, the resale of the Norge and other equipment, and the proceeds from the official book of the flight and Amundsen's subsequent lectures. As a result, the expedition's net cost was low. The Aero Club of Norway had complete charge of all financial arrangements and served as business manager of the flight.

As we looked at the open water of the fjord, we remembered our promise to Commander Byrd of a different kind of bay. Would he think we had deliberately deceived him? Then we remembered that all during the winter of 1925 the coast of Spitzbergen had been open, only to close up just before our arrival in the spring. Perhaps it would do the same thing again. It did. On April 28 a great storm broke, with a whipping gale and snow driving thickly ahead of it. The thermometer dropped down almost to zero Fahrenheit. Then the ice from the north moved in and jammed the bay full of churning floes.

On April 29, when the air had cleared, though the gale still blew, the SS Chantier, Commander Byrd's base ship, arrived at the edge of the shore ice. On board were Byrd himself, his pilot, Floyd Bennett, and their Fokker monoplane, the Josephine Ford. Inasmuch as the newspaper dispatches of the time intimated that there was ill feeling between our two expeditions and that we tried to impede Byrd, I wish to state exactly what happened.

The damaged Heimdal was tied up at the wharf, occupying the entire space. Byrd radioed that he wanted to come in with the Chantier and start unloading. The officers of the Heimdal said it would be foolhardy to move their disabled vessel out into the ice during the storm. We wirelessed that information to Byrd, and the Chantier stood outside until the storm moderated. When it was safe to do so, we moved away and made room for her.

Three days of intermittent blizzards had buried our railroad under five feet of snow. It took our gang several days to shovel out. The wind-driven floes had packed against the shores. Cold weather continued, and down the middle of the ice-locked fjord a smooth strip froze solidly, giving Byrd the runway we had guaranteed him.

Meanwhile, the Norge with its international crew had been plying up from Rome. Because of rough weather to be expected on the North Atlantic in spring, the airship followed an inland route. The first leg of the voyage carried her to Pulham, England, where there was a mooring mast. On this flight Major Scott, commander of the R 34 on its transatlantic voyage, served as assistant pilot. Next, the Norge flew to our own mooring mast at Oslo. The third leg took her to Gatchina, near Leningrad, where the Soviet government had placed a shed at our disposal. Riiser-Larsen and Nobile had gone over this whole route together in advance. The Norge reached Gatchina April 15 and waited there, Kings Bay being not quite ready for her.

Among other things, the Aero Club, which had charge of all general arrangements, had provided us with an elaborate weather-reporting service—the best any polar expedition had had up to that time. It even included an expert on electrical static—Dr

Behounek, of Prague. Our chief meteorologist was Dr Malmgren, a Norwegian. Malmgren was an Arctic type. He had gone on so many scientific expeditions into the North and had lived so many years of his life in danger and solitude that he had developed chronic polar nerves. During the crossing he would sit in his place in the crowded car looking out of his window, oblivious to everything but his job. To get his attention in the noise of the engines, I leaned over once or twice and touched his shoulder. Each time he jumped as if I had fired off a gun beside his ear. Poor Malmgren was one of those who perished in the Italia disaster two years later.

On a flight such as ours, over the top of the world in an airship, the weather would be perhaps the most vital factor in either success or failure. It was therefore necessary that the expedition have the most expert weather bureau possible to procure. It operated in two sections. Malmgren himself flew with the Norge. His assistants remained at Kings Bay gathering and relaying weather reports from all over the earth. As these came to the airship by radio, Malmgren corrected a weather map on a small blackboard attached to the wall of the radio room behind his seat. Thus we always had an up-to-the-minute picture of the weather which the navigator had only to turn around to see. The ground force used the radio of the Heimdal, which was more powerful than the shore station at Kings Bay. When we were in flight, they sent messages to us direct, but these same signals were also picked up and relayed by the powerful Norwegian wireless station at Stavanger. I may note here that until the airship's radio iced up when approaching the Alaskan coast, all these messages came through regularly. At every moment we knew what weather to expect ahead.

By the middle of April this service was functioning at Kings Bay. Twice a day the expedition was receiving weather reports from a ring of stations surrounding the Arctic—from Alaska, Canada, Iceland, Norway, Russia, and Siberia. The mimeograph was turning out weather maps of a type never before produced—intercontinental. Here in America we see weather charts with storms reaching from Georgia to the Maritime Provinces, or a high-pressure area extending from Alaska to the Great Lakes. At Kings Bay our maps showed "highs" embracing Alaska, the North Pole, and the Ural Mountains; "lows" running from Greenland to Archangel, Russia.

Though the weather was still tempestuous, the chart looked so favorable that on May 2 we radioed Nobile and Riiser-Larsen at Leningrad to start north. The Norge droned up through Finland and Lapland to our mooring mast at Vadsö, Norway. Here again a message reached her to proceed. Early on the morning of May 7 the big white ship appeared at the mouth of the fjord and floated up the bay over the ice as sedately as any liner. It was a little gusty that morning, but everybody took a hand with the ropes, and soon the Norge was safely housed in its canvas hangar.

We exulted in her flight North, which was nothing short of triumphal. At a bad season of the year she had flown over nine countries and five seas considered to be the most windy and foggy on the globe, had covered 5,000 miles in 103 hours of flying time, had battled snow, fog, and strong head and side winds, always moving into sinking temperatures, and had come through on time and without a serious mishap. One of her engines broke a shaft as she neared Kings Bay; but, since she could make her speed with two engines, that did not delay her. After this demonstration our confidence was complete that she could make the much shorter voyage to Alaska.

It was necessary to repair the engine; and, while waiting for the moment of perfect weather across the whole Arctic Basin, we made a final change in her. She had flown up from Rome carrying four water-ballast tanks. We replaced these with as many fuel tanks of equal weight, since gasoline would serve as well as water for ballast. Thus equipped, she carried nearly seven tons of gasoline, giving her a range of 4,400 miles—twice the distance to Alaska. Also at Kings Bay we impregnated the water of the engine's cooling systems with glycerin, to prevent freezing in the radiators.

With two expeditions, one a big one, preparing for the Far

North, Kings Bay had awakened from its winter sleep into the most activity it had ever known. Social amenities went on. We entertained the members of Byrd's party on the Heimdal, they entertained us on the Chantier, the coal company officials entertained us both on shore. Up to this time we still thought Byrd was planning to fly to Greenland to institute his search for Crocker Land.

Early one evening Byrd came alone to us on the Heimdal.

"Gentlemen," he announced, "tomorrow morning I am taking off and flying straight to the North Pole."

Amundsen fairly bored him with his eyes as he answered: "That is all right with us."

We both wished him luck but were appalled to discover that he had come up to Kings Bay utterly unprepared to meet the possible contingency of a forced landing on the Arctic ice. That they might not be completely lost if compelled to land, we supplied Byrd and Bennett with snowshoes. I gave Byrd my own pair. Next day, after Bennett had failed to lift the Fokker, with its heavy load of gas, off its runway, we seized the opportunity to take our own carpenter off his work for the Norge and have him build a light sledge for Byrd's plane. In his book *Skyward*, Byrd acknowledged our aid to his flight.

The following morning—May 9—the roar of an airplane awakened both Amundsen and me at two o'clock. We rushed out of our cottage just in time to see the Josephine Ford climbing up above our heads. She passed inland, gained the requisite altitude, and disappeared over the north wall of the fjord. The sound of her engines quickly faded away.

I would be less than honest if I maintained that Byrd's North Pole flight was not an annoyance. As for his reaching the Pole first, we didn't care a rap about that, speaking strictly from the explorer's standpoint. Not the North Pole but what lay beyond it was our goal. Nobile, however, grew excited when he learned of Byrd's plan and urged us to forestall him.

"I can have the Norge ready in six hours," he pleaded.

Amundsen vetoed him with an uplifted hand.

"Not at all," he said. "This is not a race but a scientific voyage to Alaska. We will wait for our weather."

The weather at Spitzbergen was ideal by this time, but the messages from Alaska were still unfavorable.

Nevertheless, we had reason to be disgruntled. In the first place, Byrd's flight divided the publicity from Spitzbergen. The Norge expedition was costing a fortune. We needed to cash in every penny we could get as its result. We wanted the complete attention of the public, so that afterwards it would buy our book, see our picture, and attend our lectures, the proceeds of all of which went back into the Aero Club's till. Our expedition was conceived ahead of Byrd's, to which indeed we were extending the hospitality of Kings Bay, and we felt that we deserved the first chance.

And there was a more serious aspect. Suppose Byrd were forced down on the ice pack, what would it do to the Norge expedition? Primarily and naturally we wanted Byrd to return safely for his own sake; but if he did not, nothing was more certain than that the Norge would have to search for him. Unless we could find him quickly, our expedition would have to be postponed for one year, at a great loss of money. There was a critical period of only three or four weeks in which we would have to make our flight, if at all. After June 1 fog blankets the whole Arctic Basin for the rest of the summer; and fog, by preventing us from seeing the regions over which we flew, would nullify most of the scientific value of such a voyage.

Therefore, it was with a double sense of relief that that same day, at 5:30 P.M., we heard the crescendo of beating propellers and saw the Josephine Ford glide over the rim of the fjord and come to a graceful landing exactly on the spot whence it had taken off. Curiously enough, Amundsen and I were the only ones out on the ice to welcome Byrd back, his own people on the Chantier not having heard his approach. There was no need for us to ask if they had reached the Pole, for the plane had been gone for exactly the time that flight took. We were genuinely overjoyed to be the first to congratulate Byrd and Bennett on a most courageous and skillful journey, one that justly went into the annals of aviation as historic.

The two weary flyers went to bed at once, but next evening we celebrated with a dinner, exchanging presents with each other. Byrd gave me the polar-bear pants and sealskin mittens he had worn in the plane. He had bought the mittens the previous year from Lomen Brothers in Nome, Alaska, ordering them by mail. After our flight in the Norge, I went into the Lomen shop in Nome to make a purchase, and the merchants at once recognized the mittens. They were greatly stirred up to learn that the mitts had been twice above the North Pole since they left the showcase.

The day Byrd flew to the Pole our weathermen told us that the weather over the whole polar basin was ideal, except for fog along the Alaskan coast. What we wanted was an anticyclone on the west side of the Pole, a condition that would give us tail winds between the North Pole and Alaska, and we would also appreciate high pressure and low temperature at Spitzbergen, conditions that would allow us to pack the maximum of hydrogen in the gas cells and thus increase the Norge's lift. Since the ship had to carry a useful load of ten and one-half tons, including the gasoline, the pilot wanted all the spare hydrogen he could get to play with when maneuvering the airship from higher to lower altitudes.

On May 9 we had exactly what we wanted in weather. The north European "high" still persisted, giving Kings Bay clear, cold weather. A new "high" had built up across the North Pole, with a stretch from Nova Zembla, Russia, to Alberta, Canada. There was a storm center in the Bering Sea, though how intense we did not know. When we reached it, we discovered that it was severe. Though May 9 was Sunday, our gang worked all day putting gasoline aboard the Norge and filling the lifting-gas cells.

On May 10 the pressure distribution continued as it had been, and both our own weather service and the Norwegian bureau at Tromsö advised us to start. Point Barrow still reported fog, but we hoped that might clear away before our arrival. On the afternoon of May 10 the Norge was ready, and at Commander Byrd's celebration dinner that evening we announced that we would start soon after midnight. During the evening, however, the wind got up again, making it risky to take the Norge from the hangar. We postponed the start until morning, and everybody turned in fully dressed and ready to go whenever the wind dropped. At 7 A.M., May 11, we were routed out of bed. We ate big breakfasts, put on our flying clothes, and went to the hangar. At half-past eight the airship, with engines running to warm them, was drawn safely from the hangar. We shook hands with our friends and went aboard, sixteen of us.

Of the sixteen, six, including General Nobile (he had been promoted to the rank of general of the air), were Italians. All the rest were Norwegians, except myself. The Italians Cecioni, chief engineer, and Caratti and Pomella, assistants, rode in the three engine nacelles. Two Italian riggers, Alessandrini and Arduino, perched on the keel above. With them was our old friend of the 1925 adventure, Omdal, serving as motor expert. At times during the flight the two Italian riggers napped in the shallow trough of the keel—a most precarious thing, it seemed to me, since if one even tossed in sleep he might have rolled out and torn through the canvas skin below to drop to a frightful death. Omdal rode on the keel to be quickly available if an engine misbehaved.

Besides Amundsen and Riiser-Larsen, the Norwegians were: Horgen and Wisting, helmsmen; Gottwaldt and Fritz Strom-Johnson, radiomen; Ramm, journalist, and Malmgren.

Lieutenant Horgen, the reader may remember, was our reserve pilot in 1925. When Dietrichson was unavailable for the Norge voyage, Horgen got the place. Oscar Wisting had been with Amundsen on many expeditions. I have already noted that he was one who accompanied Amundsen on the overland dash to the South Pole. Strom-Johnson was the radio operator on the Heimdal. Olonkin, who had been "Sparks" on the Maud and was originally engaged as assistant to Gottwaldt, flew up from Rome on the Norge but at Kings Bay developed an abscess of the ear. Strom-Johnson volunteered to serve in his place. Frederick Ramm was

also a veteran of our 1925 expedition, having been the reporter
who covered the news of it from Kings Bay for the Norwegian
press. Now he was in the Norge as correspondent for the New
York *Times,* sending his dispatches to Oslo, where they were
forwarded to America. His message from 90° N. was the first news
dispatch ever printed containing the words "The North Pole" in
the date line.

Oscar Wisting needs more than a single line of description, since
he was another "character" of the North—a more remarkable one
than Malmgren. He was the master of the Maud when Amundsen
negotiated the northeast passage in that vessel, and afterwards he
continued on with Dr Sverdrup in his explorations. At the end of
1925 Wisting, though he was married, had been away from home
seven years, much of that time drifting in the Arctic.

Finally the Maud got back and Wisting went home at last. At
his house he found a telegram from Riiser-Larsen asking him to
come to Rome and join the Norge crew. Wisting obeyed. After
seven years of voyaging, he saw his family only one day and then
was off for another year of it.

He was the most bashful man I ever knew. He had great difficulty in speaking even to his friends, and before a stranger he
turned into a mute. There was a story about him—perhaps only a
legend—that he received a medal from the King of Norway *sitting
down.* If there is any point of etiquette insisted upon in royal
courts, it is to stand in the presence of a king, especially when the
king is about to pin a decoration on one. When the king entered
the chamber to honor Wisting, that veteran's legs refused to
function. King Haakon at once understood the inarticulate hero's
difficulty and went through the ceremony as if nothing were
amiss.

Oscar Wisting died since I began to write these recollections
(December 4, 1936). He had been pensioned off as curator of the
Fram, which had been turned into a floating museum at Oslo.

When sitting in the cabin at the start, one could look up into
the twilight of the envelope under the gas cells and see what
resembled the loft of a storage house. All our supplies were there,

lashed to the braces or to the tubular metal of the keel—tents and sleeping bags, skis and snowshoes, a big canvas boat, guns and ammunition. Conspicuous were the three flags—Norwegian, Italian, and American—to be dropped at the Pole. Our food supplies were there, too. We carried the same diet we had had aboard the planes in 1925—pemmican, chocolate, oat biscuits, malted milk—nearly a thousand pounds of it, allowing a pound a day per man for sixty days. In the car itself we had only, besides the insulated cask of greasy meat balls I mentioned, two or three thermos flasks of hot coffee apiece and individual cold lunches packed by the faithful Berta, Superintendent Knutsen's housekeeper.

This, though there was no help for it, was a most faulty way of loading an expeditionary airship. A better way would have been to increase the size of the cabin and pack all Arctic supplies in with the passengers. Had the Norge been driven down to the ice, the collision would have sheared off the car, and the envelope, rid of our weight, would have bounded into the air, taking with it all food, travel necessities, and everything else we needed to support life. That was precisely what happened to Nobile's dirigible Italia two years later, when some of the survivors of the crash died of starvation.

The cabin of the Norge, a basket framework floored and covered with canvas, was but thirty feet long and six feet wide. Canvas partitions divided it into three compartments—the pilothouse forward, a central room for the navigator-captain, observers, and weather service, and a radio room aft. These partitions, however, were little more than suggestions, wide arched doorways cut in them giving a view from one end of the car to the other. A corner of the radio cubicle was curtained off as a toilet.

On the walls hung portraits of King Haakon and Queen Maud which Amundsen had had on the Fram in Antarctica. There was also a picture of the Virgin, which the Italians installed. The Pope gave the Italian members of the crew a special audience in Rome before their departure and blessed for them medallion pictures of the Madonna, which they wore on chains around their necks. Most of them also wore bracelets with gold identification tags. For a good-luck piece, on the wall hung, pressed between panes of glass, a four-leaf clover given to the expedition by Major Scott, the British dirigible pilot.

We had all been coached in advance in the safety rules for the flight, and a copy of these rules was pinned up in the cabin. Nothing was ever to be thrown overboard. The propellers were all aft of the car and, when spinning, might be shattered by even a small object hitting them. No one could walk on the keel gangway except on rubber soles, for fear of striking sparks in an atmosphere of gasoline vapor and escaping hydrogen. No smoking, of course. For hot food we must rely entirely on the coffee and soup in the thermos bottles. We carried primus stoves, but they were in the rigging, to be used only if we were forced down.

To spare every ounce of weight we could for the fuel, we all agreed in advance not to carry any extra clothing or personal effects beyond what could be put into an ordinary rucksack. Our riggers, for instance, dressed in overalls and canvas sneakers, though they had warm flying clothes over them. I wore only slacks, flannel shirt, and sweater, but over them I had on Byrd's polar-bear trousers and my own reindeer parka. Most of us in the cabin had on ordinary town shoes, but in the cabin were big canvas overshoes filled with senna grass into which we could thrust our feet. Nevertheless, the temperature remaining low during the entire flight, we all suffered more or less from cold, especially when in'fog. When the sun shone it warmed the canvas sides of the car a little.

Having made such sacrifices, taking with us not even an extra pair of socks apiece, we were rather startled to see General Nobile climb aboard, carrying his little terrier Titina done up in a dog sweater. Titina was the only female being aboard on the flight. She stayed most of the time under her master's sleeping bag in the folding armchair in the pilothouse—the one chair in the cabin. But Titina really behaved very well—as well as you could expect of a dog cooped up in a tiny crowded space for three days and nights.

After Nobile boarded the Norge, the rest of us came on. Though we had succeeded in raising the useful-load capacity of the ship up to almost eleven tons, with all weights being estimated we knew we were figuring very closely. The original plan was to carry nine-teen men, including five Italian riggers; but since the principal service of the riggers was to assist in a landing, they were not in-dispensable. After ten of us were in the cabin, the engineers in their nacelles and Omdal aboard, the lines in the hands of the ground crew began to sag a little. Alessandrini and Arduino, the riggers, climbed in, and the ropes went limp in the groundmen's hands. The airship was in exact equilibrium. We therefore closed the cabin door, leaving behind three riggers who had flown up from Rome.

Every man now took the place assigned to him. Nobile's seat was in the bow at the port side of the pilothouse. Behind him was a control board with signal wires to the engines and cords running to the hydrogen exhaust valves and ballonets. Across from Nobile was Horgen at the wheel of the lateral rudder, controlling direc-tion. Behind Horgan sat Wisting at the elevator helm, in control of climbing or descent.

Riiser-Larsen's place was on the starboard side of the middle compartment, where he had a little table for his maps and cal-culations. On the floor at his feet were his sextant and other navigational instruments. A slot cut in the middle of the floor accommodated the drift indicator. Malmgren, as I have stated, was at the back end of this compartment, his blackboard weather map on the partition behind him. Amundsen, Ramm and I sat in the other three places here, changing about as we pleased. I say sat, but actually there were only three or four folding camp stools in the car. We stood up, squatted on our heels or cross-legged, sat on ruck-sacks, or even sprawled on the floor, when we could find leg room. There was little comfort. The two wireless men in their booth aft, however, had stools and narrow shelves for tables.

The morning had advanced so far that the sun began to warm the balloon, and the hydrogen cells, pumped full at night tempera-ture, became overinflated. Nobile released gas, and the ship lost lift. A pull at some cords dumped the contents of several sandbags suspended under the cabin, and the handlers' ropes once more tautened. Everything was ready. The idling engines were shut down completely; and at 8:55 A.M. Nobile shouted in Italian from his window: "Let go the ropes!" An instant later Riiser-Larsen repeated the order from his side in Scandinavian, and slowly and without a sound the great airship began to rise.

The morning had brought a flat calm, and our ascent was almost perpendicular. Nobile dumped more sand, and the movement accelerated. It was so smooth, so even, as to suggest planetary motion. We were not rising; we were poised, and the world was falling away from us as if lowered by hydraulic power. The walls of the fjord leisurely went downward past us. Familiar faces, uplifted toward us, grew indistinct and then unrecognizable. From behind the fjord mountains rose up, glaciers and infinite snow fields glittering in the sun. Kings Bay became a toy town set in an immense white plain.

Then came a phenomenon for which we were not prepared. Swarms of gulls and other polar birds flew out from their rookeries in the cliffs to inspect this huge new cousin of the air. The air vibrated with thousands of flashing wings and shrill, excited cries. In the stillness of our cabin we could hear the roaring of the Josephine Ford far below, as Byrd and Floyd Bennett took off to bear us company during the first stage of our journey.

We rose above the fjord, and once more the North spread out under our eyes. The Byrd plane climbed up to us, its engines scaring away our feathered escort. Signal bells rang, and the engines started. With the dignity of an ocean liner, the ship came around, headed for the mouth of the bay. There we turned northward to maneuver for the meridian of the Kings Bay wireless station, which we were to follow to the North Pole.

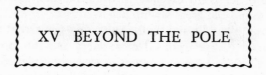

XV BEYOND THE POLE

FOR HALF AN HOUR the Norge moved at its calm fifty miles an hour up the Spitzbergen coast, past a majestic procession of glaciers and snowy peaks. The Byrd plane, much faster, literally flew rings around us. The Norge's motors were far enough back to allow easy conversation in our canvas gondola, even over the length of the car. The temperature at Kings Bay had been about ten degrees below freezing, but the upper air was colder. Thin clouds scarcely obstructed the sun at all.

As we passed Amsterdam Island, a snow-buried rock flung off the northeast corner of Spitzbergen, we looked down the glacier-striped north coast of this most northern of accessible lands. A slight mist hung above the glacier butts, but through it we thought we could see the ice cupola of North East Land, where we had landed the year before. Now Riiser-Larsen took landfall and radio bearings to control his magnetic compasses.

We worked eastward and adjusted the ship along the Kings Bay meridian, then set the sun compass for the North Pole. Let me note that our flight proved to be the longest meridional voyage—that is, travel on a due north and south line—ever recorded. After a final swing around us, Byrd and Bennett waved farewell and turned back. Below us lay the crinkled water of the Arctic Ocean; but far ahead on the horizon a "blink"—that shining band which ice reflects into the sky—showed that the polar pack was still there.

To the four of us who had flown this route in 1925, the trip to the Pole could not be called eventful. Two hours after leaving the hangar we reached the fringe of the pack, and then the pack itself. It was just as it had been, piled and broken, a vast sweep of white desolation, silent, mysterious. Our practiced eyes told us that the few narrow crooked leads were studded with ice blocks and newly frozen over. At first we saw a few seals, a few polar-bear tracks, an occasional little auk, but after Lat. 84° N. there was no more life.

A small calamity occurred. Berta's lunch hampers contained sandwiches and hard-boiled eggs. When we opened them to eat, we found the eggs split and frozen hard as granite pebbles. It was beyond the power of human jaws to crack them. The sandwiches were also frozen stiff. They were still edible, but the bread squeaked as we chewed it.

At Eighty-seven Forty-four Nobile reduced speed for a few minutes and descended within a few hundred feet of the ice. Though we were some few miles east of the place where we had come down in the Dornier-Wals, it was essentially the same region that had so nearly swallowed us up. We called to Omdal, and he clambered down from the rigging to stare with us at the ferocious scene below—exactly as it had been: tumbled ice, pressure ridges, inadequate leads. I think every one aboard the Norge shared the satisfaction of four of us that we were not now in airplanes.

Exactly as it had been, even to the fog. A black bank lay ahead of us. We climbed and eventually rose to 3,000 feet to surmount the woolly sea, in which the sun haloed the dirigible's shadow with a huge complete rainbow. It had taken us twelve hours to fly from Spitzbergen to the scene of our former disaster. The sun had completed its southern swing and was in the northwest quadrant. As we flew over the fog, it drew closer and closer to the north.

The fog dismayed us. Was it to continue for the rest of the voyage? If so, we might reach Alaska without knowing whether any land masses lay on the American side of the Arctic. For three hours, our speed now checked by a northeast head wind, we fled above this great fog bank. Our only consolation was that the breeze would be a tail wind when we turned for Alaska. Stavanger, in fact, was assuring us by radio that we would have such a wind.

The sun was almost due north, and we kept watching the chronometers for midnight. The moment came, and I started a new day in my diary—May 12. May 12? In the bustle and absorption of getting away on our flight, I had forgotten the significance to me of May 12. My birthday—I was forty-six years old! Ramm, the news hawk, heard my exclamation and sent a dispatch about it. A little later I received a radiogram of congratulation signed "Your friends in Kings Bay."

About this time another personal dispatch came aboard the Norge. It was for Gottwaldt, informing him that the king had that day decorated him with the Golden Medal of Merit. Gottwaldt was the Norwegian navy's chief wireless expert.

But the fog began to thin out at last, and at 1 A.M. we had it behind us. After Lat. 88° N. there had been several holes in it through which we saw that the Arctic was still an ice-locked sea. At about 1:15 A.M. Riiser-Larsen knelt at his window with his sextant, and we knew that the North Pole was close at hand. The sun had come around to the east, on our navigator's side of the car.

To the layman I think I can explain the simple method by which we determined that we had reached the Pole. From radio bearings, sextant observations, the sun and magnetic compasses, and drift corrections, we knew that we were exactly on the meridian of our course. The ship's true speed had been determined by frequent sextant observations for latitude. Riiser-Larsen knew that we should be at the Pole approximately at 1:30 A.M., May 12, Kings Bay meridian time. He knew the height the sun should have at the Pole at that moment. He set his sextant for that height and held it to his eye, ready, the bubble level keeping the instrument horizontal. If all these calculations were correct, the instant the image of the sun covered the bubble in the sextant we would be on the exact top of the world.

When Riiser-Larsen knelt down at his window, a silence fell over the cabin, broken only once when Riiser-Larsen admonished Horgen to hold the ship very true and steady to its course. Minutes dragged. Then Riiser-Larsen, with his sextant to his eye, announced calmly: "Here we are!"

At once Nobile rang the engine bells, and the motors shut down. A dirigible having little momentum, the Norge stopped almost immediately. I saw Oscar Wisting in the pilothouse turn around and look at Amundsen. Amundsen returned his stare, and neither said a word. They were now the only men ever to reach both poles. Until very recently only two men had ever seen this spot at all; but here, almost within forty-eight hours, that ice below had twice echoed back the roars of aviation engines.

We now took care of the little ceremony of planting flags at the Pole. The riggers and engineers were summoned to the gondola to watch. We bared our heads, Amundsen dropped the flag of Norway, then I the Stars and Stripes, and finally Nobile the Italian ensign and some Italian societies' flags. The staffs of these flags were provided with vanes to make them drop straight and stick their steel points into the ice. They all stood upright on the pack, the light breeze we had come to know so well barely lifting the banners.

The engines were started at half speed, and for an hour or more we circled over the Pole at a low altitude, three hundred feet. There was really nothing to see—ice, ridged by pressure, fewer leads in it perhaps, but no doubt drifting and eddying like all the rest of the pack. Since all directions now were south, the setting of a course to Alaska was a matter of angles—twelve degrees to the left of the meridian that brought us up from Europe. We set the sun compass for this track and at 2:30 A.M. started full speed south.

And now Amundsen had his little joke with me. He said I had celebrated my birthday prematurely. The moment we left the North Pole on the Point Barrow meridian, we were in Alaska time. It was no longer 2:30 A.M., May 12, but 3:30 P.M., May 11. We had the afternoon and evening of May 11 to live over again. The sun, which an hour before had been in the northeast, starting its southern swing that brought official day, was now in the west, beginning its night phase in the north. Though I had already celebrated two hours and a half of my forty-sixth birthday, I still had to wait nearly nine hours for it to begin.

Another point I should mention is the behavior of the magnetic compass when navigating across the North Pole. Many people suppose that a magnetic compass is of no use at the North Pole, but that is not true. The magnetic attraction for the needle is weak; but, fortunately for polar navigation, the Geographic Pole is almost as far away from the Magnetic Pole as is Spitzbergen. On the route up from Kings Bay the compass points from west to southwest. At the Pole itself the variation is, of course, 180°, the needle pointing due south on a meridian of northeastern Canada. From the Pole to Alaska the compass points southeast and east.

I should also note that on the charts of the Arctic and Antarctic, where men have never been, the isogonics, or lines of magnetic variation, are drawn from theory. Nevertheless, though on the known parts of the globe services are continually in the field measuring variation and keeping track of its changes, Riiser-Larsen found the isogonics on the Arctic charts surprisingly accurate, and I was to repeat that experience myself some years later in the Antarctic. This was most important to us when bringing the Norge in to the Alaskan coast through heavy fog.

For Amundsen and me, the real interest of the voyage began at the North Pole. We then entered the largest unexplored area left on earth. That journey of fifteen hundred miles began with perfect visibility. The ship flew at an average altitude of 1,200 feet, giving us a view of fifty miles or more in every direction. We kept watch always for land, but there was always the same ice under us.

After leaving the Pole, most of us tried to sleep, but we found sleep almost impossible during the entire voyage. The noise, the cold, the uncomfortable positions, and the fact that men were always moving about and stepping over one drove sleep away. The best we could do was nod a little when sitting or sprawling on the floor.

At 7 A.M.—for convenience we continued to use Norway time— we came to a hypothetical spot on the map hitherto unseen by man, the so-called Ice Pole. The Ice Pole, at Lat. 88° N. and Long. 157° W., is the geographical center of the Arctic ice mass, the edges of which are all explored and known. Looking down upon it, we could also believe that it was actually the physical center of pressure, the pivot around which the whole polar pack was drifting. It was nothing but a chaos of barricades and ridges, without ever an open lead among them. We agreed that surface travel of any sort would be impossible here.

Two hours later, when we were twenty-four hours out of Kings Bay, we reached Lat. 86° N. and were halfway to Point Barrow. We had used less than one third of our gasoline. For this entire distance we had had almost perfect visibility. Since Sverdrup had already established the nonexistence of land masses between Siberia and the North Pole, we could say with assurance that the eighty-sixth north parallel embraces no land at all. If our mode of travel had permitted us to make a sounding of the ocean at this point, the scientific results of our expedition thus far would have been complete.

But at this point our troubles began. At the Pole itself we had looked forward with some confidence to a perfect voyage to America, but it was not to be. Between 88° and 86° N. Lat. a few scattered pools of fog lay on the ice, but at 86° fog began in earnest and continued during the rest of the flight.

At first we flew above it in clear sunshine, since the bank only reached up to an altitude of a thousand feet; but after a while, as the fog continued to thicken, this became impossible. With the radio working well, however, and the accuracy of the Arctic isogonics already established, the ship could still be navigated truly. Our chief concern was over the fact that we could no longer see the surface of the earth. I would not give the impression, though, that this whole fog area was solid. There were numerous breaks in it, some of them big ones, so that we were able to make an adequate observation of the sea all the way to the Alaskan coast.

After about an hour of blind flying, our radio reception grew fainter and finally ceased altogether. The aerial had iced up. This antenna was a wire 450 feet long trailing from the after end of the gondola, under the radio room. Fog particles froze to it in the form of milky ice, until, when the radio failed, it resembled a long flexible rod of porcelain. The air propeller, providing power for the wireless, iced over, too, and finally locked, leaving only the storage battery for the radio. Gottwaldt and Strom-Johnson wound up the aerial and cleaned it several times, but in vain. As soon as it was dropped it iced over again. Increasing static added to the difficulty of reception. As a matter of fact, we received no more wireless messages south of 80° N. Lat., and later we learned that our own signals failed at about that point.

This was serious on two counts. It stopped our weather reports just when we were entering the region where the weather factors were almost unknown to us. Secondly, it deprived us of radio bearings, leaving our navigator at the mercy of the magnetic compass and such sun observations as he might be lucky enough to make.

Up to this moment our weather service had functioned perfectly. We could hear Kings Bay until the end, though the powerful Stavanger signals were much stronger. Stavanger was now relaying North American weather reports to us, and so were some of the government stations in Alaska. The last report we got from Alaska told of the cyclonic center still stationary over the Bering Sea.

We soon realized that we were entering the influence of that disturbance, though it was yet a thousand miles away. Whenever the fog bank thinned we rode over the top of it, only to discover now that the sky had become overcast with clouds at a very high altitude. Once or twice the sun broke through long enough for Riiser-Larsen to make a quick celestial observation and check our position. The tail wind that had accompanied us all the way from the Pole dropped to nothing, and after a while we began nosing through a faint but freshening breeze from the east. With no steady sun, the sun compass was useless. Moreover, the fog gradually iced up the compass periscope until it went out of business.

There was no more nodding or drowsing for anyone now. The situation was too anxious. All afternoon of May 12 (Norway time) the Norge drove southward, often flying between clouds and fog. Through breaks we frequently observed the polar ice and found its character much the same as the ice of these latitudes on the European side—floes massed together, leads running east and west. By evening (morning, Alaska time) clouds and fog began to merge in one woolen mass. At 8 P.M. May 12 (9 A.M. in Alaska) we came out into an open area, and there was sunshine long enough for Riiser-Larsen to use his sextant. We were only 350 miles off the American continent.

But it took us the rest of that night or day, whichever one calls it, to make those 350 miles. Almost at once we got into weather so thick that our navigator could not snatch another sun observation until four o'clock, ship's time, the next morning. The east wind strengthened, and to keep from being blown out toward Bering Strait the ship was headed into it a little, reducing our flying speed to forty miles an hour or less.

But we could not fly all the time. Presently the Norge developed the alarming symptom of being down by the head. The bows of the envelope were enameling themselves in ice. Snow squalls, too, were beginning to add to the airship's difficulties. At this point Malmgren proved invaluable. Nobile turned to him for advice; and the meteorologist, no longer having to keep his weather map, turned his entire attention to scientific observations of the amount of ice being formed at various heights.

During the rest of the voyage Malmgren made dozens of these rime tests, as he called them. They determined the best altitude for flying through the fog. Sometimes they sent us high, where the fog was thinner. Sometimes we almost grazed the ice pack itself, the temperature there being so low, the rime would not make. Once, when it was icy at every level, we tried climbing over the fog, but at the highest altitude we could reach without risking a dangerous loss of hydrogen there was still fog.

Fog made our cabin miserably cold, and it was especially hard for Riiser-Larsen, Malmgren, and the two radiomen, who had to work with their bare hands. A new note of peril sounded. One of the riggers dropped down into the cabin with the news that the engine propellers were detaching fragments of ice from the outside braces and wires of the nacelles and blowing them as projectiles through the envelope under the keel, making holes which the men above were patching.

We all knew now we were in the critical stage of the flight. If ice plates or large splinters went into the propellers, smashing them, the flying blades would most certainly be shot up through the balloon, tearing open the hydrogen bags and forcing an immediate landing. Or, even if this extreme disaster did not occur, with disabled engines the ship would be powerless and impossible to navigate in the grip of an Arctic cyclone. As if sensing the peril, the terrier Titina, who had slept most of the way from Spitzbergen, now jumped from her chair to the floor, where she cowered and whimpered. She did this several times during the last part of the flight.

The bombardment of the envelope by ice particles continued. By standing up in the cabin, we could hear the pieces hit the taut fabric. Once a big piece ripped through and made a hole so large that the dirigible had to be throttled down while the riggers repaired the break. Thus hour after hour the Norge battled on. Malmgren kept giving us the safest levels. The weight of ice on the bow could still be balanced by shifting the gasoline ballast. Most of the time the ship limped along on two engines while the riggers and engineer chipped ice from the propeller blades of the third.

Meanwhile, through breaks in the fog or when we dropped low to avoid riming, we had observed the sea change appearance. Leads became wider and more numerous, they gave way to loose fringe floes, and finally open water showed under us, whipped by a rising gale. Yet the whole Arctic north of Alaska is much more heavily iced than it is on the European side, where the Gulf Stream pushes back the floes and thaws them. Open water and masses of floes succeeded each other alternately, and for miles out the ice was jammed against the shore.

When Riiser-Larsen got his four-o'clock shot at the sun on the morning of May 13 (Norway time), we discovered that the ship was holding a true south course practically on the meridian we had chosen at the North Pole—twenty-one miles west of it. This was magnificent navigation—blind flying for hours, having only the oscillating magnetic compass for direction and only yesterday's weather map on which to base estimates of drift. Moreover, Riiser-Larsen was making no particular effort to keep on the meridian. We were now aiming not at a particular point, such as the Pole, but at a coast line 700 miles long. Yet, though we did not know it until later, our navigator brought the Norge in so close to Point Barrow that we were actually sighted from that town, and the government telegraph there sent out the first news that our expedition had crossed the Arctic.

At the time he made that observation Riiser-Larsen, after averaging our speed during the last eight hours, announced that we could expect to see land soon after 6 A.M., ship's time. The wind, which had started to blow from the southeast, was backing to the northeast. Fog conditions had improved. As we approached the coast we had several miles of visibility, the ship no longer gathered rime, and the fusillade of ice against the keel had ceased. At 6:50 A.M. Riiser-Larsen, who for some time had been studying the southern horizon through his binoculars, sang out: "Land off the port bow!" He had been observing it for several minutes but wanted to make sure before he spoke.

We all got out field glasses and scanned the distance ahead. The ship was now running above packed shore ice, and all that was to be seen, thirty miles or more away, was a faint black line in the solid sheet of white. The course was altered to the southeast, giving us a rough, quartering headwind, and it was an hour before we came in. The black line proved to be a string of immense boulders on the beach itself. Behind them the snow-laden coastal plain, flat and almost as low as the shore ice, lost itself in fog.

We came over the beach at 7:50 A.M., Norway time, having made the voyage from Spitzbergen, 2,000 miles, in a little less than forty-seven hours, including two hours spent at the North Pole. Scientifically speaking, the expedition was ended. We could conservatively claim to have looked down upon a hundred thousand square miles of unexplored territory. We could tell geographers that there is no Keenan's Land north of Point Barrow, no land at all between Alaska and the Pole. We had established the scientific fact that the North Polar Region is a vast, deep, ice-covered sea. The white patch on the top of the globe could now be tinted blue.

But though our mission as explorers was achieved, we still had the task ahead of bringing the Norge and ourselves to a safe landing. From this point on it becomes more intelligible to speak in terms of Alaska time, since we had now come down to a latitude where, in mid-May, night was still night and day day. By that reckoning, we came to the coast line at 8:50 P.M., May 12; and thereafter, through a black night and a long, wild, fog-choked day we battled for our lives.

Our first problem was one of route. Had our radio been in order, it is probable that we would have climbed and set a southeast course for Fairbanks, in the heart of Alaska, weather conditions there being calm and fair. We did not know that, however, and agreed with Nobile to cut south overland and drive straight for Nome, where, under the high bluffs of the Seward Peninsula, we could expect shelter from the northerly storm which was continually increasing. But we were not certain where we were, having only Riiser-Larsen's calculation that we had come in west of Point Barrow. Amundsen said that the coast to the eastward looked like Point Barrow country, which was familiar ground to him. We therefore decided to run down the coast southwest until we could find some feature we could identify, and from that point set a course for Nome.

In this direction we had the wind, which had now reached gale force, straight behind us, and we drove along at immense speed into constantly thickening weather. It was necessary to fly low in order to distinguish the wintry shore from the frozen sea at all. In about an hour we came to a collection of roofs which Amundsen, to whom the place was home, unhesitatingly pronounced to be Wainwright. Omdal, who had been with Amundsen at Wainwright in 1923, confirmed this opinion, even declaring that he could identify some of the men staring up as the Norge fled like a ghost through the fog.

We had our landmark, but we did not turn inland as we had planned. The interior looked too ominous. The Endicott Mountains should have been in plain sight at Wainwright, but they were lost in the smother of the storm. We did not dare drive into them on the wings of a sixty-mile wind. So we kept on southwest, following the coast line.

But soon even that became impossible. We had to fly lower and lower to see the beach. Lofty capes and headlands began jumping out of the murk ahead, and we fairly grazed them as we went over. It was too precarious. Furthermore, our flight down from Point Barrow had already showed us that the latest charts were not correctly showing the contours of the coast. We did not know what to expect ahead, and so our navigators gave up and rose to a higher altitude to fly blind as best they could.

I cannot go into all the details of that night of peril. It was an experience to test the courage of the stoutest heart. The wind reached the hurricane force of seventy miles an hour or more. The Norge flew literally between the devil and the deep blue sea. Over land the fog was frozen dry and blew off the envelope. Over water it formed rime ice on the ship. We had our choice—to lose the icing danger but risk going into a mountain, or avoid the mountains and take on a weight of ice that might force a landing.

Both dangers nearly brought us to disaster. Once in the twilight hills that were really the top of a mountain leaped up at us from below. We were so close that the weight on the end of the trailing antenna bumped, and the wire had to be wound in. When the brief hours of darkness ended, the dirigible had gathered so much ice forward that the men in the rigging had to ride on the extreme afterend of the keel to trim the airship. Let me note here that when the Norge finally landed, it was sheathed in a ton of ice.

Thus it went on. The Alaskan day of May 13 wore on. We hadn't the slightest notion of where we were. Indeed, all of us, including Riiser-Larsen, thought it likely that we had been blown south of Nome and were heading toward the Aleutian Islands. Once during the morning a break showed us open water below and distant shore ice on which were the igloos of an Eskimo village. Nobile turned the ship in that direction and descended, nosing into a blustering wind. We hoped we might actually go low enough to ask the Eskimos where we were.

But the wind made such a maneuver too dangerous. Over the village we wheeled and drove south again. I had a fleeting glimpse of a dog team, scared by our roaring apparition in the sky, running away, its Eskimo driver, hooded in his parka, gazing after his animals in despair. Then the fog swallowed us once more. Riiser-Larsen thought this open water might be the eastern end of Norton Sound, which would put Nome now northwest of us. Omdal, who had been watching, bore him out in this. Omdal declared that in the distance beyond the Eskimo village he had plainly seen Anvil Mountain, a well-known landmark. But all the rest of us had been looking, and nobody else had seen anything that even resembled a mountain. It was simply a hallucination for Omdal. After more than sixty hours without sleep, the last thirty in the shadow of disaster, the men were all "seeing things."

As we knew later, the shore we had glimpsed was that of Kotzebue Sound, north of Nome and the Seward Peninsula. Following Riiser-Larsen's theory, however, we now turned west and for some hours traveled in that direction, with the wind partly behind us. The one ray of cheer was that the storm had begun to moderate. The hurricane had dropped to a gusty half gale. When our watches indicated that it was noon, Alaska time, there were indications that the fog was breaking. The sky grew luminous, and once we ran into a hole at the bottom of which we saw a rocky, snow-bound land.

Riiser-Larsen thought now he could get a sextant observation, and Nobile put the airship into a climb. We had to rise to a dangerous altitude—nearly four thousand feet—before we came out into bright sunshine. The sun now was higher than we had seen it for many weeks, so high that Riiser-Larsen could not sight it out of the car. He therefore took his sextant and other instruments and climbed the duralumin ladder in the bow of the balloon and made his observation on the flat glacéed top of the envelope.

With a single observation, Riiser-Larsen could determine only the latitude, which his sextant told him was 67° 30′ N. This was slightly north of the Arctic Circle and at the least calculation 165 miles north of Nome. But we must be farther than that, since the Nome meridian cuts 67° 30′ in the middle of Kotzebue Sound. Land was under us now. Therefore, we must be on the north shore of Kotzebue Sound, well to the eastward of the Nome meridian.

Riiser-Larsen had scarcely returned with this information when a shout from the radio room drew the attention of all. The two radiomen had taken this fogless opportunity to wheel up and clean the antenna. They dropped it just in time to hear the end of a strong radio signal almost due southwest. The station signed off without identifying itself. The assumption could only be that this station was Nome. We hastily drew a northwest diagonal from Nome to cut 67° 30′ and made the startling discovery that we were over Asia—well back of East Cape, Siberia.

Then came the moment of greatest danger in the entire flight. Having a course that we could now follow to a landing place, the airship would not respond to its vertical helm and could not be forced down into the fog. The sun was so high and warm that it was expanding our hydrogen cells to the bursting point. Nobile did not dare release gas, lest when the cold pinch of the fog came we would lose all buoyancy and plunge to destruction. As a last resort everyone on the ship except Nobile and the two helmsmen went forward on the keel into the nose of the balloon, dragging gasoline tins and cases of pemmican with us. Wisting then put the vertical helm hard down, the ship tilted, and the engines finally forced us through the roof of the fog. Then we all had to scramble aft once more to keep the cooling dirigible from going into a straight nose dive.

At this high altitude the gale still blew at seventy miles an hour or more, driving us far inland during the hour we were in sunshine. Going back, it was all head wind and slow travel for a while. It was late afternoon before we reached the Asiatic side of Bering Strait. But as we came lower, the wind abated until near the surface of the ground it was only a strong breeze. Better still, the fog was lifting all around, giving us almost perfect visibility crossing the strait, though the sky was still overcast.

As soon as we got out of fog, the two radiomen picked the ice off the trailing antenna, giving us reception once more, so that we could get steady radio bearings on Nome. Nome, we learned, had calm weather, and a crowd of men was waiting to help land the dirigible; but we were all exhausted and were determined to come down at the first favorable opportunity. We rounded Cape Prince of Wales about six o'clock in the afternoon and an hour later came in sight of a village which proved to be Teller.

It was relatively calm in the lee of the Seward Peninsula. The frozen bay in front of Teller offered a landing field. We maneuvered overhead for an hour or more while the riggers constructed a sort of sea anchor—a canvas sleeve sixty feet long filled with all sorts of heavy objects that gave it a weight of 600 pounds. To this were attached two ice anchors. It was expected that the weight of the sleeve would hold down the cable and cause the ice anchors to bite in.

While we hovered above the village we debated the method of landing, and then occurred the disagreement with Nobile I mentioned previously. It must be borne in mind that up to this time no modern dirigible had ever been landed without the aid of a trained ground crew. Distrustful of the ability of greenhorns to hold the Norge, Nobile was for breaking out the canvas sides of the gondola and all making a jump for it together, letting the airship go. Riiser-Larsen, mindful of a property worth $46,000 to the expedition at that moment, insisted that we must leave by the cabin door one by one, each man jumping for a landing rope as he emerged. Amundsen and I sustained Riiser-Larsen, whose order therefore prevailed.

As it turned out, the landing was not difficult. Circling lower and lower, at 500 feet we let down the anchor. Just as it touched, a puff of wind caught the balloon, and we went bowling along toward shore at a great rate, the anchor sliding. Just in time, the gust released us. The anchors took hold, the engines stopped, Nobile blew out a hydrogen ballonet, and the airship slowly sank. The men of Teller came running out on the ice. The ends of our landing ropes reached their fingers, another ballonet was blown out, the car bumped on the ice. As Nobile pulled rip cords, we all sprang out and caught ropes; and the great bag, its ice-sheathed fabric sagging into its ribs, came to rest, a hundred yards from the nearest cottage.

Half blind with fatigue, Amundsen and I walked ashore together. For three days and nights we had been without sleep and under a strain. For two days we had been reduced to gnawing at blocks of chocolate and frozen bricks of pemmican for food. We were even suffering pangs of thirst, since long ago the coffee and tea in our thermos flasks had frozen solid. We came up on the same beach from where, as a young man twenty years earlier, I had looked out across the unknown North and wondered what was there. Now I knew. I had completed a great circle in my life, though I was too weary then to realize it. Not until the next day did I stand here again and think such thoughts.

When it became evident that the lost Norge, about which Alaska's wires and radio were talking, was going to land, the good women of Teller had rushed to their cookstoves. By the time the crew had deflated and secured the airship and had brought the instruments ashore, hot dinners were ready for us. Too exhausted to do more than mumble our thanks, we gorged and then tumbled into beds to sleep, most of us, for twenty hours or more.

Next afternoon the Italian crew started to dismantle and crate the dirigible for shipment to Italy as soon as navigation opened up. The rest of us started out to see the sights of Teller. The village boasted one civic attraction—a cage of white Arctic foxes. One of our Norwegians felt in his pocket a sample of the lamented hard-boiled and harder-frozen Spitzbergen eggs and tossed it into the cage. A fox picked it up to bolt it, but a puzzled expression came upon its face as the egg failed to break between its teeth. It dropped it, and another fox picked it up, only to be disillusioned in turn. Presently they were all running around in circles trying to get the egg.

That was enough. We rushed to our hampers for frozen eggs and pitched them into the cage, two at a time. A more enterprising fox would get both, stuffing them into its cheeks like a case of double mumps. The others would give pursuit of the swollen-faced fox, round and round the cage. We laughed until the tears rolled down our cheeks.

Leaving the Italian crew behind, next day we went overland to Nome to wait for a ship south and write and send our little account of the voyage to the New York *Times,* according to the contract.

It occurred to me that I might as well read that document, and I pulled it out of my pocket.

"Why," I exclaimed to Amundsen, "it says seventy-five thousand words. That's a whole book!"

Amundsen shrugged his shoulders. He hadn't read the contract, either.

I cabled to the *Times:* "Must be some mistake. My copy of contract reads seventy-five thousand words."

The newspaper answered: "Your copy correct."

I wired: "Physically and mentally impossible to write seventy-five thousand words."

Back came the answer: "We hold you to your contract."

There was nothing else to do. For an office we hired a room in the Nome Hospital. Then Riiser-Larsen, Malmgren, Ramm, Amundsen, and I chained ourselves in and in three weeks turned out seventy-five thousand words with five thousand added for good measure.

During this time Amundsen and I boarded with an estimable lady of Nome named Mrs Johnson. Mrs Johnson was an old-timer of Alaska, a real sourdough. She was hearty and husky with a loud cheerful voice and a limited number of expressions. Also she was an excellent cook. Amundsen had known her for years.

On the day of our arrival she served us a roast wild goose, which she had bought from the Eskimos. Recovering as we were from starvation, Amundsen and I polished off the entire bird at a sitting. Two days later we began to think wistfully of that feast.

"Mrs Johnson," said Amundsen that morning after breakfast, "do you suppose we could have another wild goose today?"

"I'll tell the world," said Mrs Johnson.

Because of the long years I had spent in solitude, I had never fallen into the habit of observing slang, and this was the first time I had ever heard that expression. It amused me immensely to think of Mrs Johnson, in her remote corner of the earth, telling the world about our goose dinner.

About every other morning thereafter we began the day with the question: "Mrs Johnson, could we have another wild goose?"

And the loud, cheerful and inevitable reply: "I'll tell the world!"

Prospectors and miners from all over northwestern Alaska were mushing into Teller to see the Norge. The expedition did a good business in the sale of our auxiliary five-gallon tins of gasoline for $10 apiece. The gasoline was for use, the tins for souvenirs. Souvenir hunters cut the airship's envelope to ribbons, but it was Italy's loss now, not ours. While waiting for the first boat of spring, to keep up interest in ourselves pending our arrival in the States, we sent to the *Times* stories about anything that interested us. I even visited several mining camps near Nome and telegraphed descriptions of them.

The day came when the old SS Victoria sailed with all of us on board, including the Italians, who had now boxed the Norge and turned it over to a shipping company. On the voyage down Amundsen busied himself with the lecture he was to start delivering almost as soon as he reached the East. We expected to create a little stir in Seattle but were not prepared for the vociferous welcome we received. The harbor was black with launches jammed to the gunwales with cheering men, women, and children.

It was all very flattering and also somewhat perplexing, since when Amundsen and I stepped to the rail to acknowledge the applause, nobody seemed to notice us. Also we became aware that the cries from below were in a foreign tongue. Seattle's whole Italian colony had come out to greet its heroic compatriots.

But still the mystery was not entirely solved. The bravos from the launches came in periodic waves. Casting our eyes upward at the bridge, we were stunned by the answer. Nobile stood there, Titina at his feet barking with excitement. But it was a different Nobile. Despite our agreement to carry no spare baggage in the Norge, in his own duffel he had slipped the uniform of an Italian general of the air. Now he was dressed in it, and every time he lifted his arm in the Fascist salute, the huzzas rose from below.

There came a June evening. The place was Brooklyn. The Academy of Music was crowded on the occasion of Amundsen's first lecture on the flight of the Norge. I sat on the platform, and the chairman introduced us together. It was my last official association with Roald Amundsen.

Though our warm friendship continued, there was no need to continue our partnership. He felt that he was through with exploration. "Aircraft has supplanted the dog," he wrote in his final book. But flying, he once told me, wasn't his game—he was too old to learn. Yet it was by flying that he perished—hunting for Nobile after the Italia crash.

Often I wonder how he and Dietrichson, who had stood so four-square with us in 1925, met their end. Was it after a long losing struggle against ice, snow, open leads, and famine or in a merciful crash to instant death? The latter, I hope, yet one may be sure that it was with no words of fear or despair on their lips. With Amundsen passed the heroic age of polar exploration with ships and dogs. He passed on the gage to the winged generation.

III

Antarctic

We are those fools who could not
    rest
  In the dull earth we left behind,
But burned with passion for the
    West
  And drank strange frenzy from
    its wind.
The world where wise men live at
    ease
  Fades from our unregretful eyes,
As blind across uncharted seas
  We stagger on our enterprise.

I FIRST LIFE

"I AM LEAVING it to younger men," Amundsen had said, with a gesture in my direction, but I was not ready yet to assume that mantle. Aviation was not his game, he had said. Was it any more mine? Certainly, the voyage in the Norge was a far cry from my youthful vision of polar exploration—the painfully established bases, the bitter journeys with sledges and dogs, the heroic battle against the elements. It was the physical challenge that appealed to me as much as anything else. The Norge and its crew were but a machine in which the explorer could sit at ease and watch unroll the panorama of the unknown.

With the completion of the Norge flight, I thought that my days in the polar regions were over. I had realized to the full my long ambition. With just pride I could claim that I as much as any other man had opened up the Arctic. There seemed to be no other worlds to conquer. I had not yet thought of the Antarctic.

Yet, in my middle forties, I could not sit down and vegetate. I was ripe for a new interest, and I found one almost immediately.

During that same summer, 1926, Dr David White, senior geologist of the Geological Survey, discovered fossil algae in the bottom of the Grand Canyon of the Colorado River. Although I had explored for the survey, I had never been particularly attracted by fossils; but fossil algae were different. The algae—microscopical one-cell plants that flourished in shallow seas at the dawn of mundane time—are the first life that emerged from the primordial elements, or the first that left any trace of itself. Those found in the Grand Canyon are estimated to have lived seven hundred million years ago. Between them and the first animal life that has left its fossils in the Cambrian rocks intervened the immense period of three hundred million years.

Fossil algae appealed to my innate love of extremes. Since 1920 I had been spending a little time each year at the Grand Canyon. That same autumn, 1926, I made my annual pilgrimage. Remembering about Dr White's discovery, I looked for fossil algae. To my delight, I found some.

I was stopping at the Phantom Ranch, down in the canyon; and one day, while my fellow guests were at luncheon, I wandered up a side canyon until I found myself in a grassy basin, full of ferns, wild flowers, and butterflies. The sun was warm, and I sat down on the grass, propping my back against a boulder, for a nap. Idly I watched a tarantula crawling along an adjacent rock, as if sizing me up. A swift shadow crossed the little oasis, and, raising my eyes, I saw a bald eagle soaring between the steep walls of my narrow place.

But I saw something else on the canyon wall—a sharp line, about five hundred feet up, dividing the granite and gneiss of the Archean crust of the earth from the sedimentary deposits that towered above for nearly a mile. The line of life and death, I mused—not death ending life but death merging into life. There, if anywhere, would be found algae traces. I found a way up to the stratum and discovered what I sought. Next day I returned with chisel and hammer and broke out a block of Algonkian red shale showing algae—my first specimens. This stone is now in the American Museum of Natural History.

In succeeding years I continued to prospect for fossil algae in the Grand Canyon, finding it good practice, since it trains the eye to be exceedingly alert and observant. In 1929 I located a fine deposit of Proterozoic fossils on the north wall of the canyon just west of the mouth of Bright Angel Creek and spent several weeks getting them out. I usually stayed on the rim of the canyon, going down on foot after an early breakfast each day, prospecting for as long as I had time, and then late in the afternoon climbing out again—a seven-mile trail that ascends for a mile—with my specimens in my knapsack. In all, I had freighted more than a ton of

rocks and fossils out of Grand Canyon on my back, a few pounds
at a time. A few specimens I kept for my own collections. The rest
I sent to Dr White, who, after studying them, gave them to the
American Museum.

It was, incidentally, this interest in fossil algae that took me in
the summer of 1930 to Labrador in company with a young New
York friend of mine, Beekman Pool, son of Dr Eugene Pool. Beekman was then a senior at Harvard and was the intercollegiate
squash champion. He had spent a summer at Dr Grenfell's mission
in Labrador and talked so much about it to me that finally I agreed
to go with him into the interior.

The result was a journey as uncomfortable but in some ways as
interesting as any I ever made. I had a special interest in seeing
Labrador, knowing that that desolate land exposed Archean and
early sedimentary rocks. In the Grand Canyon it was water that cut
through the sedimentation to the basic crust. In Labrador the
erosion had been from ice. Untold ages of glacial movement had
ground off the entire sedimentary crown of that vast peninsula. It
seemed likely that I might pick up some fossil algae there.

From that point of view the expedition was not much of a success, principally because of lack of time. The travel proved to be
much harder and slower than we expected. When we started in,
we had a journey of 800 miles ahead of us and just 45 days to catch
the last boat of the season leaving Battle Harbor for the south. The
result was that we had to keep going every minute. There was no
time for any prospecting.

Labrador consists of a high central plateau so level and flat that
it is half under water, being full of lakes, large and small, connected by broad sluggish rivers. At the edges of the high land the
terrain slopes off sharply, and many swift rivers, full of rapids and
cataracts, carry off the heavy precipitation of the plateau. The
rivers are especially numerous on the west and south slopes, falling
into Hudson Bay and the Gulf of St Lawrence. On our trip we
had to make sixty-nine portages, most of them on the way up to
the top.

We went up the Moisie River, outfitting at Seven Islands, the

Hudson's Bay Company post at the mouth of the Moisie on the St Lawrence. Here we bought two canoes and hired a French-Canadian guide and two Indians for polemen and paddlers. Our outfit weighed 1,200 pounds, including provisions for two months.

Going up the Moisie it was pole, pole, all the way, backbreaking, monotonous work in which the canoes did not seem to move against the torrent. But even that work was a relief from the torture of the black flies and mosquitoes. I thought I knew something about insect pests, but the black flies of Labrador were like one of the plagues of Egypt. We saw plenty of bare tipi poles on the way in but never a camp. The country was absolutely deserted, and we knew why. The Indians would not go in to hunt until fall, when frosts had killed off the swarms of black flies. Even game had fled from them. On the whole trip we saw only one moth-eaten little black bear.

We wrapped undershirts around our necks and tied up the bottoms of our trousers, but the black flies got in just the same, and our ankles swelled with their bites. One of them bit me on the eyeball, and for a few days I had an inflammation that put me in misery. The Indians along the St Lawrence are all pious Catholics. When making the contract with us, ours demurred about working on Sunday. We compromised by giving them a half day off Sundays, but the flies were so bad they swallowed their scruples and poled and portaged all day every Sunday. We knew that when we reached the watershed the flies would disappear.

But there were compensations. Our French-Canadian guide could make the best boiled beans I ever tasted. He would put in a layer of beans, then a layer of salt pork, another layer of beans, another of salt pork, and so on until the pot was full. Then he simmered them all night. They were wonderful for men working as hard as we were. We ate them three times a day. When we were just coming out of Labrador, we gave half a pot of them to some Indians at the first trading post we reached. I have always regretted that act of generosity.

The Moisie was full of big salmon going up to spawn. At the first falls they were jumping by thousands. Beekman Pool leaned out here and caught several big ones in his arms. One of the portages on the Moisie was three miles long. It took us three days to freight our load of half a ton across the muskeg bogs. At the end of three hundred miles of such travel we came at last to the watershed. The heavy timber pinched out, the Moisie became quiet, and there ahead was a little lake, the first of thousands on the upper plateau.

But this lake was a sight no one could ever forget. It was the end of the poling journey, and here all canoe parties abandoned their poles. It was Indian custom to plant the poles straight up in the bottom of the lake. For generations the hunters had been doing this, and the whole shallow lake bristled like a porcupine with abandoned canoe poles. This was also the limit of the hunting range, since there was little game in the sparse timber of the lake country. Beyond this there were no more tipi poles, and at night we had to pitch our tents on the quaking bogs. Near the canoe-pole lake was another on the banks of which were many Indian graves.

From this point on it was all paddle work as we groped toward streams that would take us to the head of the Hamilton River, down which we were to descend to the Atlantic. The water in these upper lakes and rivers was icy. Our hands swelled with the cold and the constant work. At night I examined such rocks as I could find near our tents, but our voyage up the Moisie had delayed us so much that we could not stop for any systematic exploration.

To make matters worse, we got lost in a labyrinth of lakes and connecting streams and for five days hunted for the trail over which we should portage to water moving toward the Atlantic. The trail is so little traveled that it consists merely of an occasional Indian blaze on a stunted tree. We cruised along the shores of lake after lake, watching for the continuation of the blaze we were following. Finally one of our Indians, sharper sighted than a hawk, noted an old campfire on a bank. It was something I wouldn't have seen with binoculars. We went in and there picked up the trail.

We struck the Hamilton River at its falls, of which we were

aware long before we reached them, since you can hear the thunder of the water for ten miles. Hamilton Falls is one of the great scenic wonders of North America, though few white men have ever been enterprising enough to go and see the sublime spectacle. The Hamilton is the largest river of Labrador and the only stream of any size that comes out on the Atlantic side. Above the falls the torrent races down a breath-taking chute and then plunges three hundred feet into a deep gorge. We stayed here a day to photograph and marvel at the great cataract. Incidentally, the "guest book" at the falls is a bottle into which white visitors put their names written on slips of paper.

The gorge of the Hamilton soon opens up into a wide valley with a succession of lakes. So, instead of the easy journey downstream we had anticipated, we actually had to paddle the whole distance. Rigolet, the Hudson's Bay post and settlement at the head of tidewater on Hamilton Estuary, was the end of our canoe journey. Rigolet may mean nothing to the average citizen of the United States or Canada, but wherever there is a Hudson's Bay post it has its fame. Years ago a young man named Donald Smith, the local factor, showed his enterprise by walking from Rigolet to Montreal in the dead of winter to carry some important information to his headquarters. This brought him to the attention of his superior officers. Eventually, as Lord Strathcona, he was for many years high commissioner of the Hudson's Bay Company.

From Rigolet a company steamer took us around to Battle Harbor to wait for the passenger boat going to Quebec and Montreal. There we had three days to wait. One morning I strolled down the main street of Battle Harbor to its terminus upon a limestone reef jutting out into the sea. There to my dumfounded gaze spread out an area of crystaling limestone two hundred feet square that was all rippled with that raised, wavelike recurring structure so characteristic of fossil algae. I had looked for algae over eight hundred hard miles in the interior of Labrador only to find them in a place I could have visited by excursion steamer.

I rushed back for some tool with which to dig out a specimen, but all I could find was a pickax. It made no impression on the glazed, surf-washed limestone of the reef, which needed a sledge hammer and chisel. The best I could do was take some careful photographs to prove my discovery.

My affection for the West had gradually centered upon two objects: the Grand Canyon and Death Valley; but, if anything, I loved Death Valley the better. Deserts had grown upon me with the years. I was always discovering new beauties in them. I never tired of the gaudy sunrises and sunsets of Death Valley or of studying its inconspicuous but teeming life, each species a triumph of adaptation. There is something about the monotony of a desert that suggests the polar wastes.

After returning from Labrador, I made my usual yearly pilgrimage to Grand Canyon to gather more fossils, and then spent the month of December, including Christmas, in Death Valley, stopping at Furnace Creek Inn. About ten miles out from the inn on one of the trails was the two-room board shack of a queer desert couple, a sort of Jack Spratt and his wife. No matter how hot the day might be, the man was always hunching up his shoulders and shivering. No matter how cold the wind blew, the wife was always red faced and warm, mopping her forehead. Since their shack was at the end of just a good walk for me, I often visited this pair and, in fact, grew quite fond of them.

The couple existed by selling desert souvenirs to tourists— principally colored bottles. The actinic force of the sun is so strong in Death Valley that an ordinary white glass bottle left out for ten or a dozen years turns purple. Transient visitors snatched up purple bottles as mementos. For a shop the shivering man had a small shed beside his shack. In front of the shed, beside the trail, every morning he posted his burro, loaded with a pack. The burro never had to go anywhere or do any work. He was merely a trade sign.

On Christmas morning, feeling full of good will toward men, I remembered this lonely couple and decided to do something for them. From the hotel newsstand I bought copies of all the current magazines, made up a pack of them, and walked out to the souvenir shack. My chilly friend was delighted with his Christmas present. He examined all the magazines, one by one, then piled them on the bench outside his shop and took me inside to show me some new things he had found.

When we emerged, we found that the burro had stepped from its pedestal and had started to make a meal of the magazines. He had finished *Cosmopolitan* and was starting in on *Saturday Evening Post* when his owner caught him. I never saw a man get madder at a dumb brute. He booted his literary burro until my heart bled for the poor animal.

While digging in the sand dunes for bottles, this man had uncovered one of the camps of the famous Jayhawker Party, which made such a disastrous crossing of Death Valley in the winter of 1849–50. He found an ox yoke, an ox horn, and charred pieces of the covered wagons, which the desperate gold hunters had burned after slaughtering their oxen for food. He found also in this old camp an English racing spur. The desert uncovered for him other curios, among them a fine Indian bow and arrow of antique make. The strangest object of all that came into his possession was a pair of homemade skis, which he discovered in a cave on Telescope Peak. Why anyone would carry skis into Death Valley is beyond comprehension.

I bought all the Jayhawker relics, my admiration for the pioneers who subdued the West amounting almost to worship. The tragic adventures of the Jayhawker and Manly parties in Death Valley during that first winter of the gold rush are famous chapters in the epic of California. The Jayhawkers gave themselves that nickname. They were not really bushwhackers of the Kansas "free-state" struggle but men, women, and children from all over the Mississippi Valley. The Jayhawkers and a fifty-wagon train guided by Captain Smith were independent caravans which were lost in the bewildering country east of Death Valley, in what is now Nevada. William Lewis Manly, a young Vermonter, climbed a high butte and in the west saw the snowy peaks of the Sierra Nevada. Both parties then turned in that direction, little aware of the sterile desert that lay between.

To both parties came the same fate—wanderings over the trackless waste that suggest those of the Children of Israel, food giving out, babies and children moaning for water, oxen being killed for meat and wagons split up for fuel. At any time Manly could have saved himself, but he preferred to remain to save all. Finding the trickle of a spring of fresh water, the party made a permanent camp, while Manly and a young man named Rogers started west on foot to bring help. They promised to be back in ten days but had to travel to San Fernando, in the middle of California, to reach the first settlement. It was twenty-six days before they returned with water and food, to find half their party dead. With a trail now broken, the remnant of the Smith outfit deserted the wagons and crossed on foot, reaching San Fernando in February 1850.

Young Manly's rescue trip remains a classic tale. The Jayhawkers had much the same experience in Death Valley. Afterwards the survivors of the Jayhawker caravan formed an association which held annual reunions that were a feature of California life until the turn of the century.

Fired by the success of the shivering curio dealer, I kept watch for pioneer traces myself and one day actually discovered an ancient camp which I could identify as that of the Manly Party. A few coals of the last campfire still lay in the sand, and I gathered up and preserved those cinders as carefully as though they had been precious gems. I found the debris of burned wagons—fire-rusted bolts, bits of hickory spokes. I uncovered an old meerschaum pipe and some ox shoes, the hoofs long since eaten by the rats and coyotes. One of these shoes I carried in my plane when I flew across Antarctica in 1935.

When recently Death Valley was created a National Park, its administration had the consummate gall to hint to me that I ought to give my Manly and Jayhawker relics to the museum they had started at Furnace Creek Inn. I told them to go to a hotter place than Death Valley. Those relics had been there all the time. The very people administering the new park had seen them but had never thought of buying them from the shivery man. Besides, I resented turning Death Valley into a tin-can paradise.

But this is digressive, since I had another purpose in mentioning Death Valley in this chapter. Once in my wanderings out of Furnace Creek Inn I took the trail to Marble Canyon, three miles away. By long practice I had trained my eye to pick out fossil algae, though I never expected to find any in the desert. Yet as I walked up Marble Canyon I saw ripple marks in the sandstone of one of the canyon walls about thirty feet up. I climbed to them and to my amazement found a great bed of fossil algae, the first ever discovered in Death Valley. Most of these I kept for my private collection, but a few I sent to Dr David White, who, before his death, pronounced them to be Pre-Cambrian specimens identical with those found at the bottom of the Grand Canyon.

But I found something else with them: fossil raindrops—by which I mean the petrified imprint of raindrops in Proterozoic mud. Before ever a tree or a shrub or even a blade of grass grew from the soil anywhere on earth, when only the algae were floating their green scum on the lagoons of the planet, this shower had fallen. The shallow seas were drying away, exposing beds of soft plastic clay. A tropical spate had splashed down, and some miracle of nature had caught its matrix and preserved it forever in stone. Now, five or six hundred million years later, in a region where only an inch of moisture falls in a year, I was marvelling at the impression of those great drops.

Never had I been so filled with awe in the presence of eternal things. Is it any wonder that when, almost exactly five years later, I looked, first of the human race, upon the great chain of mountains running down through Antarctica in the American Quadrant, the memory of those fossil raindrops should have flashed up in my thoughts? I did not have to grope for a suitable name for those peaks. Without hesitation I called them the Eternity Range.

II ARCTIC DE LUXE

GRADUALLY the desire was building in me to go exploring once more at the ends of the earth. The virus put into my blood by the receptions Amundsen and I had received in Norway and the United States began to breed a ferment. As several years went by in relative inactivity for me, I felt as if I had dropped out of the world. I was restless, almost desperate for something to do.

Yet I had firmly resolved never to go again into the polar regions except as the head of my own expedition. My expeditions with Amundsen I regarded as training for independent work, and I had learned much from him. The very resolution I had made to travel henceforth alone, however, kept my ambition vague and indefinite. I must first work out my own plan; and it must be for some worthy scientific end, not for the mere adventure. I had not yet thought seriously about the Antarctic, knowing little about it.

Meanwhile, polar exploration by air grew more and more active, as every year the airplane improved in dependability and range. In April 1928 Sir Hubert Wilkins, the Australian aviator and explorer, and his pilot, Carl Ben Eielson, flew from Alaska to Spitzbergen in an airplane, landing on the ice 600 miles northwest of Point Barrow to sound the depth of the ocean and successfully taking off again. The Antarctic summer of 1928–29 found Wilkins flying from a ship along the coast of Graham Land in the Pacific and American quadrants of Antarctica.

Byrd's transatlantic flight in 1927 drew world attention to him. In January 1929 he took a big expedition to the Ross Sea and on the shelf ice beside the Bay of Whales built the largest and most comfortable base camp ever set up in either the Arctic or Antarctic.

After spending the winter there, Byrd, his pilot Bernt Balchen, and two others in November flew to the South Pole and back and followed this with an eastward flight which discovered the mountainous Marie Byrd Land. Riiser-Larsen was already in the Antarctic with ship and plane, and in January and February 1930 made several exploratory flights along the coast in the African and American quadrants east of the Weddell Sea. The following year Sir Douglas Mawson, of Australia, flying from the research ship Discovery II, explored 2,500 miles of the Antarctica coast in the Australian and African quadrants. By the end of 1931 there was little of that vast ice-locked coast line which had not resounded to the noise of mechanical flight.

It was evident that the Antarctic was to be the great field for future exploratory aviation. There was little left in the Arctic to attract the pathfinding flier. The Antarctic—a continent surrounded by oceans rather than an ocean girt by continents—was of much greater importance to humanity. Except for the narrow sector cut out by Amundsen, Scott, and Byrd, the interior of Antarctica, a land mass almost as large as North America, was entirely unknown.

The spring of 1930 I spent in Schloss Lenzburg, in Switzerland, and there, in June, Wilkins came to see me. He brought to me his plan for operating a submarine under the Arctic ice, for which he needed financial support. As he outlined the scheme to me, I grew enthusiastic for it but was even more struck by Wilkins himself. He was a man, I discovered, exactly to my taste. I have often told him since that had he lived in our West during the pioneer days, he would most certainly have been a frontier marshal two-gunning some wild district into law and order.

I consented to attach my name to the submarine expedition as scientific adviser, though I had no intention of accompanying Wilkins on his voyage. In our conversations at Schloss Lenzburg we talked about Antarctica, and I gained the impression that if I ever cared to organize an Antarctic expedition, Wilkins would be willing to enlist as my adviser.

Trial trips of the submarine, the training of a crew, and the excitement of departure took up the spring. Wilkins finally sailed from New London, and I was left in New York to fret at the summer heat and dream of green glaciers, rushing streams, and canoes, when out of a clear sky came an invitation to me to join the Graf Zeppelin as Arctic navigation expert on a projected flight into the Far North. The giant airship was inaugurating a new kind of summer cruise—into the Arctic itself, where the staunchest of cruise steamers would not dare to venture.

I snapped at the opportunity, going, too, as explorer for the American Geographical Society; and just three weeks later—the morning of July 24—I was aboard the Graf as she rose from her hangar at Friedrichshafen. It was a fascinating trip.

From Friedrichshafen we flew to Leningrad via Berlin, Sweden, and Finland, stopping in the former Russian capital long enough to see a little of its night life under Soviet rule. The Graf Zeppelin was the first dirigible ever to fly into Russia. Herds of cattle stampeded under us, I saw three runaway hay wagons dashing over the steppe, and the human inhabitants of one isolated hamlet fled for refuge into their houses.

Leaving Leningrad at 8 A.M., July 26, we flew northeastward, passing above Archangel at 1 P.M. That town of 10,000 inhabitants was one vast lumber yard—the biggest in the world. The roofs of the dwellings disappeared between the stacks of logs and newly cut timbers. Here we altered the course to almost due north, flying over the White and Barents seas toward Franz Josef Land. About dinnertime we crossed the Arctic Circle, the thermometer steadily dropping. That night we had a low midnight sun. All fifteen passengers aboard were scientists, prepared for a little discomfort. When we went to bed we crawled into sleeping bags; and they were needed, too, for the outside temperature was in the low forties Fahrenheit.

All next morning we flew along the Nova Zembla coast, though out of sight of that land. At 2:45 P.M., July 27, we began flying over ice—flat, loose, broken fields of it, not conglomerated tumultuously like the fringe of the true polar pack—and the temperature dropped almost to the freezing point. An hour later we sighted Franz Josef

Land, which is really an archipelago of about one hundred and fifty islands, most of them covered with ice the year round. About five o'clock we came down and poised low over open water at Hooker Island, one of the most northerly land points on earth—farther north than Spitzbergen and almost on the latitude of the north coast of Greenland.

Here there was a Russian government weather station, and off it was anchored the Russian icebreaker Maligin. We had a sack of mail for the Maligin, and they sent over a boat for it. In the stern sheets was a vaguely familiar figure waving a greeting to me. When he came aboard the Graf Zeppelin and shook hands, I had to look twice to recognize him. It was Umberto Nobile, whom I had not seen since our Norge flight of 1926. He had aged visibly since then. The Italia disaster had made a different man of him. As he left in the bobbing boat of the Maligin, which was still looking for Italia survivors—waving good-by as he stood unsteadily in the stern—the scene held an element of pathos that I can never forget.

Thirty minutes only here, and then we spent the rest of the afternoon three thousand feet high, recording the Franz Josef group with our mapping camera. I was able to report to the American Geographical Society that Albert Edward Island and Harmsworth Island, shown on all the charts, do not exist. This was real exploring despite its luxury. Over the Franz Josefs we sent up some of our self-broadcasting radio sounding balloons. One that went up to 35,000 feet recorded a temperature of 40 degrees below zero. It was weird to keep on receiving messages from these robot operators sometimes for twenty-four hours after a free balloon was released.

From Franz Josef Land, which we left in the sunlit small hours of July 28, we headed eastward for the little-known Nicholas II Land. No man had ever penetrated or even seen that ice-locked island, perhaps the one point in the Northern Hemisphere farthest from civilization. It is forever ice locked. No ship can reach it. We came to it about five-thirty in the morning, looking down upon a black, flat, snow-free coastal plain. The dark ground was patched with colors that suggested mosses and lichens. Ice rivers glinted in deep gorges cutting through. I had never seen anything more beautiful.

All that day we flew down the west coast of that lovely solitude, coming eventually over more rugged, wintry country—snow peaks and hanging glaciers between them. The weather was warming, and fog began to choke the valleys and canyons. Toward evening it closed in altogether—heavy rolling banks of fog above which only the mountaintops showed. The fog prevented us from making any accurate estimate of the size of Nicholas II Land, but in our clear flight we had made an important geographical discovery. Nicholas II Land is, in reality, not one island but two islands separated by a narrow channel.

In fog we cruised across the strait separating Nicholas II Land from the mainland and spent the rest of the night, in clear sunshine and now with perfect visibility, flying over the great Taimyr Peninsula in northern Siberia. This desolate region, almost exactly halfway between Spitzbergen and Alaska, impressed me more than anything else I saw on the voyage. A Russian trapper once crossed this treeless wind-swept barren—in winter—but there is no other record of any crossing that I know of. Thousands of wild reindeer, grazing on the tundra, fled in panic from the apparition we made in the sky. Our camera-mapping of Lake Taimyr was the first survey ever made of that vast fresh-water sea.

From Taimyr west across the open Arctic Ocean to fly down the long narrow island of Nova Zembla, of which, since it is frequently visited, I need say nothing except that its mountains, a continuation of the Ural Range, are among the most beautiful in the world. Then back to the mainland again, across the Arctic Circle, and down through Russia, sleeping most of the time, since we had all been more or less continuously awake in the Arctic. I remember being roused by the steward at 3 A.M., July 30, with the news that we were over Leningrad. Looking down from my cabin window in the early dawn, I saw the Winter Palace. Soldiers were waiting to receive us at the airport, but, with his sixth sense as a navigator of the air, Commander Eckener kept on. An hour later fog shrouded Leningrad.

Next day we stopped for an hour or so at Berlin to discharge some of our passengers and receive an official greeting. At 4 A.M., July 31, the Graf Zeppelin was fast to her mooring mast at Friedrichshafen, having flown more than eight thousand miles in less than six days. It seemed like a dream.

But in one respect it was no dream. The sight of Arctic ice and unknown lands had fired me with a zeal for exploration such as had not burned within me since my first meetings with Amundsen. I knew now that I would go again, and soon. In New York I waited impatiently for Wilkins' return. He came at last, and one evening we spread out before us the map of Antarctica.

III PLANNING

IT WAS a question of bases and a question of which side of Antarctica to approach. Wilkins, who alone of moderns had even touched the desolate, barricaded coast of the Pacific Quadrant, told me of the difficulty of setting up expeditionary bases from which to operate. Lack of bases, or of strategic spots on which they might be established, had held up Antarctic exploration while the sledges, ships, and aircraft of venturers were crisscrossing the more accessible Arctic.

As to the side of approach, we virtually had a white ticket. Except for the narrow wedge carved out between the Ross Sea and the Pole by the tracks of Shackleton, Amundsen, Scott, and Byrd, and the eastward extension of Marie Byrd Land, five million square miles lay entirely unknown. Virtually the "whole boundless continent" belonged to the Antarctic explorer in 1932. His predecessors had merely stood on the edges and claimed for their countries icy empires they had never seen.

Yet one sector of Antarctica appealed to the map reader as

more logical for attack than the others. Southeast of Cape Horn the berg-choked Weddell Sea cuts into the continent almost to the eightieth parallel of south latitude. South of New Zealand the strangely ever-open Ross Sea washes the 200-foot face of the polar ice cap winter and summer at an equally high latitude. A chord drawn across the vast peninsula between these two indentations is 1,700 miles long and penetrates into the continent to a point almost exactly midway between the coast and the South Pole.

What lay along this track? The most interesting question was that of mountains. The Nordenskjöld Expedition of 1902 had established the fact that the Antarctic Archipelago,* which borders the Weddell Sea on the west, is really an extension of the Andes Mountains after a dip under the Drake Passage south of Cape Horn. Amundsen had discovered the Queen Maud Range of mountains at the South Pole, and they pointed roughly in the direction of the Antarctic Archipelago. Could it be possible that the Queen Mauds were connected with the peaks of the Antarctic Archipelago? If so, we had the spectacle of one system of mountains extending from the Equator to the Pole.

That—and whatever else the circumpolar continent could reveal to me—I proposed to find out.

There was an even more cogent reason for choosing this sector for exploration. In 1928–29 Byrd had established his Little America at the Bay of Whales, an indentation off Ross Sea. This was a veritable little town staunchly built on the shelf ice—a refuge for any expeditionary party that might come to grief in the interior. There was no other refuge on the entire continent, and there is none now.

*Since I wrote these pages, the British Graham Land Expedition, under Rymill, seems to have established the fact beyond question that the central spine of what all previous charts have called the Antarctic Archipelago is in reality a peninsula and part of the mainland of Antarctica and that the supposed Stefansson Strait, which was thought to cut off Graham Land from continental Antarctica, is, in fact, a deep fjord. It would appear, therefore, that the name Antarctic Archipelago can properly apply only to the South Shetlands and the islands on both sides and off the tip of the Graham Peninsula. The reader will bear this in mind when meeting the many future references to the "Antarctic Archipelago" in this book, understanding that in that term I also include the peninsula.

My first idea, however, was to provide a base ship with a plane-launching apparatus, steam along the coast of the Pacific Quadrant, and make deep nonstop thrusts into the heart of the continent, catapulting the airplane off the deck of the expeditionary vessel.

For this, my first independent expedition, I proposed to secure the most expert and experienced men I could engage. Wilkins, veteran of both polar regions and a most thoughtful and sanely courageous man, had already joined with me as expeditionary assistant in charge of bases and the base ship. For my pilot I wanted Bernt Balchen, who had flown Byrd's plane to the South Pole. Balchen was receptive but, after consideration, decided against the catapult scheme. It was too risky. The chances of failure were too great.

Our next idea, then, was to attempt a nonstop flight from the Ross Sea to the Weddell Sea and return. This was a distance of 3,400 miles, but dependable airplanes were being turned out with that range and more. It was our intention to take off from the ice at Little America, though using our base ship as headquarters. I went to Balchen with this idea, and he agreed to make such a flight with me. He stipulated, however, that we should have a meteorologist with the expedition. I could not quite see why that was necessary. Without radio reports from the whole length of the route, a meterologist could only guess at conditions out of range of his instruments. However, I conceded the point, and when we finally sailed we had a weather sharp on the ship.

As I studied the problem and learned more and more about Antarctica, I began leaning toward a different plan. Why should it be a nonstop flight? The chances were that the weather would force down any transcontinental plane in Antarctica, anyhow. Well, what of it? Pilots of planes equipped with skis were landing on and taking off from the snow in Alaska, along Hudson Bay in Canada, in Norway, and in Russia and Siberia as a regular thing. From what I could learn from men who had visited Antarctica, the ice surface of that continent was no more difficult for a ski plane than the snow fields of the North, if as difficult.

Moreover, a leisurely crossing, coming down for surface observations or to camp during bad weather, would be much more valuable scientifically than a dash across at 150 to 200 miles an hour. I took the plan to Balchen. He thought it over and agreed to make such a flight. It was consequently written into Balchen's contract that we were to land whenever necessary on account of weather or to take observations. This is important for the reader to remember.

Next came a question of a suitable airplane. There had recently been formed at Inglewood, Cal., a group of expert aviation builders and engineers called the Northrup Corporation. I knew of the excellent work done previously by these people and decided to entrust them with the design and construction of a plane for my Antarctic flight. My airplane was therefore the first to be built by Northrup, the prototype for the several hundred commercial and military planes produced since by that company.

It was an all-metal, cantilever, low-wing monoplane powered with a Wasp 600-H.P. engine, which gave it a top speed of 230 m.p.h. Fully loaded with gasoline, it had a cruising radius of 7,000 miles—the longest range of any airplane yet built. It was one of the first American planes to be equipped with wing flaps to reduce landing speed and could land at 42 m.p.h. The wing span was 48 feet, the hull length 31 feet. The low wing was especially adapted to Antarctic flying, since two men could quickly scoop out trenches. for the skis, allowing the wing to rest flat on the snow, where the wind could not get under it. The broad blunt skis, when finally fitted on, were ludicrously like a pair of giant shoes.

This ship inaugurated the famous Gamma class of Northrups. Everybody was enthusiastic about it when it came from the factory. Captain Frank Hawks, the speed pilot, bought the second model. Wilkins said it was the Rolls-Royce of airplanes. Balchen, who had stayed at the factory during the three months of its construction and who had flown it East to be taken down and shipped to my base ship in Norway, said it stepped out three years ahead of world aviation. He wanted to make the Tokio flight in it. Balchen often said frankly that exploration meant nothing to him, except as it called for expert aviation. With him the performance of a plane was the whole thing.

In Norway I had seen the fishing trawlers—staunch and sea-worthy boats, yet small enough to be maneuvred easily in ice. Wilkins agreed with me that this type of vessel was ideal, and I sent him to Norway to buy one, which he did—the Fanefjord, a herring boat built for the Bay of Biscay. She was a single-deck vessel of 400 tons built in 1919 of Norwegian pine and oak. Her power was a Bolinder semi-Diesel engine. She could do seven to eight knots and had a cruising radius of 11,000 miles. Her slowness was the only fault one could find with her; otherwise she was the best ship in the world for the work. She smelled strongly of fish at first, but that wore off. After we fitted her with sails, we could get nine knots out of her in a favorable wind.

Thus in travel equipment the expedition had the best that money could buy, and I never had any criticism to make about any of it. In fitting the Fanefjord for the Antarctic, the most important thing done was to sheathe her from stem to the widest part of the hull, nearly amidships, with oak planking covered by three-quarter-inch steel armor plate for icebreaking. We also gave her a fore-and-aft rigging, put in a new electric lighting system, and re-modeled the inside of the hull to give living quarters for fourteen men. There were six private cabins, located amidships and aft, which meant that all our scientists and technical men had to sign on and serve as members of the crew, living in the forecastle. The captain, chief engineer, and first mate, Wilkins, my airplane pilot, and myself had cabins.

This vessel I christened Wyatt Earp after the famous frontier marshal of the West. On this, my own expedition, I could indulge every whim and fancy that did not interfere with its efficiency, and one of my whims was to imbue the whole enterprise with the spirit of Wyatt Earp, the bravest man I ever heard of.

I am frankly a hero-worshiper and a sentimentalist. For years I have made almost a cult of the memory of Wyatt Earp. I have spent much time collecting every souvenir and trinket I could find associated with that unbelievably brave man. Only the other day I secured, after a three-year effort, the hair-trigger six-shooter with which he fought his famous battle with Ike Clanton's gang. I hang this gun in its holster over my bedpost, wherever I may be, and I expect to keep up this custom to the end of my life.

I don't suppose any vessel ever sailed before so filled with the presence of the figure whose name it bore as was the Wyatt Earp when it set out for the Antarctic. In the ship's library were two books about Earp: *Wyatt Earp, Frontier Marshal,* by Stewart N. Lake, and *Tombstone,* by Walter Noble Burns, author also of Wilkins' favorite American book, *The Saga of Billy the Kid.* Everybody on board read these two volumes, the Norwegians who understood English translating to those who didn't. Most of them had never heard of Earp before the voyage.

In my cabin hung Wyatt Earp's cartridge belt. When I made the flight at last, I had this historic trophy on the Polar Star. On one of my fingers I wore a plain gold wedding ring which the widowed Mrs Earp had given me in memory of her famous husband. Wyatt Earp wore this ring during his Tombstone days, and he in turn had received it from his father. The ring, therefore, saw three generations of pioneers. Judge Earp wore it when he crossed the continent from Missouri in '49, it heard the roar of guns as Wyatt Earp helped subdue the lawless frontier, and finally I carried it on the first crossing of Antartica.

What appeals to me most in the career of Wyatt Earp was his domination over men. Let me quote from a review, published in a San Francisco paper, of Stewart Lake's book:

"Three decades—the sixties, seventies, and eighties—saw the extermination of the buffalo, the coming of the railroads, and the peak times of the mining camps. No one ever lived who epitomized those three phases so definitely as did Wyatt Earp. He entered the Western scene at the beginning of its most vivid era, and when he put away his guns that era was ended. On the buffalo range, in cow towns, in Dodge City, Deadwood, and Tombstone he altered the course of Western history by his domination over men and events."

That seems to me the complete statement. It explains why Wyatt Earp has done more for me than any other figure who ever lived.

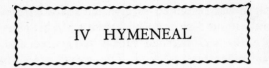

IV   HYMENEAL

THIS PROGRESS had not been made quite without interruption. Since I had inherited Schloss Lenzburg I had gone to Switzerland often to visit it, and in 1932 I had planned such a trip. Accordingly, in the summer, when I had decided in principle upon an Antarctic expedition, but before I had ordered either the airplane or motor ship, I went abroad to keep my rendezvous with the ghost of Frederick Barbarossa.

At the castle I kept busy brushing up on my navigation. I purchased a Leica camera to carry on the Antarctic flight and practiced taking pictures with it. When my legal term of residence was over, I went to Paris, engaged passage home, and waited for the boat, impatient to get back to New York and buckle down to the concrete job of organizing my expedition.

Then—and it must have been fate—two days before I was to sail from Cherbourg I suddenly changed my mind about going. Although I was fairly expert in the use of a camera, having carried one for many years, I was dissatisfied with the results I had been getting from the Leica. On my coming expedition I could not afford to slight any detail. I had every reason to expect that I would fly over mountains; therefore, the photographs I would take might be the most important record I would bring out. From a good photograph a geologist with a microscope can often determine the nature of rocks and mountains and therefore know something about their origin and history.

The best photographer of mountains in the world was Walter Mittelholzer, whose airplane Leica shots of the Alps are familiar to all lovers of camera art. Mittelholzer directed the airport at Zurich, Switzerland, and I thought he might be willing to give an amateur pointers on mountain photography. Almost on the impulse of a moment, I canceled my passage and took a train for Zurich.

Mittelholzer was delighted to give me Leica lessons, especially when he understood their purpose. I went up in his plane with him, we circled peaks and threaded valleys and passes, and I snapped his cameras under his direction. The entrance to Mittelholzer's flying field was a turnstile. As I approached this to leave after my first lesson, I saw a young woman just coming in—a slender, long-limbed, dark-haired, brown-eyed young woman, very trim and professional in a flying suit. I looked at her; she looked at me. Then we passed on through the turnstile, in opposite directions.

Next day I saw this vision again, and I asked Mittelholzer who it might be.

"Ach, Meester Ellsvort'," he replied, "dot ees a countryvooman of yours—Fraulein Ulmer. Come—I prrresent you."

So he introduced me to Miss Ulmer. We chatted together for a few moments. Mittelholzer was teaching her to fly. Then we discovered a common bond of interest. She was born in Pottsville, Pa., near where I had spent five years of my life as a student in the Hill School. I had to find out all about the old place before I'd let her go up for her flying lesson. What a duffer I had been at Hill! And was Epps Candy Parlor still there? Yes, still there—crowded every Saturday with boys from the Hill. . . .

I protracted my camera instruction for two weeks, greatly to my technical and domestic advantage. My Leica shots of the Antarctic mountains were as good as I could wish; and at the end of my two weeks in Zurich, I, a lone eagle for fifty-two years and almost a creature of the womanless parts of the earth, was engaged to marry Mary Louise Ulmer.

Her father, lately deceased, was Jacob S. Ulmer, a banker and industrialist of Philadelphia and Pottsville. His father was a naturalized American citizen, coming from Stuttgart, Germany. Her mother's people were the Dyers, of Pittsburgh, who traced back to England via Virginia and Rhode Island.

Since our marriage we have discovered that we are both quite fascinated by our ancestors. I have told of the trip we made to Hartford, Conn., to trace Ellsworths. We also went to Rhode Island to hunt colonial Dyers. In a case in the Providence Museum we saw a gentleman's silk suit of wig-and-powder days—the first silk suit worn by any man in America. It belonged to William Dyer, brother of the Virginia ancestor. Still, it does not do to probe ancestory too deeply. We also discovered a Mary Dyer who was burned as a witch in Rhode Island.

Mrs Ellsworth was educated at Miss Bennett's School in Millbrook, Conn., and had lived a great deal of her life abroad. We were married the following spring—May 23, 1933—in New York at the Little Church around the Corner. In all, I have been at home just about six months since then, and until 1936 we had never spent Christmas together. Even our wedding trip took us to rainy, chilly New Zealand, where I met the Wyatt Earp.

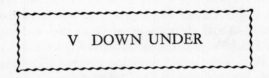

V DOWN UNDER

REFITTING the Wyatt Earp, purchasing and assembling supplies, engaging a crew and a scientific staff, shipping the Polar Star to Oslo and loading it aboard the expeditionary ship, and a thousand other details of preparation took up the winter and entire spring of 1933. Early in July the little ship started out on its 18,000-mile trudge to New Zealand—nearly a 4-month voyage for her. She sailed by way of Cape Town, the Indian Ocean, and Melbourne for Dunedin, our jumping-off place near the southeast corner of South Island, New Zealand. All of the Antarctic party were aboard except myself.

I started from New York in August, traveling with my wife and her mother, Mrs Ulmer. We first flew to California on a commercial transport plane, and I was a wreck when we arrived. Every place we stopped, whether in the dead of night or not, reporters were at the airports to interview me about this harebrained thing I was going to attempt. I got no sleep at all. Finally, when I refused to come out and see them, they came to my window and said: "If you don't come out, we'll come in."

One place we made a landing during a blinding thunder squall and broke off the tip of a wing against a tree. During the excitement of that small accident, I got a reputation for coolness I scarcely deserved. I was fast asleep through it all.

In San Francisco people said to me, when I had told them something about my project: "Oh, then your flight will be about the same as from New York to San Francisco—twenty hours?"

I answered: "Yes, just about the same—only different."

We sailed from Los Angeles and ten days later, at Honolulu, caught the Matson liner Mariposa for Auckland, where, in September, we found the antipodean winter still hanging on. We went to the National Park south of Auckland to climb mountains and keep fit, but the weather was so cold and miserable we gave up and took a boat for Pago Pago, capital of American Samoa back in the tropics, to wait there until spring arrived in New Zealand. The Wyatt Earp was not due in Dunedin for weeks.

In Pago Pago we stopped with the governor, Captain Landenburg, U.S.N., who occupied a cool, tropical frame house on top of the bluff at the entrance to the harbor. The harbor itself, really the crater of an immense extinct volcano, is one of the most beautiful in the world. The sides of the crater frame it like the seats of an enormous amphitheater. Banana trees thickly clothe the mountain from the ridge to the beach, and in the morning sun the green fronds look as if they were waxed. I so fell in love with Pago Pago I swore that after I had crossed Antarctica I would return there to live, but I changed my mind completely after I shook off its spell.

After a week in this lovely place, we sailed away, the flag on the mast in front of the governor's residence dipping in salute as our steamer nosed out to sea. We went this time to Christchurch, South Island, so as to be nearer Dunedin, but found it, if anything, windier and colder than Auckland. There were great herds of cattle near Christchurch, and they all had blankets tied around their bellies to keep them warm, the first time I ever saw such a thing. We found the people most kindly and hospitable, but they all lived in English-type houses with open fires and no steam heat, and we Americans could not get warm.

At Christchurch we would have three sunny days, then three days of rain, fog, and cutting winds in regular succession. But though the weather was wintry, nature insisted that it was spring. Neither my wife nor I had ever seen more beautiful spring flowers —the hawthorn hedges white and pink with bloom, hillsides golden with gorse and mimosa. The hills were covered with a green succulent tussock grass on which grazed thousands of sheep, which were just then dropping their lambs.

Except for the mountainous scenery, in New Zealand one could easily imagine himself in England—the hawthorn hedges, the eternally green pastures, the coal fires and drafty halls, even the English menu of mutton and cabbage, day after day. But excellent mutton, and another English delicacy, whitebait, is abundant at Christchurch. The hotel served whitebait fritters; and my, they were good! If you ordered eggs, unless you specified hens' eggs, you were likely to get ducks' eggs. Tea was the universal beverage; coffee, hard to get; coffee with cream, unknown.

Twice during our stay at Christchurch I walked forty-two miles to the seaside fishing port of Akaroa. This was where Scott's ship Discovery came in with the news of his tragic death. The sheltered bay teemed with domestic swans, and the tavern served me swans'-egg omelet, my first introduction to that dish. It takes a high place on my list of local delicacies.

For another excursion I chartered an airplane at Christchurch and flew three hours to Franz Josef Glacier. After viewing this natural wonder, I engaged a guide, intending to cross the mountains on foot and descend to the hotel on the other side. Before we got halfway up to the pass a terrific storm set in. My guide and I found a deserted log hut beside a natural hot spring, and there we sheltered three days as it poured torrents every minute.

Lincoln Ellsworth and Mary Louise Ulmer (Later Mrs Lincoln Ellsworth) before Their Engagement, Schloss Lenzburg, Switzerland, 1932.

SOME OF THE WORLD'S FINEST SCENERY—BUT SELDOM A HUMAN EYE TO SEE IT!

Among the Large and Small Islands of   Make It Impossible   to Land   a Plane
the Antarctic Archipelago, Black Rocks   along   Most   of   This   Coast.   The   Sheer

By that time we had eaten all the food in our knapsacks. If we were not to starve to death in the midst of plenty, we would have to get out of there, rain or no rain. It was coming down cats and dogs, but we started back, soaked to the skin after the first few minutes of it. Dry gullies that had crossed the trail had become torrents which we had to ford, wading waist-deep. The howling gale drove into our very bones. Fortunately, this country was full of hot springs. We were sopping wet, anyhow, and so every time our teeth began to chatter we waded into a hot spring and sat down in it to warm up. Thus we got out without serious mishap.

Radio reports from the Wyatt Earp told of her approach, so we went to Dunedin, 200 miles down the east coast of South Island from Christchurch, to meet her upon her arrival. Dunedin, the third largest city of New Zealand, proved to be a hospitable place, its Scotch population extending us a warm welcome. Antarctic explorers are an old story to them. Many expeditions have started from Dunedin, Scott's and Shackleton's among them.

I have never seen people with less curiosity than the Dunedinites. While we were in Dunedin, a British cruiser came into the harbor and sent its company ashore to parade with music and banners. In any American community, from New York City to a village, such a parade would have lined the curbs with spectators, and a crowd of small boys would have trotted beside the bass drummer. The Dunedinites paid not the slightest attention to it. The trumpets brayed, but the local population merely glanced casually over its shoulders and went about its business.

When the Wyatt Earp came, we went down the bay in a launch to board her. How proud I was of my little ship, thus soberly and faithfully finishing her long voyage! This was the first time I had seen her. And how glad to greet my comrades again—Wilkins, Balchen, Chris Braathen, our engine mechanic, and Lanz, a Brooklyn boy whom I had engaged as radio operator! Balchen's appearance gave me a hearty laugh, for he was wearing the belt and knife of a typical Norwegian sailor.

There I met my crew—captain, two mates, chief engineer, cabin boy, and five sailors before the mast. All but the cabin boy, Larsen, were veteran Norwegian whalers, men who had been brought up in the ice and who had all been in the Ross Sea before not once but many times.

There were anecdotes to tell about the Norwegian doctor we had signed for the expedition. On our three cruises into the Antarctic we had queer luck with our doctors, as my story will show. This one, who hailed from Oslo, was a serious, well-meaning man who at least could produce the diploma of an M.D. On the way south through the Atlantic, Bernt Balchen developed a touch of appendicitis, and it was hazardous for him to go into the ice in that condition. Therefore, the Wyatt Earp put into Cape Town, South Africa, for Balchen to undergo an operation.

Our faithful medico saw him through it as far as he could, accompanying the pilot to the hospital, standing by while he went under the ether, and marching with the stretcher into the operating room. Then at the sight of the first incision he fainted dead away. Fortunately, there was nothing else that ever required his professional attention. Once in the Ross Sea I asked him for formalin in which to preserve some fish specimens. He gave me a handful of moth balls.

The Wyatt Earp reached Dunedin on November 9, and there she stayed about a month, refueling, taking aboard the final supplies, and giving the men a rest from the sea. We provisioned her for two years, allowing for eighteen men, and her fuel tanks held enough oil for ninety days steaming. On December 10, 1933, we sailed from Dunedin for the Bay of Whales. My wife and her mother went back to the States to watch the outcome from there.

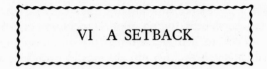

VI A SETBACK

THE LITTLE WYATT EARP, 135 feet long and drawing 15 feet of water, soon showed me what a wonderful sea boat she was. We were scarcely out of sight of New Zealand when we ran into a terrific storm and for three days had the wildest sea we experienced all the time we were in the Far South. The Earp fairly rolled her rails under. In the tiny dining room, which ran along one side of the vessel amidships, though we dampened the tablecloth and screwed on fiddles, we were always having to snatch flying crockery out of the air. Seas breached clear over her, and we had to wear rubber boots at our meals. The cabins and forecastle, though, were dry.

But the Wyatt Earp came through it without damage. In better weather we settled down to our routine, everybody taking a hand in operating the ship. I took my four-hour trick at the wheel every evening right after supper. There was not much room anywhere to stretch one's legs. Two tiers of gasoline drums, wired to the rails, prevented the pleasant passenger-ship custom of the daily constitutional around the deck. There was no general cabin to assemble in, only the narrow dining room in which everybody ate, sailors and all. In fact, when off duty the most comfortable place to be in was one's bunk.

We had a small library—a few volumes we picked up in New Zealand, and a set of paper-bound classics from Everyman's Library presented to us by the publisher. Wilkins brought a little library of his own—doctoring books and old books of philosophy mostly. He also brought a small phonograph and a batch of records with him and played them at night as he read Nietzsche or fussed with some contraption he was working on. At Nordenskjöld's camp, which this narrative will reach later, Wilkins found a vise. He set this up in his cabin and afterwards spent many hours at it polishing agates which he picked up on the Antarctic islands.

The members of the crew when off duty lay in their forecastle bunks and read or slept, or sat on the floor playing some Norwegian game with a pack of greasy cards. The assistant engineer had a fiddle on which he played lugubrious music. Each bunk was curtained so that its occupant could shut out the light if he wanted to sleep.

At the end of a week we reached the pack ice closing off the Ross Sea. It was heavy that year, and we spent twenty-two days in it worming through a distance of 454 miles. It was back, drive ahead, collide with ice, stop, and back again. During a single watch one day the bridge rang 169 signals to the engine room. As a result of this constant backing and going ahead we wore down our gears until we lost our half speed altogether. For thirteen of the twenty-two days we were at a standstill, locked in the ice.

On Christmas we had a grand celebration. We were fast in ice that day, and there was nothing to do but maintain a watch on deck. The doctor (meaning the cook this time) put together a big Norwegian dinner. Somebody mysteriously dug out of the hold a small evergreen tree that had been put aboard at Dunedin for the purpose. Decorations were found for it; and then a big surprise —presents for everybody from Mrs Ellsworth. Each man got a box of candy, several packages of chewing gum, a metal puzzle, and a mouth organ. There was plenty of music in the forecastle after that. Aquavit and whisky flowed, and everybody was merry.

In the rigging of the vessel hung the carcasses of several wild pigs which Balchen had shot when hunting during the time the Wyatt Earp stayed in Dunedin. He also brought back one young porker alive, and it became his pet on the ship. It had three broken ribs but was otherwise intact. This animal was a regular jack rabbit for speed. No matter how securely it might hide itself on the Wyatt Earp, it was sure to turn up at meal hours. It seemed to be able to tell time.

On any such expedition there has to be someone to serve as clown or as the butt of witticisms. The bos'n was ours on the Wyatt Earp. He was a Norwegian who, when sober, was taciturn to the point of being a mute. When drunk, he could open up a little, though only upon one theme—the grandeur of the Yangtse Kiang River in China.

"The Yangtse," he would say slowly and impressively, "is the finest river in the world."

If he were pressed for reasons to substantiate this statement, he merely repeated: "The Yangtse is the finest river in the world."

That summed up his conversation. We nicknamed him Yangtse Bill.

Yangtse Bill had great pride of craft. One day when cold sober, the Wyatt Earp steady in the ice, he fell down the forecastle ladder, hit his head on a beam, and got a black eye. He was so ashamed of this lubberly performance that he kept out of sight as much as he could until his eye cleared. He would not even eat with the others but sneaked into the dining room after everybody was gone.

The Wyatt Earp gave us a Christmas present that day which was not quite so pleasant. In the midst of our party the shaft of the electric generator broke, and we had no more electric lights during the rest of the voyage. This made no difference on deck, since we had now raised the sun until it was swinging in its circle above the horizon twenty-four hours a day. It was dark inside, though, and until we got back to New Zealand the cabins reeked with the smell of kerosene lamps.

On January 9, 1934, we moored to the edge of the heavy bay ice in the Bay of Whales; and the crane set the Polar Star, which had been assembled, ready for flight, in Dunedin, down on the level snow. Little America, where Byrd and his party were about to establish themselves for their second stay in the Antarctic, was twelve miles south of us. On the twelfth Balchen and I took the plane for thirty minutes out on a test flight over Amundsen's old South Pole trail. Everything worked perfectly. We were ready for the great attempt.

Then in the night came disaster. The evening before we noticed that the ice front, pounded by heavy seas, was breaking off a little. Balchen took some of the men and moved the Polar Star ·inland about a mile. Sir Hubert Wilkins questioned whether that was far enough. Balchen said it would be better to take it back farther, but it would be safe for the night. Everybody was tired. Next morning we could all take a hand and move the plane back to the Ross shelf ice.

About four o'clock in the morning shouts ringing through the ship brought everybody up on deck. In my cabin I heard a rumbling like distant cannonading. On deck I saw an amazing spectacle. Cracks were running everywhere through the thick bay ice as heavy swells kept moving out *from underneath the great ice cliffs of the Antarctic Barrier.* Within fifteen minutes the Bay of Whales, which had been a snow prairie, had become a grinding mass of ice cakes and floes for five miles inland. The Polar Star was marooned on a small cake little larger than herself. Presently this cake, caught in the crush, split in two, dropping the skis and hull into a crevasse. Only the wings were holding the airplane out of the bay.

It took sharp work for six hours to save the plane. Men tumbled over the rails of the Wyatt Earp, dragging boats with which to cross the leads. Three landed on the split cake with the Polar Star. Lines were thrown from an adjoining floe, and eventually the plane was hauled up upon safer ice. The motorship maneuvred through the leads until finally it drew alongside the floe of the rescue party. The Polar Star was swung aboard, a pitiful sight—skis fractured, one wing bent, unflyable. The expedition was off for that year at least. Only a factory could put the airplane back into condition.

There was no use crying over spilled milk—nothing to do but pack up and go home. Technically, the responsibility was Balchen's, but I am not blaming him, since I would probably have done the same thing myself. He had spent two Januaries at the Bay of Whales and had never seen it behave that way. The old whalers on the Wyatt Earp had never known of such a cataclysm. I have always believed, since the Ross Sea calmed that night, that the disturbance was seismic. There was, in fact, an earthquake in India

that same day. It could have been the result of an unknown erup-
tion of lonely Mount Erebus, Antarctica's single active volcano.

So we turned the Wyatt Earp northward. Try again; that was all
I could do. As the semi-Diesel started, huge pieces of the barrier
were toppling into the sea with a booming like distant claps of
thunder. It was an expensive accident for me. The expedition had
been costing $5,000 a month for running expenses since spring.
The cost of the Polar Star was $37,000. Against that I had a syndi-
cate contract with the New York *Times* and the North American
Newspaper Alliance for the exclusive news of the expedition.
Since nothing had occurred but the accident to the plane, there
would be little revenue from that source. I had also received money
from the National Geographic Society.

On the voyage up through the ice I renewed the contract with
Bernt Balchen and a few of the others. The doctor—the M.D. from
Oslo—we were shipping back to Norway.

Coming into Dunedin, the Wyatt Earp, fighting the tide and
having no half speed, smashed her nose against the dock. The
whole trip was unlucky. There she remained to be repaired and
conditioned for another voyage to Antarctica. In Dunedin we found
an oil tanker about to start for California. I arranged to ship the
battered Polar Star on this vessel; and Braathen, the engine mechanic, and Lanz, our radioman, snatched the opportunity to go
home and see their people. Balchen was also staying with the
airplane. I waited in Auckland to catch the good old Mariposa for
San Francisco.

VII FRESH START

DISCOURAGING AS IT WAS, the accident to the Polar Star
was to benefit the expedition in more than one way. In the first
place, during the year improvements had been made in the Gamma

model of Northrup airplanes, and these were installed in my ship when it went to the Inglewood factory. It came out of the shop a better job than it had ever been, as Balchen knew after he had given it a test flight from Los Angeles to New York and return.

But more important, the delay gave me time for a more mature consideration of the whole plan for the projected flight. It became obvious that the project to fly across Antarctica from the Ross Sea to the Weddell Sea and return was faulty in several ways. For one thing, it put both our salvationary eggs—the Wyatt Earp and Little America—into a single basket. Should the plane crack up at the eastern end of the route, the occupants would face an impossible foot journey of a thousand miles or so over the ice cap. Moreover, on such a long flight, everything would have to be sacrificed for gas. If the plane were damaged anywhere in the interior, the flyers would have scanty equipment indeed with which to reach safety. They must virtually bet their lives on the performance of the plane itself.

In the third place, experience had now showed us what we had known before from hearsay: namely, that it is impossible to get into the Ross Sea and reach the Bay of Whales before the month of January. Yet January is a poor month for Antarctic flying. The best months are October and November. After December 1 the fogs set in.

The logical thing, therefore, seemed to be to base with the Wyatt Earp on one of the islands of the Antarctic Archipelago which border the Weddell Sea on the west, and, choosing the good weather of October and November, fly across to Little America and wait there until the Wyatt Earp could break through in January. While this plan would add between three hundred and six hundred miles to the distance across Antarctica proper, still it gave us a much shorter route than the round trip first proposed. It would enable the plane to carry a sledge, a tent, food supplies, and camping equipment without which it would be foolhardy to venture into the icy continent.

Besides, in Wilkins I had with me, as a member of the expedition, a man familiar with the Antarctic Archipelago, having been the first to explore it since Charcot in 1909. But even Wilkins knew none too much about those mountainous masses of land, buried under glaciers and snow and almost perpetually fogbound. He knew, however, that certain of the islands, perhaps because their rocks are warmed by volcanic action, remain snow free even in winter. He felt certain that we could find a base from which to take off.

The archipelago offered us one further advantage. Its southernmost and westernmost fragment of land is Charcot Island, which lies a short distance off the supposed Antarctic coast at the seventy-fifth meridian west of Greenwich. When in the flight I should cross the seventy-fifth meridian, I should be almost halfway to Little America but only about three hundred miles from Charcot Island. The route therefore offered three havens in the event of an accident to the plane. Moreover, of all the islands of the archipelago Wilkins knew Charcot best, having flown clear around it in 1929. He therefore could describe its landmarks and thus make easy a rendezvous, if the Wyatt Earp had to come there to pick us up.

All this was predicated upon the plane's ability to communicate with the ship by radio. What our plans should be in the event of radio failure I will come to later on.

All the way back to the States I considered these points, and by the time I reached New York I had made my decision. The destination of our next voyage would be the Weddell Sea side of Antarctica. The new plan for a straight transcontinental flight from my base ship to the Ross Sea now brought up seriously the problem of a polar diet. On the first attempt we had not bothered much about diet but had carried only a standard polar diet, since we planned to be away from the Wyatt Earp only twenty hours at the outside, assuming the flight to be successful. On the Wyatt Earp it was not necessary to think of a condensed, lightweight, scientific diet, since the ship could and did load whatever food we fancied—twenty tons of the best of everything, including even fresh meat. Quarters of beef and carcasses of hogs and lambs, tightly wrapped against sunshine, hung in the rigging, keeping sweet and unspoiled in the natural refrigeration of the Antarctic climate.

But now it was a different question. It was quite possible that my pilot and I would have to subsist for weeks in Little America. I had no idea if Byrd had left any food supplies there and so could not count on it. We should have to carry in the Polar Star our entire food supply, which therefore must be highly concentrated and scientifically balanced.

Accordingly, as soon as I reached the East, I engaged Dr Dana C. Coman, of Johns Hopkins University, who had been dietician with Byrd on his first expedition to Antarctica, to come with mine as dietary expert. Since Coman was also a physician, he could serve as our doctor as well. The diet he worked out for me, though lightweight, compact, and balanced, offered much more variety than the one I had known with Amundsen.

That spring I went as usual to Switzerland. When we returned, my wife and I went at once to Hawaii, staying several weeks that summer at the Crater House. The SS Monterey, with Balchen, Braathen, and Lanz aboard and the Polar Star in the hold, called, but I waited for the Mariposa. A pleasanter trip I never took than the voyage on her from New Zealand to San Francisco, and she had become my favorite boat on all the seven seas. Dr Coman joined me in Honolulu, and we sailed south together. My wife went back to New York to watch the drama of the flight from that point of vantage.

Spring in New Zealand was wet and cold as ever; but I paid little attention to the weather this time, proceeding direct to Dunedin, where the Wyatt Earp had already returned after a voyage up to Auckland to receive the Polar Star from the SS Monterey. The damage to the bow and to the machinery of the motor ship had been repaired during the winter. Final supplies were going aboard, and we were about ready to start. My old crew was intact except for a single change. One of the Norwegian sailors had signed on a ship going back to Europe. His place had been taken by a Dunedin boy, a novice in the Antarctic, who turned out to be a good man.

Through the courtesy of the Dunedin Harbour Board we had enjoyed free dockage during the entire winter. Everything had been done to assist us and make our stay in that fishing port enjoyable. When we sailed, Dunedin gave us a formal farewell, and both the mayor and our local agent, Mr Tapley, declared that the Ellsworth Expedition was the most popular of any that had ever visited their town.

The Wyatt Earp presented a much more shipshape appearance than she had on the former voyage. Better stowage had succeeded in putting almost everything in the hold. Besides the two tiers of gasoline and oil drums around the rails, the only other bit of freight on deck was our motorboat Verona, lashed to the hatch top. This was in marked contrast to the usual expeditionary ship, its decks piled high with crates and all sorts of lumber.

I wish I could convey to the reader some idea of the immense detail of stocking a polar expedition, the hundreds and thousands of different articles required—sea stores, land stores, engine spares, camping and ice-travel equipment, food, clothing, fuel, technical instruments, and countless other things. As one item, we carried wheels and pontoons for the plane as well as skis. There are few standards to guide one; it's all a matter of individual experience. Our lading included enough Texaco aviation gas to fly the Polar Star 12,000 miles at racing speed, and in the bunkers was enough oil to drive the Wyatt Earp a similar distance. Our food stores would subsist twenty men bountifully for two years.

The equipment indeed was complete and perfect in every way except for one trivial omission and one entirely unsuspected inclusion. In spite of every check, there were no connecting rods—those short bits of steel by which a gas engine's pistons are attached to the main shaft—in the spare parts for the Wasp motor, and, through some slip of our protection system, we had taken aboard in Dunedin the nucleus of a colony of highly prolific rats. Both the omission and the inclusion made plenty of trouble later.

We sailed from Dunedin on the morning of September 19, 1934 —seventeen men outbound on the quest that had baffled Shackleton, Wilkins, Riiser-Larsen, and three other expeditions since 1914—

the crossing of Antarctica from the Weddell Sea to the Ross Sea. It was the brightest goal of all polar exploration. The personnel of the expedition was as follows:

SCIENTIFIC PARTY

Lincoln Ellsworth, leader
Sir Hubert Wilkins, technical assistant
Bernt Balchen, pilot
Dr Dana C. Coman, medical officer
Lanz, radio officer
Dr Holmboe, meteorologist
Chris Braathen, motor mechanic

CREW OF WYATT EARP

Captain Holth
First Mate Olsen
Second Mate Liavaag
Chief Engineer Holmboe
Assistant Engineer Bigsth
Larsen, cabin boy
Boatswain
Three deck hands

I have never known a drearier voyage than that of the Wyatt Earp from New Zealand to Deception Island, southeast of Cape Horn—four thousand miles of wind-lashed ocean, gales, blizzards, and hurricanes, the laboring motorship half buried under the boarding combers, never a sunny day, scarcely a sunny hour, dead reckoning all the way. We rolled and wallowed at seven knots an hour across the most desolate stretch of water on earth. During the entire twenty-six days we did not meet one vessel. No whale's gleaming back broke for a moment the tortured monotony of the sea. There was no gull or auk, no life at all. When we reached Deception Island we were all as bleached out as if we had been in the hospital. Our eyes watered in the unaccustomed glare of the snow fields.

But though we were only a smothered dot on a deserted ocean larger than the North Atlantic, we were constantly in touch with our relatives, friends, and business connections in the United States, in New Zealand, South America, and England. Messages went back and forth every day. Radio has robbed the "perilous seas" of their romance and deprived the rover of his isolation. Outside, a wild sea and lonely horizon; inside, the radio buzzing about gasoline supplies and syndicate rights, and a phonograph playing jazz!

We all felt sorry for Dr Coman, who was seasick the entire way. He lay in his forecastle bunk, his cap always pulled down clear over his eyes, turning a greenish countenance toward his visitors. I asked him once how he had managed with Byrd on the voyage to Little America.

"I don't know," he moaned. "I only remember the high lights."

Sheer starvation drove him out to eat after eight days. He managed a full meal but was immediately felled by another attack of *mal de mer*. Poor chap, he had an unhappy time of it!

Deception Island was picked as our destination for two reasons. Its northing made it likely that it could be approached in October, when more southerly islands were likely to be walled off by ice. Still, one could never tell about Deception Island, which is perhaps why it received its name. Octobers had been known when the island was locked in heavy pack ice stretching hundreds of miles. We counted, however, on good ice within the bay for our aviation field. Among our various data we had two November observations of bay ice in Deception Harbor. In 1919 it was six feet thick; in 1929, two feet.

Secondly, Deception Island offers one of the few caravansaries Antarctica affords—an abandoned Norwegian whaling factory in which even a strong expedition could, in need, shelter.

During the long run to Deception we had but a single interest, other than the duty of standing watches, to bring us on deck—to watch for the elusive Dougherty Island. Whalers had several times reported the island at approximately Lat. 59° 20' S. and Long. 120° W., but both Shackleton and Scott visited that spot and found no land.

One day we thought we saw it at about the position given above. Through thick, snowy weather loomed a mass with a jagged sky line and which therefore did not resemble the usual table-topped iceberg of the Antarctic. Not until we drew within a mile of it did we see that it really was a berg. What seemed to be crags and pinnacles of rock were hundreds of penguins perched around the edges of the berg and riding far from their habitat. Thinking perhaps that Dougherty Island had sunk and that the berg had stranded on it, we observed it for a while but saw that it was afloat and drifting with the current.

The most violent weather of the entire voyage overtook us just as we approached Deception Island. Visibility dropped so low that we did not raise Smith Island at all—that 6,000-foot outpost of the South Shetlands. By dead reckoning we had passed Smith Island when we ran into a howling blizzard, the wind blowing with hurricane force from the north. Early in the morning—October 14—breakers ahead, seen just in time, made us turn south. After two hours of wary steaming, a towering rock, surrounded by many jagged outcrops, loomed through the driving snow. The ship's officers identified this as Castle Rock.

All three bridge officers of the Wyatt Earp and most of the sailors had been at Deception Island before on whaling vessels, and this was familiar water to them. Taking bearings on Castle Rock, we now groped through the storm toward another landmark, Sail Rock, a flat slab of stone rising vertically two hundred feet above the sea. At noon we had this islet abeam and close beside us.

It was fifteen miles from this point to Deception Island, now due north, with foul ground intervening. Snow driving horizontally ahead of the wind stung the faces of those on watch and drove tears from the corners of their eyes, the drops freezing on their cheeks. Nevertheless, we shouldered ahead, the engine at full speed, as we were now taking the hurricane right over the bows. Towering waves roared over adjacent reefs, drift ice was being blown into lines, visibility was but a few hundred yards. Only men daring, able, and knowing what they were about would have taken a vessel into such a place.

About two o'clock in the afternoon the tall cliffs guarding the entrance to the bay rose dimly through the murk. The sea was quieter under the immediate lee of the island, but the high wind still made the ship hard to manage. A swaying iceberg, insecurely grounded outside, half blocked the narrow passage—only one hundred yards wide—into the bay. We squeezed through; and then, to our dismay, saw only open water.

But though in a landlocked harbor, we were still none too safe. Deception is the most curious of Antarctic islands, having the form of a South Sea atoll; but, instead of low coral banks, those of Deception rise three thousand feet. It is the crater of an extinct volcano which in past ages blew off its top and later subsided into the sea. We could see nothing of that now. Even the drifted shore close by was indistinct. Down the slopes from the north howled willy-willies, laden with old granular snow, twisting the Wyatt Earp in their grip and lashing the bay to fury. The little ship nosed her way to the whaling anchorage off Port Foster. We had just begun to make out the outlines of the big factory and the workmen's houses, when a thick snow-squall shut out everything, making it unsafe to anchor just then. To put in the time, we took a turn to the back of the bay to look for the hard, smooth ice on which we had counted, but there was none. The bay was ice free. Our take-off field did not exist this year.

Greatly disappointed, we steamed back to the factory, where we succeeded in anchoring. All that afternoon and night the storm continued unabated, so that we saw nothing of the island. At midnight there was a sudden lull, the barometer dived below twenty-nine inches, and for some minutes ensued a dead calm, a light snow drifting down. We were in the eye of the hurricane. Then the wind struck again, from the south this time and hard as a board. Low and laden as she was, the Wyatt Earp swung around sharply on her cable, her stern only a few yards from the beach. Scarcely had she streamed herself into the wind when drift ice, coming in through the mouth of the bay, bore down on her, rearing up on the taut anchor chain, grinding along the stout sides of the Wyatt Earp, and threatening to lift her up on the beach. By morning we were thoroughly packed and frozen in, the temperature falling fifteen degrees below the freezing point.

The south wind soon blew away the snow clouds. Just after breakfast the sun broke through, and the dazzling heights of the island were revealed to our eyes. There was a rush for skis and snowshoes, and everybody dropped overboard and crossed to shore on the ice. Dr Holmboe, the meteorologist, and I tried to climb to the top of the mountain to see Graham Land, to the south, but long before we reached the summit the wind was blowing us off our feet and we had to come down. Holmboe estimated the force of the gale at well over a hundred miles an hour.

Balchen, meanwhile, had been prospecting for a landing field and reported that the deep snow left by the blizzard on the lower slopes offered an excellent chance for a take-off. The new snow fields seemed likely to last for a month. Consequently, we decided to unload here and use Deception Island for our transantarctic flight.

Rain, sleet, and high winds followed the hurricane, and it was five days before he could even unload the Polar Star and drag its members up the steep beach. Ten more days elapsed before the plane was assembled ready to fly. On October 29, the day this work was finished, I had a narrow escape from death. Skiing rapidly down the glaciated slope of the mountain, I broke through an unsuspected snow bridge and found myself clinging by elbows and arms to the top of an abyss of blue ice, the bottom of which I could not see. By carefully distributing my weight, I managed to climb out, returning badly shaken to the ship.

That evening, after a day of sunshine, snow squalls set in. We had the heating apparatus under the plane's engine, expecting to make a short test flight. The weather defeated us there, but it was deemed advisable to run the Wasp engine a little while before making everything snug for the night. The starter was thrown in, but after a half turn of the propeller there was a terrific jar and a snap like a pistol shot, and the engine stalled. Examination showed a broken connecting rod. To prevent corrosion during the sea voyages, the cylinders of the engine had been filled with heavy

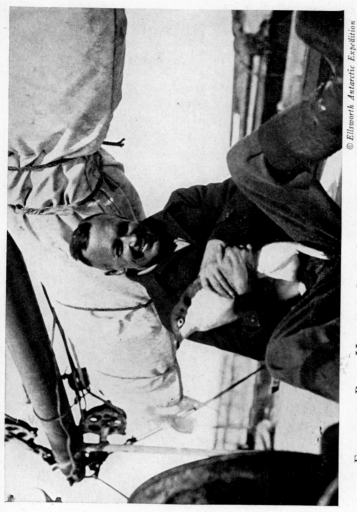

© *Ellsworth Antarctic Expedition*

ELLSWORTH PLAYS HOST TO A SAUCY LITTLE "NEIGHBOR" IN ANTARCTICA

While Waiting for a Break in the Weather at Deception Island on the Second Expedition in 1934, Some of the Men Collected Penguin Eggs and Caught Several of the Birds and Took Them on Shipboard. These Adélies are among the Few Creatures Living on the Ice-covered Lands of the Far South.

© *Ellsworth Antarctic Expedition*

ONLY THE SNOW-CHOKED ENGINE PROJECTS ABOVE THE SURFACE WHEN A BLIZZARD ENGULFS THE POLAR STAR

Here Is Striking Evidence of How the Weather Island. It Seemed a Hopeless Task Shoveling out the Defeated the Second Expedition. Two Members Snow from Around the Plane. First Storms, Then lubricating oil. The enormous pressure built up as the piston head attempted to force this viscous stuff out of the combustion chamber of one of the cylinders proved too much for the connecting rod.

The boxes of spare engine parts were at once broken open, and a search of many hours ensued for connecting rods. We had none. By some mischance they had not been included in the spare parts, though everything else was there. It went to show what attention must be given to detail in the preparation of a polar expedition. The most trivial oversight may wreck the plans and efforts of months.

Fortunately, it was still early in the season, and Chile was not far away, its southernmost port, Magallanes, being about a thousand miles from Deception Island—a thousand miles of the roughest water in the world, off Cape Horn. By radio we arranged with Pan-American-Grace Airways for the spare rods, and the Wyatt Earp started north, five of us—Dr Coman, Dr Holmboe, Balchen, Braathen, and myself—electing to stay with the Polar Star on Deception Island. Though the whaling factory buildings had been badly wrecked by wind and snow, the dwelling houses were in good condition. We camped in one of them, making ourselves as comfortable as we could.

Byrd said of Bernt Balchen: "Balchen can do more things well than any man I ever knew." After observing the pilot at close range during the sixteen days the Wyatt Earp was gone, I could heartily echo that opinion. The man's versatility was amazing. Besides being a good navigator and a pilot with few peers, he was a marvelous man on skis, the use of which he had learned when he was an officer in the Norwegian army. On the trail he was tireless. After he and Braathen had torn down the Wasp engine ready for repair, to find an occupation for himself he built a light sledge suitable to be carried in the plane. No Norwegian professional sled builder could have turned out a better job. This same sledge I finally carried across Antarctica.

Besides this, he was a good cook. He did the cooking for our little shore party on Deception Island, and we fared better even than at the hands of the Wyatt Earp's cook. Had he chosen a career in art, he would have been successful, for he could draw and paint like a professional. He made beautiful sketches of Deception Island and other scenes along the archipelago. Today Balchen is associated with Riiser-Larsen in the management of the Norwegian national airways.

Balchen was moody and temperamental during this voyage, subject to sudden fits of temper. Once, just as we were sitting down at table, Dr Coman let one of the cats into the dining room of the whaling-station cottage. Balchen picked up the animal and threw it against the wall.

During our wait for the Wyatt Earp I spent all the time I could up on the mountain collecting geological specimens and practicing with the Leica camera. But there was not much good weather. Fog and rain alternated with high winds and blizzard, but the tendency was all toward thawing. Gradually the snow fields on which we were relying thinned. When the Wyatt Earp returned on November 16, patches of black volcanic cinders could be seen all through the snow. Ten days later, the repaired engine ran perfectly, and we were ready for flight; but fog and mild temperatures persisted, and all the snow had disappeared except two narrow stretches less than four hundred yards long.

Hope of flying with skis from Deception Island that season had to be abandoned. We loaded everything, including the fully assembled plane, back on the Wyatt Earp and on November 27 sailed south in search of a new base.

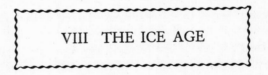

VIII   THE ICE AGE

OUR PLAN was to run down the northwestern side of the Antarctic Archipelago as far as Adelaide Island; if necessary, choosing inside passages and looking for snow fields or level glacier over which the plane could ski, or, better, thick smooth shelf ice near some shore. We left Deception shortly after noon and late that evening were off Trinity Island, which is close to the coast of Graham Land. We could barely see Trinity, however, because of a thick snowstorm.

At that point we headed slightly more to the southwest toward the head of De Gerlache Strait, navigating carefully because of the many icebergs, rocky islets, and reefs with which these waters are infested. Morning found us in the strait, which runs between Graham Land and two large islands, Brabant and Antwerp. South of Antwerp Island Bismarck Strait runs between that island and a jutting headland of Graham Land, and after threading Bismarck Strait one is again in the open ocean.

We encountered little ice in De Gerlache Strait next day until near its southern end, and then heavy ice forced us back when we were almost in sight of the ocean. Bismarck Strait was locked tight. Our next plan was to pass out to sea between Brabant and Antwerp islands, but when we reached that strait the weather had become too thick and snowy for us to risk ice in that narrow place. At this point we held a conference as a result of which I decided to give up the Adelaide Island plan altogether, skirt clear around the archipelago by the north, and try the shelf ice in the Weddell Sea.

Though the tall peaks of the islands and of Graham Land were shrouded in mist, we had clear visibility below during much of the passage of De Gerlache Strait and looked upon some of the most glorious mountain scenery in the world. Vast cliffs, tinted in many beautiful pastel shades, spaced off immense glaciers presenting to the sea sheer ice walls 300 feet high. Behind in lofty chasms hung glaciers of the Swiss type, their drip coming down in bridal-veil cataracts.

As we lined the rail of the Wyatt Earp to marvel at beauty surpassing anything the Arctic could offer, veritably we were gazing at the edge of the last great remnant of the Ice Age. Looking at these eternal masses of moving land ice, we could imagine what North America was like when the North Polar ice cap came down as far as New York and Philadelphia. Antarctica really is a single huge conical glacier, seven thousand feet thick, flowing down on all sides from the Pole itself over a descending series of plateaus. The flow is sluggish but steady—forty-six yards a year. Here is a body of ice so great that if some shift in the earth's position should bring it vertically under the sun, the world would have a new Deluge above which only a few Ararats would show.

Yet the warm cycle, which has already erased the Ice Age from our own continent, except for a few splinters in the highest mountains of the West, is operating steadily upon Antarctica. Each year it breaks off around the edges a little faster than it flows down. In January 1936, when I was going up to Australia from the Bay of Whales on the Discovery II, that floating laboratory took soundings every four hours. A hundred miles out from Little America the Ross Sea suddenly shallowed. Dredges were put down, and we found that we were riding above an old terminal moraine left on the ocean's bottom. In no distant past the Antarctic ice cap had extended out that far.

The rate of recession is estimated at about one tenth of a mile a year. If the process continues, in seven or eight thousand years from now the Antarctic continent will be a warm, sunny land, as habitable as any temperate region is today.

One thing struck our Norwegian seafarers with surprise. Usually at this season De Gerlache Strait is alive with whales feeding on plankton—sea scum composed of myriads of minute plants and animals—but now we saw no whales or any plankton, either. We were to discover later that the deep-sea shrimp, which swarm in these waters and form the chief sea food of Antarctica's animal life, had all but disappeared.

In entering the Weddell Sea from the northwest we were well aware of the risk of it. The Weddell Sea pack ice is notoriously the most treacherous along the entire Antarctic rim. It is all old, heavy, steel-blue shelf ice, screwing and piling up under pressure. But it is especially dangerous in the northwest corner, where without warning the pack will move in and jam against the mountainous barrier of the islands and Graham Land, crushing like an eggshell any vessel caught in the cul-de-sac.

There were records of only three ships ever having ventured into that corner, and one of them was lost. In December 1893 a daring Norwegian whaler, Captain Larsen, took his ship Jason through Antarctic Strait, remained a few days in the Weddell Sea, and escaped. Nine years later Larsen commanded the Nordenskjöld Expedition's steamer Antarctic. In February 1902 he landed the Swedish Baron Nordenskjöld and his party on Snow Hill Island in the northwestern end of the Weddell Sea and again got out, promising to return the following December. In December, however, he found the region impenetrable. He therefore landed three men—Gunnar Andersen, Lieutenant Duse, and a sailor named Grunden—at Hope Bay on Antarctic Strait to make their way on foot to Snow Hill and tell Nordenskjöld not to expect rescue until the end of the summer.

In February 1903 the Antarctic returned once more to the Weddell Sea to pick up Nordenskjöld, this time to be caught by the ice and wrecked. Whalers rescued Larsen and his people, who brought out the news of Nordenskjöld's plight. In December the Argentine government sent down the cruiser Uruguay, which reached Snow Hill Island, took the Nordenskjöld party off in a hurry, and slipped out of the Weddell Sea just as the pack closed in.

The whole story of the Nordenskjöld Swedish Expedition is one of the most thrilling in polar annals; and from the standpoint of scientific achievement, few expeditions into either the Arctic or Antarctic ever had its success. Baron Nordenskjöld, son of an equally famous Arctic explorer, was only twenty-five years old in 1902. After the Antarctic deposited him and his men on Snow Hill, they built a stout hut for a base and during the winter made sledge journeys to the coast of Graham Land and over the Weddell ice as far south as Lat. 66°.

When their ship failed to come in December, the young scientist spent the summer making geological studies and collections on the snow-free islands of the Weddell Sea and along the Graham coast. A second winter found them still prisoners. In October 1903, while exploring on Graham Land, Nordenskjöld met three ragged skeletons painfully making their way southward. They were Andersen,

Duse, and Grunden, the party left at Hope Bay by the Antarctic nearly a year earlier.

These three men had made heroic efforts to get through to Snow Hill during the preceding summer but had been turned back by conditions. They had taken from the Antarctic only enough food for that journey. When the summer passed without bringing rescue, they faced a winter desperate indeed. Beside a penguin rookery they built a stone hut for shelter and in it managed to survive on what few penguins they could kill.

Both Andersen and Duse were scientists attached to the Nordenskjöld Expedition. In spite of starvation, they amassed at Hope Bay an important collection of Jurassic fossils and rock specimens, storing it in their hut when they started south in October for Snow Hill. Ice conditions were so menacing in November that the cruiser Uruguay did not dare stop in Hope Bay, so the Andersen-Duse collection was abandoned.

This expedition revealed for the first time that Graham Land and the mountainous islands of the Antarctic Archipelago are an extension of the Andes Mountains. The fossils told a fascinating chapter of geologic history. They showed that the primitive plant life of the Jurassic Age, identical in many respects with that of South America, was also more varied and abundant, proving that at one time the climate of Antarctica was at least subtropical. More significant still, Nordenskjöld did not find a single fossilized vertebrate animal on Antarctica, nor has any other explorer. No four-footed land animal exists in Antarctica today. The deduction is clear. In Jurassic times Antarctica was connected with the northern continents. Some great convulsion cut it off on all sides by abysmal deeps. The polar continent then rose higher, the cold set in, and the ice stopped evolution before the first land animals appeared.

It was toward this risky corner of the Weddell Sea that our little converted herring boat jogged northward from De Gerlache Strait. The second morning out from Deception found us plugging up through Bransfield Strait in threatening weather, our course laid to round Trinity Peninsula. All day long the Wyatt Earp rolled and pounded in the shallow choppy water off North Graham Land.

About midnight we turned the cape into Antarctic Strait, facing
the Weddell Sea. The wind had risen to a full gale, driving sleet and
fog from the southwest; the sea in the channel was very high. It
was foolhardy to risk a possible encounter with the Weddell pack
in such thick weather, and we ran into Hope Bay to ride out the
storm.

In the morning conditions were as bad as ever. I tried to go
ashore to hunt for the Andersen-Duse collection of fossils, but the
weather was too much for me. Hurricane gusts were blowing down
over the glaciers at the back of the bay. The water was too deep
for anchorage and too rough for a small boat. We drifted about the
bay until noon. Then, the weather thick as ever, we sailed south,
anyhow, defying the ice. All night we crept down through the
strait. In the morning the gale blew the sky clear. Except for a few
bergs, no ice was in sight, and we made a good crossing of Erebus
and Terror Bay.

We now approached the three most curious islands of Antarctica
—Cockburn, a mere dot in the Weddell Sea; Seymour, much larger
and south of Cockburn; and, largest of all, Snow Hill, separated
from Seymour on the south by only a narrow channel. All three,
due perhaps to volcanic warming, are snow free the year round, and
a spectacular sight they present against the wintry heights of big
James Ross Island behind them.

Cockburn proved to be only an incongruous reddish-brown
mountain rising abruptly two thousand feet. Seymour looked like
a segment of the Bad Lands of the Dakotas, darkly barren and
desolate, silhouetted against the snow and glaciers of Ross Island.
Before we could catch a glimpse of Snow Hill, a dense fog blew
over the sea, reducing visibility to a few yards. We groped down
past Seymour and Snow Hill Island, not seeing the latter at all,
then kept on. In the late afternoon we began running through
fringe ice that grew heavier and heavier. Just at dusk of the sub-
antarctic spring evening, we came to the true edge of the Weddell
shelf ice.

It was a wild, weird scene—the dull twilight, the gale roaring in
the rigging and past our ears, the smother of fog, and the

tumultuous, grinding pack at the edge of the shelf. I had never seen more wicked ice, even in the Arctic. For just an instant the fog parted. There on a floe, regarding us with calm dignity, sat an emperor penguin, the first I had ever seen since I watched Shackleton's in the London zoo so many years ago. The fog closed in again, and we lost him.

Chris Braathen mourned, "I wanted that penguin."

Chris had become our official penguin snatcher and skinner. Those strange birds fascinated him, and he had perfected a technique of capturing them. Chris would spot a colony of Adélie penguins. He then sneaked up on them behind a pressure ridge, dived over, and grabbed. It was risky, for even an Adélie penguin can break a man's wrist with a blow of its stubby wing.

The year before, when we were fast in the ice off the Ross Sea, Chris caught two Adélies at a dive. One he stuffed into an empty coal sack. On the Wyatt Earp the bird emerged with its beautiful white vest badly smudged. It was dreadfully ashamed of its appearance and sulked around the deck all day. If the other penguin approached, the dirty one drove it off.

I always think that emperor penguins must have been originally animals that have somehow moved backward in evolution. The emperor is the only wild bird that produces its young in the dead of winter in temperatures as low as seventy-five degrees below zero. Its nest is a circle of stones. The female penguin lays its egg on its broad, scaly, webbed foot, and thereafter the male and female penguins vie in holding and warming the egg. When the fledgling is hatched, the parental jealousy breaks out in battles. To escape the family row, the young one crawls into a crevasse, where it usually freezes to death. Scott's naturalist estimated a 75% mortality among young emperor penguins.

The common Adélies are a daffy race, spending all their time in sociable groups, dancing, jumping, and cavorting around in a most senseless way. Emperors, who are solitary, will have nothing to do with these silly cousins. The emperor is much bigger, standing four feet high. It has a yellow breast and a soft, liquid eye, like a deer's. Unlike the little Adélies, it will not fight a man.

Adélie penguins nest everywhere along the archipelago, but only one emperor rookery was ever found. Scott made a hundred-mile sledge journey to discover it. On Deception Island we took eggs away from Adélies by substituting round stones under them. The birds did not seem to mind. The eggs were not bad in omelets, but boiled—ye gods! Tough as rubber balls and fishy besides.

Our voyage to the shelf ice was fruitless. A mild season had pitted its surface with holes and coated it with loose refrozen crystals on which a heavy plane could not ski. All we could do was turn back, break a passage through the pack, and make for Snow Hill Island in the final hope that there we might find a field serving our purpose. It was the fourth day since we had left Deception. The date was December 2. Already the best flying season had passed.

Nordenskjöld's hut, we knew, was on the west side of Snow Hill Island, facing James Ross Island across the narrow Admiralty Strait. Navigating carefully through fog, we tried to get through between Snow Hill and Seymour islands to anchor off the hut but found the water too shoal even for the Wyatt Earp. So we dropped the anchor on the Weddell side to wait for the weather to clear, and a weary crew of men turned into their bunks.

When we awoke, fog and gale had gone, and the sea was calm. The twenty-five mile length of Snow Hill Island lay clear before our eyes—the most theatric island of the archipelago. The northern tongue of it—a low coastal plain perhaps twenty square miles in area—was brown, stony, and barren. Behind that the island had a turtle back formation, rising on gentle slopes to a height of 900 feet; and this whole flattened dome was clothed in a glacier which, being white, has given the morsel of land its name.

With three or four of the others I went ashore at once to explore. Forty-four days of searching here met their reward. Snow Hill, our last resort, was giving us almost perfect landing fields—on the glacier itself. The glacier, I discovered, was of the so-called continental type—i.e., thin, slow moving, and without crevasses. About a mile inland, at the 500-foot level, lay a flat plateau of ice broad enough for a take-off on trial flights with a light load. On top was a big sweep of perfect ice from which the Polar Star could fly with its full load. My spirits, which had been lower than the barometer, now rose to a keen pitch of anticipation. It did not seem that there could be failure now.

The glacier presented to the sea a barrier front only ten feet above high tide, forming a natural wharf. The Wyatt Earp was moored alongside, and the assembled plane lifted over on the ice. Under her own power she easily taxied up the glacier to the first flying field. Sledges were brought from the hold of the Wyatt Earp, and, three men to a sledge, the crew began the work of hauling two tons of gasoline and oil up the icy slopes.

Meanwhile, I had crossed the island and found Nordenskjöld's hut. Obviously, I was the first man who had visited it since the Swedish Expedition fled for their lives in November 1903. The evidences of the hurried departure were as plain as though the thing had happened yesterday. The mummies of three white sledge dogs lay in front, just where they had fallen when shot. Near them was a pair of rusty ice skates and a pair of shoe trees, dropped in flight. Piled against the cabin were several cases of canned sardines, pepper and mustard, and cakes of chocolate. The chocolate tasted good as new, but none of us quite had the stomach to try vintage fish. Nordenskjöld's sledge was also beside the hut, which was strongly guyed with wire at the four corners to hold it against the hurricanes.

Inside were the same evidences of flight. Clothing, boots, and other equipment were scattered over the floor. On a table at a window stood an old-style gramophone with about a dozen cylindrical wax records. A big clock on the wall had stopped at three o'clock. A stove was set up, cooking pots hung on nails, eating utensils and dishes were on the shelves. Everything was in an excellent state of preservation. We found a curious type of telegraph instrument and personal trinkets of all sorts.

All of these relics I carefully salvaged and preserved and later presented them to the American Museum of Natural History.

But the most curious object of all in the hut was a cone-shaped block of blue hard ice partially filling the room. Every member of my expedition visited the hut during the days that followed and speculated upon the origin of that huge block. Since the wind had broken out the cabin's windows, the consensus was that it had been formed by snow blowing in, though how snow could pack and make ice so crystalline or a cake so shapely nobody could say. However, we all accepted that explanation.

The following spring a Swedish exchange professor at Yale looked me up in New York after all this story had been published. He had been the botanist with Baron Nordenskjöld and was curious to hear the story of their abandoned camp thirty-one years later from my own lips. I told him all I could think of, while he kept nodding in remembrance. He remembered the shooting of the dogs and everything else. For a souvenir I gave him an old-fashioned penwiper I found in the hut. On it were embroidered the crossed flags of Norway and Sweden, the two countries having been united under a single crown in 1903.

Just before we parted I told him about the mysterious dome of ice in the hut.

"We always did mean to mend that leak in the roof," he told me.

There was the explanation. The crystal block represented thirty-one years of thawing and dripping.

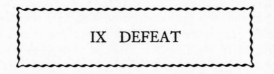

IX   DEFEAT

ONE ADVANTAGE enjoyed by my expedition of 1934–35 I have put off mentioning until now. The Byrd Expedition was still at Little America. Through Admiral Byrd's courtesy, the radio operator at Little America sent us his local weather report twice a day. Having an exact knowledge of the weather at both ends of the transantarctic airway, our meteorologist, after becoming familiar with the average movement of the continental pressure centers, could make a fair guess about conditions to be met en route.

Here is one of our weather reports as a sample:

SNOW HILL ISLAND, Dec. 5.

Little America—
> WIND—South, less than 10 m.p.h.
> BAROMETER—Rising for two days. Still rising.
> TEMPERATURE—Falling (with S. wind), 15° to 11°.
> VISIBILITY—Four miles.
> CLOUDS—Overcast; stratus.
> FORECAST—Conditions likely to change.

Wyatt Earp—
> WIND—Calm to E.N.E. less than 10 m.p.h.
> BAROMETER—Rising for two days. Still rising.
> TEMPERATURE—Steady, 30° to 32°.
> VISIBILITY—Forty miles.
> CLOUDS—Light alto-cumulus 8.
> FLIGHT FORECAST—Landings probably required.

It will be seen from the above that December 5, 1934, was a favorable day for the flight if carried out according to my plan of making landings in bad weather. But Balchen had begun to raise a most disquieting issue. He was urging that we carry a third man in the Polar Star when we took off for the great flight. I protested that such a change might and probably would ruin the whole enterprise. A third man could be taken only at the sacrifice of gasoline or of camp and travel equipment on which our lives might depend, if the plane were damaged in landing. Balchen's argument was that it might take three men to clear a runway and put the plane into the air even if undamaged.

This proposal was so violently at variance with my whole scheme and theory of the crossing that I could not believe that Balchen really meant it. I felt certain that when the right moment came he would go through with that contract—believed it until the incredible event proved my belief ill founded.

But if Balchen had been as eager as I to fly to the Ross Sea, we could not have done so immediately, since from December 5 to December 18 we had a constant succession of gales and blizzards, with scarcely an hour of sunshine or decent visibility. The front of the Snow Hill glacier began to break off, making it necessary for the Wyatt Earp to move out to safe anchorage. One day in the storm we saw once more an emperor penguin floating past us on an ice cake—the same emperor, we all agreed, we had seen at the edge of the shelf ice some miles to the south, since it was the only emperor penguin we saw during our entire stay.

This time he did not escape us. We sacrificed him to science and discovered that the bird was starving. Its stomach was entirely empty, there was no fat on the carcass, and it weighed but sixty-two pounds. The average full-grown and well-fed emperor weighs seventy-five pounds. Since the chief food of this species of penguin is shrimp and plankton, usually abundant in Antarctic waters, it was evident that food supplies had disappeared along the coasts of Graham Land.

Our second engineer, Bigsth, about this time developed an outbreak of boils, giving the doctor a patient.

At every opportunity I could get during this stormy interval, I went to the island to hunt fossils, often in company with Dr Coman. The snow-free tip of the island offered a prolific field for the geologist. The blizzards melted here as fast as they fell, keeping the ground muddy. The tract was absolutely barren except for lichens and mosses. Through the mud were scattered thousands of sandstone nodules which, when cracked open, occasionally revealed fossils. On the sides or ravines lay fossil logs of a prehistoric Sequoia-type tree, which is related to an evergreen conifer now growing in both South America and Australia. Some of the fossil wood showed the holes of the boring marine worm, teredo, showing that this land, when heavily timbered, once sank beneath the sea. The other fossils were all those of marine life—various mollusks, sea urchins, corals, etc.

In all I collected 150 specimens of 28 species, three of which had never been found in the Antarctic before. These, augmented by the ones found at Nordenskjöld's hut, form the largest Antarctic geological collection in the United States. They are in the American Museum of Natural History.

December 18 brought us our first entirely clear day since we landed at Deception Island two months before. We seized the chance to give the Polar Star its necessary test flight. It took us all day to dig the plane out of the drifts, gas it for a few hours flying, and load emergency equipment. After a late supper Balchen and I took off, flew to the southern end of the Nordenskjöld Coast, and returned, landing on Snow Hill just at midnight, having been gone two hours and a half. The repaired engine functioned perfectly, and we had been in constant two-way radio communication with the Wyatt Earp during the entire flight.

To me had been revealed a panorama of surpassing beauty. These were the longest days of the year for the Southern Hemisphere. Though outside the Antarctic Circle, Snow Hill Island and its region now had a midnight sun, just grazing along the edge of the southern horizon. That long semisunset worked a transformation in the vast frozen expanse of the Weddell Sea, tinting it with rosy light in which the flat-topped icebergs gleamed like rubies.

Conditions were so good that evening and the barometer so high and steady, there was little doubt in my mind that next day, the nineteenth, would see us off for Little America. So confident was I that I radioed to the New York *Times* and the North American Newspaper Alliance an advance story of the flight plans to be released for publication upon receipt of a "flash" from the Wyatt Earp that we had started.

But next day occurred one of those sudden weather changes to which we had grown so wearily accustomed. Snow squalls blew out across the Weddell Sea; the barometer was dropping. Surely I had a just grudge against Graham Land weather. Snow, gales, and overcast skies persisted until the end of the month. Our Christmas celebration was a glum affair. At last I was facing the bitter thought that the flight might be impossible this year. We had already long overstayed our time in this dangerous region—no other ship had ever dared to remain so long. Only the fact that the hard winds had blown invariably out of the west had kept the pack ice off the Wyatt Earp. Any easterly gale would bring disaster. The ice was gradually closing in, cutting off escape. The whole north now seemed full of it, though our mariners could see from the top of Snow Hill that Antarctic Sound, the exit between Join-ville Island and Cape Trinity, was still open. It would be a question of reaching it through inside passages.

On December 30 occurred another break in the weather. The snow clouds cleared away, the wind dropped, and a sounding broadcasting balloon, sent aloft, reported light airs as high as ten miles up. Flying weather was also perfect at Little America. Once more the Polar Star was dug out of the snowdrifts and now fueled for 2,500 miles. By night she stood poised and ready at one end of her runway. In the tent beside her were Balchen's and my flying clothes. The hour of the take-off was set at 4 A.M. next day, that being the best hour, from a navigating point of view, for the start.

With a little more speed in preparing the Polar Star we might have taken off that day. For the first time since we reached the Antarctic, Dr Holmboe, the meteorologist, had written on his fore-cast: "Probability of straight flight." Successive disappointments were making me nearly frantic to go, yet there were men of my own party who were drifting into the opinion that the risks were not worth while. We kept waiting and waiting—for what?

Dr Holmboe went up to the plane early in the afternoon, soon after he had made his morning forecast. Balchen, coming up some hours later, asked him what he thought then.

"I think it's all right," said Holmboe.

"I don't believe it," Balchen said.

Balchen had demanded a meteorologist with the expedition, yet now he would not accept the expert's judgment. Still, I had to re-member that Balchen himself was a good man at foretelling weather.

Next morning fog shrouded the island and sea so heavily that we could see only a few yards. I was almost glad of it. Defeat by the weather I could accept philosophically and try again. As the new year dawned, it was evident that the expedition was over. There was such a thing as stretching our luck with the pack ice too far. We waited two more days. The bad weather still held, and on January 3 we started to pack up and clear out.

The morning was spent in bringing down to the glacier front the extra drums of gasoline and oil from the landing field. Meanwhile, the weather showed signs of clearing. The snowfall had stopped, and the wind was dropping. When we went up in the afternoon to dig out the Polar Star once more and bring it down to the ship, the sky was cloudless. Dr Holmboe brought the afternoon weather report. It showed good conditions at both ends of the route, though there was a probability that thick weather would force an early landing on the Weddell Sea end.

On an impulse I said to Balchen: "Let's make a try! What do you say?"

"All right," he answered instantly and at once began to warm the engine.

Wilkins insisted that we have a hot meal first. The primus stove was started in the tent to boil pemmican and coffee. Jubilantly I wrote a dispatch for the American press:

"Flash—Balchen and I took off at seven this evening, heading for the unknown. The great adventure so long awaited is at hand. The motor is warming up, and soon its roar will be breaking the silence that veils the earth's last great unknown, as Balchen and I wing our way across Antarctica, with the opportunity of all that pertains to the opening of a continent for the last time in human history."

There was more along this same line. In an hour the motor was tuned up for flight, and Balchen and I, in Arctic flying clothes, were in our places. This impromptu start was going to make navigation hard, since I now had no time to work out our positions in advance, to be checked only by instruments on the plane. However, better a little inaccurate navigation than not fly at all. The hour of the start offered difficulties, too. We had always chosen 4 A.M. (8 A.M., Greenwich civil time) before, since a start then, if we maintained expected speed, would bring the sun due north and in a position for easy sextant observation from the starboard window, just as we were halfway across the continent. I would have to get my sextant shots as best I could.

The heavy snow on the runway, after weeks of blizzards, had blown into long undulations, called sastrugi, and these made it hard for the Polar Star to take off. Whenever the heavy ship, now weighing nearly four tons with its full load, gained much speed, it bumped in a racking manner over these unyielding waves. What wind there was blew down the slope of the best take-off area. Checked by sastrugi, the plane could not get off on the upgrade. After an hour of such taxiing, Balchen grew impatient. He set the movable pitch propeller at the most advantageous angle, we strapped in, and then the pilot boldly slid the Polar Star over the top of the dangerous south slope of the glacier and, now in a side wind, opened the engine out to 1780 r.p.m. In a flurry of snow we shot down the grade at dizzy speed, and next moment the plane was in the air. We circled the Wyatt Earp in farewell and then headed south, climbing slowly to 3,000 feet.

Following down the glacier-plugged southern coast of Ross Island as far as Cape Longing, we then turned out across the frozen Larsen Bay, coming in at the Seal Nunataks. From this point on everything is so choked and buried under ice and snow that it is difficult to distinguish land from sea. Nunatak is an Eskimo word for an isolated peak rising above land ice, though it seems that the Seal Nunataks, of which there are seven in a row, are islands.

Having been busy noting my observations in my diary, I looked up and was surprised to find that the peaks of Graham Land, which a moment before had appeared off to the right, through my starboard window, were now on the left-hand side. We had turned back! We were heading north! I shouted a question to Balchen.

"Bad weather," was his laconic response.

It did not seem bad to me. There was a squall ahead, but it was only a little wisp of one with the glow of the sun showing on both sides of it. So at last I began to realize the truth. Balchen was not going to go through with this flight unless he found absolutely

perfect flying conditions, and they were something we might have
to wait years to find. Two years of planning and work were going
by the board. I knew that Balchen was a good judge of weather
and that by turning back we might be escaping a storm—yet next
day we had ideal weather at the Wyatt Earp. I shall always believe
we could have gone through.

We flew northward right up through the heart of Graham Land.
Discoveries slid under the wings of the Polar Star. The prominent
topographical feature marked Cape Sobral on the latest charts I
found to be really an island. Behind it I saw an immense new fjord,
crevassed and walled with glaciers, cutting back northwest into the
Nordenskjöld Coast for thirty miles. Five uncharted islands, three
fjords, and several conspicuous mountain peaks were the trophies
of the flight, the result of which drastically changed the map of
the eastern side of the archipelago. Toward the north end of
Graham Land I observed a low pass through which could be
described the peaks of the South Shetland Islands, a hundred miles
north.

We landed on the Snow Hill glacier two hours and a half after
our take-off, having flown about four hundred miles. I dropped
over the side of the plane and floundered down through the snow
to the launch. Balchen could tell how I felt. Wilkins, who had come
up, asked Balchen about it.

"Ellsworth can commit suicide if he likes," said the pilot, "but he
can't take me with him."

On the Wyatt Earp I pulled myself together, resolving to re-
trieve as much as I could from the ruin of my hopes. I sent a
dispatch to the newspapers, blaming everything on the weather,
which indeed was atrocious that summer, and telling about the discoveries made during the flight. I even left the inference that I
might try again next year, though I was far from feeling that way
privately.

We all knew that this ended the expedition of 1934–35. It was a
question, in fact, whether we had not made our inconclusive
journey at the cost of having to spend the winter on Snow Hill
Island, even possibly at the cost of the destruction of the Wyatt

Earp and the necessity of having to put others to the trouble and expense of rescuing us.

Winds that had held westerly were now shifting into the eastern sector, and the loosening pack was slowly closing in on us. Already the north looked shut. Yet there was the airplane up on the glacier, and bad weather moved in, giving us another succession of gales and blizzards. It was not until January 9 that we were able to bring the Polar Star down to the sea and make it fast on the deck of the Wyatt Earp. There was a remote chance left that we might yet make another attempt at the great flight. At the Weddell Sea entrance to Antarctic Sound and therefore near the edge of safe and open water lay Dundee Island, its plateaus and coastal levels offering possible take-off areas.

In the afternoon of January 10 we steamed north from Snow Hill, sheltering that night behind Seymour Island, as a strong northeast wind blew and snow fell thickly. That gale brought the pack in still more heavily, but next morning we started to buck our way through it, backing and then ramming the armored bow of the Wyatt Earp into the floes. All that day and the next we put the hard-won miles behind us, crossing Erebus and Terror Bay with the greatest difficulty.

When I went to sleep on the night of the 12th, the movement of the ship was still the regular succession of backing, forward lunges, and collisions. Next morning the movement was steady, and I thought we had got through. As usual I went back to the galley for a cup of coffee. As I passed his door Wilkins called out, "Do you know where we're bound for now?"

I said, "No."

"Snow Hill Island," he replied calmly.

All desire for coffee left me. In the night the Wyatt Earp had reached Antarctic Sound, only to find the ice packed so heavily in that passage, our only egress, that no vessel could have broken through. So we were doing the only thing we could do—retreating sixty miles to wait for the northerly gale that might clear out the ice and save us.

This time we came down the sheltered west side of the island

and anchored off Nordenskjöld's hut, where the Wyatt Earp was relatively safe from the moving floes. For five days the pack held us there, then, as it showed signs of loosening, we started north again, and late that evening reached Cape Gordon, the eastern tip of Vega Island, having come thirty-five miles in sixteen hours. The nights now had four hours of darkness, and to pass that period we tied up to a floe on the north side of the cape, where there was an open pool under the steep sandstone cliff.

Not long after the ship had become quiet a yell from the watch brought everybody on deck. The wind had shifted, and our pool was visibly closing. Heavy floes, filled with steel-blue shelf-ice fragments, bore down on us. It seemed only a matter of an hour or so until the Wyatt Earp would be smashed against the precipice. There was no sleep for anyone that night. The floodlights were turned on, and everyone worked hard to be ready to abandon ship. Men in the hold brought out emergency rations and checked emergency packs containing clothing and food. The lifeboats were reprovisioned and swung out ready for launching; water casks, replenished. If the ice caught us, our plan was to drop overboard, drag the boats and supplies to some large floe, and drift to open water.

But that necessity never came. About four o'clock in the morning the light wind shifted, the ice pressures relaxed, and the danger was momentarily over. We took advantage of the opening leads to push northward once more. The press grew worse as we went. Six hours of struggle put us under the frowning barrier of North Graham Land. Fridfjof Sound looked impassable and to venture into it suicidal. Yet to remain where we were was out of the question. To retreat meant a winter in the Antarctic with the possible loss of our ship. We kept on.

Then it was that the little Wyatt Earp really proved her staunchness. By sheer power she butted a way through blue tumbled ice a few yards at a time. Now and then a wisp of a lead gave her a few minutes respite. Ahead loomed a dark "water sky." As we neared Antarctic Sound we saw that the same wind which had so nearly brought our destruction against Cape Gordon had also cleared that passage. We broke through to the open water at last and were unimpeded except for a few bands of pack ice spanning the strait.

As we came near we saw that the entrance to Hope Bay was being bombarded by scattered floes of ice moving swiftly southward. On the way down I had promised myself to return and look for the fossils which Andersen and Duse were supposed to have left there. So we went into Hope Bay. We found the hut the marooned men had built but no fossils. Some other visitor had anticipated us. Dundee Island? It was walled off by miles of ice. There was no chance of getting in there.

From Hope Bay we went to Deception Island, where at the whaling station we dismantled the Polar Star and stowed it once more in the hold of our base ship. The men working below complained of the many rats. On January 21 we sailed from Deception for Montevideo, Uruguay, where I had decided to lay up the Wyatt Earp until I could decide about the future.

I was in no frame of mind to make any decision then. All I could do was think, write a little, and try to plan anew. All I had for two years of effort were a collection of fossils, of primary interest to geologists and the credit of making a few minor geographical discoveries. But that great unknown continent, the fringes of which Wilkins, Charcot, Riiser-Larsen, and others had seen, had been denied me. I had seen only known islands and limitless ice.

If Balchen would not do it, could I even hope to find a pilot willing to make the flight? At the time I thought not. I might come back year after year, wasting my life and substance in the chase of a rainbow for its pot of gold. The difficulties seemed insuperable; yet always came the memory of icy land and icy sea crowded with flat-topped bergs, delicately purple at noon, liquid gold when the sun declined to its midnight position. That mocking beauty called me back.

Once during the voyage from Snow Hill Island to Montevideo I spoke to Balchen, expressing regret over our failure.

"You can't buck the weather," he replied.

Balchen had his side of the story. He told Wilkins afterwards that in the camp on Deception Island, when the five of us were waiting for the Wyatt Earp's return from Chile, he had made up his mind that he could not rely on a single man for sufficient assistance in the event of a forced landing. That was when he began asking for a third man in the plane. He had decided that he would not attempt the flight with me alone, unless conditions were such that we could make it nonstop.

Balchen grievously disappointed me, but that has not lessened my esteem for him. When the following year our radio broke down and the world did not hear from me for two months, the magazine *Time* insinuated that I had deliberately silenced the radio to build up publicity for myself. One of the first to speak up in my defense was Bernt Balchen.

As if we had not already had enough bad luck, no sooner was the Wyatt Earp north of Cape Horn than we were beset by a plague of rats. In the warm weather the teeming descendants of the colony taken aboard at Dunedin erupted from their cozy hold and swarmed all over the ship. They killed and ate one of our cats. When one morning I saw a big one clinging to the ceiling of my cabin, we declared war. With sticks and clubs we went after them, slaughtering 169 on the deck and killing dozens of others below. All leather stowed in the hold was gone—our muhluk boots, even the webbing out of snowshoes.

From Montevideo I crossed to Buenos Aires and went by plane, via the West Coast and Miami, to New York.

X NEW BLOOD

IN NEW YORK it was not an encouraging pat on the back but a well-meant attempt to dissuade me that sent me back to the Antarctic once more. Upon arriving I went to Mr John Wheeler,

head of the North American Newspaper Alliance, to see if after
my two failures he would be interested in another contract for
exclusive news from an Antarctic expedition.

"What do you want to go back there for, Ellsworth?" he said.
"You'll lose your life. Try something else—something easier."

That advice, which represented the sensible, comfortable world,
crystallized my determination. I was not to be defeated—I *would*
cross Antarctica by air. The memory of that three-hour flight
—infinitudes of molten ice—fired my ambition anew. I informed Wilkins and then announced to the newspapers another
trial.

Balchen was returning to Norway to enter commercial aviation,
and for a new pilot I turned to the North. For the airmen of
Canada and Alaska, landing on and taking off from snow on skis
was an everyday job. My advertisements, sent to various aero clubs
and aviation companies, brought several applications. I finally narrowed down my choice to two men—Herbert Hollick-Kenyon and
J. H. Lymburner, both of Canadian Airways.

Hollick-Kenyon was an Englishman, a Londoner, who had emi-
grated to British Columbia when a boy. He had learned flying with
the Royal Air Force during the war and afterwards remained in
the service as instructor. In 1928 he resigned and joined the
Canadian Airways as a transport pilot, flying out of Winnipeg. He
was thirty-eight years old, married, and the father of two children.
Lymburner was an Ontario farm boy, aged thirty-one, and married also. He was a pilot with Canadian Airways, flying from
Montreal.

As pilots their qualifications were quite different. Hollick-
Kenyon had much the more experience—6,000 hours in the air as
against 1,600. Much of Lymburner's 1,600 hours, however, had been
with skis and floats along the eastern shore of Hudson Bay. Hollick-
Kenyon had done much ski-flying, both day and night, and had
also flown in the Canadian Arctic.

But their chief difference lay in their special talents. Hollick-
Kenyon, with an average pilot's knowledge of engines, was a
wizard at the controls when in the air. Lymburner, a good flier,

knew no celestial navigation but had a genius for engines. It was hard to say which talent was the more important in a flight such as I proposed. I ended by engaging both men—Hollick-Kenyon for chief pilot, Lymburner as reserve.

The Byrd Expedition was returning from Little America, which was going to be deserted the following year. Accordingly, we would have no need of a meteorologist, since we could judge local weather conditions as well as an expert. In our interview Hollick-Kenyon agreed to this omission. He thought my plan of starting in good weather and taking a chance on the rest, landing to ride out storms, was perfectly feasible. He spoke as if it were nothing at all —all in the day's work.

Dr Coman did not care to return to the Antarctic, and I engaged another medical officer for the expedition, an M.D. who, for reasons to appear later, can be left nameless here. One point was causing me concern. If our flight project carried through as planned, Hollick-Kenyon and I might have to stay in Little America for two months or more before the Wyatt Earp could break through to us. To carry provisions on the plane for that period meant a load that would subtract from our flying range.

Accordingly, in April I wrote to Admiral Byrd, asking if he had left in Little America any food we might use and, if so, where it was stored or cached. It was many months before I received an answer.

Early in May, with my wife, I sailed for Europe to make our annual visit to Switzerland. When that was over we took the Graf Zeppelin to South America, disembarking at Rio de Janeiro. We were early but had promised ourselves an outing with Sasha Siemel, the famous big-game hunter, after jaguars in the jungles of Brazil. I had met Siemel, about whom the novels *Green Hell* and *Tiger Man* were written, that spring at The Room, a New York club for hunters. There to Colonel Theodore Roosevelt, and some others, including myself, he demonstrated his method of killing a jaguar with a spear. The jaguar waits on the limb of a tree when chased by dogs, then in charging jumps to the ground first and

takes off from there. "And," said Siemel, "to stand waiting to receive the flying charge of a jaguar on the point of a spear is the
greatest moment in life."

Siemel was a professional hunter, taking contracts to clean the
jaguars off the big ranches in central Brazil. On one ranch he killed
sixty-two, spearing several of them. We wanted to see him do it
and accepted his invitation to drop in on the way down to
Montevideo.

The story of our two weeks with Siemel in Matto Grosso is off
the line of this narrative, so I will touch only its high lights. We
killed no jaguars but had other adventures, among them a funny
encounter with revolutionists and a lively fight with a peccary I
had shot and wounded. We were in a swamp all the time—perhaps
the biggest swamp in the world—camping on the islands. Mrs Ellsworth got a touch of blood poisoning from wading so much.
My most vivid memory is of lying in my hammock under a
net at night and hearing the rustle of the vampire bats crawling through the dry leaves on the ground to attack our horses
and hounds. Our dogs were always anemic from their bites,
and one morning I saw four clinging to a horse. They do not
fly to their victims but crawl up their legs. Their teeth are so
sharp that an animal cannot feel the bite; and they do not suck
blood, as is commonly supposed, but lap it as it flows from the
cut.

Emerging from the interior at Santos, I heard the disquieting
news that the Polar Star had had a mishap on a test flight, though
Wilkins' telegram assured me that the damage was not great. At
Santos I bade good-by to my wife, who returned to the States
from there. I boarded the Italian liner Augustus and went down to
Montevideo.

There I found everything ready for the start. The plane was good
as new, having required only a patch on the wing. Kenyon,
Lymburner, the doctor, and the engine mechanic I had engaged in
New York were on hand. Captain Holth had left, and we made
changes in the navigating crew, advancing First Mate Olsen to cap-

tain and promoting Liavaag, our former second mate, to the rank of first mate. Olsen's younger brother became second mate. Engineer Holmboe and Larsen, the cabin steward, were still with us, as was also Lanz, my radio operator.

I had only to call on the port authorities to thank them for the favors extended to the Wyatt Earp—free harbor dues and also freedom of the port, relieving us of having to use a pilot—and the little ship could sail on her third invasion of the Antarctic. I also said thank you to Mr Gordon-Firing, Norwegian consul at Montevideo, for his efforts in facilitating our work there and making our stay pleasant.

On a fine spring afternoon in October we started South again, our first destination being Magallanes, Chile, the most southerly port in the world, where the Wyatt Earp was to fuel. There we picked up the last letters that could reach us until we emerged from the Antarctic. At Magallanes I received from Admiral Byrd a radiogram answering my letter of the previous spring. It merely told me of the disposition of the gasoline and oil which I had shipped to Little America the preceding year but promised a later message about food supplies.

With full bunkers and two years provisions in the hold, we sailed from Magallanes on October 28, 1935, and five days later were standing off Deception Island, blocked by heavy pack ice blown together by a westerly gale. It was two days before we could break through to the whaling station, where we intended to assemble the Polar Star before proceeding southward. For the fourth time the luck of the Wyatt Earp had held at Cape Horn. We had the usual jumping sea and strong wind, but it was a whisper compared with what the Howling Sixties can do.

A funny but rather vexing incident enlivened the voyage. Our new doctor was a talkative soul who speedily made himself unpopular with the silent Norse. They began to cold-shoulder him. One day at mess our flag-waving medico accused the whole Norwegian breed of clannishness. High words ensued, and Second Mate Olsen planted his fist on the doctor's chin and floored him. When his rage cooled, the mate apologized to me and then sought out the doctor to beg his forgiveness. The doctor merely sulked in his bunk and would not listen. Next morning we were amazed to find the following notice posted:

During the rest of the voyage I will give no professional services to the members of this expedition.

It was signed by the doctor.

Though the South Shetlands were heavily iced in, off to the south showed plenty of "water sky." It took us a week to assemble the plane and lash it on the deck, ready to be lifted ashore and flown. On November 11 we moved out of Deception Harbor, bound this time for Dundee Island. No more Snow Hill Island for us, no more chances taken with the treacherous Weddell pack. On our first voyage down we had had a chance to observe the apparently level areas on Dundee Island, which had the further attraction of lying at the edge of safe waters. We intended to use it if we could.

As we had suspected, there was little ice this year around the Antarctic Archipelago. Dundee Island was enclosed by a half-mile hem of shelf ice, but it was solid and fast to the shore and only offered the Wyatt Earp a quay to which she could tie up and unload. But when we inspected the island itself we saw that we had found the ideal flying base. There were magnificent sweeps of hard snow; and, if all the possible flying fields sloped a little, that fact did not disturb our pilots.

Wilkins, who in exploring the Graham Coast independently had met all the flying difficulties which I had experienced on the previous voyage, said to me: "If I had known five years ago what this island was like, you would not be trying now to be the first to fly across Antarctica."

We chose a base at the northwestern end of the island, on the sheltered passage between Dundee Island and lofty Joinville Island, eastern outpost of the archipelago. By November 18 the Polar Star had been test-flown and stood at the tent on the flying field loaded, gassed, and ready for the great moment.

XI PREPARATIONS

ALL THE AUGURIES pointed to success. For as far as we could
see, the Weddell Sea was open. Polar spring kept smiling upon us.
Storms were the exception. Even the fog stayed away.

Indeed, we had rather an embarrassment of good weather.
Although the temperature hovered at the freezing point, dropping
a little during the midnight twilight, the sun by day thawed the
snow surface of our runway enough to make it "sticky" for the
plane's skis. Our first attempt to take off for the great flight failed
for that reason. In packing snow the plane could not get up enough
speed to lift its full load.

Favorable conditions and the likelihood of a start any morning
put much extra work on me, as navigator. Each evening I had to
chart in my navigation book and precalculate our assumed positions on the flight course, since the observations at those points
varied with the sun from day to day. As a preliminary to flying over
known territory, no navigator would go into such detail, since he
would always have landmarks and radio bearings to correct his
celestial observations en route; but over the unknown it was worth
all the time it took—three or four hours of close mathematical
figuring every night. Such a precomputed route would serve as a
check to the navigator, informing him if he were badly in error in
his flight observations of position.

To do this I first plotted a great-circle course between Dundee
Island and Little America. Upon this I next marked fourteen
equally spaced positions, each representing the location of the Polar
Star at the end of an hour's flying. By maintaining a ground speed
of 155 m.p.h., which we hoped to do either by throttling down in
a tail wind or by opening out the engine in a head wind, the

fourteenth hour would bring us to Little America, approximately
twenty-two hundred miles away from Dundee.

The first three hours of the flight would be down the Graham
Land coast to Stefansson Strait—an explored region. After that, the
hourly positions of the plane, assuming a non-stop flight, should be
as follows:

4th hour—Lat. 72° 11' S., Long. 67° 33' W.
5th hour—Lat. 74° 00' S., Long. 74° 41' W.
6th hour—Lat. 75° 42' S., Long. 76° 49' W.
7th hour—Lat. 77° 16' S., Long. 83° 13' W.
8th hour—Lat. 78° 39' S., Long. 91° 16' W.
9th hour—Lat. 79° 45' S., Long. 101° 15' W.
10th hour—Lat. 80° 28' S., Long. 113° 10' W.
11th hour—Lat. 80° 45' S., Long. 127° 06' W.
12th hour—Lat. 80° 28' S., Long. 141° 02' W.
13th hour—Lat. 79° 45' S., Long. 152° 57' W.
14th hour—Lat. 78° 39' S., Long. 162° 56' W.

Position 14 is approximately that of Little America.

My nightly task was to take these assumed positions and for each
one precalculate the sun-elevation and azimuth curves for the date
and hour. Such calculations would enable me to set my sextant
quickly in the plane for the precomputed altitude of the sun. After
our midmorning failure in thawing snow, we set 4 A.M. as the
starting time, since then we could rely on a frozen surface. The four-
o'clock start was also convenient, as I have explained since, if we
maintained schedule, we should reach the middle of the unknown
just at noon, local time for that position, putting the sun due north
and therefore well placed for a sight out of the starboard window.

A word here about time on polar airplane flights. Because of the
pinching together of the meridians as they approach the pole, local
time changes so rapidly during flight that it is less confusing to
use Greenwich civil time throughout a long voyage. Dundee Island
is south of Newfoundland, putting its local time about four hours
behind that of Greenwich. A 4 A.M. start therefore meant a start at
approximately 8 A.M., G.C.T. (the actual time being 7:44 A.M.,

G.C.T.). Since Little America is west of Honolulu, the flight represented a time spread of something like seven hours—a local-time loss of that much. To avoid needless confusion in radio messages, etc., the polar flier uses the fixed Greenwich civil time.

On this expedition I took no dietician, retaining the diet prescribed for me by Dr Coman the previous season. To the pemmican which formed the backbone of Amundsen's diet, Dr Coman added oatmeal and bacon as staples, besides such minor delicacies as bouillon cubes, fresh butter, raisins, and dried apricots, not only giving variety to the meals but to some extent avoiding what the radio announcer politely calls "faulty elimination"—that bane of the polar explorer. The daily ration was as follows:

FOOD	WEIGHT IN OUNCES
Pemmican	6
Biscuits	10
Bouillon cubes	½
Bacon	1½
Oatmeal	1½
Butter	2½
Powdered milk	4
Sugar	4
Chocolate	2
Raisins	1
Malted-milk tablets	¼
Dried apricots	¾
Total weight	34 ounces.

To this list was added, unweighed, tea, salt, and a little pepper mixed with the salt. The diet provided a man with 4,800 calories per day, all from easily assimilated food. We loaded aboard the Polar Star 150 pounds of this food, proportioned as above—enough to feed two men five weeks.

Dr Coman also wrote out the standard menus for breakfast, lunch, and supper, as follows:

BREAKFAST: Apricots (3 apiece), oatmeal, biscuits and butter, tea and sugar.

LUNCH: Biscuits and raisins, chocolate and malted-milk tablets, tea with sugar. (Tea kept hot from breakfast in thermos bottle, and no cooking required.)

SUPPER: Bouillon, pemmican, bacon, biscuits and butter, tea.

In actual practice, I have to confess, we didn't stick very closely to Dr Coman's menus. For breakfast my pilot and I usually only boiled up some oatmeal and bacon together and ate it with some dried apricots and called it a meal. At night we varied the diet with pemmican. But we found this very satisfactory. In fact, if I go into the Antarctic again, I will choose this combination for my ration, adding to it only oat biscuits and butter.

For the reader interested in the technical details of a polar expedition, let me list now some of the other articles loaded aboard the Polar Star. Besides clothing, which I shall describe later, I had in my rucksack, among other things, soap, comb, toothbrush and powder, a pair of hair clippers, a 38-caliber revolver with one box of cartridges, a tube of lanolin (an unguent for chapped skin), two pounds of psyllium seeds, eight tins of smoking tobacco, two plugs of chewing tobacco, safety razor and blades, two dozen boxes of matches, a pound of dried coca leaves, six ounces of guarana— a mild stimulant like coffee which I found in Brazil.

What, someone asks, do you do when you run out of razor blades? I had the answer to that, too—a whetstone. Neither Hollick-Kenyon nor I chewed tobacco, but we carried the two plugs to cut up for our pipes if we ran out of ordinary smoking tobacco. The only book on the plane was a small Bible, which I had in my rucksack.

Stowed in the plane were also a hand sledge, knocked down, a silk tent with poles, an emergency hand-driven radio trail set and three bamboo fish-poles for its antennae, two shovels, a coil of Alpine rope for possible use in descending on foot from mountains, a handsaw for cutting snow blocks, reindeer sleeping bags, sled harnesses, and so on. For kitchen equipment we had enamel mugs, tablespoons, forks, plates and cooking pots, tea towels, and a wash basin. We also put aboard a sewing kit containing darning wool, coarse linen thread, and needles. For cutting anything at meals we had only our sheath knives.

In the cockpit besides my navigation equipment—charts, sextants, nautical almanacs, drawing instruments, pencils, and notebooks—I carried two mascots. One was a Micky Mouse given me by my wife and the other the 1849 ox shoe I found in Death Valley. I carried six flags. One was the U.S. standard flag, made by my niece, Clare Prentice, which I meant to raise when claiming territory for the United States. The rest were as follows: a U.S. flag from Hill School, the flag of the National Geographic Society, the flag of the Quiet Birdmen, the Yale flag, and the New York Athletic Club flag. All of these last five were to be returned as relics after being carried across Antarctica.

I should also speak here of our radio equipment for the flight. The Polar Star's own radio could transmit on any wave of the band between 20 and 80 meters, with a power output of 100 watts. It received power from a 400-watt generator coupled directly to the engine. To operate the radio when the plane was on the ground, we carried a portable 300-watt generator turned by a small gasoline engine. In addition, we had with us an emergency transmitter and receiver, operated either by hand or foot power, which could be mounted on the sled, and which could broadcast on any wave length from 30 to 100 meters with a power of 15 watts. With so many safeguards, we hoped to keep in touch with the Wyatt Earp at all times, no matter what happened on the route.

As soon as I reached Dundee Island and gave the plane its test flights—one with Hollick-Kenyon and one with Lymburner—it became evident that we might start out for the Ross Sea at any time on short notice. I therefore prepared a sort of manifesto of instructions for the guidance of my base party should my pilot and I meet disaster in the interior and be unable to communicate with them by radio. This I posted in the Wyatt Earp, keeping copies for Hollick-Kenyon and myself. The text was as follows:

TO WHOM IT MAY CONCERN:

It is my intention to fly from Dundee Island to the Bay of Whales, Ross Sea, on a more or less great-circle course. In case of a forced landing from which no communication by wireless and no further progress by our own plane can be made, before reaching Lat. 69:30, I would expect to follow the Larsen ice barrier to Robinson Island and Robertson Island, then follow through the Crown Prince Gustave Channel and reach Hope Bay as a rendezvous, possibly looking for depots and leaving notes on the southwest corner of Robinson Island and on the southeast corner of Robertson Island and on Cape Longing.

In case of a forced landing from which no communication by wireless and no further progress by our own plane can be made, after passing Lat. 69:30 and before reaching Lat. 72, I would make for Cape Pierre Baudin, Marguerite Bay, passing through Bourgeois and Lallemand fjords, thence along Matha Bay to Cape Evensen and expect to find notes or depots at each or one of these places. If by chance the route to Pitt Island is impassable on foot, I should expect to make the southeast corner of Beascochea Bay the rendezvous.

In case of a forced landing, etc., between Lat. 72 and Lat. 75, I would expect to make for Mt Martha, Charcot Island, and remain there until relieved, looking for a depot on the southeast corner of Charcot Island.

In case of a forced landing, etc., between Lats. 75 and 80, I would turn north to the edge of the land-fast ice and then eastward to Mt Monique, Charcot Island, expecting to remain there until relieved and looking for a cache on the southwest corner of Charcot Island.

In case of a forced landing, etc., between Lats. 80 and 81 and before reaching Long. 130, I would make for Mt Mabelle Sidley to leave a message and look for a depot and possibly remain there with the expectation of being relieved. However, if there is no food obtainable at Mt Mabelle Sidley and we have food sufficient to enable us to reach Mt Grace McKinley, I might decide to leave a note at Mt Mabelle Sidley and proceed to Mt Grace McKinley.

In case of a forced landing, etc., after passing Long. 130, I would make for Little America, following the course laid down for the airplane. At Little America last year, through the courtesy of Admiral Byrd, I laid down 500 gallons of gasoline and some lubricating oil, and with these supplies there is twenty or thirty days food rations. I have no information from Admiral Byrd as to the amount or disposition of his supplies or if any were left at Little America; and I am not much concerned about that, for once we are at the Bay of Whales we will find many seals and penguins, and with our own supplies we will be able to live until the latter part of January or later, if the Wyatt Earp should be delayed in reaching us.

(Signed) LINCOLN ELLSWORTH.

A perusal of this statement will indicate the scrupulous attention to detail a well-found polar expedition must give. These instructions applied only to rescue in the event of an accident, so that the expedition might be self-sufficient and save the explorer from having to call on others for help. But everything else had to be managed with equal forethought and care. Take the item of food, for example. Our plan called for us to carry on the plane 150 pounds—five weeks supply. But why five weeks? The most critical hour of the projected flight, when the plane swung south of Lat. 80°, would put us at our greatest distance from food— 400 miles from the land-fast ice at the edge of the Pacific Ocean, where we could expect to find seals and penguins. At twelve miles a day we could travel that distance in just about five weeks.

XII   FRUSTRATED

NOVEMBER 19 was the day we tried a midmorning start only to fail to lift off the thawing surface. Our flying field was a low hill or ridge at the northern end of the narrow island, with gentle slopes down both sides. To the northwest and also to the southeast we had downhill runways more than a mile long. The snow fields were level sweeps lined over with sastrugi so shallow that they were little more than ripples. On top of the ridge we established our gas dump and made our starts from that point.

On the twentieth we actually started at 4 A.M., local time. Roaring down a frozen runway, the Polar Star lifted her gross weight of 7,600 pounds in less than half a mile. It was a great thrill for me to realize that at last, after three years of effort, we were off for the frozen continent with a full load of fuel, good weather, and every prospect of success.

But this feeling was not to last long. We had flown but an hour and a half and were only a little south of the point reached by Balchen and myself when Hollick-Kenyon informed me that the fuel flow gauge was in danger of bursting. Bumping over the sastrugi at the start had broken the glass, and only a bulging celluloid film was holding back the gasoline. Should that give way, it would flood the cockpit and force a landing. Accordingly, we turned back, setting the plane down on Dundee Island at about seven o'clock in the morning after three hours and ten minutes of flying.

All the short trip had shown me was that the Weddell Sea was open for two hundred miles at least.

Each thwarted attempt entailed work for the ground crew— hauling gas and oil up the long slope to the dump. Yet it was not all work for the expedition. We had our amusements on Dundee Island these days, though for theater, movie, and radio hour we had only an interesting rookery of Adélie penguins near by and a lot of big Weddell seals that were always sunning themselves on the bay ice near the Wyatt Earp. These seals were the tamest wild animals I have ever seen. Not only would they not move out of one's way, but they enjoyed having their sides scratched with sticks, rolling over on their backs like contented kittens.

The weather held good, indicating a start next morning, November 21. This time, I felt in my bones, we would make it. The others must have shared my confidence, for the sledge haulers, after finishing their work that day, built at the dump a cairn of empty gasoline drums, weighting them with stones. This was to be the monument to the great flight.

We kept adhering rigidly to our time schedule. At 4:10 A.M. I was shaking hands with everybody, while Hollick-Kenyon started the warmed engine. The day promised perfection. It was absolutely still and cloudless at Dundee, the temperature just at the freezing mark. On the southern horizon was a little haze, pinkish in the low sunshine, but that was the only indication of any disturbance. Just at 4:16 A.M. (precisely 8 A.M., Greenwich civil time, which I will now continue to use) Hollick-Kenyon gave her the gun, and three minutes later we were climbing above the island.

At 8:05 we straightened out for the south, climbing slowly with our heavy load. At 8:30, from an altitude of a mile, I was looking down over the heights of Ross Island at our familiar Snow Hill Island. Beyond, the Weddell Sea dimpled in the morning sunshine. Familiar scenes passed below—Robertson Island at 9:15, Cape Framnas at 9:55. We still flew above open water, but off to the southeast the Weddell Sea was filling with pack ice. Haze lingered in the south, spreading to the southwest.

After Robertson Island it was all territory new to me. Robinson Island slipped past at 10:20, Cape Northrup behind it. Over the Weddell Sea, now white with pack ice, the atmosphere was clear, but the weather was thickening over the land and the ice barrier. A few miles south of Robinson Island I could not take a drift observation because of ground fog. Mount Ranck, at the southern end of Graham Land, came into view at 11:30, and five minutes later I stared across the entrance of Stefansson Strait.

That geographical feature is still much debated. Is it a strait cutting the Graham Land mass off from the continent or a fjord running back westward into the Antarctic Andes? Nobody knows for sure, though scientists are inclining to the opinion that it is a fjord. If so, it is an immense one, for we could see its walls back for thirty miles, where they lost themselves in cloud and fog. I observed that it was much narrower than Wilkins had suspected— not over a mile or two wide in places. Also the Finley Islands north of it were much closer together than the chart showed.

The air grew very bumpy off the mouth of the strait. Ahead, everything was closed in by fog, but a blue patch of sky appeared, and we hoped we were through the worst of the bad weather. At the clear edge of the sea I identified Cape Eielson—a low headland

of the continent itself, buried under ice and studded with nunataks. Dropping, pitching, and swaying, at 6,000 feet we flew through
the tattered, upheaved ceiling of the cloud bank, which rose ever
higher ahead of us. Just at noon, G.C.T., a violent pitching of the
plane indicated that we were crossing the continental shore of
Hearst Land and at last were over territory where men had never
been.

Uncertain as to what lay ahead, Hollick-Kenyon put the plane
into a climb. Suddenly through a rift I saw a great mountain peak
ahead and to the left, and therefore due south of us. Although we
had reached an altitude of 7,000 feet, it loomed high above us. A
minute later several other peaks had come into sight ahead, both
to left and right, and, as we climbed, more and more appeared—
jagged, rocky summits piercing the clouds to a height of ten and
eleven thousand feet—until finally we confronted a great range
crossing our track diagonally from north to southeast and extending off to the southeast at least seventy-five miles.

This was the greatest hour of my life. Obviously here was a
mountain system of major importance, and our eyes were the first
to behold it! They had been here almost since mundane time
began, for I could plainly see what I thought was stratification
and therefore placed them as of sedimentary origin. In my exalta-
tion, as I stared with awe at the sublimities of these silent peaks,
into my mind flashed the memory of the fossil imprints of raindrops I had found in Death Valley. At once the true name for
these mountains came to me, and I wrote it down in my diary—
the Eternity Range. Later, observing three central summits a little
higher than the others, I gave them the names, in order from
north to south, mounts Faith, Hope, and Charity.

But we were not to climb over these mountains so quickly as I
have implied. Aiming for what seemed to be a pass between
peaks, Hollick-Kenyon was finding the ship "heavy." It climbed
sluggishly, the temperature dropping at each new level. Unable to
take drift observations, we sensed that we were in a strong head
wind. Amid flying fragments of cloud and fog, the Polar Star
climbed, as a gale swept over this ridgepole of Antarctica and tried

to bear us down. Meanwhile, though we did not know it, the land was rising as rapidly as we were. At 10,000 feet through a hole we saw rocks only 800 feet below us. The temperature had sunk to zero.

We climbed to 12,000 feet and then had the entire cloud field beneath us and only a limpid sky and sunshine above. Everything was fogged in up to the 10,000-foot level, the stark peaks and high glacier-choked passes rising above that curtain. We had gained this altitude at the expense of distance, but now, straightening out on the course, we made better speed, and the range moved steadily under us. Far ahead over the cloud field were indications of more mountains, but there the cloud bank seemed to rise to the stratosphere, shutting us off like a wall.

Nevertheless, since everything was functioning perfectly on the ship, I assumed that we would fly through it, according to plan. In fact, I was so busy with camera and notebook that I was scarcely noticing Kenyon at all. Then at 1:05 P.M., G.C.T., I became aware that he was banking to turn.

"What are you doing?" I yelled. "Keep on to eighty, if possible."

(By that I meant 80° W. Long., the edge of unclaimed land.)

He only shook his head and kept turning, making no explanation. Was this to be forever my fate on this crossing? Was I always to be frustrated? Then I cooled down when I observed that instead of doubling back on our course, northeast, Kenyon was steering almost due east. I thought I understood his plan—to head for the Weddell Sea, where we had seen good weather, land on the shelf ice, and wait for the mountains to clear up.

This short leg of the journey gave me a vivid idea of the strength of the gale we had been bucking. Although our positions over Hearst Land will never be accurately known, since we could take no ground observations, it is unlikely that we made more than one hundred miles in an hour of flying. With that same wind on our tail we came back to the Weddell Sea in thirty minutes.

But there we attempted no landing, since the weather looked clear to the northwest over Stefansson Strait. It was a good plan to land in that shelter, provided we could find suitable ice. Accordingly, we followed the coast north, rounding Cape Eielson at 2:12, G.C.T., then heading west up into the strait. But again Kenyon attempted no landing, flying well above the mountainous walls of the supposed passage. After twenty minutes on this course we wheeled and flew back for a short distance, then swung north and west again, moving in above the Finley Islands. Then a little later the plane made a complete circle to the left and straightened out to the northeast, the direction of Dundee Island. Kenyon passed me a note:

"Couldn't go up the strait. Clouds and snow right down to the bottom. Have told ship we are on our way back."

So once more we had retreated before the weather. But what of the plan we had so long discussed—to land in bad weather and wait it out? That seemed to have gone into the discard. I saw Kenyon munching a biscuit. He passed me a note: "I've just had lunch. Have you?"

I didn't answer. Lunch! All the way back I tried to decide what I would do about this fiasco, scarcely observing anything from the plane, taking no pictures, entering no notes. We reached Dundee about three o'clock in the afternoon, local time, landing at the foot of the hill near the ship. A party was waiting for us. Without a word I dropped down to the snow and started for the Wyatt Earp. Wilkins was coming toward me.

"What happened?" he asked.

I made no reply but kept on over the bay ice. Kenyon was following behind. He and Wilkins spoke together, and then I heard Wilkins exclaim: "If I had known this was to be a one-day flight, I would never have joined the expedition."

Aboard the Wyatt Earp I dumped my belongings into my cabin and strode out to the afterdeck. Wilkins and Kenyon presently came aboard, and Wilkins joined me on deck.

I said to him: "Tomorrow I'm trying again, but I don't want Hollick-Kenyon. I'm going to take Lymburner."

Wilkins pleaded with me to reconsider. "Lymburner is tired out from working on the engine," he said. "Kenyon at least now knows the route to Stefansson Strait. There's that much gained."

But I was still too upset to listen. Wilkins left me, and then Hollick-Kenyon came out.

"I understand," he said, "that you would prefer Lymburner on the next flight. That's quite all right with me."

He was so earnestly sincere in his attitude that I instantly relented. I could not doubt that he was as anxious as I to have the expedition succeed. In returning to Dundee Island he had, after all, only used his pilot's judgment. True, it was our agreement to land in bad weather, but to have attempted a landing in fogged mountains would have been sheer suicide. Then, the plane had burned so much gas over Hearst Land fighting the head wind it was doubtful if we had enough left to make the Ross Sea. Having had to turn back at all, in such circumstances, it was better to go clear back and refuel for a fresh flight.

Such considerations, however, came to me later. At the moment I could only remember Hollick-Kenyon's great qualities as a flier. In the air he was superb.

I answered him, "No, Kenyon, I want you." Then I added: "But we should have camped in the strait."

"Well," he said thoughtfully, "that was a very narrow place. If we had come down in there, with our load I don't know how we'd ever have got up again."

"All right," I said, "but next time we won't turn back."

XIII   THE FLIGHT

AT ONE O'CLOCK next morning—November 22—I was roused from sleep by Larsen, the cabin steward, shaking my shoulder.

"How's the weather?" was my instant query.

"The weather looks fine, sir," he said, and there was a note of curiosity and respect, almost of reverence, in his tone. To Norwegians exploration is the greatest of all human businesses.

It is a queer feeling to come out of sleep and a warm bunk and realize that one's hour has arrived to start out into the unknown. I sat on the edge of my berth and thought: "Well, here I am—I've waited three years for it."

I dressed hurriedly in clothes for the flight. First I put on a suit of silk-and-wool underwear, then one of heavy camel's hair, then camel's-hair socks, over which I pulled a pair of heavy wool ski socks. Next, a gray wool shirt, then ski breeches. This was wintersports clothing I bought at Saranac Lake three years earlier. I had worn it on all three Antarctic expeditions and found it the most satisfactory dress for polar weather I had ever discovered.

On my feet first I put on a pair of moosehide moccasins, then a pair of rubber-soled canvas boots with a drawstring to tie them tightly around my pants just below the knees to keep out snow. This footgear combination was a mistake which made trouble for me later. Over my shirt I wore, fur side turned in, a Siberian squirrel parka which Amundsen had given me. This was as far as I dressed before eating breakfast.

I stepped into Hollick-Kenyon's cabin to see how he was getting along. He was shaving with his electric razor. Hollick-Kenyon was the most fastidious man I ever knew on a polar expedition. He always shaved every morning, no matter how hard the circumstances; and every night before supper, if there was even a chance to melt snow, he always sponged down to his waist—in marked contrast to Balchen, who had a fine viking scorn for soap and water.

His dress for the flight was somewhat different. Underneath, he wore the warm camel's-hair socks and underwear; but for outer clothes he had an ordinary pair of tailored trousers, a heavy blue jersey, and over that a lumberman's plaid shirt. For footwear he used only the canvas boots. So careful was he of his clothes that at the end of the expedition his trousers still retained their crease.

I went into the galley and put down a mess of bacon and five fried eggs, finishing with a second cup of hot coffee. Hollick-

Kenyon joined me there but ate more sparingly. By half-past one we were putting on our outer flying clothes—knitted wool caps that pulled down over the ears, helmets and goggles, heavy fur gloves, and heavy reindeer parkas, worn fur side out. Each of us carried an extra pair of sealskin breeches to wear should we encounter extraordinarily low temperatures, and in our pockets we had woolen face masks for the same emergency.

At 3 A.M. Hollick-Kenyon and I left the Wyatt Earp on snowshoes to climb the 1,400-foot slope to where the Polar Star lay groomed ready for flight. We purposely kept down our pace to avoid dampening our clothes with perspiration. At the aviation camp I found everything ready. Lymburner had been there since 12:30 A.M., tuning up the engine.

Wilkins was also at the plane, having been there for hours, going over everything. And here I wish to pay my tribute to the man whose singlehearted devotion to my Antarctic enterprise contributed so much to its ultimate success. It was a fine stroke of fortune when I secured the services of Sir Hubert Wilkins and the advantage of his long experience in polar exploration. His conscientiousness had no limits. The expedition and its great object came first with him, and nothing else—not sleep, food, or personal comfort—counted. At our numerous failures he had been as chagrined as I. His concern embraced everything from the broadest plans and policies down to the smallest details. This morning, for example, he had thought to prepare lunch boxes for us, including thermos bottles of hot tea.

And I remember so well that January afternoon when Balchen and I made our snap decision to attempt the transantarctic flight. The weather was fine, the plane ready to go, but Wilkins would not let us start until he lighted the primus stove and cooked a big pot of pemmican for us. I never appreciated pemmican so much before. A hot meal is a great thing at such a time.

On November 22 the Polar Star was a hundred pounds heavier than at the previous starts. When I was working out my navigation the afternoon before, Wilkins came to confer with me. He was worrying about the food at Little America. We had not heard from Byrd, so there was a possibility that Little America had been cleaned out when the Byrd Expedition left it. We were relying upon finding seals and penguins there, but the season before there had been none in the Weddell Sea. They might also disappear from the Bay of Whales. There was always a possibility of radio failure, and Wilkins might not be able to relay the information to me, if he heard from Byrd.

He therefore proposed that we double the food load aboard the Polar Star and thus, whatever happened, be able to subsist on a decent ration at Little America until the Wyatt Earp could reach us in January. The plane had been taking off so easily with what was supposed to be its maximum load that it ought to handle the extra weight. I agreed to try to carry 100 pounds more of food. That evening we loaded aboard 40 pounds of pemmican, 20 of oatmeal, 10 each of sugar and butter, and 20 of biscuits, raisins, nut meats, and tea. To compensate a little, we abandoned our heavy skis and carried only our 3-foot snowshoes.

I said good-by to my companions who had so loyally followed me through the vicissitudes of three years, and as Kenyon busied himself with last adjustments I had only one thought: *This time we must succeed!* There was a finality about it all I had not experienced before. Only subconsciously did I hear the whir of the propeller and mechanically note "8:05" (G.C.T.) as we took off to the south in renewed pursuit of the unknown.

We followed as before the already explored coast of Graham Land for five hundred miles until we came to Stefansson Strait, again observing the unusual phenomenon at that season of the Weddell Sea quite open for the first three hundred miles. At 12:22 G.M.T. we crossed the strait. The compass bearing of the coast was SE 138 and W. 242. The low black conical peaks of Cape Eielson rose conspicuously out of a mantle of white on our left.

We climbed to an elevation of 13,000 feet, where the temperature was 22 degrees below freezing, and were again over the unknown, the vast mountains spreading out on all sides. But how different was this ascent from yesterday's! The air was almost smooth, and instead of fog, cloud, and a heavy headwind, we had only a gentle southeast breeze and visibility of 150 miles in every direction.

In the clear air we could now see the mountains in all their sublimity. It falls to the lot of few men to view land not previously beheld by human eyes, and it was with a feeling of keen curiosity not unmingled with awe that we gazed ahead at the great range across which our route lay. Bold and rugged peaks rose sheer to an elevation of 12,000 feet above sea level. Suddenly I felt supremely happy for my share in the opportunity to unveil the last continent in human history.

We were indeed the first intruding mortals in this age-old region, and looking down on the mighty peaks I thought of eternity and man's insignificance. So these first new mountains we saw will, I hope, in the future bear the name Eternity Range.

On our long slant it took us three hours to cross the range. I thanked my stars now that I had given myself instruction and training in mountain photography with the Leica, for I had magnificent opportunities which it would have been a crime to muff. Actually I took thirty-one snapshots of the Eternities, and nearly every one was excellent. The system lay in three parallel ranges divided by high plateaus. Mounts Faith, Hope, and Charity were in the middle range. Strikingly contrasted to these rugged Hearst Land mountains were the low-topped Graham Land ranges we had followed south, which dwindled down into isolated peaks as they neared Stefansson Strait. Undoubtedly both ranges are of sedimentary origin. The Hearst Land mountains—at least that section over which we flew—were a loosely formed range with none of the crowded topography of peaks with glacier-filled valleys and high crevassed bottoms such as pictures of the Queen Maud Range show. We saw neither glaciers nor crevassed surfaces in crossing.

On we went, the mighty panorama of the Antarctic continent unrolling before our eyes. At the end of three hours the mountains beneath us gave place to a great polar ice plateau from which emerged a few nunataks, the last evidence of the mountain chain we had just passed. We were flying at an altitude of 10,000 feet.

About this time Kenyon noted in his log: "Beginning to fly hands off." This gives an idea of the serenity of conditions.

At 16:15, G.C.T., when we were yet 950 miles from our destination, the radio broke down, due to a defective switch and antenna lead. Since we had left the Wyatt Earp, Lanz, the radio officer on the ship, had been complaining to us of imperfect reception. Many of our signals came in a jumble. Later we found the trouble in a defective switch leading to the trailing antenna. At 16:15 Hollick-Kenyon passed me a note, reading: "Transmitter out of action. What shall we do?"

I answered: "Keep on to eighty."

Eighty degrees west longitude was my first objective. There we would enter unnamed and unclaimed territory which I proposed to claim for the United States, naming it for my father. Even to repair the radio I did not want to land before 80° W.

The failure of our radio, however, gave the world the impression that we were lost in the heart of Antarctica. Had there been no such invention as radio, we would eventually have emerged from the Antarctic with our expedition an acknowledged success in every particular, even to the maintaining of the time schedule. As it was, the silencing of our wireless voice set in motion two efforts to rescue us.

Fortunately, the plane's radio failed on a note that gave our friends every confidence in our safety. Had it cut off abruptly after hours of perfect transmission, there might have been reason to fear a disaster; but our last signals, as they faded into silence, were telling of good weather. I quote them from the radio log of the Wyatt Earp:

15:48—WELL I ESTIMATE THAT WE ARE AT SEVENT . . . ONE . . . EREABOUTS . . . MY GUESS IS . . . AT THAT . . . PECT STILL CLEAR . . . TO S . . . IGHT DULL . . . LITTLE NO WIND.

That is easily translated. Hollick-Kenyon then thought that we had reached 71° W. Long., or thereabouts, that the flying prospects ahead were clear, though to the south the light was dull, and there was little or no wind. No hint of disaster in that message. Moreover, fifteen minutes later Lanz caught our signals again but could not read them. The trouble was evidently a simple failure of the radio.

This was the view taken by everyone connected with the expedition and by every explorer familiar with the Antarctic. Stefansson, interviewed in New York, gave us three chances in four of being safe. Wilkins was privately assuring my wife of his belief that we had reached Little America, though her confidence in my safety never flagged. While the sensational press was headlining "The Ill-fated Ellsworth Flight", Byrd voiced the opinion that we were in Little America, citing his own experience when several members of his first expedition were "lost" for a week in the Rockefeller Mountains, near Little America, because their radio had gone out of commission.

About the time the radio failed, on the distant right horizon a mountain range with isolated black peaks became visible, which faded out twenty minutes later. After forty-five minutes a few more peaks showed on the same sky line; and in another twenty-five minutes more mountains—120 to 140 miles distant—appeared on our left (south) horizon, and also a few peaks on the right.

The Polar Star droned along, nearly a mile above an unbroken desert of snow. There were no marks now by which we could determine drift or ground speed accurately. Now and then a puff of wind blew a little snow, so that we could determine surface wind direction. Once Kenyon passed me a note: "So this is Antarctica! How do you like it?"

I penciled back: "100 per cent."

In my diary I made the observation: "No landmarks visible. Only a limitless expanse of white."

Half an hour passed, and it became very hazy ahead. Below it was dead flat, with a patch of sastrugi on our left. One hundred and ten miles farther on—again to the left—we came abeam of a solitary little range about seventy-five miles long, to which I took bearings. It was symmetrically formed with peaks rising to 13,000 feet—and all clustered into a central mass, which dwindled down at either extremity to merge with the plain around. I named it

Sentinal Range and its central peak Mount Mary Louise Ulmer, after my wife.

Fifteen minutes later, on the south horizon and one hundred miles distant, appeared a long black flat-topped range which visibly extended through at least one degree of latitude. This appeared to be the last of the mountains we were to see, for ahead and around swept only a vast plateau meeting the horizon in a vista of white. Throughout the journey, so far, visibility had been from 120 to 150 miles.

For two hours longer we flew on, with nothing ahead to break the monotony of the level ice plain stretching out beneath. At 20:35, G.C.T., Kenyon passed me his logbook with a fresh entry reading: "Water sky dead ahead."

A water sky is that dark blue appearance of the sky over water when seen across ice. The only body of water ahead of us that could possibly account for this phenomenon was the Ross Sea. Ten minutes later Kenyon handed me this note: "I really have no idea where we are, but our courses, carefully steered, should put us close in."

Logic agreed with him. We had been in the air nearly thirteen hours; and such a flight, in a plane as fast as ours, should have carried us almost across the continent from Dundee Island. Yet the position of the sun—indicating early afternoon, local time—disputed that assumption. As we were soon to find out, it could not have been water sky that we saw but only some darkening of fog or cloud. But, before we were through with it, this queer land played us so many tricks of illusion—setting pitfalls where none existed or raising unseen obstacles for our feet, plaguing us with mirages, deceiving our ears with sounds—that I sometimes wondered if we had not both gone crazy.

At the end of another hour the water sky vanished and gave way to cloud. We had been in the air nearly fourteen hours and had flown over one thousand miles of continuous mountains. Visibility was getting poor. We determined to land and take an observation, for we had no gas to spare.

The snow on the high plateau was granular and packed so hard the skis of the plane made little impression. And let me interpolate here, each time we landed it was easily possible to pick out smooth surfaces free from sastrugi. During the blizzard we experienced at Lat. 79° 58′ S., Long. 114° 15′ W., which I will tell about later, the wind was from the east to the southeast, and the snow was of a hard, fine-grained texture. Throughout the whole period of flight over the continent the drift in relation to our course was never more than five degrees and constantly toward the same direction. In fact, during the whole middle section of the flight, from the time of reaching the high plateau until we started on the downgrade to the Ross Barrier, we did not have anything but easterly and southeasterly winds. Only twice did it blow from the north, and then only for short intervals. It never did blow from the west. On the downgrade and after reaching the barrier itself, the winds were from the south.

Before I leave this first leg of the flight, let me note that I was able, when over the mountain area, to make many photographs, but once over the plateau there was little to be shown by photographs. Science demands proof, but does not the evidence of these lofty mountain ranges and high plateaus discovered on the flight carry the thought that they are but units in a great mountain system that traverses Antarctica? Does it not suggest that the highlands of Graham Land, which must be regarded as a continuation of the South American Andes, link up with the mountains of Victoria Land on the Ross Sea, and that the Queen Maud Range itself is but a connecting link in this great chain, forming the backbone of Antarctica? Further, does it not seem to imply that a sea-level channel between the Weddell Sea and the Ross Sea does not exist?

The surface elevation at our first landing place—Camp I, as I call it, since we made four landings on the crossing—was 6,300 feet, and the plateau extended with slight undulations in all directions. We climbed out of the plane rather stiffly and stood there, looking around in the heart of Antarctica. Then I noted that the fuselage was crumpled. Kenyon thought it must have been done on the take-off, but more likely our landing was responsible for it, for we came down so hard I thought my teeth would go through my head.

Eventually we fixed our position as Lat. 79° 12′ S., Long. 104° 10′ W. I am now certain this was correct, though I confess I made one sextant reading before landing that caused me considerable wonder. According to the reading, we were in the immediate vicinity of the South Pole, whereas I knew we were more than six hundred miles away. The index error-adjustment screw of the instrument had worked loose without my knowing it. Had we continued reckoning with the error thus created, we might have learned rather more of the unknown than would have fitted agreeably into our program.

This reading—since we had not yet discovered the sextant error, it could only be regarded as approximate—showed that we were almost on the most inaccessible point of the whole route. The Pole lay 650 miles south of us, the coast line of the continent 450 miles to the north, and our destination, the Bay of Whales, 670 miles ahead. We stood in the heart of the only unclaimed land in the Antarctic—in the whole world.

I felt a very meek and reverent person. To think that I, of all those who had dreamed this dream, should be permitted its realization! For the moment I lost all sense of the troubled beginning, had no thought for the journey ahead. I was content, grateful. . . . So here I raised the American flag. The area extending from Long. 80° W. to 120° W. I named James W. Ellsworth Land after my father. That part of the plateau above 6,000 feet I called Hollick-Kenyon Plateau.

Altogether we remained in Camp I for nineteen hours, taking sextant observations at three-hour intervals. After taking the first observation, we set up our tent, moving our primus stove, food supplies, dishes, and sleeping bags into it. When we had a mess of oatmeal and bacon cooking, we crawled out to take a second observation. I must explain about our tent, which was specially made for the expedition. The tent itself was of silk fabric, highly windproof. It was sewed to a canvas floor, so that no snow could blow in under the sides. The "door" was a long sleeve or bellows of silk through which we crawled in and out. When crawling back in the first time, unable to see where I was going, I bumped our oatmeal off the stove, and we had to cook dinner all over again.

In Camp I we had ample time to consider the seriousness of our difficulty with the radio. At the time the plane set ceased to function, opposite Charcot Island, we were not particularly concerned because we had two other safeguards—the portable generator for use when not flying and our hand-driven trail set. Now the question came up of repairing the switch and operating our radio with the portable generator. Because of the disappointing speed the Polar Star had shown thus far on the flight—for some still unknown reason averaging little more than two thirds of what we had expected—it had become questionable if we had enough fuel left to carry us across. Consequently, we abandoned the idea of using the plane's radio at this camp, since we felt we could not spare a spoonful of gas for the generator.

The best we could do was set up and work the trail set. The Wyatt Earp did not respond, though we tried several short-wave lengths. And I may add that up until the time we were forced to abandon the plane sixteen miles from the Bay of Whales, we were faithful to predetermined schedules for broadcasting. After the exhausting task of turning a frozen hand crank for ten-minute intervals, while standing in a biting wind with the temperature below zero, all we ever heard from the ship was the sentence, "We can't hear you," and the name, "Mount Grace McKinley." The defect was not in our receiver, for upon three separate occasions we got time signals from the powerful Buenos Aires station, which fortunate reception enabled me to keep track of my chronometer error. Exact Greenwich time of a sextant altitude of the sun is essential for taking out the necessary elements from the Nautical Almanac to establish a line of position.

Although we heard no more calls from the Wyatt Earp, there was always the possibility our messages were getting out. So, night after night we kept sending at the appointed hours in the hope that we could forestall any anxiety for our safety. We also sent out innumerable general calls.

Then one day when we tried to crank the trail-set generator with frozen bearings, we stripped a gear and put it out of business for good. We could not get at it to repair the gear, because the back of the generator was soldered on. Thus, when we finally abandoned the Polar Star to hunt for Little America on foot, we left the useless trail set with the plane, because of its weight. I may also state that I have been asked many times why we did not use the radio left at Admiral Byrd's old base. The answer is that we were never able to locate any radio equipment there beyond reminiscent towers and dangling wires.

On November 24 we took off from Camp I at 17:03, G.C.T., which was shortly before noon, local time. The weather was fine, though the horizon ahead looked thick. It was astonishing how easily the Polar Star, lightened by the consumption of so much fuel, got off this hard surface of snow—a swift breath-taking lunge of fifty yards or so, and she was in the air. It was all the more remarkable because of the altitude of the plateau—more than a mile above sea level.

This flight was to be short. The weather speedily thickened as we drove westward, and at the end of thirty minutes we landed. I was not sorry, being greatly disturbed about my navigation. I fully realized the gravity of flying through a trackless continent without an accurate knowledge of our position all the time. As we again unloaded the plane and pitched our tent, I told Hollick-Kenyon that here in Camp II we would remain until we fixed the position beyond doubt.

That resolution I was unable to keep, though for three days of varying thick and clear weather we tried strenuously to get an accurate observation. We took no less than thirty careful sun altitudes. Nevertheless, in all thirty, each date, hour, and minute, when reduced to position, gave a hopelessly large spread. Something was radically wrong. After struggling with lines and figures for three days and getting only a rough approximation of our whereabouts, in great uncertainty we took off once more in what we hoped was the general direction of Little America.

The civil engineer may well ask why we did not study the sextant and find out what was wrong with it. My only excuse is the conditions under which we worked. There can be a great difference in the way a man's mind functions in a comfortable office or study and in a dark icy tent, hands numb with cold, realizing that life itself may depend on his calculations. Though the mercury outside stayed near 15 degrees Fahrenheit, a certain amount of snow clung to our canvas boots. This melted in the tent, and the canvas soaked in the water. Our feet became permanently wet as a result. The leather moccasins I had unwisely worn began to shrink with dampness, impeding blood circulation in my feet, with serious consequences to me later.

Yet they say blessings often come in disguise. For geographical science my faulty sextant proved to be a blessing. Had it been accurate, one or two sets of observations at each stop would have checked with our estimated positions, and we would probably have let it go at that, well content to be within ten or twenty miles of complete accuracy. As it was, we took many observations which enabled scientists later, when the sextant's error had been computed, to fix the position of our Camp II certainly within a mile of its true place. Checking back from that, they could put the Eternity Mountains, the Sentinal Range, and other landmarks I discovered on the new map as accurately as any ground survey could do.

The late afternoon of November 27—23:55, G.C.T.—saw us flying again, but it was to be only for fifty minutes. The weather became so thick we could scarcely see to land. Evidently we were on the downgrade to the Ross Barrier. Our position, ascertained later, was 114° 45′ W. Long., 79° 58′ S. Lat.

No sooner had we pitched our tent than a blizzard broke upon us. For three days we lay in our sleeping bags, trying to keep warm. It was minus 5° Fahrenheit and so cold I had to take my fur parka from beneath my bed and draw it over my feet and legs inside the sleeping bag. I thought surely the tent would go with us inside it, as the floor cloth on which we lay was sewed to the sides of the tent. We were spared this unceremonious flight only because the pegs holding the guy ropes had frozen so firmly in position that even a forty-five-mile gale could not tear them out.

When the blizzard abated we were able to cut snow blocks with which to erect a shelter to windward of our tent. No doubt it helped, but still the blasts of wind bellied in the tent on Kenyon's side and kept him sliding over almost on top of me, as we tried to rest and sleep.

Seven days—that is, until December 4—the storm delayed us in this cheerless Camp III. During this period we came to a momentous decision. Though it was questionable if we had enough motor fuel left to reach Little America, we agreed that it was best to fix the plane's radio and operate it with the portable generator, even if it meant a shortened flight and a sledge haul at the western end of the route. That day I had written in my diary: "Suppose the Wyatt Earp is already starting to lay bases for us along the coast, knowing nothing of where we are." This we wished to avoid, and we were also anxious, both of us, to let our people know of our safety.

Kenyon had no difficulty in putting the big radio set in order. We strung the antenna on bamboo poles, ready for 21, G.C.T., or with us about 2 P.M., which was one of our scheduled broadcast times. To warm the engine of the generator and start it, we had to bring it inside our tent. The exhaust soon blackened the interior and us, too, with greasy soot. Thus, in addition to the general discomfort, grease and dirt became the order of the day. We were never able to heat enough snow on the little cooking primus to wash with.

But then, with everything ready, we waited for the scheduled hour. We started the portable engine, Kenyon flashed our position, switched in the receiver to listen for Lanz's answer. And just at that moment the magneto burned out, and our radio was dead. Lanz, perhaps fishing for the short wave of our trail set, never got our message, nor did anybody else.

Thus one thing after another went wrong in this wretched blizzard camp. The valve of the primus stove started to leak air, and constant pumping was necessary to keep the flame going. Eventually we found a way of fixing that. But those three days spent in our sleeping bags had not been all time wasted, for by studying our sextant we finally found the trouble with it—the loose index lock nut. Since all but our first observations had been consistent with each other, the question was, how much had the index slipped before it caught again? If we could find the degree of error, we could correct all previous observations. It was Kenyon who discovered how to do it.

On December 1 the storm moderated and gave us a fairly good day, with intervals of sunshine. We crawled out through our tent bellows, grimy as Hottentots, to find our plane almost buried under drifts. We spent practically the entire day digging it out. Of all abominable jobs in polar regions, next to "man haul" the worst is shoveling snow. It is dry, fine as flour, sifts into everything, and packs hard as rock.

We discovered that the whole inside of the tail of our plane was one solid block of snow. Being slenderer than Kenyon, it fell to my lot to crawl in among the control cables and struts and bail it out. Using a bucket and pemmican mug, this job took me one whole day.

But in the intervals of sunshine on December 1, we took observations with the sextant again. It was a question of how to adjust it correctly once more. Kenyon happened upon the simple expedient of putting the bubble on the snow horizon, then setting the index at zero and locking it there. We both of us instantly realized that this would give a roughly correct set. (Afterwards we found it to be within four miles of absolute accuracy.) When we managed to get sights at the sun thereafter, they put us practically on the eightieth parallel and just past the one hundred and fourteenth west meridian. We were still more than five hundred miles from the Bay of Whales!

In spite of everything we were in good spirits that evening. We knew our position to a certainty, and we felt sure that next day we would complete the flight. Yet when we awoke a buffeting wind, snow, and thick weather kept us grounded. We shoveled out the drifts continually, ready to pull the Polar Star out of the crater forming about it.

All this time the weather kept bitterly cold. As long as we remained in our sleeping bags, I was all right, but when we began to work outside, trying to free the plane, my shrunken moccasin got in its bad work. I lost sensation in my left foot and the power of moving my toes. I seemed to have no foot. How horrified a man is in civilization when he thinks he has frozen a member of his body, yet in this camp I did not even take off my socks to look at the foot. I gave it no thought at all.

Two comforts were left—the hot meals we had morning and night and a pint bottle of grain alcohol Wilkins had slipped into the baggage for us. Every evening we took a nip from that bottle before eating. When the storm was at its worst our only excursions outside the tent were to use the trail wireless three times daily and to fill our 4-liter bucket with snow for water in which to cook our morning meal of porridge with bacon boiled in it and the evening meal of pemmican.

Though we carried on the plane three months emergency food rations, we were not obliged to adhere strictly to our diet allowance, as we ate only twice a day, and even then were never, for some reason or other, very hungry. In the morning we had a mug of oatmeal with cubes of bacon boiled in it, milk, sugar, and oat biscuit with butter on the side. In the evening we had a mug of pemmican, oat biscuit and butter. I thrived on this simple diet, just as in 1925, with Amundsen, I never grew tired of our menu of hot chocolate morning and night and pemmican at noon. Intense interest and enthusiasm for the task have a strong influence upon one's mental attitude toward conditions to be met.

As the cold, snow, and wind persisted, only to get out of that hole became our ambition, irrespective of weather or how far we could go. For clarity let me repeat the chronology of Camp III. During the first three days, when the blizzard was at its height, we remained in our sleeping bags most of the time. On the fourth and fifth days we shoveled and cleaned out the plane, took observations and fixed our position, and repaired and then burned out the radio.

That fifth night—December 2—we turned in, vowing we would pull out next day, whatever the conditions. Our position indicated that we must be near the western edge of the high plateau. Soon the ice cap would be dropping down toward the Ross Barrier. Perhaps at a lower altitude we would find better weather. But when we awoke next morning, we found that it had snowed heavily, and we had another big shoveling job ahead of us.

Nevertheless, we bent our backs to it, determined to keep our resolution, and by noon had the plane clear. The next task was to get it up out of its hole. We unloaded everything and then, with the canvas hood over the motor, we put the fire pot inside for forty-five minutes to warm the engine—as we always did before starting. Then we cranked the engine. After a couple of weak turns the propeller would stop with a choke. Five times we did this, with the same result. Kenyon knew better than I what was wrong, and, after connecting the antenna wire from the radio battery to the starter, he had the propeller going in no time. Then we pulled out of the drift.

Next, under a forbidding sky, we loaded everything back on again, finally striking and packing our tent. But before we could stow the tent away in the fuselage, a heavy storm broke from the southeast—thick snow and a high wind. We could do nothing but secure the plane, pitch camp again, and start the primus stove.

Thus ended the sixth day of our imprisonment at Camp III. It was the lowest moment of our crossing. Recklessly we drained the last of our pint of alcohol, then prepared supper. My left foot remained numb and seemed to have no toes at all. Outside, the storm raged.

Hollick-Kenyon was a quiet chap. His silences made even the Norwegians seem talkative. During the weeks we were together in Antarctica—the only human beings on a continent—he volunteered but two remarks that were not answers to questions or pertaining to some work in hand. Now, as we ate our pemmican, he suddenly uttered the first of them.

"Maybe this is all meant to try us out," he said.

I was startled to realize how nearly he had voiced what was in my own mind, and I remembered the beautiful promise in the old hymn:

*So long Thy power has blest me, sure it still
Will lead me on.*

That was my spirit and my faith. By this I do not mean to imply that I was enjoying the experience. Quite the contrary. As I turned in that night I wrote disgustedly in my diary: "God forbid this airplane stuff anyway!"

It might have seemed a slender thread indeed to which we clung, had we but given thought to it. There we were—two lone human beings on an ice-capped continent the size of North America. Perhaps this thought brought us closer together. Catastrophe might be lurking just ahead, should the frail man-made contrivance of metal and wood, lying inert and lifeless beside our little tent, grow weary of its mission and set us adrift there where hundreds of miles separated us from our destination. True, the coast was but 450 miles to the north, but even so, there might be a hundred miles of pack ice between it and open water. There would be seals, of course, and perhaps penguins, but after that, what? While one learns to accept disappointment and even defeat in those regions, the thought of a month's haul on foot was anything but inviting.

But the snow held off that last night. In the morning—December 4—though the sky was lowering and full of menace, we prepared to get away as quickly as we could. By eleven o'clock, local time, we had the fire pot under the engine and nearly everything loaded aboard. At 11:30 Hollick-Kenyon started the engine. I climbed in, put on my flying helmet, and took a last look at our late camp. Then I wrote in my diary: "I suppose our snow wall will stand for a long time. I thought it would be our mausoleum."

The Polar Star lifted from the new snow better than we expected. At 11:38 A.M. (19:15 Greenwich time) we were in the air. The weather was anything but promising, with thick horizons all around and a sullen sky overhead. Yet one hour later the whole universe became filled with a golden light, and within a few minutes we were flying under a blue sky with a clean horizon all around. The surface of the ice cap had dropped to an elevation of 4,500 feet above sea level and was steadily falling away in great undulations.

Evidently the storm area had been hanging stationary near the western edge of the Hollick-Kenyon Plateau.

We crossed into Marie Byrd Land about 19:45, G.C.T. After two hours and fifteen minutes of flight the ground surface was much lower, the ice indicating its drop by many great crevasses. This would have been a bad place for a forced landing. We flew over crevasses for about an hour, at the end of which time the surface elevation was about one thousand feet. There the plain smoothed out again, and in about half an hour we decided to land. We came down at 23:10, G.C.T., after three hours and fifty-five minutes of flying.

We had two reasons for landing—to check our exact position, since we knew we must be close in, and to ascertain the state of our fuel tanks. We had used up lots of gas climbing over the Hearst Land mountains and in our three subsequent take-offs. But the tank, when we examined it, seemed to have enough gas for another hour's flying. And at the end of three hours we had our position—Lat. 79° 15′ S., Long. 153° 16′ W.

What an afternoon! The snow sparkled like jewels. There was no wind. Once more it was good to be alive, for we were off the high plateau and on the Ross Barrier at last, 980 feet above sea level—and only 125 miles from our destination, with fuel enough to reach it.

Restless and anxious to be off again, we slept very little that night. At 8:58, local time, next morning we took the air, and at 9:50 we reached the north end of Roosevelt Island, sixteen miles south from the Bay of Whales—although at the time we did not know it was Roosevelt Island. Confusion as to just where we were was due to the fact that we were using two maps which did not agree as to the location of this island.

But at that moment something else was commanding our complete attention. All during this last hour of flight a great water sky had been building higher in the north. Then all at once, as we came past Roosevelt Island, we saw it—slate-colored open water on the north horizon, looking almost black in contrast to the white expanse across which we gazed. The Ross Sea!

There was the goal at which so much Antarctic exploration had aimed, and we had reached it. Behind this moment lay three years of planning, work, and travel, heartbreak and hardship, failure, discouragement, and renewed determination—and at last there it was. We had crossed the continent from the Weddell Sea to the Ross Sea.

At such moments in the storybooks men are supposed to make memorable remarks, but in actual life behavior seems to be different. What happened was this: As soon as the open water appeared in the north, Hollick-Kenyon turned around and looked at me. I expected him to say something, but he did not. Nor could I think of anything to say. I stared back at him, that was all. Then we resumed our individual tasks. After all, what was there to say?

A little later the Wasp engine, after twenty hours and fifteen minutes of faithful performance since we left Dundee Island, began to falter. Next instant, our fuel tanks completely out of gas, the propeller was flopping without power. Hollick-Kenyon picked his spot; and at 10:03 A.M., local time, December 5, the Polar Star like a weary bird came gently to earth.

XIV GROPING

BY DEAD RECKONING we had come down within four miles of Little America and to the south of it, and the sextant roughly confirmed this position. But where was Little America? Any place in a trackless, white, unmarked region of twenty-five or thirty square miles, no doubt blanketed under snow with only a wireless mast and a few stovepipes showing above the surface—something that one would have to fairly stumble upon to locate.

In lieu of roads, milestones, and direction signs to guide us, we had a pocket compass, a sextant, the Roosevelt Islands or Mountains—they are mere bumps in the ice—for a landmark, two charts which did not agree upon the location of the Roosevelt Islands, and in the north the dark water sky above the Ross Sea.

Although, geographically speaking, we had "arrived", it was evident that the camp itself might still be as elusive as the proverbial needle in the haystack.

We were in no hurry to begin the search, realizing that we must prepare for it thoroughly. Therefore, we spent the rest of the day considering plans, pitching camp, and securing the Polar Star. This last we did by digging broad trenches two feet deep in which to settle the skis, so that the wing rested upon the snow. Next we unloaded our excess food supplies from the plane and piled them on the skis, where they would serve to weight down the airplane and at the same time be in a well-marked cache.

That afternoon as we worked, we noticed off to the northeast a small mysterious black object that puzzled us a great deal. It seemed to be about three miles away, but, except that we did not believe it was part of Little America, we could not think what it could possibly be.

After our evening pemmican that day, we computed our distances and times and discovered that the Polar Star's average ground speed from Dundee Island to the Ross Sea had been only 102 m.p.h. This was a little different from the 155 m.p.h. we had expected to maintain, having even thought that we might have to throttle down to keep on such a slow schedule.

Since in her test flights at home the Polar Star had shown that she was one of the fastest heavy airplanes yet built, I have never found any satisfactory explanation of her slow flight across Antarctica. It may be that the air drag of the skis was unexpectedly strong. The crumpled fuselage may have had something to do with it. The fact remains, however, that she averaged but 102 m.p.h.

The black object in the northeast so excited our curiosity that next morning—December 6—we decided to hike over to it and find out what it was, hoping it might give us a clue to the location of Little America. Distances on the ice, we were to discover, were deceptive. The three miles stretched into nearly six before we saw that it was an empty 5-gallon gasoline tin stuck up on a pole to serve as a beacon. We drew close enough to it to read the words stenciled on the tin—"Byrd Antarctic Expedition." But between us and the beacon intervened a great crevasse in the ice, so we turned back. Nevertheless, the beacon gave us the assurance that we were near Little America.

A ten- or twelve-mile march on snowshoes over the ice was enough for one day, so we decided to stay another night at this place before starting out on our hunt. Perhaps two nights, for we had to unload and assemble our sledge. It was much warmer here than up on the high plateau—the thermometer always at freezing or a little above. The surface snow was soggy at noon. My "lost" foot began to recover sensation.

Next morning, the seventh of December, as we were getting the sledge members out of the Polar Star, Hollick-Kenyon climbed up on the wing and, standing there and studying the horizon, made what seemed a great and fortunate discovery. Off to the northwest *he thought he saw Little America*. I joined him on the wing and, after carefully scrutinizing the silhouettes to which he called my attention, agreed with him. I should note here that we brought no field glasses on the Polar Star. Binoculars are of little use on a jarring airplane in flight, and we anticipated no difficulty in finding the Byrd base at the flight's end.

At any rate, what we saw certainly resembled that camp on the ice. On the horizon were irregularities that could well be a collection of snow-covered buildings. More significant, there was a spire which looked like the wind generator for the radio plant, very much iced up. The group of objects seemed to be about four miles away, which would correspond precisely to our dead-reckoned position.

In our excitement we dropped our work, strapped on our snowshoes, and started out for the place, traveling light. Once more we were deceived by Antarctic distances. After two hours, when we had covered at least four miles, our goal seemed no nearer, though our eyes still gave us the same story of hope. So we returned to the plane, aware now that it was too long a trek to the "town" to attempt without the sledge, yet as confident as ever that within a few hours we would be in the shelter of Little America.

We spent the rest of the afternoon and all of next day, December 8, putting the sledge together, a much more difficult job than we had imagined. On the morning of December 9 we were ready to go. On the chance that we might find no food at all in Little America, we packed fifteen days rations on the sledge, also putting on our primus stove and its fuel, as well as dishes. Last, we stowed our sleeping bags on the sled but packed little else. Since the plane and the town were in sight of each other, we could travel back and forth at our convenience and bring on the rest of our stuff. We even left our tent set up beside the Polar Star, since we would need to sleep there when we made subsequent trips back to the plane.

December 9 was the warmest day we had experienced in the Antarctic. The runners of the sledge sank into the soft snow; its 200 pounds of weight and load dragged horribly. At the end of a mile the sweat was dripping from our chins. We peeled off our heavy parkas and our caps, putting them on our load. Kenyon even threw away his jersey. Bareheaded, we bent once more against the harness straps and so kept on mile after mile, resting every fifteen minutes while we unclogged the meshing of our snowshoes.

Seven hours of such work, traveling about two miles an hour, and then a cruel disillusionment—the "town" turned out to be only a high pressure ridge of ice. The "buildings" were heavy blocks, the "tower" was a big upended cake, its thin edge toward us. It was a lesson to us never to travel again over the ice without full equipment, for now we had no tent and no sextant.

There was nothing to do but go back for them—a mere fifteen-mile trek over soggy snow! We stopped long enough to cook ourselves a meal of pemmican, then left the sledge where it was and started back with empty knapsacks, the sun beating down on us out of a cloudless sky. Traveling light, we made better time on this journey, reaching the plane about the middle of the evening. By then we were men fit for a rest.

However, we did not take it. We struck the tent and stuffed it into one of the rucksacks, together with some tins of tobacco and other odds and ends hastily picked up. The sextant went into the other rucksack, and the man who carried the sextant also shouldered the tent poles. We lighted our pipes and had a smoke as we sat for a few minutes on the Polar Star's wing, then set out once more for the sledge.

This was the most grueling phase of the whole experience. Though by the clock it was night, in the warm spell the temperature did not drop to freezing. The tent pack weighed fifty pounds, and the sextant and tent poles made no mean burden to carry on such a journey. Our snowshoes sank into the soft wet surface. At each step I could hear the water sogging in my moccasins.

We took turn and turn about with the heavy tent pack—fifteen minutes of slogging on, then four minutes to rest, clean snowshoes, and change burdens. During the whole seven hours of this march I don't think we spoke half a dozen words to each other. Men on long and arduous trails don't talk. There is nothing to talk about. Each one knows the other's thoughts, anyhow, and wastes no breath on speech. The novice, too, soon learns on such marches to keep single file. This aids in trail-breaking; also when walking abreast there is a feeling of competition in speed and a sort of compulsion to keep up conversation. It is a strain.

An hour before we came to the sledge we could see it—a tiny speck in the limitless expanse of white. Silence and desolation, and we the only inhabitants of the Antarctic continent! We reached our journey's end on the morning of December 10, having been twenty-four hours without sleep and having traveled forty-five miles, freighting three hundred pounds over a third of that distance. Hollick-Kenyon dropped his pack on the sledge and flung himself down in the wet snow.

"Am I tired!" I heard him mutter.

Due to my long training on trails, the journey did not seem to bother me as much as it did Kenyon. Indeed, I honestly felt that, bad foot and all, I could, under stress of necessity, have kept on indefinitely.

We pitched the tent in a hurry. Not stopping to cook, we broke out of the baggage a box of mixed nut meats and ate our fill. Then, wet with perspiration as we were, we crawled into our bags and for ten hours slept like dead men.

When we emerged late that afternoon it was with the resolution to do no more day traveling. At night we could usually expect frozen snow over which to drag that heavy sledge. But two days later fogs set in, making it cold twenty-four hours of the day, so we went back to day marches again.

Soon after we had arisen we took sights and plotted our position in latitude as about twelve miles south of the mouth of the Bay of Whales, which itself is fifteen miles long, Little America being on its east bank. If our observation was correct, then the bay, or the southern tip of it, must lie either east or west of us. It was a question of which direction to choose. Off to the west the land seemed to rise almost into foothills. It seemed to us, therefore, that we would not be likely to find the head of a bay in high ground. To the east it was lower, so it was in that direction we headed at first when we had struck camp after our breakfast, or supper, if you prefer.

There was a terrible load on the sledge for two men to pull— three hundred pounds at least. Whenever we stopped to rest, snow froze to the runners and had to be scraped off before we could pull again in unison. It was a lucky thing that we brought snowshoes instead of skis. We could never have hauled that sled over the icy slopes of the sastrugi with skis.

After a while Hollick-Kenyon wanted to jettison or cache some of our load, but I vetoed the proposal. For a while we argued about it. He was banking on finding Little America soon. It was true that we might stumble upon the buried, deserted town any hour but equally true that it might take us days and days to find it. As leader, I was responsible for Hollick-Kenyon's safety and my own. I did not dare travel without enough food to last through a very complete search.

To make matters worse, that first night a heavy fog drifted in, and from that time until we found the camp we were never without fog. Sometimes it closed us in so thickly we could see only

Two of Antarctica's Rare "Growing Things"—Beards and Icicles

Lincoln Ellsworth after Two Months without a Shave. No Washing Was Possible During This Time, for the Fuel Supply Was too Scant to Permit Melting Snow Except for Drinking and Cooking. Dark Glasses Were Worn to Prevent Snow Blindness from the Glare, Which Seemed Worse on Cloudy Days.

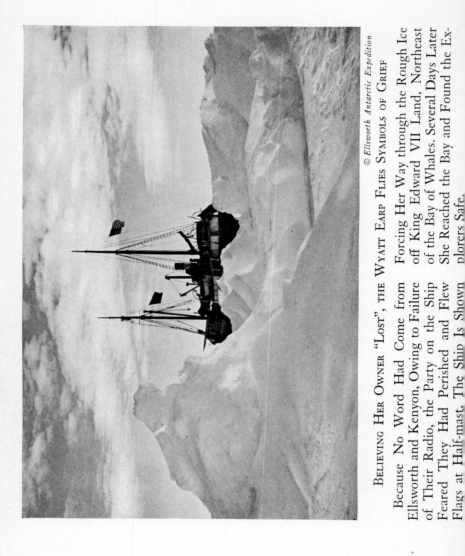

© *Ellsworth Antarctic Expedition*

BELIEVING HER OWNER "LOST", THE WYATT EARP FLIES SYMBOLS OF GRIEF

Because No Word Had Come from Ellsworth and Kenyon, Owing to Failure of Their Radio, the Party on the Ship Feared They Had Perished and Flew Flags at Half-mast. The Ship Is Shown Forcing Her Way through the Rough Ice off King Edward VII Land, Northeast of the Bay of Whales. Several Days Later She Reached the Bay and Found the Explorers Safe.

a few yards. At other times the Ross water sky loomed above it, and the sunshine filtered through. The night sunlight in December in Antarctica is unlike anything else in the world. The sun seems as high at midnight as at noon, it burns the skin just as much, and causes snow blindness as easily, yet it is cold sunshine, while that of the day is warm. In fog the night sun suffused the air with a weird light.

I will not attempt to unravel the confused, nightmarish memory of the next days. We adopted a regular system with the sledge—pull fifteen minutes and rest five. A day's work consisted of eight or ten hours, with six hours of actual pulling. We estimated that we traveled ten miles a day. We had to estimate, for there was nothing we could see by which to measure our distances. To keep direction we had Hollick-Kenyon's pocket compass.

As we toiled over the frozen snow, hour after hour, with nothing but fog around us, we began to feel loss of equilibrium. There was a tendency to start falling over. And there were other queer illusions. One of them was to be startled by the impression of a hole in the surface right ahead of one's feet. One instinctively braced himself for a step down, only to be jarred to the top of one's skull next instant as one's foot struck level ground. There had been no hole at all. At other times we felt sure we were going downhill, but the sledge ropes were taut as ever.

I found myself falling into long reveries about nothing at all. Hollick-Kenyon grew more and more silent. A little querulously, I asked him one day why he didn't talk more. He told me he was cursed with a bad temper and that it was better for him not to talk. I guess we were both getting "polar nerves."

Once, at the end of a day's march, the fog cleared a little, and I suddenly cried out: "Water!"

There, plain as day in the northeast, appeared a considerable expanse of open water. Hollick-Kenyon looked, too.

"That's right," he said. "It *is* water!"

We thought it was the Ross Sea—or perhaps even the bay itself, ice free earlier than usual this year. Knowing how fog magnified distances, we did not attempt to reach it that night; but, not to miss the welcome view the first thing when we awoke, we pitched the tent with the opening facing the water.

Then to celebrate our good fortune Kenyon that evening fried a mess of bacon. While he was doing so, the impulse came to me to examine my left foot, which remained numb day after day. I removed boot, moccasin, and my two pairs of socks, then hastily put them back on again, all my appetite for the savory feast gone. My whole foot seemed to be one water blister.

Neveretheless, I did not worry about it. On such a journey one learns to accept all misfortune with stoical resignation. No use to worry—that's polar religion. And it is easy not to worry. Life is all work, work, work—dull, brutish toil that leaves no place for fear or any other strong emotion. I never felt sorry for myself, since this thing had been my own choice. I only felt sorry for those outside, waiting and worrying without word from us.

Next morning when we crept from our sleeping bags we looked eagerly for the water that would guide us to Little America. A chilly fog was shrouding the ice, and we could see nothing. Nevertheless, we knew the direction of the water and set out for it by the compass. That day we made fourteen miles instead of our usual ten, but we never came to the water. It had vanished. It is a mystery I will never solve, for I cannot believe we were looking at a mirage.

The air was clearer next day, and we followed north toward the water sky. Our one desire now was to reach the Ross Sea. We were utterly lost, keeping on the move only to get somewhere else. During silent hours we toiled onward with the sledge—the same dreary routine of stopping every fifteen minutes to knock the snow clods from our snowshoes. We were thinking of making camp when ahead we observed a considerable rise or long ridge— a surprising feature after days on the dead level of the shelf ice. We had fair visibility at this time, and we decided to keep on to the top of the ridge, which seemed about two miles away, hoping that from the crest we might see Little America or some beacon or landmark that would guide us there.

As we neared the ridge we thought it likely that we were in for a change of weather. In the distance we could hear a sound like that of a rising wind. If wind, it would at least blow away the fog, we thought. In less than an hour we reached the foot of the slope. Wriggling out of the sledge harnesses, we went up light. At the crest we instinctively sprang back, so startled were we by what we saw. We found ourselves looking straight down 200 feet into the black tumbling water of the Ross Sea. What we thought was wind was the thunder of waves dashing against the foot of the ice cliff far below.

We stared at this spectacle only a few moments, then went back to the sledge and beat a hasty retreat. The shelf ice is always sloughing off at the barrier edge. After our long flight and our almost equally long sledge journey, we did not want to end by being dumped into the ocean. We withdrew a mile inland and there made camp, aware that if we played our cards right we were near salvation. And high time, too, for we only had three days of fuel left for the primus stove.

It was a question of following the ice coast to the Bay of Whales. But which direction should we follow it, east or west? If we turned the wrong way, we would be almost as badly off as when lost on the shelf ice. Day and night meant little to us now. We slept only a short time, then spent several hours reconnoitering in the fog. To the east the barrier face stretched off in a straight line. To the west it began to curve inland. We decided to go west.

Keeping well back from the edge, we followed first a southwest chord that should bring us out to the barrier again by a short cut, if it followed its curve. After a couple of hours of travel, we reached it again, but now looked down upon a different scene— a wintry scene—flat, low ice under the beetling crags of blue shelf ice. It was the Bay of Whales at last. We kept down along its east shore—tough pulling, for it was all long sastrugi here. About the middle of the afternoon we came to a place where stood two American caterpillar tractors together, almost buried under the snow. There was no doubt about this place—Ver-sur-Mer, Byrd's port for Little America.

Although we had already traveled fifteen miles this day, we decided to keep on. Directions were now sure. Little America was almost due south along the shore, though how far away we did not exactly know.

Actually it was six miles away, and we went on to complete a march of twenty-one miles, having sledged in all a distance of more than one hundred miles in the search. The actual distance of the Polar Star from Little America, we learned later, was sixteen miles.

Following down beside the bay, we noticed presently that the trail was marked by orange-colored flags on bamboo sticks frozen in the ice. These flags were spaced about half a mile apart. We did not realize that Little America was such a distance from Ver-sur-Mer. In fact, at one time we almost thought that the orange flags might mark the trail to Byrd's hut, where he spent the winter alone, and that we were going in the wrong direction. When we had followed these flags nearly three hours, Hollick-Kenyon said that if in one more hour we did not reach Little America, he would favor camping for the night. We were very tired by this time.

The trail lay over the crests of long icy sastrugi. A little while after Kenyon had spoken, we topped the rise of one of these and looked down upon the most desolate remains of past habitation I ever beheld. It was the Byrd camp, but now appearing only as a sparse thicket of masts, poles, stovepipes, and guy wires protruding above the snow. All else was level white.

We dug near a stovepipe until we found a glass skylight. This we broke, then, after knotting loops in a sledge rope to make a ladder, we let ourselves down and found we were in the radio shack. Icy, bleak, and deserted as it was, it seemed cosy to us after our weeks in the sooty tent. It was Sunday, December 15— the end of the twenty-third day since we left Dundee Island.

Then I had a surprise for Kenyon. For three years I had been carrying in my knapsack two small bottles of Napoleon brandy my wife had given me to celebrate my crossing of Antarctica. That moment had now come. I produced the bottles and opened one. It contained the best brandy I ever tasted—brown, fiery, yet smooth as velvet. Hollick-Kenyon took a sip and really smiled.

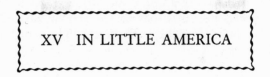

XV IN LITTLE AMERICA

IT WAS MY IDEA to make it a good celebration and drink the second bottle of brandy at once, but Hollick-Kenyon demurred.

"Let's save it for Christmas," he said.

Since Christmas was only ten days in the future and the brandy the only alcoholic cheer we had, I consented.

We found the radio shack to consist of two rooms. That into which we had broken was the operating room, where the Byrd radio instruments had been set up. Behind it was a room lined with bunks, where the radio staff had slept. This we occupied, first clearing out all the snow that had sifted in and exposing the skylight above. There was a stove in the bunk room and a sack of coal, and presently we had a hot fire going and were very warm and comfortable. The only light in the bunk room came from the half-buried skylight, but the obscurity was a blessed thing after the glare of the Antarctic summer. How we slept that night, after a good supper of pemmican!

Next day we made ourselves shipshape, adopted a routine, and settled down to a Christian way of living. My sore foot seemed to get better in spite of my misuse of it. The numbness persisted, but I found I could walk on it quite comfortably. Hollick-Kenyon at once resumed his precise personal habits, shaving every day. That was a little too much for me, though—melting snow for shaving water, and so on. I was content to shave about once every two weeks.

We cut a tunnel and steps down to the door of the shack, then explored for supplies, finding two more sacks of stove coal, a bag of hardtack, and half a drum of "white" gasoline—all the primus fuel we ever found. In the radio shack itself was a big five-pound tin of strawberry jam, some orange marmalade, a can of George Washington coffee, and several bottles of malted-milk tablets. The tunnels connecting the various buildings at Little America were lined with boxes, but all we opened were empty. However, by searching the camp thoroughly we found enough food to live on for three months.

We divided the duties of the camp. Hollick-Kenyon was cook. I did the rest of the housework and kept the shaft clear of snow. Fuel for our heating stove was evidently going to be scarce— though we did find two more sacks later—and to conserve coal and fuel, we agreed to stay in our sleeping bags fifteen hours a day. This was the routine adopted: We had supper at 9 P.M., local time. At midnight we turned in. We got up at three or four o'clock the next afternoon and had breakfast. After I had cleaned everything up, I put on my parka and snowshoes and hiked to the tractors at Ver-sur-Mer, six miles each way, to observe the condition of the bay ice and watch for the Wyatt Earp. I usually got back home just in time for supper.

One day—it was shortly before Christmas—Kenyon accompanied me to Ver-sur-Mer, and we dragged the sledge on which was loaded our tent and poles. We set up the tent at the tractors, and near it we planted firmly in the ice a bamboo pole with an orange bunting flag fastened to it. I also put a note inside the tent, informing whom it might concern that we were at Little America. Tent and flag were a prearranged signal to inform Wilkins, when the Wyatt Earp should enter the bay, that we had arrived.

While I was away on these walks, Hollick-Kenyon would rummage around through the cabins for what he could find. He was the official food hunter. He usually had some treasure trove to show me when I got back from Ver-sur-Mer. The very next day after our arrival he found a lot of bully beef with some bottles of chili sauce, Worcestershire, and tabasco. We had meat every day after that but always made our stews too hot with seasoning.

They gave me indigestion and made me long for the old diet of oatmeal and bacon.

In almost every cabin Hollick-Kenyon dug up books—mostly detective stories. He had stacks of them in his upper berth. In one of the houses he found a tin of pure-sugar hard candies, in another a small tinned plum pudding, which we saved for Christmas. One great discovery was a package of prepared pancake flour and a can of maple sirup. A five-pound tin of blackberry jam came to light. He also found a carton of tins of Dill's Best smoking tobacco. How I hated it! But I had at last run out of my good New Zealand tobacco which I had bought in Auckland the year before. Hollick-Kenyon said the New Zealand tobacco was the worst he ever smoked. Each man to his taste.

At first we slept a great deal in the unaccustomed darkness of the cabin. It was really cozy there, especially in the evening when we had the fire going. We put up with a cold cabin during the day to save coal. In the shack, deep under the snow, we didn't even know what the weather was like outside, except that when the stovepipe rattled that meant wind, drifts, and a shoveling job for me in the morning. Hollick-Kenyon was always stoking up the fire. He kept the cabin much too hot for me.

That view of a supposed town which we had had from the wing of the Polar Star had been bad luck for me. In our eagerness to reach Little America we did a slipshod job of selecting supplies to pack on the sledge. Then, after our disappointment, when we returned to the plane, we were too tired to think of anything except the tent and sextant. As a result we left several things behind we could have used in Little America. There was one serious omission for me—my glasses. I left them in the cockpit of the Polar Star, and as a result I could read nothing and could write only with uncertainty. This at least doubled the boredom of the wait for me. Hour after hour in his upper berth Hollick-Kenyon lost himself in detective stories, while I had only my thoughts for company.

I lay in my bunk one evening, merely putting in the time, when my fingers touched a wad of chewing gum somebody had stuck on the frame underneath. I debated with myself two days whether to chew it. I really yearned for that quid to chew on hikes through the snow. Then when I returned from the tractors one evening Hollick-Kenyon proudly produced two packages of chewing gum he had found.

In the camp kitchen we came upon a pile of frozen seal meat which Byrd had had for his dogs. We who had more or less contemplated subsisting on seals at Little America now turned up our noses at this stuff. We were living on the fat of the land. At least, it was the fat of Antarctica. Every other day we had boiled bully beef, alternating it with Dr Coman's spicy pemmican.

A curious thing happened to us during the first, or sleepy, period of our stay. One day Hollick-Kenyon woke me from sound slumber by climbing out of his bunk—rising a little early, I thought, for my watch said just twelve o'clock. He went outdoors but returned a moment later, a perplexed look on his face. He saw me looking at him.

"Say," he said, "do you know what time it is?"

"Why, yes," I answered. "It's just noon—twelve o'clock."

"That's what I thought," he said, "but, by George, the sun is dead south! It's midnight!"

We had lost twelve hours somehow. We must have slept twenty-four hours without a break.

But it grew dreadfully monotonous for me in the isolation into which I had been thrown by the loss of my glasses and by Hollick-Kenyon's absorption in his stack of mystery stories. Lying in my bunk, I began to long for that other bottle of Napoleon brandy. So queerly does imprisonment in the polar regions affect one's character that I was too perverse to come out frankly for drinking it at once. No, I had to pretend that I was keeping to the original plan. Just as once in the Arctic I took a subtle revenge upon poor old Feucht by eating my oat biscuits after he had finished his, so now I laid a sly plot against Hollick-Kenyon.

One evening before supper I said to him: "Well, tonight's Christmas Eve. We'll drink the brandy to celebrate."

"Tonight?" he exclaimed. He got out his notebook. "According to my diary, today's the twenty-third—two more days until Christmas."

"You're wrong, Kenyon," I said calmly. "Those twelve hours we lost must have mixed you up."

So we drank the brandy, and Hollick-Kenyon changed the dating of his diary. After supper he examined his notes again, and I heard him grumbling: "Lost a day! Don't see how I could have done that." December 24th we celebrated as Christmas, dining in state off bully-beef stew and our plum pudding.

Nature herself speedily punished me for this lie. In scheming for the brandy, I had quite forgotten that a total eclipse of the sun was to occur in Western Antarctica on Christmas afternoon. It came—a weird and wonderful phenomenon when seen across the vast snow fields—and I was exposed. To get out of it, I confessed shamefacedly that I must have made the dating mistake myself.

By the end of the year we mutually abandoned our routine of fifteen hours a day in bed. We were completely "slept up." So we began rising early in the morning and keeping warm as best we could until it came time to fire the stove at night. There has been an implied criticism of us that we did not at this time return to the Polar Star and bring back the wireless apparatus to operate from Little America. Those who find that fault simply do not know what conditions are like in the Antarctic.

In the first place, we were uncertain about the exact position of the Polar Star in relation to Little America. It might mean a long hunt to find it. Indeed, after some heavy snows in early January, I expressed a doubt in my diary whether we ever would find the plane. If it were snowed completely under, only a lucky chance would bring it to light again. If we spent days hunting for it, fresh snows might blot out our own trail and make a return to Little America exceedingly difficult. At any rate, besides our tent and other camp supplies, we should have to pack on the sledge food and fuel for at least ten days. For travel-worn men it was too great an ordeal to contemplate. We had crossed Antarctica safely. Why risk our lives further?

When the Wyatt Earp finally arrived, my people put one of
Byrd's tractors into commission to carry gas back to refuel the
Polar Star, which had been found by one of the reconnaissance
flights of the plane brought down to aid in a possible hunt for us.
The tractor followed a direct route to the Polar Star and dropped
into a crevasse, from which it was rescued with difficulty. Those
with the tractor discovered that, owing to the crevassed nature
of the ice, we had by chance taken the only possible direction at
the start by which we could have reached Little America. So, had
the two of us started out to hunt for our plane again, we might
have found the journey impossible.

There was plenty to call us back to the Polar Star besides the
natural human wish to communicate with our friends and dear
ones. By New Year's Day I would willingly have paid a thousand
dollars for my reading glasses. In the plane was food enough for
two months. Indeed, necessity might drive us back for that
eventually. One of my most precious relics, Wyatt Earp's cartridge
belt and holster, was still in the cockpit. Sometimes I thought I
would regret its loss as much as that of the plane itself.

On December 27 there was a heavy snowfall, the first we had
seen since leaving the high plateau. On January 6, 1936, began a
four-day blizzard, our shaft drifting full every night. Cooped up,
my nerves grew edgy. Two men cannot live together under such
conditions without getting on each other's nerves. Each tiny difference in habit becomes an irritation.

Before he left for Antarctica, Mrs Hollick-Kenyon presented her
husband with two briar pipes having very long stems. He kept
them alternately hot. We lacked pipe cleaners, and Hollick-
Kenyon's pipes gurgled with nicotine. How maddeningly familiar
became the routine at night, when Kenyon sat devouring his
novels! From my bunk I could not see, but I could hear. The
intermittent gurgling of his pipe. Thirty minutes of this, then a
swipe to throw out the juice. Next, the lid of a candy tin coming
off. Then the crunching of teeth on hard candy.

Hour after hour of it, as I lay in my dark berth, my mind almost
a blank. I had long since extracted all the enjoyment from my

daydream of the reception I should receive when I emerged victoriously into civilization.

On one such evening Hollick-Kenyon broke his continuity of gurgle, swipe, and crunch to make his second and last original remark of our weeks on Antarctica. It was the day after the January blizzard. I had walked to the tractors that afternoon to find more seals than ever upon the bay ice and the bay itself clear within half a mile of Ver-sur-Mer. The annual mid-January breakup was near, and ships could soon get in. I told Hollick-Kenyon about this on my return.

That evening an unexpected silence fell over the cabin. Then Hollick-Kenyon's voice spoke out.

"Have you any dogs at your home?" he said.

I told him I hadn't, and he resumed his reading. I never knew what prompted him to ask the question.

I loaded my pipe for my after-supper smoke but fell to thinking about some subject and let two matches burn out in my fingers before lighting up with the third.

"You must be president of a match factory," Kenyon remarked.

"You use a good many more matches than I do," I retorted.

Nothing pleased me now. I even began to complain of Sir Hubert Wilkins' delay, though by our prearranged schedule I was not to expect the Wyatt Earp in the Bay of Whales before January 22 and was not to be concerned if it did not arrive until February. Yet on January 14 I wrote in my diary:

"Will the Wyatt Earp never come for us? Wilkins said five or six weeks to come the 3,000 miles from Dundee island, and here it is almost seven. One can't sleep all the time, and it's awful not to be able to read. My glasses are in the plane along with all my flags and souvenirs."

The truth was, I was sick. My left foot was troubling me again. I refused to admit to myself that the trouble came from the frostbite. The sole had begun to crack open, causing me anguish when I walked. I told myself the rawhide webbing of my snowshoe had bruised it. I had taken so many twelve-mile walks to Ver-sur-Mer and back that I had worn the webbing loose. Red streaks up my leg and swollen glands under my knee and in my groin should have told me I was developing a gangrenous condition, but I wouldn't let them tell me anything. I wouldn't even look at the foot. I didn't want to know what was wrong with it, since I couldn't do anything about it.

On January 14 I gave up and stayed in bed, telling Hollick-Kenyon I was resting my foot to let it heal. By this time I was running a temperature, and my brain was confused. For the fifteenth this was my only diary entry: "The first penguins this year at the Bay of Whales. One flopped on the skylight as I lay writing. *One month today since we arrived here!*"

At ten o'clock that night Hollick-Kenyon roused me from a sort of stupor. He was rustling a piece of note paper in his hand.

"Read it," he said nonchalantly. "It's probably from Wilkins."

I was wide awake in an instant.

"Wilkins?" I excitedly replied. "Is he here?"

"No," said Hollick-Kenyon, "but this just dropped."

Then he explained how down in our dugout home, fifteen feet beneath the surface of the snow, he had heard the roar of an airplane and had scrambled up the shaft just in time to see a small parachute descending through the mist. I got up at once. The note was signed by Lieutenant L. C. Hill, commander of the British Royal Antarctic Research Society's ship, Discovery II. It directed us to start for our tent at Ver-sur-Mer on foot and meet a party of his men, whom he was sending ashore. With this note came a parcel, the contents of which we spread out on our table— packages of chocolate, raisins, and a can of very sweet, concentrated orange sirup.

"Why should I walk?" I said. "We'll have to come back and pack our stuff, anyhow. I've got a sore foot. You go on alone."

"All right," Kenyon answered. "Expect me back in about three hours."

He left at once. I went back to my bunk and tried to sleep, but sleep had left me. It was curious that as long as our food supply was limited I never felt very hungry; but now, with relief at hand, feverish as I was, I developed an enormous appetite. At midnight

I got up and cooked for myself a huge meal of bacon, hot cakes and sirup, and coffee. Recklessly I heaped some of our last remaining coal on the fire.

Hollick-Kenyon did not return in three hours, and I went back to bed again. But I could not sleep. For hours I rolled and tossed —and grew hungry. At six o'clock in the morning I got up and prepared another big meal, firing up the stove with the rest of our coal. Chilling with fever, I could not get the cabin hot enough. I expected people to come any minute, so I gobbled my breakfast down fast, unwilling to share a mouthful of it.

Then more hours in bed. When at noon—fourteen hours after the plane had dropped the note—nobody had yet appeared, I got up, dressed, and started out on foot. I had proceeded about a mile when through the fog, which magnified everything frightfully down there, I saw what looked like a small army approaching me. Actually it consisted of the first mate and five sailors from the Discovery II. So I turned back with them for Little America.

When we descended into the radio shack, and the mate saw all the bunks there, he told his men they could lie down if they were tired after their march. I thought to myself: "My gracious, if a six-mile ski trip does them up this way, what would they be like after ten hours in a sledge harness?"

But instead of resting, they wanted to eat and asked if I had anything.

"Hollick-Kenyon said you had," they insisted.

I invited them to help themselves. They cleaned up everything, especially praising tea made with snow water, the first any of them had ever tasted. They said it was the best tea they ever drank, though I could tell no difference between snow-water tea and any other. After that they stripped the shack of everything they could find for souvenirs—calendars, strainers, anything— they helped me pack the sledge with our stuff, and we started for Ver-sur-Mer. On the way back we made a stop for the sailors to eat some chocolate while I waited, my teeth chattering from fever.

As soon as I arrived on board the Discovery II, Captain Hill gave me a stiff drink of whisky. Then the doctor took charge of me—a hot bath, my first in two months, and then to bed in the chief scientist's cabin, the best quarters on the ship. My temperature was 102°. While I was in the commander's cabin Hollick-Kenyon walked in, smiling, clean shaven, and debonair in borrowed clothes that fit him—a suit, muffler, and camel's-hair coat.

He told me that when the first shore party met him alone, they thought one of us was dead. He assured them of my safety, and they took him to the Discovery II first. He hadn't slept a wink since leaving me but had talked all night to the fascinated officers of the research ship. For once the floodgates of Kenyon's conversation had been down.

From Captain Hill I learned at once that the Wyatt Earp was near, slowly breaking her way through the pack ice outside the Ross Sea. He and Sir Hubert Wilkins had been in touch with each other by wireless for more than two weeks. Late Sunday afternoon, January 19—three days ahead of the schedule set on Dundee Island—my staunch little boat came into the Bay of Whales. Her flags were at half-mast.

My foot had responded to medical treatment so rapidly that I was able to go over to the Wyatt Earp as soon as she tied up to the edge of the shelf. How happy I was to see again comrades I had learned to love so well during three years of voyaging! Reproachfully I pointed to the half-masted flag and told Sir Hubert he couldn't have had much confidence in me to mourn my death before he had proof of it. He said that I flattered myself. Just before the Wyatt Earp reached the Bay of Whales, Lanz picked up a radio bulletin from London announcing that the king was dead.

Lieutenant Hill having offered me the hospitality of the Discovery II, it seemed to me that I ought to go up to Melbourne to thank the Australian government for sending the fine research vessel to my aid. Wilkins urged this, too. Sir Douglas Mawson, the famous Australian explorer, had been especially concerned about my safety, sending to the Discovery II his own sledges from the Adelaide Museum. Captain J. K. Davis, Australian director of navigation, had done everything to expedite the departure of the ship.

Leaving my people to the week's work of bringing in and dismantling the Polar Star (which one of the Australian planes had already located), I shook hands all round, promising to meet them in New York. Then I boarded the Discovery II and started north.

XVI NOT "RESCUED"—
"AIDED"

GRATEFUL AS I WAS to the Australian government and to the Discovery Committee in London for dispatching their expensive vessel to me—a steel ship, incidentally, and therefore one that ran a risk in butting through heavy ice—regretful as I was at having caused others all this trouble, nevertheless I have to state that the voyage of the Discovery II to the Bay of Whales was unnecessary.

For my own reputation as an explorer I must insist that my Antarctic Expedition was self-sufficient. I allowed myself five weeks in which to cross Antarctica. We actually reached Little America in three weeks. The Wyatt Earp was instructed to pick us up at Little America on or after January 22, 1936. She actually arrived on the nineteenth.

At no time were we "lost", in the sense that we did not have a general idea of where we were or were unable to proceed. At no time was Wilkins, on the Wyatt Earp, at a loss as to what to do next. At no time were Hollick-Kenyon and I in desperate straits. We experienced discomfort and even hardship, but we always had food, heat, shelter, and available transportation; and, though we encountered difficulties, we overcame them as best we could and pressed on steadily to a successful end. Our whole program went through as projected; and, if there were a few bumps in it, these had been anticipated and discounted.

Had our radio not failed, the world of the streets would have hailed the crossing of Antarctica as a most intricate and difficult undertaking in exploration carried through without a hitch. As to the charge that I suppressed the radio for the sake of publicity, I would have had more publicity and the newspapers a more dramatic story than our mere "disappearance" gave them, had I been able to send a daily account of our fortunes—how we fared during the long blizzard on Hollick-Kenyon Plateau, for example, or in our blind wanderings through the fog at the Bay of Whales.

Earlier in this narrative I have given in full the open letter I signed on the eve of departure from Dundee Island, telling what I might be expected to do in Antarctica in the event of a forced landing. In addition to this, Sir Hubert Wilkins and I discussed thoroughly what he would do on the Wyatt Earp if a mishap or disaster overtook the Polar Star during the flight. Sir Hubert summarized these understandings briefly, and I carried a copy of his summary across the continent. It read as follows:

The procedure discussed is that if the plane has passed Lat. 75°, Long. 75°, an endeavor will be made in the U.S.A. to secure an amphibian plane fitted with skis in place of wheels, the machine to have a range of about 1500 miles on floats or skis with an extra load of pilot, navigator, and 500 pounds of provisions, some of which will be cached, if necessary. 1500-miles range will reach from points previously reached by ships to any point of Ellsworth's route and return to position accessible to ships. The amphibian will be flown to Magallanes. Meanwhile the Earp can proceed to Magallanes, meet airplane there, then proceed to Bay of Whales and fly food to Mt Mabelle Sidley and Mt Grace McKinley. The food caches in each case need not necessarily contain more than 300 pounds of food, for at Charcot Island seals and penguins have been observed, and from Mt Mabelle Sidley and Mt Grace McKinley the men can walk to Little America. At Charcot Land and at Little America the men can winter, if necessary. As to time of action in the South, the Wyatt Earp can, if nothing is heard before December 1, reach Magallanes December 1. Plane reaches Magallanes December 7. Meet the plane there, say latest December 15, then reach Charcot Island in ten days (25th), allow seven days for laying the Charcot Land depot, distance to be flown, 150 miles each way, then

THE OWNER COMES ABOARD!

After Two Months on the Antarctic Plateau and at Little America, Lincoln Ellsworth and Hollick-Kenyon Board the Wyatt Earp at Bay of Whales. Overhead Is the Plane Flown from Kansas City to Magallanes, Chile, and Then Brought South in Case It Should Be Necessary to Search for the Flyers.

THE FRINGES OF ETERNITY

These Peaks of the Eternity Range   Later This Great Mountain Range
Were Photographed Two and a Half   Dwindled into Isolated Nunataks, Which
Hours after the Polar Star Crossed   Gave Way to the Level Antarctic Plateau

travel to Bay of Whales in 19 days, arriving Jan. 22nd. Allow one month for laying depots at Mt Mabelle Sidley and Mt Grace McKinley —distance to be flown, 500 miles and 250 miles each way respectively —then, leaving Bay of Whales Feb. 22, return to Charcot Island with favorable winds in 17 days. Arrive Charcot Island March 11th. Visit caches within a week and then leave Antarctica before the freeze-up.

In addition to these written instructions for both the air and the base parties, we agreed upon and printed out on cards a code of signals by which men on the ground could communicate with an airplane by laying out strips of orange bunting in various formations. Planes were to reply by dipping, circling, jazzing motor, cutting figure eights and letter *S's,* etc., or by dropping notes by parachute.

Thus it will be seen that, if we had to be rescued from Antarctica, I proposed to carry out that rescue at my own trouble and expense. So confident was Wilkins in our essential safety and the integrity of our plans that on December 10—seventeen days after the last word was heard from us—when the Australian government had announced its intention of dispatching the Discovery II to the Bay of Whales, he sent to Director of Navigation Davis, at Melbourne, the following wireless message:

ON MY BEHALF PLEASE EXPRESS SINCERE APPRECIATION TO THOSE RE-SPONSIBLE FOR EFFORTS IN CONNECTION WITH ELLSWORTH'S EXPEDITION, BUT EMPHASIZE THAT UNLESS UNLIKELY DELAYS ARE EXPERIENCED, ELLS-WORTH'S EXPEDITION'S OWN PLANS WILL MEET ALL REQUIREMENTS UNTIL MID-JANUARY, AFTER WHICH WOULD BE TIME, IF NECESSARY, ACTUALLY TO DISPATCH DISCOVERY WITH PLANES TO BAY OF WHALES. ELLSWORTH IS ADEQUATELY EQUIPPED AND PROVISIONED AND UNEXPECTS RENDEZVOUS UNTIL ABOUT END OF JANUARY. WE HAVE NO GOOD REASON TO BELIEVE THAT HE HAS NOT ARRIVED. NOTWITHSTANDING ALL THIS, PREPARATIONS SHOULD BE MADE.

The reply of Captain Davis was that the Australian government considered the immediate dispatch of Discovery II justified, since any airplane search of the Bay of Whales area would have to be carried out by February 1, if at all.

Now let us follow the movements of the Wyatt Earp after the Polar Star whooped down the slope of Dundee Island and disappeared into the south behind a cloud of kicked-up snow. We got away just in time, for the good weather broke next day and was followed by a succession of fogs, snowstorms, and low clouds. After our radio failed, Lanz listened and buzzed our call letters constantly, but concentrated on four hours fixed by prearranged schedule. The schedule for Lanz was as follows:

G.C.T.		Wave Length—Meters
12	Send	35.2
12:05	Listen	35
13	Send	24.2
13:05	Listen	28
21	Send	24.2
21:05	Listen	28
22	Send	35.2
22:05	Listen	35

On November 25, two days after we left, Kenneth Rawson, navigating officer of the Second Byrd Expedition, radioed the Wyatt Earp the position of various food caches left by Byrd in Antarctica—particularly those at Mount Grace McKinley and in the Rockefeller Mountains close to Little America. One sentence of the message read as follows: "At Little America there is ample food and coal in the tunnels, also a cache of trail rations in the southeast radio tower." Thereafter, Lanz always repeated this message to me on his schedules, but of course I never heard him.

Meanwhile, Mrs Ellsworth, Bernon Prentice, Charles S. McVeigh, Trubee Davison, and others of my friends in New York formed a committee to take charge of that end of carrying out our emergency plans. To avoid any danger of being trapped by ice in the Weddell Sea and to be in a strategic position for either a dash to South America or the Antarctic Coast, the Wyatt Earp sailed from Dundee Island on November 26 for Deception Island.

Drums of gasoline were left both on the beach at Dundee and at our cairn on top with duplicates of the following notice affixed to them:

Lincoln Ellsworth and Pilot H. Hollick-Kenyon left here November 23rd to fly to Bay of Whales, Ross Sea. When their radio was last heard they were at approximately Lat. 76° S., Long. 79° W. It is hoped that they are at the Bay of Whales, but a request has been sent to Ellsworth's representatives in New York to provide an amphibian plane for use in laying depots at Charcot Island, Mt Mabelle Sidley, and at Mt Grace McKinley, which are prearranged rendezvous. The MS Wyatt Earp proceeded on November 26 to Deception Island, there to await information from the representatives in New York with reference to the relief airplane. The flights to lay depots will be made if Ellsworth and Kenyon are not heard from, or if they are not found at the Bay of Whales.   (Signed) HUBERT WILKINS.

Unable to find a suitable amphibian plane, the New York committee chartered a Northrup Gamma monoplane—a lineal descendant of the Polar Star, except that it was powered with a Cyclone engine. The owner-pilot, Russell K. Thaw, was engaged to fly this ship from Newark Airport to Magallanes. However, taking off with his mechanic, William H. Klenke, Jr, at Atlanta, Thaw crashed. Neither flier was injured, but the plane was too badly damaged to proceed.

At once the Texaco Company, through Captain Frank M. Hawks, offered a twin of the damaged Northrup. This my committee chartered in Kansas City, engaging the crack transport pilot Dick Merrill to fly it to Chile with Mechanic Klenke, which he did via Yucatan, Cristobal, Guayaquil, Lima, Santiago, and Bahia Blanca, Argentine—8,000 miles in 40 hours of flying.

The chronology of events at this time:

November 27—Wyatt Earp arrived at Deception Island.

November 30—Wyatt Earp sailed for Magallanes.

December 4—Wyatt Earp arrived at Magallanes.

December 5—Australia announced its intention to send the Discovery II to the Bay of Whales.

December 9—Thaw plane cracked up at Atlanta.

December 13—Merrill left Kansas City with the Texaco North-rup.

December 19—Merrill reached San Antonio, Argentine, and delivered his plane to Lymburner, my reserve pilot, who that same day flew it down, 1,000 miles to Gallegos, Chile, to be fitted with pontons sent up from the Wyatt Earp by truck.

December 22—The Northrup relief plane, Texaco 20, fitted for depot-laying work along the Antarctic Coast, reached Magallanes and was loaded aboard the Wyatt Earp, which that same evening sailed for Charcot Island.

December 23—The Discovery II sailed from Melbourne for the Bay of Whales, via Dunedin, New Zealand. The vessel had not hurried departure, since she could not expect to break through to the Ross Sea much before January 15. The Discovery II carried two airplanes, pilots from the Royal Australian Air Force, sledges, and extra rations for long marches over the ice.

Wilkins and the Wyatt Earp reached the heavy shore pack ice off Charcot Island on December 28. The pack extended out sixty miles from the island and mainland coast, but, even so, it was compressed by a strong gale blowing from the north. There were no leads in the ice offering still water from which the Texaco 20 could take off with pontons, and the sea was far too rough to attempt even to launch the plane.

These conditions, interspersed with fogs and snows, persisted day after day. On December 31 Wilkins gave it up and started for the Bay of Whales to keep his schedule. He had never really believed in the necessity of laying a food base on Charcot, anyhow, since when our radio failed we were well beyond that point, and our plane was flying well. If we were not at Little America, he would have to return to Charcot at the end of the summer. Meanwhile, he had observed many seals and penguins on the Charcot ice which could keep us from starvation until the Wyatt Earp arrived in March.

For the rest of the voyage Sir Hubert was in daily touch with the Discovery II, coming down from New Zealand. With him for a while it was a race, as for the honor of the expedition he tried to reach the Bay of Whales first and thus allow us to accomplish our own "salvation." But when he found out that this meant over-working the engines through 1,000 miles of heavy pack, he desisted and allowed the British ship to get in ahead.

There is little more to tell of the transantarctic story as I know it at first hand. The voyage up on the Discovery II was a sheer delight—hot salt-water baths daily, good food in fine variety eaten off china upon snowy linen tablecloths. The chief scientist's cabin which I occupied was luxurious. It contained a splendid library of books, nearly all relating to the Antarctic. The ship's surgeon soon discovered my lack of glasses, canvassed everybody on board, and found a pair of spectacles that fit me well enough for read-ing. We took a month coming up from the Bay of Whales. I'm glad it wasn't all time wasted for the research vessel. Even while waiting for the Wyatt Earp to get in, the Discovery II made scientific investigations at Discovery Inlet, sixty miles west of the Bay of Whales. And it was on the voyage north that her sound-ing apparatus discovered the moraine in the Ross Sea.

In Australia I received a royal welcome. Among those who met me at Melbourne was Sir Douglas Mawson, who had traveled a thousand miles from Adelaide to do so. My official host was Captain Davis, the director of navigation. He took me every-where, always a little worried lest I should someday appear too stylishly dressed for democratic Australian taste. I think he sus-pected me of having a silk hat concealed somewhere in my polar baggage. As the guest of the government I couldn't spend a cent for anything. They took me for a four-day visit to Mount Buffalo National Park, also on a three-hour flight from Melbourne to Canberra, the capital, where I lunched with Prime Minister Joseph A. Lyons.

Among the pleasures in Melbourne was my discovery that my favorite liner, the Mariposa, was sailing for America in ten days. I was on her for the entire voyage, my wife boarding the steamer in Honolulu. At Los Angeles a squadron of airplanes met the ship in my honor, while army stunt fliers looped and did other evolutions overhead. The governor of California sent his personal representative to greet me, while delegations from the Los Angeles city administration and the chamber of commerce made a welcoming committee. During the two weeks we remained in Los Angeles we rode in official cars with police escorts.

Then came a great day in New York—an April day—when the Wyatt Earp, having soberly chugged up the west coast of South America and gone through the Panama Canal, arrived in New York to receive an official welcome and be thrown open for the city's inspection.

On her deck was lashed the assembled Polar Star, which had now traveled something like 65,000 miles in order to fly a critical distance of 2,300 miles. She was as good as new but far too dear a relic in my eyes to be permitted to grow old and go to aviation's boneyard. So I presented her to the Smithsonian Institution. Hollick-Kenyon was with me in New York, and we planned to fly down to Washington together in the plane and make the presentation with a flourish. But an unromantic inspector for the Department of Commerce took a look at that crumpled fuselage and refused to license her to fly at all. It seemed ironic to me, since we had flown her in that condition over a thousand miles of Antarctic ice. It was with difficulty that we obtained permission for Hollick-Kenyon to fly her down alone.

After that there were luncheons and dinners, presentations and other honors, all capped on a summer day when Congress, by its act of June 16, 1936, voted me a special gold medal—"for claiming on behalf of the United States approximately three hundred and fifty thousand square miles of land in Antarctica between the eightieth and one hundred and twentieth meridians west of Greenwich, representing the last unclaimed territory in the world . . ."

That, I suppose, should be a sufficient crown for a career which began in such fumbling fashion. And yet I still feel the old nostalgia. Exploration—the contest of mind and physical powers with the blind forces of nature—gets into one's blood. I find myself restless, unhappy in spirit, trying to grasp some settled peace wherein I can be content. There is more for me to do—I a vigorous man with years of strong life ahead of me. My whole training has been wrong for sedentary existence. I find myself repeating a favorite stanza of mine:

> *Who has known heights and depths shall not again*
> *Know peace—not as the calm heart knows*
> *Low ivied walls, a garden close,*
> *The old enchantment of a rose.*
> *And though he tread the humble ways of men,*
> *He shall not speak the common tongue again.*
>
> . . . . . .
>
> *Who has trodden stars seeks peace no more.*

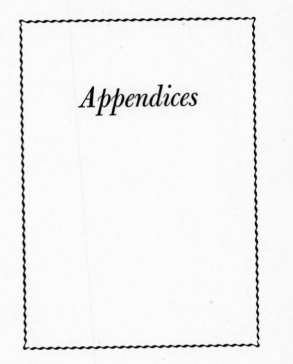

Appendices

APPENDIX I

The Ellsworth Trans-Antarctic Flight Preparation and Background

[From an address entitled "The First Crossing of Antarctica" delivered by Mr. Ellsworth at a meeting of the Royal Geographical Society in London, November 30, 1936, and published in the March, 1937, issue of the Geographical Journal.]

AFTER my flight with Amundsen in the *Norge* from Spitsbergen in 1926, over the north polar basin to Alaska, restlessness and desire nagged me until I was able to settle on the last great adventure of south polar exploration: the crossing of Antarctica.

A crossing of the area between the Ross Sea and the Weddell Sea seemed to offer the best possibility of solving the major problem in the Antarctic. Does the Andean massif which dips at Magellan Straits, rises to form the grand mountain chain of Graham Land, and dips at what is believed to be Stefansson Strait, rise again in Hearst Land and continue until it joins the polar plateau and the mountains of South Victoria Land; or, if it does rise in Hearst Land, does it dip again to form a depression or a below sea-level channel connecting the Ross Sea with the Weddell Sea?

Numerous plans and many preparations had been made to carry out a trans-Antarctic journey. Shackleton in 1914 lost his ship before he reached the starting-point. Wilkins was foiled two years in succession by failing to find a suitable aeroplane field from which to start. Watkins, after much preparation and endeavour, failed to get started from England. Riiser Larsen was carried away from the barrier edge by the breaking up of the ice, and did not get started on the actual journey.

By the time I was able to turn my attention to the problem a great advance had been made in the machinery for aerial transportation, and

I believed that it was no longer necessary to risk the lives of many men who by their sheer physical endeavour would fight their way slowly through storms, starvation, blizzards, and snow blindness, struggling for many weeks against tremendous odds across what might prove to be a monotonous stretch of sastrugi-featured snow: or, if mountains were found to exist between the Weddell Sea and the Ross Sea, find themselves in a maze of overhanging glaciers, steep-sided valleys, and faced with unscalable cliffs such as could be seen in Graham Land.

I myself would have preferred to have been with the vanguard of polar explorers, and am happy in the knowledge that neither the North Pole nor the South Pole were first humbled by conquest by aeroplanes. Nevertheless it would not do for us to lag behind the times. Change is the law of the world itself.

> *"The hills are shadows, and they flow*
> *From form to form, and nothing stands."*

says Tennyson. And so our method of approaching the mystery and romance of Nature's last stronghold against man's invasion had to change.

My own experience with aeroplanes in high latitudes had given me some knowledge of the possibilities of aircraft in polar conditions. I knew that low temperatures would not be a great obstacle to flight. I had experienced the fact of landing far from my base and setting out again for a safe return. I knew that aircraft engines in 1932 were reliable for many hours' service without overhaul, and I had studied carefully the Antarctic conditions as far as they might affect the use of the aeroplane.

In spite of the general impression created by the books on Antarctic travel, which are filled with descriptions of bad sledging trails, hazy outlines, sudden blizzards and hard-lipped sastrugi, I found that even the written accounts of previous expeditions really encouraged the belief that machines might be landed safely on most of the surfaces encountered in the past. A thorough search through the diaries of Scott, Shackleton, Mawson, and Amundsen revealed that the surfaces they found on their sledge journeys, both on the Ross Barrier and on the polar plateau, would afford reasonably good landing fields for modern aeroplanes, provided of course that the weather was such that these surfaces could be seen.

For instance, in Scott's published diary of his journey to the Pole he mentions soft snow, heavy and rough surfaces, and some surfaces distinctly good, but he actually mentions sastrugi on five days only during the thirty days it took him to travel from the edge of the Barrier to the foot of the Beardmore Glacier which leads up to the polar plateau. Only on one occasion did he mention sastrugi 12 inches high, and then they were "widely dispersed." The other sastrugi seen must have been lower and probably would not have interfered with the safe landing of an aeroplane. From this it was clear that only a small percentage of the actual Barrier surface would be unsuitable for forced landings.

On the way up the glacier Scott mentions sastrugi "not more than three inches high." There were crevasses and undulations and soft spots of course; one would expect to find these in the fairly steep-sloped area leading up to an altitude of 9000 feet. But it was hardly necessary to consider the glacier surface in relation to Antarctic flight, for any aeroplane flying over them would, in case of engine failure and a forced landing, be able to glide above the glacier surface to the lower level of the Barrier.

When once over the plateau and beyond the "third degree" camp, Scott found the surface difficult for sledging, but not until after five days' marching did he come to sastrugi which were rough and confused —it was so rough in fact that Scott decided to abandon his skis, which he had used up to that time. But the rough condition was limited in area—a cross-section of probably less than 5 miles; for when they came to the end of the sastrugi Scott says they went back for the skis, a trip which resulted in a delay of only an hour and thirty minutes. Onward to the Pole, and between the dates January 7 and 17, sastrugi are mentioned only four times, and then only in relation to the general direction of the winds. He refers to rough surfaces only once, on the 15th, near the Pole, and there the sledges "bumped over the ridges."

In Amundsen's account of his journey from the Bay of Whales to the Pole he mentions sastrugi only five times, and only when on and near the glacier, in the draw of the mountains, did he find the surfaces exceedingly rough.

The general description of the surfaces encountered by Sir Douglas Mawson and the members of his parties was not so encouraging; but then Sir Douglas was travelling in comparatively low latitudes, between 69° and 70°, and his route lay over the sloping ice-sheet not far from where it meets the open water: a condition likely to induce high winds, crevassed areas, and sastrugi. Mawson's Magnetic Pole party led by Bage travelled farther from the continental edge, but was not more than 120 miles from the sea. Bage mentions sastrugi only twice during the first 75 miles of travel, and lists the snowy wind-drifts only once as being 1 foot high; the others must have been lower. Later on he remarks on sastrugi 6 inches high, then for three days very few. After that they travelled for five days over fairly good surfaces, then he mentions "some old sastrugi," then "surface smoothly polished."

Notwithstanding the difficulties which were actually encountered by Mawson's sledging parties in the Adélie Land area, Bickerton did use an air-screw tractor, in reality an aeroplane minus its wings, and taxied it several times over a route 10 miles long. The surfaces on any part of that route if suitable for taxiing must have been suitable for an emergency forced landing.

It is only logical to assume that conditions inland from the Adélie Land would provide food in the form of seals and penguins. The fuselage of the Northrup *Gamma* was large enough to accommodate a pilot and navigator, a sledge, skis and snow-shoes, sleeping-bags, tents, engine covers, and heating stoves required for conveniently starting the engine in cold weather. The machine was of course equipped with a two-way wireless as well as an emergency radio outfit. The final design incorporated a 600-h.p. Wasp engine, giving a possible speed of 215 miles per hour. It had sturdy, short, and wide skis made of wood, sheathed with metal. The skis were interchangeable with wheels and pontoons, so that we might use the machine on any type of surface. A unique feature was the flaps, a very new feature in 1932, which permitted us to land at the comparatively low speed of 50 miles an hour and take off in a short distance.

After the aeroplane was selected it was necessary to find a ship which would accommodate the machine in the hold for safe transport through the stormy waters we should cross to reach the Antarctic. My first plan, based on the assumption that in the Ross Sea, at the edge of the great Ross Barrier, was the only place where I could be certain of finding an unloading point for the plane on skis, was to fly from the Ross Sea to the Weddell Sea and return on a triangular course.

My ship would have to brave the stormy areas south of New Zealand, and have sufficient range to journey round the Pacific sector of the Antarctic ice edge to pick me up, should I be compelled to land on the Weddell Sea side or abandon the plane en route and walk to some part of the coast. I finally selected a staunch, single-deck, motor-driven Norwegian fishing-boat of 400 tons. She was built of Norwegian pine and oak in 1919. I sheathed her with oak and armour plate for service in the pack-ice. Her engine was of the semi-Diesel type, and I installed tanks for fuel sufficient for cruising 11,000 miles at a speed of 7 to 8 knots. I named the ship the *Wyatt Earp* after an unbelievably brave frontier marshal who more than any other man of his time typified the empire builders of the western United States.

The *Wyatt Earp* could carry supplies for two years as well as the aeroplane in the hold, where it was well protected from the weather. This left our decks clear, except for the explosive gasoline, which was carried in drums lashed to the deck rails. There was room in fact to have carried another plane on deck, but I finally decided against taking a duplicate machine for two reasons. First by exercising infinite care with the machine while preparing it for flight, and by flying only in fine weather, landing only in clear weather, and in time to lash it down before being overtaken by storm, I could be reasonably sure of safety from damage. A skilled pilot, landing under such conditions, would protect us from the danger of accidents to the personnel and leave us in a position to walk away from the machine if it was necessary to abandon it. Secondly, two aeroplanes would have meant two or more pilots and other additional members of the expedition, and in all an extra cost far in excess of the actual and initial cost of the machine.

Economy has not always been the first consideration in polar exploration; and while it is necessary to spare no expense in providing adequate equipment, there is no reason why expeditions should be absurdly expensive or luxurious. It is impossible of course to value discovery in dollars and cents, but all attempts at discovery should be organized with some consideration for the magnitude of possible results compared with the amount of money involved. In this relation the use of aeroplanes has made it possible to lower the cost of exploration and discovery.

An expedition equipped for flying needs less personnel, and can expect to cover more miles for less expenditure of energy and money than could be done when using the dog-team method. For detailed scientific research the dog-teams may be necessary, but my efforts were to be purely in the nature of discovery, to open the way for future research to follow. To achieve my purpose I believed that by carrying sufficient food and equipment in the plane, we could if required spend several weeks on the journey, and if by chance our plane was wrecked we could either hold out until my ship could return to civilization, pick up another plane, and come to our rescue, or else meet us at a predetermined point to which we might walk, and where we might find additional native food.

Adequate radio precaution would assure us of communication with our base at all times, and to cover this I prepared not only for two-way radio communication from the plane but carried as well a complete engine generator set for use when the plane was on the ground, and a complete hand-driven set for use when sledging. This, we believed, would take care of all emergencies. But we were wrong, for during our flight a terminal inside the sending set, and which we could not reach, burned out. While we were on the ground between flights we maintained the prearranged schedules three times daily, but the signals sent out by the engine generator set were never heard. The oil in the hand-driven generator froze stiff and stripped its gears.

Believing that we had ample fuel we did not conserve our supply either when climbing to high altitudes over Hearst Land or during the various landings, and this brought us to a landing out of fuel when within 16 miles of our goal. There was no useful radio gear at Little America, and with a frozen foot and considering the difficulties of crossing the terribly crevassed area and pressure ridges which lay between Little America and our plane, I did not think it possible to haul equipment and fuel sufficient to bring the machine to Little America, where in time it might have been possible to repair the wireless set. So after the set failed, when we were about half-way across the Antarctic continent, we were out of touch with our base. We did however pick up time signals on three separate days from a station at Buenos Aires, and this made it possible for us to check up on our chronometers and establish our positions.

With the exception of our wireless, our equipment served its purpose admirably. There was no difficulty with the aeroplane equipment because of the cold. Wherever we landed on the plateau surface the snow was smooth and hard packed. The skis sank less than an inch, and we had no difficulty in landing or taking off, or in securing our plane so that it was safe during the blizzards we experienced. This shows that a carefully selected machine and suitable equipment, in the hands of a skilled pilot, will serve for preliminary reconnaissance in the Antarctic. Even in the mountainous areas we crossed in Hearst Land there appeared to be many places, which would be difficult to reach by dog-team, where we could have landed safely.

An aeroplane can carry more and bring back more specimens than a dog-team could haul, and although much time might pass while waiting for reasonably good weather, the speed of travel when the weather is good and the excellent visibility to be had when travelling by plane more than compensate for the delay. Therefore I think that with the aeroplane we can reveal the last remaining unknown regions on the face of the earth.

APPENDIX II

Details of the Flight
(Same source as Appendix I)

So much for our plans and the way in which they failed in certain points. The details of the flight have appeared already in the publications of American societies, but a brief summary of them will still be in place here.

In 1933 I had planned to make the flight in the opposite direction, from the Bay of Whales to the Weddell Sea, and in January 1934 had landed the aeroplane on the bay ice which, after a successful trial flight, broke up in a gale and crushed the machine so extensively that we had to abandon the attempt.

In September 1934 we were back in New Zealand ready for another attempt; this time to make the flight from the Weddell Sea to the Ross Sea, because an earlier start was possible in that direction owing to earlier break-up of the pack-ice about Graham Land. But the weather was altogether against us, first at Deception Island and later at Snow Hill Island on the east coast of the Archipelago, where we found a suitable flying base. We made a start on 3 January 1935, but were soon driven back by bad weather. In the whole of that season, and we were there for three months, we had less than twelve hours of flying weather. Returning from Snow Hill Island we were caught in the pack and got free with difficulty, and for the third attempt we chose a safer base, Dundee Island, some 80 miles north of Snow Hill, which we had marked on the return from the previous attempt. The *Wyatt Earp* reached Dundee Island again in November 1935 with Sir Hubert Wilkins and five others who had been on all three expeditions. For pilot on this flight I was fortunate in obtaining Mr. Herbert Hollick-Kenyon, who had obtained leave from Canadian Airways; he had much experience of flying in sub-arctic conditions.

At the summit of Dundee Island, about 500 feet above sea, there was an almost unlimited snowfield with an excellent take-off slightly downhill. Supplies and fuel were hauled up on sledges and personal equipment carried by the plane during test flights. The weather was favourable and we took off on November 21 in clear weather for what we hoped would be the main flight, but after about 600 miles our fuel gauge clogged, so that we were forced to return, and landed after ten and a half hours in the air. We had realized from our experience on the first two expeditions that the only way to fly in the Antarctic is to start in good weather, and if it turns bad to be prepared to land and await the return of better conditions. So this time we took no meteorologist on our base staff, feeling that it is impossible to forecast in the Antarctic.

Next day the machine was refuelled and the engine tuned up again by the mechanics. The weather promised to remain clear, and Hollick-Kenyon and I were called at 02.00 on the 23rd. (All dates and times are Greenwich Civil Time.) We ate a hearty breakfast and then dressed in heavy clothing, with snow-shoes. We purposely made slow time walking the 5 miles to the plane, because we did not wish to get our clothing damp with perspiration before taking off. After two hours we reached the place where the *Polar Star* lay ready for flight. As Kenyon busied himself with last adjustments I had only one thought: "This time we must make it."

When we took off to the south at 08.04 on November 23 the weather was clear, the temperature −3° C., and the sea a turquoise blue which gave a marvellous reflection on the mountains. By 08.30, as we flew along the coast of Ross Island, we had climbed to 6400 feet and the temperature had dropped to −10° C. Weddell Sea was quite open for the first 300 miles—unusual in the Antarctic springtime. For 600 miles we flew along the eastern coast of the Antarctic Archipelago, until we came to the frozen channel which we identified as Stefansson Strait. It appeared to be not more than 3 miles wide, much narrower than is shown on the map of the American Geographical Society, and we could not see far enough to determine whether it actually connected the Weddell and Bellingshausen seas, or was merely a deep fjord, though we had risen to more than 13,000 feet.

So long as we had landmarks for checking the plane's ground speed and position we made careful notes of dead reckoning, and found that our ground speed was lower than expected, but was 120 m.p.h. or more. By 09.30 we noted that there was some wind and later that we were drifted too far to the east, and our course was altered to allow for this.

The low, black, conical peaks of Cape Eielson rose conspicuously on our left, and with keen curiosity we gazed ahead at the great mountain range to be crossed. Bold and rugged peaks, bare of snow, rose almost sheer to some 12,000 feet above sea-level. Impressed with the thought of eternity and our insignificance, I named the new mountains the Eternity Range, and the three most prominent peaks on our right Faith, Hope, and Charity, because we had to have faith, and we hoped for charity in the midst of cold hospitality. They were in striking contrast with the flat low peaks of the Antarctic Archipelago which we had followed south, peaks which dwindled into low isolated nunataks as we neared Stefansson Strait. The range which we were now crossing was loosely formed, with none of the crowded topography of peaks and glacier-filled valleys with crevassed bottoms.

After three hours the mountains beneath us gave place to a vast polar ice plateau from which emerged a few nunataks, the last relics of the mountain chain just passed. We were flying at 10,000 feet, which was the average altitude of our flight. During the first hours of the flight we had constant two-way radio communication between the ship and the plane. But at 16.15 I logged: "Transmitter out of action. Only thing is to go on." We had traversed 1000 miles and were yet 1300 miles from the Bay of Whales. We sighted several isolated mountain peaks, but these soon faded out on our right about 16.20. Forty-five minutes later other peaks showed on the same skyline, and in another twenty-five minutes more mountains 120 to 140 miles away appeared on our left horizon, and also a few peaks to the right.

Sun sights taken at 16.53 and 18.54 gave a fix which appeared to show that we were more than 200 miles west off our course: as will be explained later the bubble sextant had got badly out of adjustment. At 17.00, when by estimation we had passed out of the Falkland Islands sector, I logged: "Long. 80° dropped American flag and named the land up to 120° west James W. Ellsworth Land. What a thrill!!!" One hour and forty-five minutes later we came abreast of a solitary little range about 25 miles away on our left, symmetrically formed, with a central pyramid rising to 13,000 feet. I named it Sentinel Range, and its central peak Mount Mary Louise Ulmer, after my wife.

Fifteen minutes later, and 100 miles distant on the southern horizon, appeared a long, black, flat-topped range which extended visibly through at least 1° of latitude. This looked like the last of the mountains we were to see, for ahead lay only a vast plateau to the horizon. At 20.30 I noted: "No land marks visible. Only a limitless expanse of white." At 20.45 Hollick-Kenyon passed me the following message: "I really have no idea where we are—but our courses carefully steered should put us close in," and it proved in the end that we had remained surprisingly close to our scheduled course, within 45 miles, though our speed had been much lower than expected. We had been in the air nearly fourteen hours; visibility began to get poor, and we determined to land and take sights of the sun for our position, for we had no fuel to spare. We had no knowledge of what the surface might be like, and it was misty on the ground but we landed safely at 21.55 on November 23, though we crumpled the fuselage in landing.

This was the first of our four landings during the crossing, and twelve of the nineteen hours here were spent in taking observations to check the position of this our first camp, which we will call Camp I. After getting one position line, it was necessary to wait two or three hours to get another line crossing the first at an angle sufficient to give a reasonable intersection. I went out once to get exercise between the observations, but the monotony of the terrible expanse of endless white got on my nerves, so that I was glad to get back into the four walls of the tent. There are twenty-four hours of daylight in this region at this time of year, and that too wears on the nerves. The temperature was 15° below freezing. During our nineteen hours here we strung up the antenna wires on the bamboo sledge poles, worked the sledging-set transmitter by hand, and kept on sending calls, both general and to the *Wyatt Earp*, but we got only one response during the twenty-two days of our journey across Antarctica, and that was: "We can't hear you." The dead reckoning position of the camp was lat. 80°28' S., long. 141°02', but our ground speed had been much overestimated; for the position as determined by our observations was 80°20' S., 104° W. And we had not then overcome the trouble with the sextant. When its index error was eventually discovered and the sights recomputed, it proved to be 79° 15′ S., 102° 35′ W. The snow on the high plateau was granular and packed so hard that the skis of the plane made little impression. The surface elevation was 6400 feet, and the plateau extended with slight undulations in all directions.

The Pole lay 750 miles south, Dundee Island 1550 miles behind us, the coast-line of the continent several hundred miles to the north, and the Bay of Whales 750 miles ahead. It was here that I raised the American flag, and so far as that act would allow, claimed the sector between longitudes 80° to 120° W. for the United States, having already in my mind named it James W. Ellsworth Land after my father. That part of the plateau above 6000 feet I called Hollick-Kenyon Plateau. We set up our balloon-silk tent and took repeated altitudes of the sun with the sextant.

After nineteen hours at Camp I we again took to the air at 17.00 on November 24 in calm weather, but looking thick ahead. We felt we must push on, for our chances of a successful crossing were decreased in proportion to the time we lost at any one place. We soon experienced low visibility, and at the end of a short half-hour we were finally forced to land again, with a ground elevation of 6000 feet. We were surprised at the ease with which we could land or take off on a hard surface. It required no more than 50 yards to rise from the snow when we left the first camp on November 24. This is all the more remarkable since we had no assisting wind, and since we were at an elevation of 6400 feet above sea-level.

At Camp II we waited three days for good weather, trying strenuously and continually, but fortunately unsuccessfully, to fix our position. I say fortunately because the number of observations we made here were useful later in tracing the error of our sextant. After getting only a very rough approximation to our position, we took off in great uncertainty about the precise direction of Little America.

This was on November 27. After 90 miles we landed in a fog, and at 02.30 a blizzard was upon us. On November 28, 29, and 30 we lay all day in our sleeping-bags with drift and gale reaching 50 miles per hour. By November 30 there were huge drifts around the plane, and the cockpits were full of snow. We were unable to get into communication with the *Wyatt Earp,* although on November 30 we got three time ticks from Buenos Aires. We were 600 miles from Little America and probably had not enough fuel left to get there. I considered this stay at Camp III as the low-water mark of our flight.

However with our prospect appearing so dark, our situation was improving. At Camp III we luckily thought of the simple expedient of adjusting the bubble of our sextant on the snow horizon when the index read zero. This showed that the sextant had after the first observation developed an index error of 82 minutes of arc, and that it had been apparently constant. We reduced it to an uncertainty of about 4′, enabling us to fix our position and to set a direct course to Little America. Once the sextant was put in approximate adjustment our navigation problem became a simple one. All observations, except the very first one, were corrected for the determined index error of 82′ and the positions reworked with impressive results.

The second observation taken in the air at 18.54 on November 23 showed that the plane was behind schedule. The big discrepancy in the estimated air speed of 145 m.p.h. and the actual ground speed is accounted for by several factors: (1) the substitution of skis for wheels causing an unexpectedly heavy drag; (2) a slightly crumpled fuselage which altered the streamline and thereby reduced the speed; (3) unexpectedly heavy head winds; (4) low temperatures which reduced the engine power output; and (5) throttling down the engine to save fuel. During the whole mid-section of our flight, from the time we left Eternity Range until we started on the down grade to the Ross Barrier, the prevailing wind blew from the east and south-east. Only twice did we have a north wind, and then only for a few minutes. We never had a west wind. But these factors hardly account for the reduction of more than 25 per cent in the speed of the *Polar Star*. The measured speed at the beginning of the flight when the plane was heavily laden, and the known speed of the plane on the last two legs, was relatively much higher, so that an extremely low ground speed of about 92 m.p.h. was made on the first and most dangerous leg of the flight.

On December 1 we spent the whole day clearing snow drifts from the plane, which was one solid block of snow. To crawl in among the controls with a teacup and clear away dry snow as fine as flour was the worst job of all. On December 3 we tried to start up the machine, but the magneto burned out. It looked as though we were 650 miles from the Bay of Whales with no hope of getting there. When the blizzard abated we were able to cut snow blocks to erect a shelter to the windward of our tent. For eight days, until December 4, the storm held us prisoners in the camp. Our only excursions outside during the blizzard

were to use the wireless three times daily and to fill our bucket with
snow for water. Our food ration was 34 oz. a man each day, but we
were not obliged to adhere to the allowance as we ate only twice a
day. Even then we were never very hungry. In the morning we had a mug
of oatmeal with chunks of bacon boiled in it, milk, sugar, and oat biscuit with butter. In the evening we had a mug of pemmican, oat
biscuit, and butter. I thrive on this simple diet, just as in 1925 with
Amundsen I never grew tired of our menu of hot chocolate morning and
night and pemmican at noon.

One morning we tried unsuccessfully to start the aeroplane motor
after warming it for an hour. The situation seemed bad, for we were
being buried deeper and deeper in the snow. We decided that we
must get out of that hole irrespective of the weather ahead, and after
eight days in the blizzard camp we put the canvas hood over the motor
and placed the fire pot inside for forty-five minutes, as we always did
before starting. Then we cranked the engine. After a couple of weak
turns the propeller would stop with a choke. Kenyon connected the
stronger radio battery to the starter and had the propeller going in no
time. With the plane unloaded we pulled out of the drift, loaded up
again, and at 19.20 on December 4 we took off into a sky which was
anything but promising. But we had not been flying long before the
horizon became clear and the sky took on a beautiful golden glow.

At 23.10 we came down to get a sight, which made Camp IV in
79° 29′ S., 153° 27′ W. It was a beautiful calm night, the boundless
snow fields sparkling like diamonds. There was no wind, we had left the
high plateau, and were only 145 miles from the Bay of Whales. Once
more it was good to be alive. We were now on territory explored by
Byrd and all we wanted was to get to our destination.

At 09.00 on December 5 we took off and at 09.50 reached the north
end of Roosevelt Island, only 16 miles south of the Bay of Whales, but
we did not know this at the time. From the air we saw the ice-free
waters of Ross Sea, the goal of my four years of endeavour. At 10.05
the *Polar Star* slackened her speed and came gently to the snow, her 466
gallons of gasoline completely exhausted. Here we made Camp V.

On December 6 we dug trenches to settle the skis in, waiting to walk
to Little America. On December 7 the south-east wind continued,
with snow squalls, and temperature round about freezing-point.
On December 8, standing on the wing of the plane and looking northwest, we saw among a lot of irregular ice hummocks, that might be

snow-covered buildings, what Kenyon thought was a wind-generating tower. Was it Little America? We thought we would trek over on our snow-shoes, but after a two-hour walk we appeared to be no nearer and returned to the plane.

On December 9 we packed our hand sledge with ten days' rations and started off, leaving our tent with the plane, and expecting to find shelter in the huts. We traveled 9 miles of heavy hauling in the soft snow, and as we neared the tower we saw that it was only an ice pinnacle. Being without tent or sextant to fix where we were we had to leave the sledge and return to the plane for both; rested an hour, and got back to the sledge at 03.00 on December 10. We made Camp VI here, and after seven hours' sleep took sights and fixed its position in 78° 38′ S., 163° 20′ W. about 12 miles south of the head of the Bay of Whales. The weather for two days had been perfect, with no wind, the sun shining out of a cloudless sky and the temperature above freezing.

On December 11 we traveled 10 or 11 miles, sledging by low sun, and had one bad pull over a crevasse. It was weary work, and it seemed as though we must be going in the wrong direction, for the never-ending expanse stretched on for ever. The low night sun cast a dull glow over the ice fields without warmth, although the sky was cloudless. Suddenly I told Kenyon I could see a line of blue water on the horizon. It was the Bay of Whales, and we had been traveling much too far west.

On December 12 however, although we marched 12 miles, we were unable to find the water which we had seen the day before. On December 13, travelling entirely by compass as before, in misty weather with snow flurries, we made another 10 miles. We approached a ridge and hoped to get an extended view. Topping it we looked straight down into salt water. We had heard the lapping of the waves and thought it was the wind, but it really was the sea at last.

On December 14 we reconnoitered and in the evening took a sight, to find we had travelled about 10 miles too far north, and must go back south. We judged that we were at the mouth of the Bay of Whales. On December 15 we traveled 15 miles and came, at "Ver-sur-mer", Byrd's unloading place, upon two tractors half-buried in snow. This gave us our position, so we dragged on up the east side of the bay, topped a rise, and looked down upon the most desolate remains of past habitation that I have ever witnessed: only a lot of masts and the stove-pipes of buildings sticking out of the snow. We broke through a glass skylight, and were able to let ourselves down into what proved to be the radio shack.

On December 16 we dug a tunnel and made steps down to the door of our shack. We found coal, gasoline, and some welcome stores. We cleaned up everything, and settled down to a routine to await the arrival of the *Wyatt Earp*. Every day I walked 6 miles down to the tractors where we had put up our tent, with two yellow streamers and a note that we were at Little America, so that the *Wyatt Earp* could know where we were.

On January 15, a month after we arrived at Little America, I was awakened at 22.00 to see Kenyon standing over me with a note in his hand. He had heard the roar of a motor overhead, although our dug-out home was 15 feet beneath the snow, and had crawled up to the surface in time to see a parachute descending through the fog which had enveloped us for two weeks. The parcel contained food, and the note was from Captain Hill, commanding the R.R.S. *Discovery II*. Within ten days after the failure of our radio the Commonwealth of Australia had sent a relief expedition, and had been seconded in this by the governments of the United Kingdom and New Zealand. As I was laid up with an infected foot, Kenyon started off alone to meet our visitors; but I could sleep no more that night, and started out in snow-shoes to learn what was up. A mile from camp I saw through the fog, which magnified frightfully in these regions, what appeared to be a whole army of men marching towards me; in reality there were six of them. We packed the sledge and started for the ship, where I was received with open arms, and learned that my own ship had been delayed by the pack-ice in the Ross Sea. Three days later a radio message told us that the *Wyatt Earp* was approaching the bay, and very soon the staunch little craft loomed up in the fog. While my party was loading the *Polar Star* on the *Wyatt Earp* I went on the *Discovery II* to Australia, where I was for twelve days the guest of the Government.

APPENDIX III

Equipment
(Same source as Appendices I & II)

At our take-off from Dundee Island the loaded plane weighed 7987 lbs. made up as follows:

Plane (empty)	3614 lbs.
466 gallons of gasoline	2796
Oil	160
Food	260
Sledge with cover and lashing	98
Primus stove, skis and tools	80
Fuel for stove	18
Sleeping-bags with wooden slats for protection against wet snow	32
Cameras	10
Sledge radio set	50
Miscellaneous and spares	449
Pilot and navigator with equipment	420
	7987

The food was principally pemmican, sunwheat biscuits, bouillon cubes, bacon, butter, milk powder, dried fruit and tea, and the full daily ration for 61 days was 34 oz. computed to contain 15 per cent protein, 28 per cent fat, 56 per cent carbohydrates, giving 4860 calories.

The pemmican was of two brands—the Amundsen type made by the Beauvais Co. of Copenhagen, and another made to the formula of Mr. D. C. Coman, of Johns Hopkins University. The latter had some pepper in it and for my part I preferred it. I always find that one or two fixed rations are better than a great variety. On this flight we had for breakfast a mug of oat porridge with cubes of bacon; dried milk and sugar, and oat wafers with butter. For supper, a mug of pemmican with biscuits and butter. I never tired of this and always looked forward to it. We must have used much less than the 34 oz. per day of our schedule.

There were two radio sets. The main set transmitted on wave lengths of 20 to 80 metres and on 600 metres. The transmitter with 100 watts output was worked by a generator coupled directly to the engine; the antenna was of the trailing-wire pattern. Until it broke down this set transmitted successfully to the *Wyatt Earp*. To energize the transmitter when the plane was not in flight we had a portable petrol engine generator of 300 watts.

The sledging radio set could transmit and receive over a wave length of 30 to 100 metres. For transmitting it was operated with a 15-watt generator, turned by hand or driven by a foot treadle. It seemed unreasonable to suppose that all these means should fail, but in fact we did fail to keep in touch with either the ship or civilization.

Radio equipment should be mounted so that it can be easily dismounted and taken apart, and nothing should be soldered which can be secured by other methods. Our principal radio set broke down apparently by a connection shaking loose, but the fault was never quite established, for the set was not properly accessible.

I myself wore during the flight, camel-hair underclothing and socks, fleece-lined socks, moose-skin moccasins, woollen breeches, squirrel-skin parka, reindeer-skin parka, chamois face mask, silk gloves, woollen gloves, dog-skin mittens, woollen cap, and snow goggles.

Hollick-Kenyon's outfit varied from this by an additional pair of socks, trousers instead of breeches. Canvas rubber-soled boots with insoles instead of moccasins, only one parka, an additional leather flying cap with earphones, and another pair of woollen gloves instead of silk.

APPENDIX IV

Navigation of the Flight

(*Prepared by Mr. Ellsworth with the collaboration of Lt. Commander P. V. H. Weems, U.S. Navy, Retired.*)

Our plane was fitted with a Pioneer drift indicator, but it was found difficult to measure drift over featureless snow. We had no means to measure the ground speed directly, and in fact it proved to be much slower than we had calculated from the known air speed of the machine and our estimates of the wind.

We had based our plans upon an average ground speed of 145 to 150 m.p.h., derived from tests of the plane with skis made at Winnipeg, though not, it is true, with the full load. We soon found on the flight that the air speed must be less than anticipated, for there was not sufficient evidence of wind to account for the reduction of the ground speed to about 120 miles on the average. We have never been able to account for this loss of speed.

In planning our navigation we had to remember that the tail of the plane hid the sun when it was within about 15 degrees of the course astern. We had chosen our starting hour so that the sun should be abeam in the middle of the flight, which should have allowed us to determine by sights that we were on our course, though not precisely where upon it; but our loss of speed would rather have defeated this intention even if the sextant had not gone out of adjustment, and in fact our observations for position were, in the end, all taken from the ground except one position line at 16h.

Our scheduled route plotted upon the map of the Antarctic in four sheets, published by the American Geographical Society of New York, provided for fourteen and a half hours' flying at 145 m.p.h. over the ground. For the end of each hour we had worked out the true bearing of the Great Circle course, which ranged from 202° at the beginning to 304° at the end, changing by two or three degrees per hour in the first half and then more rapidly. To this we applied the compass variation, which changed from 14° east at the start to 105° east at the finish, its total change and its rate of change being curiously similar to the change in the true course but of opposite sign. In consequence the magnetic course varied very little, being constant over the first half at 188° or 187° and then varying irregularly up to 199°. It was due to this happy accident of the compass variation balancing the change in the true bearing of the Great Circle course that we kept very close to our course, although on the first half of the flight we were far behind our scheduled time. Instead of having to change course by a number of degrees per hour we were able to fly upon a fixed compass bearing for fourteen hours, and were relatively little off our course at the end of that time.

We carried a Bausch and Lomb bubble sextant of Bureau of Standards Type C; a high-grade watch by Patek-Philippe; an American *Nautical Almanac* with the new table of Greenwich Hour Angle, and Ageton's tables (Hydrographic Office No. 211) with blank computing forms adapted to these tables. In preparation for the flight begun on November 21 we had computed curves for the altitude of the sun at scheduled points in order to be able to solve the position-line problem by inspection. It is worth while to work many hours in comfortable quarters if it saves only a few minutes of work in the air.

We were however compelled to turn back on November 21. We did this computation all over again for November 23, but little use was actually made of these prepared altitude curves, because first of the accident to the sextant, and secondly of the long delay in camps en route.

The bubble of the air sextant is set in adjustment by a lock-nut. It seems that this must have worked loose between the first and second sights in the air on November 23, for the results worked from these two observations were impossible and, similarly, the sights obtained when we descended at Camp I had no reasonable solution. Our long delay at Camp II enabled us to take a great number of sights, and eventually to determine that the bubble, after having slipped so that the index error was about 82', had since remained constant, and when this was determined we were able to work back and reconcile the sights made on November 23.

We used a 7-inch Aperiodic magnetic compass (Pioneer Company), and it gave excellent performance. We made no attempt to compensate for all deviations since over-compensation makes the compass sluggish in the neighbourhood of the Magnetic Pole.

Due to the difficulties of accomplishing accurate navigation in flight it is most important to accomplish as many details as possible of this important work in advance. Fortunately, this can be done. For example, the compass is carefully adjusted and swung for deviation. The variation for the area to be covered is carefully selected to the proper date. The proposed dead reckoning courses and distances are carefully computed and plotted. Finally a large portion of the celestial navigation work may be done in advance, though, as in the case of our flight, this procedure might entail extra work. It is worth while to work many extra hours in comfortable heated quarters if it saves only a few minutes of work in the air.

We carefully computed the altitude of the sun for the various dead reckoning positions and times. Due to the delays we had to make these computations several times, and then due to a freak accident with the sextant, little use was made of the pre-computed altitude curves so carefully worked out.

Because of the nature of the flight over unknown territory, an important part of the actual work on the flight was in connection with navigation, and since this is the subject most difficult for the beginner to master, and further because we were able to bring out a fairly complete record, this will be included. Obviously, those reading this as laymen should pass over the technical part and leave it to those who are vitally interested in the methods and results and the careful study of the actual navigation accomplished.

Analysis of Flight. As part of the flight preparation, a careful analysis of the navigation problems was made in advance. This data was originally based on a take-off from Snow Hill Island. Actually, the final take-off was from Dundee Island, 66 nautical miles to the northeast. Since this change in the point of take-off made little change in the Great Circle courses and distances previously computed between Snow Hill Island and Little America these computations were used in laying down the courses and estimated positions.

The course selected was the Great Circle course, or shortest route. The flight over this course was intended to be made at a constant speed of 150 miles per hour (130 knots). Instead of determining locations along the course of their distance from the starting place, the flying time was used in this analysis.

The Great Circle course, its vertex and points on the course were computed using Ageton's Tables (H.O. No. 211).

Latitude and longitude of initial and final positions were taken from the American Geographical Society's Map of the Antarctic, in stereographic projection. The scale of this map in latitude 71° is 1:4,000,000.

One of the reasons for selecting this course was that it was believed that the Queen Maud Range, the high land at the bottom of the Weddell Sea and Graham's Land's southern-most islands may meet at a point somewhere between latitudes of 75–80° South and longitudes 60–80° West. Also if high islands should exist in the locality of the unknown coast-line between longitude 120–80° West, these might be located and perhaps some solution be found to the problems of the far northerly extension of the shelf ice in these regions.

The 7″ Aperiodic magnetic compass used in the *Polar Star* gave excellent service. We made no attempt to compensate for all deviations since over-compensation has a tendency to make the compass sluggish in the magnetic polar regions—where at best the directive force is

weak. We had no serious difficulty in steering the correct compass
course.

Deviation Table. The Master Compass of the *Polar Star* had a maximum deviation of 7 degrees on Northerly magnetic headings. Knowing the approximate compass courses to be flown, the compasses were
carefully checked on these headings.

To steer chords of the Great Circle course across Antarctica radical
changes had to be made in the true course. By a coincidence, however,
the change in variation largely compensated for the changes in the
true course with the result that changes of only a few degrees had to
be made in the compass course. This calls to mind that Clyde Pangborn
was able to fly across the Atlantic on one compass course due to somewhat similar conditions. The following table shows the Greenwich
Civil Time we planned to change course, the true course to be flown
for each hour's run, the average variation, and the corresponding magnetic and master compass courses:

GREAT CIRCLE COURSES

FROM SNOW HILL TO LITTLE AMERICA

G.C.T.	T. Course	Var.	M. Course	Dev.	Master Compass
0800	202°	14° E	188°	5° E	183°
0900	204	17 E	187	5 E	182
1000	206	19 E	187	5 E	182
1100	209	22 E	187	5 E	182
1200	212	25 E	187	5 E	182
1300	216	29 E	187	5 E	182
1400	221	34 E	187	5 E	182
1500	227	39 E	188	5 E	183
1600	235	46 E	189	5 E	184
1700	245	52 E	193	5 E	188
1800	256	63 E	193	5 E	188
1900	269	80 E	189	5 E	184
2000	283	93 E	190	5 E	185
2100	294	100 E	194	5 E	189
2200	304	105 E	199	5 E	194

We passed Snow Hill about one hour late on this planned schedule,
and our ground speed was far under what we expected.

The compass course, except for drift allowance, was kept practically
constant at approximately 185 degrees for the first half of the flight
and at approximately 195 degrees for the last half of the flight.

In order to reduce the navigation work during the flight, the altitude and azimuths for the estimated hourly positions were computed in advance and plotted as curves on cross-section paper. In spite of the obvious advantage of this new technique, the trouble with the sextant prevented the full use of this data. Normally, an observed altitude referred to the curves would give at once and without further calculations the "altitude difference" or error in assumed position as determined by the usual longer methods.

In practice, the azimuth would ordinarily not be used since the observer forms a mental picture of his line of position when the altitude difference is picked from the curves. Little would be gained by plotting the line of position in extenso on the chart. If the observer is too close to the observed body he would simply alter course or speed or both as may be required—or else hold his course and speed and know the amount he is off schedule.

The final take-off at 08.05 on November 23, 1935 was merely the last of numerous similar experiences over a period of three years. We started off beautifully and travelled nearly 600 miles when a leaky fuel gauge forced us to return. After 10½ hours of flying, we landed back at Dundee Island to make preparations anew. Many weary hours the crew worked hauling gasoline to the hilltop, checking the engine and repairing the gauge. No one complained. Work and anxiety are inevitable parts of exploration.

The track we hoped to follow was carefully plotted on two navigation charts made on the previous expeditions by the versatile Bernt Balchen.

Repeatedly, we computed the altitude and bearing of the sun for the assumed schedule of time, course and speed we would follow, but with each delay, the computed data of course needed to be reworked. Due to the convergence of the meridians in the high latitudes over which we were to pass, it was not practicable to keep the watches set to local Civil Time. Instead, we kept our watches set to Greenwich Civil Time which simplified the problem of navigation and made it easier to keep the correct time.

The night before the final take-off, I worked out new pre-computed altitude and azimuth curves of the sun while the men laboured with the plane. Actually, all this pre-computed data was of little practical use due to the fact that the sextant reading was in error, and to the further fact that the speed of the plane was reduced by an unexpectedly large amount due to the wind resistance on the skis and to head winds. However, the work we did in advance did no harm and the practice of doing it was good training. I therefore strongly recommend that every possible figure be handled before a flight is started, since it is much more difficult to do the same operation in the air and besides, time is an important item to keep in mind. One can afford to work an hour on the ground in order to save a minute in the air.

A final check was made on the timepiece we selected for giving us the correct Greenwich Civil Time. We carried a second-setting watch on the ship, and this was a time-saver for routine work, but on the flight itself we carried the best timepiece available, a large Patek-Philippe watch in a silver case. This watch gave excellent results and was most valuable in the determination of positions by celestial navigation.

We used a Bausch and Lomb Aircraft Sextant (Bureau of Standards Type) which except for the index slipping gave excellent results. An advantage in the use of this type sextant is the fact that the size of the bubble, once adjusted, required no further attention from the time we left Dundee Island till we reached Little America.

We used the Greenwich Hour Angle tabulation in the 1935 American Nautical Almanac. The Greenwich Hour Angle is tabulated directly and displaces the equation of time formerly used for working celestial navigation problems. The new arrangement is a distinct advance over the old arrangement.

For reducing observations to position, I selected H.O. No. 211 (Ageton's Tables) as being the most suitable. One big advantage of these tables over other "short" methods is the fact that the dead reckoning position instead of an assumed position is used for working lines of position. Also, it is convenient for working the Great Circle courses and distances. And finally it is small, strongly bound, and indexed.

We used the Aircraft Plotter, a celluloid protractor with a scale, and found it to be a convenience.

It must be remembered that there are very few navigation charts of the Antarctic and no topographical maps of the unknown areas over which we flew. In other words, of the four usual methods of navigation—Pilotage, Dead Reckoning, Radio Navigation, and Celestial Navigation—the first had to be ruled out after passing Cape Eielson, while, because of the early failure of our radio transmitter we could make little use of radio in connection with navigation. The greatest value of radio in connection with our navigation problems was the timely reception of time signals from the powerful station at Buenos Aires at the very time that we were making strenuous efforts to fix our position in the bleak plateau of Antarctica.

I feel that the very difficulties and mishaps that we had with our navigation equipment helped to provide us with useful data that otherwise we would not have preserved. I refer especially to the fact that the index lock-nut to our sextant slipped, giving us a hopelessly erroneous result. Only by careful analysis of the observed data and the fortunate fact that after the sextant slipped out of adjustment it remained at or near the same setting while a large number of observations were made were we able to make use of these observations. Had the first observations taken shown us our approximate position it is likely that we would have taken a minimum number, say three sets of observations at each camp. As it was, we reduced the first observations we made only to find that the results were indeterminate. Then we anxiously observed and reduced other observations only to get the same hopeless results. After repeated observations, we became convinced that the sextant was in error, and to correct the greater portion of the obvious error, we adjusted the index to read zero when the reflected image of the snow horizon was at the centre of the bubble horizon.

A careful check on the observed data shows that all observations taken at Camp Gamma, about thirty in all, were excellent, and together serve definitely to fix the position of the plane at that station, and thereby fix the position of Mt. Mary Louise Ulmer and other important landmarks within narrow limits, say within two or three miles. Had the conditions for working navigation on the Antarctic plateau been as conducive to careful work with figures as one would find in a comfortable office, we might have saved ourselves the mental hazard and physical hardships of many hours of nerve-racking work with numb fingers and distraught minds.

We might further observe that air navigation is in itself a broad and difficult science to master both theoretically and practically, and that the navigator should really be a specialist in his line without too many other disturbing factors. In our case, while both Hollick-Kenyon and I could do fairly good work in celestial navigation, neither of us were especially expert at the job and had many other things to do on the flight, such as to fly the plane, operate the radio, lead the expedition, keep a record of the flight, get as many photographs as possible, take drift observations, keep track of the plane's dead reckoning position, and finally to shovel many tons of snow and to live under the most difficult conditions in Antarctic surroundings. Therefore, we offer no apologies where our navigation work was not 100 per cent, though we do feel that the flight as a whole was successfully navigated and that our record stands as the best to date of any similar undertaking.

Still a further reason for giving in considerable detail the actual accomplishments in navigation is the fact that we were fortunate in having some new and efficient equipment not available to explorers of the past.

Valuable lessons may be derived from a study of the navigation problems involved on this flight. All methods of navigation were utilised. The rapid convergence of the meridian, the rapid change in variation, the lack of pilotage charts over Antarctica, the difficulty with the radio equipment and with the sextant, together with the long distances and dangers involved, make the navigation problems of this flight especially suitable for study.

It was planned to refer observed sun altitudes to the Curve of precomputed altitudes. Unfortunately, this was made extremely difficult by two factors:

(1) The sextant index lock-nut accidentally slipped, giving an error in observed altitudes of 82' too much, and

(2) The ground speed, after passing Cape Eielson had dropped from about 120 m.p.h. to about 90 m.p.h.

Under normal conditions the observed sun altitudes when referred to the curves would have given at once, and without further calculations, the altitude difference found by solving the spherical triangle in the usual way for a line of position. At first thought, it would appear that the method of pre-computed altitude curves failed. Actually, the curves gave, even in this unusual case, all the practical information to be desired from a complete solution for a line of position.

In this case we would have assumed a position far from the plane's actual position, and the resultant altitude difference, or indicated error in position would have included both the sextant error and the altitude difference due to incorrect assumed position. In fact the results in each case would have been approximately the same, the curves giving the information without confirmation.

Where this is within one to two hundred miles of the scheduled position, the pre-computed altitude method should be for practical purposes as accurate as separate solutions for lines of position. Under normal conditions a plane should not, even for a 2000 mile flight be more than 200 miles, or 10 per cent off schedule.

After flying fourteen hours, and when visibility was seriously reduced by haze, we landed the *Polar Star* at 2155 G.C.T. to fix our position and to await better weather.

Immediately after landing a series of sun observations were taken. It was at once apparent that something was radically wrong with the observations, but at first this was a puzzle to us. About 9 hours of the 20 hours spent at Camp Desolation were occupied in taking and reducing sun observations.

It will be noted that near the vertex of the Great Circle course, that is, in the highest latitude, the plane making 150 statute miles per hour, or 130 knots, would cross approximately 15° of longitude, so that the *Polar Star* with sufficient fuel could have continued round the world at about 80° of latitude and kept the sun at one bearing.

Valuable lessons may be derived from a study of the navigation problems involved on this flight. All methods of navigation were utilized. The rapid convergence of the meridian, the rapid change in variation, the lack of pilotage charts of the Antarctic, the difficulty with the radio equipment and with the sextant, together with the long distances and dangers involved, make the navigation problems of this flight especially suitable for study.

It should be pointed out that in the part of Antarctica we crossed, one cannot fly, except by instruments, in other than perfect conditions, that is to say clear sunshine. This is because, except for a few mountains on the coast, there is absolutely nothing by which the eye can gauge distance when the sun is hidden. With the sun hidden by fog, the snow and fog blend into one hazy mass.

Therefore, when we did fly, we could see immense distances, possibly 140 miles on each side of our course. If we call this only 100 miles, our band of visibility was 200 miles, and for the 1500 miles of unexplored distance, this made a total area of 300,000 square miles added to mapped areas. However, this narrow ribbon across Antarctica still leaves plenty of unexplored territory for future explorers.

The *Polar Star's* speed from Cape Eielson to Camp Desolation was reduced by head wind, skis, crumpled fuselage, mountain flying and low temperatures from a planned speed of 150 m.p.h. to about 95.

This resulted in a loss of about 523 miles on the schedule for this leg, or a mean lag of about 262 miles. This error in D.R. caused the plane to be steered about 12° to the right of the Great Circle course. Fortunately, this error was mostly compensated by an increase of approximately 10° in the easterly direction, so that the resultant error in course due to being behind schedule was about 2°.

The distance from Cape Eielson to Camp Desolation was approximately 900 miles. An error of −2° for this distance would place the *Polar Star* 900 x 2/60=30 miles to the right of the course.

It is interesting to note that Camp Desolation was actually about 40 miles to the right of the scheduled course. This was the first of four landings that we made during the crossing and we passed 12 of our 19 hours there making sun observations to check our position. The dead reckoning position of the camp was lat. 80° 28′ S., long. 141° 02′ W. At this time we had not mastered the trouble with the sextant, so our position was considerably in error as determined by our observations, which gave lat. 80° 20′ S., long. 104° W. Later, by working back and by correcting the sextant errors for the original observations, we found the actual position of Camp Desolation to be lat. 79° 15′ S., long. 102° 35′ W.

After 19 hours at Camp Desolation we took off again, only to be forced to land again a short half hour later. We named the second landing place, Camp Gamma, where we again set up our tent and waited three days for good weather. It was here that we made strenuous and fortunately unsuccessful efforts to accurately fix our position. Strange to say the trouble we experienced with the sextant resulted in a more accurate ultimate fix of the position of Camp Gamma, from which the positions of the landmarks observed in flight on November 23rd could be the better determined. Had one or two sets of observations checked with our estimated position it is probable that we would have been content and made no further observations. As it was, the observed date, when reduced to a position, gave a hopelessly large spread indicating that something was radically wrong. Being uncertain and realizing the seriousness of our situation, we continued to take careful sun observations. In all, we took no less than thirty careful sun altitudes with the corresponding times. After struggling with this data three days, and getting only a very rough approximation of our position, we took off in great uncertainty in the general direction of Little America.

Our next landing after about 90 miles of flight was at our third camp which we called Camp Winnipeg. In retrospect I consider our stay at Camp Winnipeg the low-water mark of our flight. The radio failure left us without communication with the outside world. Luckily we thought of the simple expediency of setting the bubble of our sextant on the snow horizon when the index read zero. This gave us an accuracy of observations to within 4 miles which was amply accurate to permit us to fix our position and set a direct course to Little America. Anyone familiar with the sextant and calmly studying the subject would soon see that the sextant could easily be set to an approximate adjustment on the snow horizon. However, all of this is "hindsight" and we offer no apologies for our apparent slowness in correcting the sextant error. We are still puzzled to know what caused the index lock-nut to slip in the first place. Since the final outcome was a happy one and since we were absolutely dependent on the sextant for finding our way, the general facts are related with the hope it might be of help to future polar travellers. Once the sextant was put in approximate adjustment our navigation problem became a simple one.

Having determined the error in the sextant, and by careful analysis of the data taken at Camp Desolation and at Camp Gamma, we discovered, by deduction, that the sextant after slipping by an amount equivalent to several hundred miles fortunately stuck fast, or nearly so, with the index reading 82' too much. We were even able to determine that this occurred between the two observations I took in flight on November 23rd. All observations except the very first one were corrected for the determined error of 82' and the positions reworked with impressive results. The second observation taken in the air at 18.54 G.C.T. on November 23rd showed the plane was behind schedule, which it was. The position of Camp Desolation was thus determined to be lat. 79° 15' S., long. 102° 35' W. as compared to the scheduled position of lat. 79° 45' S., long. 152° W., and Camp Gamma at lat. 79° 22' S., long. 107° 30' W.

The big discrepancy in the estimated air speed and the actual ground speed is accounted for by several factors: (1) The substitution of skis for wheels causing an unexpectedly heavy drag, (2) A slightly crumpled fuselage which altered the streamlining and thus reduced the speed, (3) Unexpectedly heavy head winds, (4) Low temperatures which reduced the engine power output, and finally (5) Throttling down the engine to husband the fuel. Strange to say that generous allowances for these factors hardly account for the more than 25 per cent reduction in the speed of the *Polar Star*. The measured speed at the beginning of the flight when the plane was heavily laden, and the known speed of the plane on the last two legs, was relatively much higher, so that an extremely low ground speed of about 92 m.p.h. was made on the first and most dangerous leg of the flight.

The few observations we got under great difficulties at Camp Winnipeg gave a definite fix at lat. 79° 58′ S., long. 114° 20′ W. Radio time signals assured us of the correct time.

Although the plane radio transmitter had ceased to function when we were 1300 miles from our destination, or opposite Charcot Island, our first rendezvous base previously agreed upon, we were not then particularly concerned because we were provided with three means of communication.

Until the time we were forced to abandon the plane, 16 miles from the Bay of Whales, we were faithful to predetermined schedules for broadcasting. Twice each "night" and once every "morning" we tried to reach the *Wyatt Earp*. After the exhausting task of turning a frozen hand for 10-minute intervals, while standing in a biting wind with the temperature minus five, all we ever heard from the ship was the sentence, "We can't hear you."

The defect was not in our receiver, for three times we got time signals from the powerful Buenos Aires Station—a fortunate reception which enabled us to keep track of our chronometer error.

We took off again on December 4th at 19 L. 10 M. CC and landed again at 23 L. 03 M. at which we called Camp Tranquille at lat. 79° 29′ S., long. 153° 27′ W., according to our determinations. We were on the Ross Ice Shelf, at last, our navigation ended.

APPENDIX V

Topographical and Cartographical Results

Condensed from two articles published by the American Geographical Society in its quarterly journal, the *Geographical Review*, under the authorship of Mr. W. L. G. Joerg, for many years in charge of the Society's program of polar research ("The Topographical Results of Ellsworth's Trans-Antarctic Flight of 1935", *Geographical Review*, July,

1936, pp. 454–462; and "The Cartographical Results of Ellsworth's Trans-Antarctic Flight of 1935," *Geographical Review*, July, 1937, pp. 430–444).

The topographical and cartographical results of Lincoln Ellsworth's Antarctic flights of November 21 and November 23–December 5, 1935, as interpreted at the American Geographical Society, are based on the original material placed at the disposal of the Society by Mr. Ellsworth, consisting of a complete set of the photographs taken by him and the observational and navigational records kept by him and his pilot, Mr. Herbert Hollick-Kenyon, on the two flights.

The photographic material bearing on topography consisted of two series of Leica film, one of 25 exposures taken on the November 21 flight and the other of 41 exposures taken on the November 23 to December 5 flight. Neither series contained any photographs taken north of the region of Stefansson Strait (or Stefansson Inlet, as it now appears to be) and the last exposure in the second series (all of which were made on November 23) was made in about 77½° S. and 88° W. Of both series Mr. Ellsworth had made a list giving the time when the photograph was taken and whether from the right or left of the plane.

Enlarged prints 4 by 6 inches were made. These were studied for coincident features and the position and direction of each photograph were plotted along the time-spacing on the routes according to the record on the list. As a result, the photographs fell into groups naturally, and this grouping and additional notes in the logs relating to features not shown on the photographs made it possible to reconstruct the major lineaments of the area traversed and classify them regionally.

Ellsworth's Leica photographs, supplemented by certain photographs taken by Sir Hubert Wilkins on his flight of December 20, 1928, were finally used to construct three maps published by the Society in the July, 1937, issue of the *Geographical Review*. These consist of (1) a map of the eastern coast of Graham Land approximately between latitudes 68°10′ and 69°35′ S., compiled on the scale of 1:200,000 and published on the scale of 1:400,000; (2) a map compiled on the scale of 1:400,000 and published on the scale of 1:800,000, showing the great linear depression (conjectured to be a fault trough) and its bordering upland features south of Marguerite Bay; and (3) a map compiled on the scale of 1:400,000 and published on the scale of 1:800,000 of the Sentinel Range, the isolated range far in the interior, almost midway between the eastern and western edges of West Antarctica.

The construction of these maps was carried out according to a technique that has been developed at the Society over a period of years on various projects of reconnaissance nature. As an aid to the method the special instruments developed at the Society, the photogoniometer and the single-eyepiece oblique plotter, were used for a large part of the work, especially in the determination of heights. By the use of these procedures it was possible to carry to completion this undertaking despite the formidable handicap presented by the fact that the photographic material, for reasons beyond Mr. Ellsworth's control, was hardly sufficient for photogrammetrical plotting of any kind, with the result that approximations were unavoidable. Photography on the flight was limited to the Leica camera with exposures 1 by 1½ inches, since it was found to be impossible to use the large mapping camera that Mr. Ellsworth had brought on the expedition. That the photographs, when enlarged, could be used with such valuable results, is a matter of congratulation.

From the photographs taken by Mr. Ellsworth there have resulted the first maps of two important areas. One of these (the eastern coastal belt south of Graham Land previously known only in sketchy outline) is about 2300 square miles in extent, and the other (the fault-depression area wholly unknown until the flight of November 23, 1935) about 9000 square miles. The results demonstrate again the value of air photography in reconnaissance exploration.

Geographical features

In interpreting the geographical and topographical features revealed by the Ellsworth photographs and the maps compiled from them, an attempt was made to correlate the findings of the Ellsworth expedition with Wilkins' discoveries in 1928 and with the work of the British Graham Land Expedition under Rymill. At the time that the maps were under construction from the Ellsworth photographs only preliminary newspaper accounts were available on the work of the British expedition which operated in or close to the two main areas, coastal and interior, covered by the maps.

The map of the eastern coast of southern Graham Land published by the American Geographical Society on the scale of 1:400,000 discloses a segment of ice-mantled coast with an outer frontage of about 120 miles conjectured to lie approximately between 68°10′ and 69°35′ S. The mountainous coastal belt, possibly a dissected scarp according to Rymill's report, is cut through by a large number of valley glaciers of low gradient, which divide it up into numerous capes and headlands, of which some apparently extend out directly to the shelf ice of Weddell Sea and others are fronted by an apron of piedmont ice, whose outer edge is marked by a line of crevasses. This stretch of coast is divided into two segments, a northern arcuate piece concave towards the sea, and a southern roughly rectilinear piece extending north and south. Both segments meet in a projecting headland.

The Ellsworth photographs in this area are also of great value in the interpretation of a number of the Wilkins photographs taken in 1928. At three places along this stretch of coast features on the Ellsworth photographs were identifiable on the Wilkins photographs. In the north the dark outliers along the sweep of Bowman Coast, photographed by Wilkins at a great distance as he was flying across the wide bight enclosed by this coast, are repeated on a number of the Ellsworth photographs. In the centre, features at the mouth of Lurabee Glacier (named Lurabee Channel by Wilkins) and at the mouth of the adjoining glacier to the north correspondingly named Casey Glacier on the new map, were readily recognizable on several photographs taken on the November 21, 1935, flight. Similarly, a single coincident feature on two photographs taken by Ellsworth and Wilkins, respectively, links two continuous photographs of the northwestern flank of Stefansson "Strait," taken by Wilkins and provides a more reliable clue than was available from Wilkins' sketch-map to the true position of this feature which the burden of evidence now points to as being a major embayment and not a through channel.

The map published by the Society on the scale of 1:800,000 represents the great linear depression and its bordering mountains discovered by the Ellsworth expedition shortly after the airplane had entered on its long cross-continental flight on November 23, 1935. Although the position in latitude and longitude is even more indefinite than that of the eastern coastal strip, the connected area represented on this map may be conjectured to lie roughly between 69½°–72° S. and 66°–71° W. The gap thus left between the coast and the first of the ranges bordering the depression on the east is by no means featureless; indeed, it is filled by mountains up to 11,000 feet high, trending southeast, that represent the main Graham Land axis but which it was not possible to photograph because of clouds. Photographs taken on the outward course on November 21, which here paralleled the November 23 course at a probable distance of some 50 miles, hence remain the only photographs available of the main axis, Eternity Range as it was named by Mr. Ellsworth.

From the distinct similarities between this map and the photographs on which it was based and accounts, which appeared in the press during the construction of a map, of a remarkable sea-ice-filled strait about 15 miles wide explored by the British Graham Land Expedition in September, October, and November, 1936, there seems strong possibility that the two are identical. The account of the British expedition describes this strait as extending about 200 miles in a S. 15° E. direction from the southern coast of Marguerite Bay and flanked on both sides by high land. Its eastern side was described as constituting the west coast of Graham Land and no sea-level channels entered it. On the basis of this evidence and of knowledge gained from other surveys made by the British expedition, it was determined that this western coast continues unbroken from at least 450 miles from Matha Bay (in 66°45′ S.) and that Graham Land is hence not an archipelago. The western side of the strait was found to be the eastern coast of Alexander I Land which, therefore, is much larger than assumed from the work of Bellinghausen in 1821 and Charcot in 1909. The Graham Land coast of the channel was characterized by eruptive rocks akin to those of the same coast farther north. On the great bluff of the Alexander I Land side stratified sedimentary rocks were exposed that yielded fossil invertebrates and plants that will probably serve to interpret the structure and age of the adjacent Graham Land mountain arc. "The strait is bounded on either side," the dispatch continues, "by such strangely different ranges that it must be one of the most impressive fault features of the earth's surface."

On the long north-south range shown in Ellsworth's photographs, from which the Society's map was constructed, exposures of stratified rock seem clearly evident in a number of places. When the two sections of the map based on photographs taken on the opposite sides of the flight route were, during construction, "hung" on the route according to the interpretation of the time record, the ranges with stratified exposures on both sides of the route fell into alignment. This would make it probable that they were continuous, while their farther continuation to the south would seem to be indicated by the ranges partly characterized by flat-topped spurs that appear in the middle ground of the final photographs of this series. Beyond (east of) this stratified range and between it and the serried massifs in the background as shown in the photographs used in plotting the southerly half of this map, with their suggestion of different rock structure, lies a long uninterrupted ice belt which, according to the plotting, has an average width corresponding closely to 15 miles.

As to the absolute position of the fault depression in terms of latitude and longitude, neither the map based on Ellsworth's photographs nor the preliminary newspaper account of the British expedition can be conclusive. Its S. 15° E. trend and 200-mile length to the end of the British expedition's sledge journey mentioned in the newspaper accounts fits well with the Society's map. Its western wall as plotted on the map would tend to indicate that it starts from the southwest corner of Marguerite Bay. From the southeastern corner, in any event, starts what is probably a secondary feature, a broad, gently-sloping glacier that leads upward and apparently in a southerly direction to a low pass beyond which another glacier occupying a depression 5 to 10 miles wide flows apparently southwest and empties into the strait in about 20 or 25 miles.

Beyond the area covered by the Society's map of this great linear depression the remaining eight photographs taken by Ellsworth portray isolated, widely separated features. The general picture is that of a vast ice plateau interrupted by occasional nunataks. Not all that were observed could be photographed.

Between 16.15 and 16.45 o'clock, when the airplane was flying about from 73°S. and 72°W. to 73¾°S. and 74°W., reference is made in the log to sighting a number of such exposures to the right of the course. Similar ones appear on photographs to the right and left, which plot approximately within the quadrangle enclosed by 74 1/3°–75°S. and 76°–78°W. At 17.20, from a conjectured position in 74½°S. and 76°W., mountains were sighted abeam to the left, estimated to be 120–140 miles away.

The last three photographs taken on November 23 represent the Sentinel Range (so named by Ellsworth). In contrast to the preceding nunataks, which, according to the time record, lie about 275 miles back (northeast) with the featureless ice plateau intervening along the line of flight, the range is a mountain feature of major proportions.

The plotting of the photographs on the Society's map of the Sentinel Range indicates that it consists of a main range and a number of sub-ranges and outliers, the whole group trending northeast-southwest from its northeastern end in about 77½°S. and 86°W. for more than the 35 miles shown up to the right border of the last photograph taken, which cuts abruptly through the main range.

Beyond (southwest of) the Sentinel Range the existence of other mountains seems indicated by the statement in Ellsworth's log at the time his last photograph was taken abreast of the Sentinel Range (19.44 estimated in 77¼°S. and 88°W.): "ahead and on southern horizon a long black mountain chain visible." The existence of these mountains is confirmed by Mr. Hollick-Kenyon. He states that at this time further peaks came into sight on the southern horizon, which he estimated to be 125 miles distant. They were so distant that it was impossible to distinguish any details of their appearance. The general locality indicated would fall within the quadrangle 78°–80°S. and 85°–90°W.

These were the last mountains observed on the flight. Beyond, for what amounts to half the distance across West Antarctica, only the uninterrupted icecap surface was met with, descending gradually in this distance of more than 800 miles from an elevation of over 6000 feet to 1000 feet near its crevassed border where it merges into the Ross Shelf Ice 150 miles east-southeast of Little America. No air photographs were taken in this 800-mile stretch.

The Antarctandes

South of the Stefansson Inlet depression the results of the Ellsworth flights seem to confirm not only the conjectured southern continuation of the Antarctandes but also the virgation, or spreading, of their axes forecast by the Swiss geologist Staub. The significance of this virgation would be that it represents the only one of the two blind ends in which the great world belt of young folded mountains frays out to the south that impinges directly on the oldland mass of Antarctica, since the other, the New Zealand-Auckland Islands-Campbell Island virgation, dies out before it reaches the southern continent.

Although all deductions must necessarily be tentative, it may be pointed out that the ranges discovered on November 21 and 23 south of Stefansson Inlet seem, in orientation and position, to fit into the prolongation of the three axes recognizable north of the strait.

The main range discovered south of Stefansson Inlet, named Eternity Range, which reaches an elevation of some 11,000 feet, forms a direct continuation of the main axis of Graham Land. It has a south-southeast trend and consists of a number of subranges whose northern ends and intervening longitudinal valleys are truncated by the Stefansson Inlet depression. Its eastern border, at least in the area observed, seems to form the western coast of Weddell Sea.

What may be termed the intermediate axis, defined by the islands west of Lallemand and Bourgeois Fiords (67½°W., between 67° and 68°S.) and by the mountain "islands" discovered by Wilkins and Rymill south of Marguerite Bay, seems continued to the south by three ranges trending north-south lying between about 71° and 74°W. and 71½° and 73½° S. Mountains seen to the south 120 to 140 miles from the November 23 track in about 81° W., and therefore lying in about 77° S. and 76° W., may also belong to this axis.

In the third, or western, axis, defined by the offshore islands Antwerp, Adelaide, and Alexander I (Charcot Island is off line), would lie the high Sentinel Range, discovered in about 86° W., between about 77° and 78° S., with its peak, Mt. Mary Louise Ulmer (over 12,000 feet), and a range located in about 92° W. and 78½° S. Nearer the coast, in the same alignment, may lie the mountains seen to the right from 77° W. on the November 23 track, which would place them in about 79° W. and 73½° S.

Between the first and second and the second and third axes the plain of the icecap, averaging 6000 feet in height, is interrupted only by occasional nunataks.

Objectives for Future Exploration

From this account it will be seen that in one remarkable flight of 2200 miles, of which 1200 miles were over wholly unknown territory, a clue has been gained to the character of one of the earth's important structural areas. Enough has been seen to show that here, in this tapering projection of the continent between Weddell and Ross seas, the interior of the icecap, unlike its counterpart of the same size in Greenland, does not completely mask the underlying topographical features. Further exploration is therefore likely to yield immediately tangible results: following the Eternity Range to the south will disclose the behavior of this major trend line and its relation to the probably shelf-ice-fringed west coast of Weddell Sea; following the other axes or crossing them farther south may throw light on their termination and their relation to the old mass of the rest of the continent; and tracing the coast on the Pacific Ocean side may confirm the inward sweep to the south suggested by the water sky observed by Hollick-Kenyon on November 23 in the conjectured position of 76° S. and 100° W. and also by the marginal location of Mt. Hal Flood and Mt. Mabelle Sidley surmised by Harold June on the flight eastward to 135° W. on the 78th parallel on November 18, 1934, during the second Byrd expedition.